Learn Cocoa on the Mac

Jack Nutting,
Dave Mark and
Jeff LaMarche

Apress®

Learn Cocoa on the Mac

ISBN-13 (pbk): 978-1-4302-1859-3

ISBN-13 (electronic): 978-1-4302-1860-9

Printed and bound in the United States of America 9 8 7 6 5 4 3 2 1

President and Publisher: Paul Manning
Lead Editors: Clay Andres, Brian MacDonald, Matthew Moodie, Douglas Pundick
Technical Reviewer: Mark Dalrymple
Editorial Board: Clay Andres, Steve Anglin, Mark Beckner, Ewan Buckingham, Gary Cornell, Jonathan Gennick, Jonathan Hassell, Michelle Lowman, Matthew Moodie, Duncan Parkes, Jeffrey Pepper, Frank Pohlmann, Douglas Pundick, Ben Renow-Clarke, Dominic Shakeshaft, Matt Wade, Tom Welsh
Coordinating Editor: Mary Tobin
Copy Editor: Tracy Brown Collins
Compositor: MacPS, LLC
Indexer: John Collin
Artist: April Milne
Cover Designer: Anna Ishchenko
Photo Credit: Weronica Meijer

Distributed to the book trade worldwide by Springer-Verlag New York, Inc., 233 Spring Street, 6th Floor, New York, NY 10013. Phone 1-800-SPRINGER, fax 201-348-4505, e-mail orders-ny@springer-sbm.com, or visit http://www.springeronline.com.

For information on translations, please e-mail info@apress.com, or visit http://www.apress.com.

Apress and friends of ED books may be purchased in bulk for academic, corporate, or promotional use. eBook versions and licenses are also available for most titles. For more information, reference our Special Bulk Sales–eBook Licensing web page at http://www.apress.com/info/bulksales.

Contents at a Glance

Contents

Foreword

Beware Dave Mark bearing new ideas.

You've probably seen Dave's name on the cover of the Apress Mac and iPhone books. Actually, his name is on the cover of **this** book. He's the Mac and iPhone series editor, he knows how to get stuff done, and I wish I had half of Dave's energy. And, if you're a friend of Dave's, he'll put you to work. He's put me to work over the years (in addition to my day job).

"Hey, MarkD, I have this idea for an introductory Objective-C book. Why don't you and Scott Knaster write it?" Sounds like fun, and it was. I still chuckle at some of jokes that we targeted to very narrow slices of nerdom.

"Hey, MarkD, Jeff LaMarche and I have this idea for an iPhone SDK book, want to be technical reviewer for it?" Sounds like fun, and it was. Then they did another iPhone book, which I got to review. I discovered that this technical reviewing thing is pretty awesome.

Just think of it. You get to read a nerdy book before it comes out. You get to learn cool new stuff along the way. Best of all, you get to poke holes in the text and code, kibitz and generally make random suggestions. And then you don't actually have to do the work involved in fixing it! **And** you get paid for it! My spousal overunit lets me keep any money I make off of books, so it's mine to play with. Daddy's camera needs a new lens.

Anyway, Dave calls up and says, "Hey MarkD, I have this idea for a Cocoa book, want to be the technical reviewer for it?" Sounds like fun. Daddy needs a new 85mm f/1.8.

So I "meet" this Jack Nutting guy via email. I GoogleStalk for anything interesting. We chat a bit. I start getting chapters to review. They're interesting. They're informative. I'm learning stuff. (oh, so **that's** how NSPopupMenu bindings work). And they've got a fun streak. I very rarely LOL in real life when I'm at the computer, but there was a time or two where I was totally C|N>K. Then I had to explain "C|N>K" to everyone in the publishing pipeline because I wrote it in the reviewer comments.

I had my doubts. Cocoa is a huge topic. The typical Mac OS X desktop application takes a lot more work, and uses a lot more technology and Cocoa classes than the typical iPhone application. Some parts of Cocoa are kind of old and crufty, it being a 20-year-old toolkit. Some parts of Cocoa are totally the new shiny. But no matter what kind of Cocoa app you're writing, you have to know something about a lot of stuff before you can really get started.

Jack's picked the current best-of-breed techniques for making applications in Mac OS X 10.5 and 10.6 (and beyond). There's enough breadth to know what you need to know, enough depth to get you up and running, and enough knowledge to dig deeper on your own.

I hope you enjoy reading this book. I truly enjoyed reviewing it.

Cheers,
++md

P.S. C|N>K means "coffee piped through nose into keyboard"

Mark Dalrymple

About the Authors

Jack Nutting has been using Cocoa since the olden days, long before it was even called Cocoa. He's used Cocoa and its predecessors to develop software for a wide range of industries and applications including gaming, graphic design, online digital distribution, telecommunications, finance, publishing, and travel. When he's not working on Mac or iPhone projects, or developing web applications with Ruby on Rails, he's usually spending time with his family. Jack is a passionate proponent of Objective-C and the Cocoa frameworks. At the drop of a hat, he will speak at length on the virtues of dynamic dispatch and runtime class manipulations to anyone who'll listen (and even to some who won't). He blogs from time to time at http://www.nuthole.com.

Jeff LaMarche is a long-time Mac developer, and Apple iPhone Developer. With over 20 years of programming experience, he's written on Cocoa and Objective-C for *MacTech Magazine*, as well as articles for Apple's Developer Technical Services website. He has experience working in Enterprise software, both as a developer for PeopleSoft starting in the late 1990s, and then later as an independent consultant.

Dave Mark is a long-time Mac developer and author and has written a number of books on Macintosh development, including Learn C on the Macintosh, The Macintosh Programming Primer series, and Ultimate Mac Programming. His blog can be found at http://www.davemark.com.

About the Technical Reviewer

 **Mark Dalrymple** is a long-time Mac and Unix programmer, working on cross-platform toolkits, Internet publishing tools, high-performance web servers, and end-user desktop applications. He is also the principal author of *Advanced Mac OS X Programming* (Big Nerd Ranch, 2005) and *Learn Objective-C on the Mac* (Apress, 2009). In his spare time, Mark plays trombone and bassoon, and makes balloon animals.

Acknowledgments

This book would never have been possible without contributions from many people. Clay Andres' expert guidance and helpful insights into the publishing process have helped keep me on track numerous times. Dave Mark's feedback and concrete writing tips have been absolutely essential; believe me, you don't want to see the first draft of the first chapter I wrote, before Dave started setting me straight. Jeff LaMarche's work on the first chapters of the book, as well as his initial outline for the rest of the book, provided a solid foundation for me to build upon. Mark Dalrymple has done a great job of examining the book's technical details with a fine-toothed comb, keeping me honest and making me look good at the same time. Brian MacDonald's vantage point as someone with great technical knowledge, but not detailed experience with Cocoa, helped uncover bits and pieces of the book that needed to be expanded or compacted. Throughout the last several months of the writing, Mary Tobin has been consistently patient and helpful with this newbie author, keeping track of the statuses of each chapter and keeping the process working smoothly. And copy-editor Tracy Brown Collins has responded to a deluge of way-past-deadline chapters with remarkable efficiency and a keen eye for detail. Beyond that, there are any number of people involved in the layout and other aspects of the production who are, to me, completely unknown and nameless, despite their crucial contributions. Thank you, whoever you are!

Apart from the people associated with Apress, a number of friends have helped in a variety of ways, at various stages during the creation of this book, either volunteering their time freely or at least answering my pleas for advice. Saurabh Sharan has given great feedback on nearly every chapter of the book, helping locate sections that needed further clarification. Joar Wingfors provided detailed commentary on several chapters, as well as a handy bit of public domain code that we used in Chapter 11. Tim Burks provided some important feedback on the final chapter. I owe a huge debt of gratitude to Tom Geller, who put me in touch with Apress in the first place; without Tom putting two and two together, I'd still be sitting here wondering if I'd ever write anything "real". Finally, I'd like to thank my wife Weronica Meijer and our children, Henrietta and Dorotea, who've put up with my many long nights and "lost weekends" as I worked on this book, and have been more patient than I could have hoped for; this book is dedicated to them.

Preface

I first encountered Cocoa as a college student in about 1989. Of course, that was before the iPhone, before Mac OS X, and before it was even called Cocoa. Back then, the seed of today's Cocoa was a part of NeXTStep, the OS that was the core of the NeXT computers. NeXTStep was years ahead of its time, and, while the lab full of NeXT workstations was woefully underused in the computer science courses, my student sysadmin job had me using them daily. As a user, I was hooked. I won't dwell on the NeXT user experience here, but just state that many of the best features of Mac OS X come not so much from the Mac of old as from NeXTStep.

At that time, there was no www, not much of a NeXTStep developer community, and very little written about the development environment apart from the impenetrable tomes that NeXT shipped with its earliest machines. I tried to wrap my head around Objective-C and the AppKit from time to time, but without any nearby experts, or much example code to look at (not to mention my actual studies which sometimes distracted me from playing with fun projects), I was basically stumped.

After college, something completely unexpected happened. A friend pointed me in the direction of a consulting firm in my city that was building custom NeXTStep apps for some pretty big customers, and I had the good fortune to come on-board. Suddenly, I had a group of colleagues who had not only been programming in NeXTStep for a while, some of them had even worked at NeXT! All it took was a bit of their expert help to get me started, and the things that had seemed so mysterious for years suddenly made sense. Within a few weeks, I learned so much I was able to start leading some training and mentoring efforts in NeXTStep development.

The point of that isn't that I'm a genius or a quick study. It's that the set of technologies we now call Cocoa are really powerful, and quite easy to learn and put to good use; but you're likely to need some help along the way. I'm hoping that this book will help nudge you in the right directions, and help you learn the essence of Cocoa programming, so that, by the time you're finished reading it, you'll have enough knowledge of Cocoa to be able to propel yourself forward and write the Mac applications of your dreams. In short, the kind of book I wish I'd been able to find 20 years ago.

Jack Nutting

Chapter **1**

Must Love Cocoa

Welcome! You must be here because you want to write programs for your Mac. Well, you've definitely come to the right place. (Here for Pilates? Third door down, on the right.) By the time you finish this book, you'll know everything you need to know to create fast, efficient, good-looking Mac OS X applications.

The key to creating a modern Mac application is Cocoa. According to Apple, Cocoa is a set of object-oriented frameworks that provide a runtime environment for Mac OS X applications. As you make your way through this book, you'll learn all about the Cocoa frameworks and runtime environment. For the moment, think of Cocoa as a programmer's assistant that takes care of much of the housekeeping that goes along with Mac development. Almost every common task performed by a Mac application, from drawing a window to blinking the cursor in a text field, is handled for you when you write programs using Cocoa, freeing you up to concentrate on the code that makes your application unique.

Cocoa provides a class for just about every one of your development needs. There are Cocoa classes for each piece of the Mac OS X user interface, from windows to menus, scrollbars to buttons, images to icons. If you can think of a user interface element you'd like to add to your own application, chances are very good that element is already implemented as a Cocoa class.

Another benefit of using Cocoa is that it is tightly integrated with Mac OS X. Build your application using Cocoa, and your application will play well with others and will interface seamlessly with Mac OS X elements like the Finder and the Dock.

WHEN IS 20 YEARS NOT 20 YEARS?

Cocoa has been around in one form or another since 1986. The technologies that we call Cocoa evolved from the NeXTStep AppKit, the application building tools developed for the NeXT platform. When Apple bought NeXT in 1996, they began building a new version of the Mac OS, what we now know as Mac OS X, basing much of the new operating system on technologies acquired from NeXT.

As Mac OS X evolved, so did Cocoa. Apple added technologies from the classic Mac OS, like QuickTime, as well as completely new technologies, like the Quartz rendering system that enables all the fancy visual effects and animation that OS X uses. They also made sure that they kept the Mac's famed ease-of-use in the process.

Bottom line: Cocoa is constantly evolving and expanding. The development tools, libraries, and frameworks you'll be learning in this book are the result of more than 20 years of experimentation and refinement.

Get a Mac and Download the Tools

Before you can begin creating applications with Cocoa, you'll need a Macintosh computer. It doesn't have to be the newest or the most powerful Mac; in fact, pretty much any Mac that's been made in the last six or seven years or so will work just fine for building the exercises in this book. As you become more serious about writing software, you may find it's worth investing in a newer or faster machine, but for now just about any Mac made this millennium will work fine for learning what you need to learn. Any Intel-based Mac, and almost all PowerPC Macs with a G4 or G5 processor will run Mac OS X 10.5 (Leopard). If you want to run the newer Mac OS X 10.6 (Snow Leopard), the PowerPC machines won't do; you'll need to have an Intel machine.

You'll also need to join Apple Developer Connection (ADC), which is Apple's developer relations organization. There are paid memberships, but the basic membership is free. You'll need at least the free membership in order to download Apple's development tools, which you'll need to do in order to write software in Cocoa. To join ADC, open up your web browser and navigate to http://developer.apple.com/mac/. If you already have an Apple ID, press the Log in button and enter your info. If you are new to Apple's online services, click the register link and create your account.

Once you are a bona fide ADC member, you'll be able to download Apple's developer tools. These tools are listed on the main Mac Dev Center page under the heading *Xcode*. The link for downloading Xcode actually downloads a full suite of developer tools, including all the software you'll need for working with Cocoa.

Once you are logged in, find the version of Xcode that's appropriate for your version of Mac OS X, and click on the Xcode link to start the download. A *.dmg* disk image file will download. Last we checked, the download was about a gigabyte, so it might take a few minutes. Once it is done downloading, double-click the *.dmg* file to mount the disk image. Next, double-click the installer file inside the disk image and start that install.

If you don't have a high-speed internet connection, you may find the developer tools on one of the CDs or DVDs that came with your Mac. That said, if possible, you should try to find a way to download the latest version.

> **NOTE:** If you've already installed the iPhone SDK, then you're all set. When you install the iPhone SDK on your computer, it also installs all the tools needed for creating Cocoa programs. Though the frameworks do have major differences, the tools are pretty much the same, so if you've done any iPhone SDK development, you should feel right at home creating Cocoa programs.

Download the Source Code

In addition to downloading and installing Xcode, you'll also need to download the sample projects that go with this book. You can find the code archive on the Apress *Learn Cocoa on the Mac* web page:

http://www.apress.com/book/view/1430218592

You'll find the source code archive in the *Book Resources* area on the left side of the page. Click the link, download the *.zip* archive, and move the *Learn Cocoa Projects* folder to a location in your *Documents* folder.

You'll also find a link on the Apress *Learn Cocoa on the Mac* web page, in the *Book Resources* area, that lets you submit and view errata. If you find an error in the book (much as we'd like to think otherwise, all books have errors) please do take a moment to report the error. This will help us make the book better in subsequent printings. We thank you in advance.

Getting Help

As you make your way through the book, you'll no doubt have some questions you'd like to get answered. Fortunately, there is a great community you can join, designed specifically for this series of books. Check out:

http://learncocoa.org

Register with the site, find the appropriate book forum and post your questions. You are sure to find other folks who can answer your questions and, who knows, after a while you might find yourself answering questions for other folks as well.

What You Need to Know Before You Begin

This book assumes that you already have some basic programming knowledge. You should be comfortable with the concepts of loops, variables, pointers, and linked lists. This book also assumes that you understand the fundamentals of object-oriented programming and are familiar with the Objective-C programming language. Starting with Mac OS X Leopard 10.5, a new version of the language was introduced, called Objective-C 2.0. Don't worry if you're not familiar with the more recent additions to the Objective-C language. We'll be sure to highlight any of the 2.0 language features we take advantage of and explain how they work and why we are using them.

NEW TO OBJECTIVE-C?

Here are a few resources that will help you get started.

New to programming? Check out *Learn C on the Mac, 4th Edition*, written by our own Dave Mark:

http://www.apress.com/book/view/1430218096

New to Objective-C? Check out *Learn Objective-C on the Mac*, an excellent and approachable introduction to Objective-C 2.0 by Mac programming experts Mark Dalrymple and Scott Knaster:

http://www.apress.com/book/view/9781430218159

Next, navigate over to the Apple iPhone Development Center and download a copy of *The Objective-C 2.0 Programming Language*, a very detailed and extensive description of the language and a great reference guide:

http://developer.apple.com/Mac/library/documentation/Cocoa/Conceptual/ObjectiveC

Are You Ready?

The Mac is a great computing platform, and Cocoa is the best tool to use to build your Mac applications. If you are coming to the Mac from another platform, you may find it a bit disorienting working with Cocoa and Objective-C. Even though you might find it hard to get your bearings at first, as you make your way through this book, we're confident that you'll soon start to wrap your head around the "Cocoa way" of doing things. With a little perseverance, it will all start to make sense.

One thing you should keep in mind is that the exercises in this book are not simply a checklist that, when completed, grant you Cocoa developer guru status. Every step of the way, make sure you understand what you just did before moving on to the next project. Don't be afraid to make changes to the code. Experiment and observe the results. That's one of the best ways to wrap your head around the complexities of coding in an environment like Cocoa.

Also, remember that we've set up a message forum for readers to discuss the exercises and content of this book. So if you get stuck, or want to chat with us and other Cocoa developers about any Cocoa programming topics, head over to http://learncocoa.org and register for the discussion forum.

That said, if you've got your developer tools installed, turn the page. If not, get to it! Then let's go!

Chapter 2

Hello, World

As you're probably well aware, it has become something of a tradition to call the first project in any book on programming "Hello, World." Following the "if it ain't broke, don't fix it" guideline, we'll stick with tradition.

Building "Hello, World"

By now, you should have Xcode installed on your machine. You should also have the *Learn Cocoa Projects* folder ensconced, safely, somewhere on your hard drive. If by some set of circumstances you don't, go directly to Chapter 1 (do not pass *Go*, do not collect $200) and reread the appropriate sections.

The first project we'll be working with is located in the *02.01 – Hello, World* folder.

Launch Xcode, which is located in the folder */Developer/Applications*. Just in case you've never used Xcode before, we're going to walk you through the process of creating a new project.

Start by selecting **New Project…** from the **File** menu, or by typing ⇧⌘N. When the New Project Assistant comes up (see Figure 2–1), select *Application* from under the *Mac OS X* heading in the left column, then select the *Cocoa Application* icon from the upper-right pane and press the **Choose…** button.

Figure 2–1. *Selecting the Cocoa Application project template from Xcode's New Project Assistant*

You'll be prompted for a project name and save location using the standard save sheet (see Figure 2–2). Type in the project name of *Hello World*. You can choose to save the project in your *Documents* folder, or you can create a separate folder to hold the Xcode projects that you build yourself. It really doesn't matter where you save an Xcode project, but you may find it easier to find them later if you pick one place and always save your projects there.

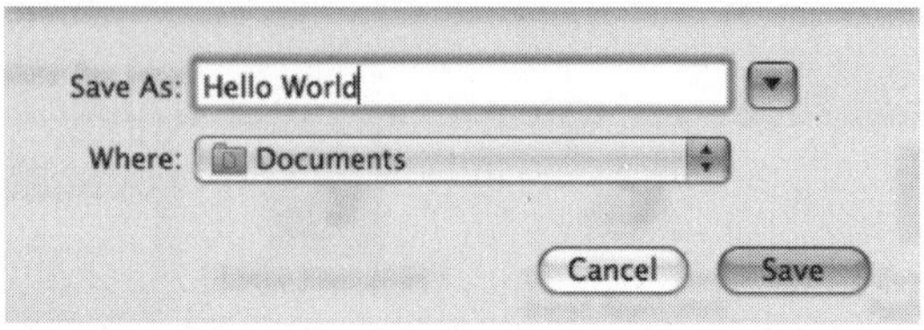

Figure 2–2. *Naming your project and selecting the save location*

Once you select a filename and location, a new **project window** will appear (as shown in Figure 2–3). Although you might already be familiar with Xcode, let's take a second to look at the project window. This is where we will be spending an awful lot of our time, so we want to make sure we're all on the same page.

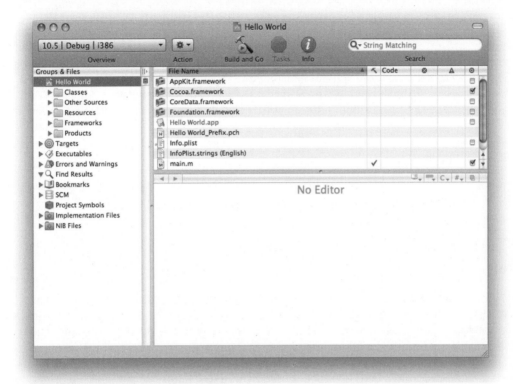

Figure 2–3. *Your project's main window in Xcode*

Your project window features a toolbar across the top, which gives you ready access to a bunch of commonly used commands. Below the toolbar, the window is divided into three main sections, or panes.

The pane that runs down the left side of the window is called the *Groups & Files* pane. All of the resources that make up your project are grouped here, as are a number of relevant project settings. Clicking on the little triangle to the left of an item expands that item to show any available sub-items. If you click on the triangle to the left of an expanded item, you will hide its sub-items.

The top right pane is called the *Detail View* and shows you detailed information about items selected in the *Groups & Files* pane. If nothing is selected in the *Groups & Files* pane, the *Detail View* shows all the files that make up your project. The lower right pane is called the *Editor* pane. If you select a single file in either the *Groups & Files* pane or the *Detail* pane, and Xcode knows how to display or edit that kind of file, the contents of the file will be displayed in the *Editor* pane. This is where you will be writing and editing all of your application's source code.

NOTE: Many developers like to get rid of the *Detail View* when they are working in the editor, so they have more screen space devoted to editing code; you can toggle the *Detail View* by pressing ⇧⌘E.

Turn your attention to the *Resources* folder in the *Groups & Files* pane. Double-click the *Resources* folder or single-click the disclosure triangle to the left of it. That will expand the *Resources* group to reveal three files that were created automatically for you. We'll ignore the first two files for the moment, and revisit them later. The third file is named *MainMenu.xib*.

NOTE: You might have noticed that *MainMenu.xib* has a disclosure triangle next to it, even though it's a single file and not a group or folder. Disclosure triangles are also used for files that are localizable, which means they've been set up so they can be translated into other languages. If you press the disclosure triangle next to *Mainmenu.xib*, you'll notice a single sub-item named after the language specified in International preference pane in your *System Settings*. Despite the disclosure triangle, double-clicking on *MainMenu.xib* will open the nib file for editing.

In your project window, double-click on *MainMenu.xib*. This should launch Interface Builder, the editor specifically designed to edit *.xib* files. (See Figure 2–4.) As you'll learn as you make your way through this book, Xcode and Interface Builder go together like bacon and eggs or, if you prefer, like Conan O'Brien and Andy Richter. The idea here is to use Xcode to organize your program's resources and code, and Interface Builder to design your program's user interface. There's more to it than that, but that's a pretty accurate high-level view. You'll be using Interface Builder throughout this book.

The file *MainMenu.xib* is known as a **nib file**. Huh? A nib file? Why not a xib file? Well, for starters, xib is awfully hard to pronounce. But more importantly, the term nib is a holdover from an earlier, simpler time. The precursors to Cocoa and to the modern Xcode/Interface Builder development tools were developed by NeXT, Inc., a company started by Steve Jobs in 1985. The name ".nib" originally stood for NeXT Interface Builder. Over time, NeXT was acquired by Apple, and the nib format evolved into a newer, XML-based format. This combination of XML and Interface Builder yielded the new *.xib* extension. Nonetheless, the name "nib file" stuck, and most developers still call their *.xib* files "nib files."

WARNING: You'll find the file *MainMenu.xib* in every Cocoa project you create in Xcode. This is a special file. Treat it as such. Do not move, rename, or otherwise annoy the file. Unless we tell you to. When your application gets launched, it will automatically load the contents of *MainMenu.xib* into memory. *MainMenu.xib* contains critical information, including your application's menu bar and main window (if it has one). Over time, you'll learn all there is to know about nib files and will be rolling your very own. For the moment, patience, and hands off.

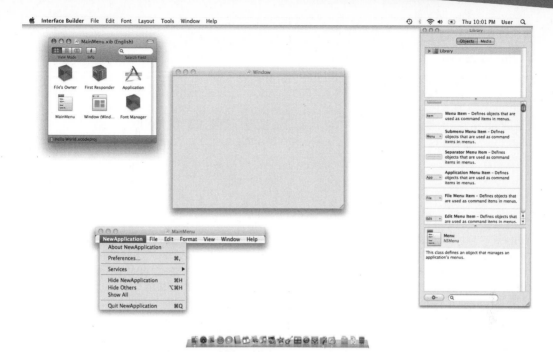

Figure 2–4. *MainMenu.xib opened in Interface Builder*

Exploring the Nib File

Once Interface Builder has launched, a series of windows will appear. A large blank window named *Window* (Figure 2–4, left middle) represents your application's main window. As you'll see in a moment, you'll use this window to lay out the contents of the window that will be displayed when your program is launched. The *Cocoa Application* project template we used to create this project assumed that you would have at least one window in your application, and it created that window instance for you.

The short, wide window labeled *MainMenu* (Figure 2–4, lower left) represents your application's menu bar. Changes to this window will be reflected in the menu bar that appears when your application is launched.

The window in the upper left corner with the title *MainMenu.nib (English)* is your nib's main window. Don't confuse this window with the window named *Window* (which represents your application's main window). The window titled *MainMenu.nib (English)* is basically the nib's main document window, which includes all the windows, views, and other objects contained in the nib. To distinguish this from the windows it contains, we usually refer to this window as the "main nib window." If you close a nib's main window, all the other windows relating to that nib will close as well.

The Library

On the right side of the screen, you'll notice a window with a smaller title bar (Figure 2–4, right side). The skinnier title bar is a clue that this window is not part of a specific document, but rather is some form of utility window. This particular window is known as **the library**. The library acts as a palette, a collection of objects you can use to build your application's interface. You scroll through the library looking for the item you want to use, then drag that item from the library into the appropriate Interface Builder window.

> **NOTE:** If you close the library, you can open it again by selecting **Library** from the **Tools** menu or by typing ⇧⌘L.

The library is divided into three primary panes, as shown in Figure 2–5. The top pane is called the organization pane, and lets you select specific groups of objects you'd like to explore. The middle pane is called the item pane. Obviously, the selection in the organization pane determines which items are displayed in the item pane. Finally, the bottom pane is called the detail pane. As its name suggests, the detail pane shows details about the currently selected item in the item pane.

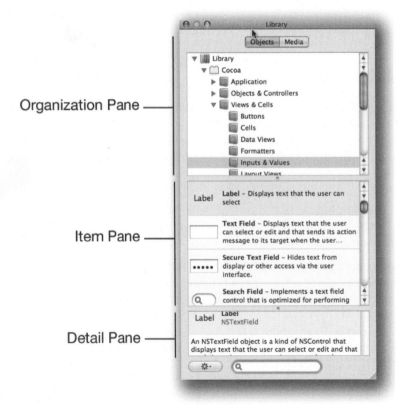

Figure 2–5. *The parts of Interface Builder's library*

Single-click the disclosure triangle next to the word *Library* in the organization pane (the top part of the library window), which should reveal a number of additional categories. The first one below *Library* should be called *Cocoa*, and it should also have a disclosure triangle next to it also. Click that one as well.

There are three sub-items under *Cocoa*. The first one is called *Application*, and contains objects that apply to your whole application, such as menus and windows. We already have all the menus and windows we need for now, so we can skip that one for the time being.

The second item is called *Objects & Controllers*. These are things that will help you manage your application data, but because we don't have any application data in this chapter, we're going to skip over this one for now, too. Don't worry, we'll return to these in later chapters.

The final sub-item under Cocoa is called *Views & Cells*. These are the various views and controls that can be used to build your application's user interface. Expand *Views & Cells*, and single-click the sub-item named *Inputs & Values* (Figure 2–6).

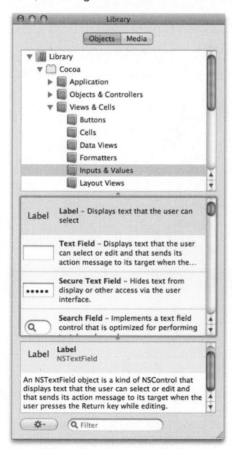

Figure 2–6. *The Library with the Label selected*

Dragging Out a Label

The library's item pane will show a list of items that can be dragged to your application window to build your application's interface. Let's drag one over now. The first item under *Inputs & Values* is called *Label*, and is used to display static text, text that the user can't edit. Let's drag a label over to the *Window* window.

In the library window, click on the first row in the item pane and drag a *Label* over to your application's main window (the window labeled *Window*). If you accidentally close your application window, you can bring it back up by double-clicking the icon labeled *Window* in the nib file's main window (the window labeled *MainMenu.xib*). Doing this will add a new label to your application's window.

> **TIP:** Instead of drilling down through the hierarchy as we just did, we could have just typed the word "label" into the search field at the bottom of the library window. This would have filtered down the list to show only those objects in the library with the word "label" in their name or description.

Now that you've got a label, let's change it. Double-click the label. It should become editable and selected (Figure 2–7).

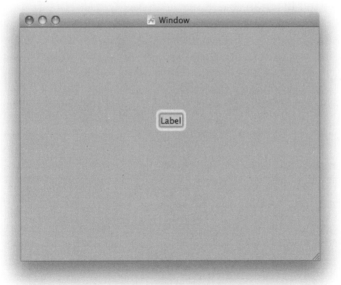

Figure 2–7. *The new label becomes editable when double-clicked.*

Because the existing text is selected, you can just type your new text and it will replace what was there before. Go ahead and type "Hello, World!", which is infinitely less boring than "Label." If you're feeling rebellious, you *could* type something else, but don't blame us if the Tiki Gods come after you!

Using the Blue Guidelines

When you're done editing the label, press return to commit the changes, which will take that label out of editing mode. Next, click and drag the label toward the left side of the window. As it gets near the left edge of the window, you should notice a dashed blue line to the left of your text (see Figure 2–8). Interface Builder uses these blue guidelines to indicate that the item you are dragging is aligned properly with the items around it. In this case, the guideline is telling you that your label is the proper distance from the left edge of the window.

> **NOTE:** One of the things that have made using the Mac such a pleasant experience over the years has been the consistency of the user interface. In the vast majority of Mac applications, you can count on the ability to press ⌘W to close a window, ⌘S to save, and ⌘P to print, regardless of what program you are in. If you're going to write software for the Mac, you should know these "rules of consistency." Apple lays out these rules in their "Human Interface Guidelines" (also know as the HIG). Interface Builder's little blue guidelines are there expressly to make it easier for you to conform to the Human Interface Guidelines. You can find a copy of the HIG here:
>
> http://developer.apple.com/documentation/UserExperience/Conceptual/AppleHIGuidelines

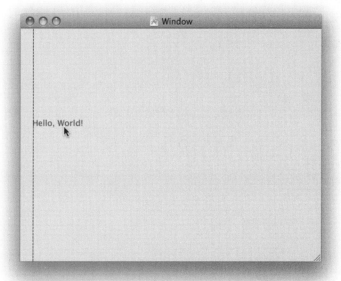

Figure 2–8. *When you move the object near the edges, blue lines appear.*

The Inspector Window

Another important Interface Builder window looks very similar to the library window, so much so that you might get them confused. This one's called the inspector. To open the inspector, select **Inspector** from the **Tools** menu or type ⇧⌘I. The inspector is typically closed when you launch Interface Builder for the first time.

The inspector is a context-sensitive window that displays information about the currently selected object. Click a window and the inspector displays information about that window (see Figure 2–9). Click your label and the inspector displays information about that label. You get the idea.

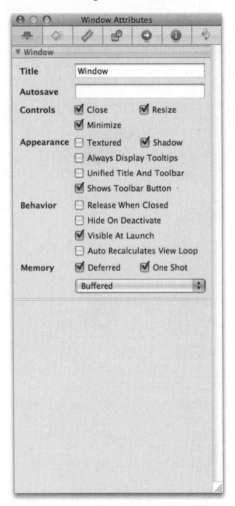

Figure 2–9. *The inspector showing attributes for the window*

Take a look at the inspector window shown in Figure 2–9. Notice the seven small tabs that span the top of the window. When pressed, each tab will turn the window into one of seven different inspector types.

There is also a keyboard shortcut for each of the inspectors, starting with ⌘1 to go to the left-most inspector (the attributes inspector, which you'll use the most) through ⌘7 for the right-most inspector. Table 2–1 lists the command-key equivalents for each of the seven inspectors.

Table 2–1. *Key Combination Shortcuts for Interface Builder's Inspectors*

Key Combination	Inspector
⌘1	Attribute Inspector
⌘2	Effects Inspector
⌘3	Size Inspector
⌘4	Bindings Inspector
⌘5	Connections Inspector
⌘6	Identity Inspector
⌘7	AppleScript Inspector

The Attributes Inspector

Let's start off with a look at the attributes inspector. If you don't see it, press ⌘1 to bring up the window, then single-click on your label. The inspector should look like Figure 2–10.

You can use the attributes inspector to change the appearance of your label. You can change attributes like text alignment, border, and scrolling behavior. Interestingly, several of these fields will actually do nothing. Go ahead and type something into the *Placeholder* field. Doesn't change the appearance of the label at all, does it?

What's going on here? When you pull a *Label* out of the library, you are grabbing an instance of the *NSTextField* class. The *NSTextField* class is used for both static and editable text fields. In an editable text field, the placeholder is that gray text you see in some text fields when they are empty, which tells you what the field is for. Figure 2–11 shows an example of placeholder text, used to indicate that the text typed in this field will be sent to Google to initiate a search.

Figure 2–10. *The attribute inspector showing all the attributes of the label that can be edited in Interface Builder*

Figure 2–11. *The search box in Safari uses a placeholder to tell you that typing text into that field will initiate a Google web search.*

When a text field is configured as a label, there's no need for a placeholder. It doesn't hurt to provide one, but it doesn't help, either.

There are too many context-specific attributes to be able to enumerate them all in this book, but we will walk through the non-obvious ones. As you make your way through the book, you'll become comfortable with most of the attributes that you'll find yourself using.

Let's change the size of the label. If the label is not selected, single-click it to select it. A dot should appear on either side of the label. These dots are resize handles, which allow you to change the size of the selected item. Most objects in Interface Builder have four resize handles, one in each corner, which allow you to adjust the size in all four directions. Certain items, like labels, only have two resize handles. The label's attributes (the size of its font in particular) determine the vertical size of the label. You don't change the height of the label by resizing it. You only use the resize handles to change the width of the label.

Let's center the label. Make sure the left side of the label is lined up with the blue guideline near the left edge of the window. Then, grab the right resize handle and drag out the label until you get to the blue guideline near the right edge of the window. Once you're done, your label should look like Figure 2–12.

Figure 2–12. *Your application's window in Interface Builder, after resizing the label*

Now, with the label still selected, bring up the attributes inspector by typing ⌘1. In the attributes inspector, look for a row of buttons labeled *Alignment*, and select the "center text" button (Figure 2–13). Also, look for a button labeled *Selectable* under the heading *Behavior*. Click that checkbox, which tells Cocoa that we want to allow the user copy this label to the pasteboard if they want. By default, labels are not selectable, but we just changed that.

Figure 2–13. *The alignment buttons in the Attributes Inspector for the label, set to centered text*

Change the Label's Color and Font

Let's make one final change to our window's content: let's change the font, size, and color of the text. If you look at the attributes inspector, you can probably figure out how to change the color of the text, but you may be wondering if it's even possible to change the font and size. Fear not: it is. But you don't change font and size in the attributes inspector.

First, let's set the color. Look in the attributes inspector for a color well labeled *Text* (Figure 2–14). If you click that, the standard Mac OS X color picker will appear (Figure 2–15), and you can select the color you want for the text. Go ahead and do that now, picking whatever color strikes your fancy.

Figure 2–14. *The color well from the Attributes Inspector used for changing the color of the label*

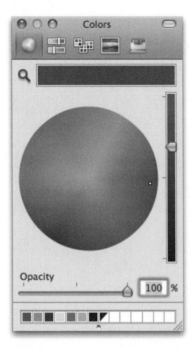

Figure 2–15. *The standard Mac OS X color picker is used for selecting colors in Cocoa applications. Here, we're using it in Interface Builder to set the color of our text.*

Interface Builder itself is built using Cocoa, and leverages a lot of built-in Cocoa functionality, such as the standard color picker. The Apple engineers do not want to re-invent the wheel any more than you do. When you write your own applications, you'll be able to use this exact same color picker with just a few lines of code or, in some situations, without writing any code at all.

Another piece of built-in Mac OS X functionality that you'll be able to use in your applications is the standard font window (Figure 2–16), which allows you to change the font, size, and attributes of selected text. Press ⌘T to bring up the font window in Interface Builder. Make sure that your label is still selected (look for the resize handles), and also make sure that your application's main window is still the frontmost window.

Play with the font window and make your text look just the way you want it to. Because this application will only be running on your machine, you can select any font and combination of attributes that you wish. When creating applications that will be distributed to others, it is important to realize that you could select fonts that your user won't have installed. In general, for standard GUI components, you're probably better not changing the fonts at all. Consistent font usage is an important part of the GUI consistency that the Mac is known for. Most labels, buttons, and other controls use the Lucida Grande font by default. You can change the size of some labels, and switch them between Bold and Regular to highlight different things, but leave the font itself as it is.

Figure 2–16. *Mac OS X's font window is available for use in all Cocoa applications. It's also used in Interface Builder to let you change the font, size, and font attributes of text you place on your interface.*

Once you have your label looking just the way you like, we'll make one more set of changes in Interface Builder. Then, we'll go back to Xcode, put some finishing touches on our application, then run it. If you're running short on screen space, you can close the font window, the color picker, and even your application's main window (the one that says "Hello World"). Just make sure you don't close the nib's main window yet (the one with the icons in it), because we're not quite done with this nib.

Using the Menu Editor

If the menu editor (Figure 2–4, lower left) is not showing, open it by double-clicking the *MainMenu* icon in your nib's main window. The menu editor allows you to edit the contents of your application's menu bar. By default, *MainMenu.xib* comes with many of the standard menu items that you would want in a Cocoa application. We'll get into the specifics of working with the menu bar later in the book, but here's a quick overview. As you build your application, you'll provide actions for the each menu item you want to support. When the menu bar is drawn, if an action to respond to an item is available, the item is enabled. If no action is available, the item is disabled (grayed out). Some actions are provided for you, such as those provided for text-related menus like **Copy** or **Paste**. For items you will never use, the best approach is just to delete them.

For the moment, don't worry about the mechanics of working with the menu bar.

Let's customize the menu bar for our "Hello World" application. If you're running Snow Leopard, the menu has been pre-configured to use your application's name in the relevant places, but for projects created on Leopard, you'll see the text

"NewApplication" in five different places in the menu bar and individual menus. All of these need to be changed to reflect the actual application name. If you're using Snow Leopard or later, you can skip ahead to the next section ("Creating Your Application Icon").

First, change the name in the application menu. The application menu is the menu immediately to the right of the Apple menu, and is named after the running application. The application menu lets the user know which application is frontmost. Because your application does not control the Apple menu, the Apple menu does not appear in the nib's menu editor. The left-most menu that you can edit here is the application menu. The menu title is **NewApplication**. Double-click the menu title. It will become editable. Change the application menu title from **NewApplication** to **Hello World** (Figure 2–17). Click on another menu or item, or type return to commit the change.

Figure 2–17. *Using the menu editor to change the application menu title from NewApplication to "Hello World"*

Remember, the application's name appears in five places. That's one down, and four to go. Next, single-click the freshly changed **Hello World** menu, which should cause the actual menu to drop down so you can edit its contents (Figure 2–18).

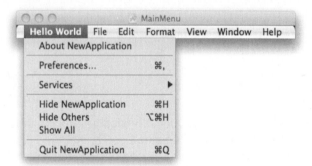

Figure 2–18. *Expanding the application menu in Interface Builder's menu editor*

Inside the application menu, there are three more occurrences of **NewApplication** that need to be changed to **Hello World**. The process here is exactly the same as it was for changing the menu name. Just double-click on a menu item to put it into edit mode, type the new value, then hit return, or click out to commit the change. Make the change to the **About**, **Hide**, and **Quit** items. Four down, one to go.

Next, click on the **Help** menu, the right-most menu in the menu editor's menu bar. You could change the single item in this menu, just as you did in the application menu. But instead, we're just going to get rid of the **Help** menu in its entirety. One reason to do this is the fact that we have no plans on supporting the **Help** menu in this particular application. More to the point, we just wanted to show you how to delete a menu.

Single-click the **Help** menu so the menu title is selected, then press the delete key. The menu should disappear. That's all five done, well done!

Save your nib file by pressing ⌘S. We're now done with Interface Builder, at least for the time being. You can leave Interface Builder open if you want, because we'll be using it in the next chapter, but close the nib file's main window because we won't be editing this particular nib any more. After closing it, go back to Xcode.

Creating Your Application Icon

One thing that all applications need is an icon. Mac OS X uses a special file format for icons, and the developer tools you downloaded includes an application named Icon Composer designed to help you create the *.icns* files you'll need. You can find Icon Composer on your hard drive at */Developer/Applications/Utilities/Icon Composer.app*.

You need to start your icon in an image-editing program such as Photoshop, Acorn, or GIMP. You should create your original file at a size of 512×512 pixels, and save it in a standard image format that supports alpha channels (transparency) such as TIFF, PSD, or PNG. Once you have your original file saved, launch Icon Composer, and drag your image to the Icon Composer window. Icon Composer will convert your image into the right format, and even let you specify different images for different sizes. This is a handy feature if you've got details in the 512×512 image that are important but which won't be readable at smaller sizes. In that situation, you can create a slightly different version for the smaller sizes to make sure that the important details can be seen no matter what icon size is used. Figure 2–19 shows Icon Composer in action.

After you've imported the image or images that make up your icon, you can save the document to a *.icns* file, which can be imported into your Xcode project to serve as your application's icon.

To save you the trouble of creating your own icon, we've provided a .icns file you can add to your project. If you'd rather roll your own, go right ahead and use Icon Composer to create a file named *hello world.icns*.

Alternatively, you can use the *hello world.icns* file you'll find in the *02 – Hello World* folder that came with the downloaded project files.

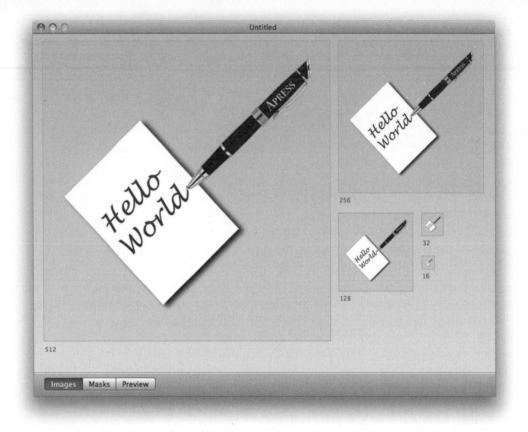

Figure 2–19. *Designing an icon in Icon Composer. Note that you can specify different versions of the icon for different sizes.*

Adding Your Icon to Your Project

Whether you created an icon yourself or you are using ours, drag your *hello world.icns* file from the Finder to Xcode's *Resources* group (Figure 2–20) in the *Groups & Files* pane of Xcode, which tells Xcode that you want to import this file into your project. You can also select **Add to Project…** from the **Project** menu if you prefer to select the file using the standard file browser rather than using drag and drop.

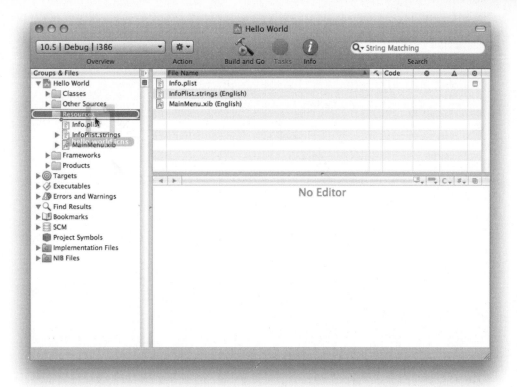

Figure 2–20. *Dragging a file to the Groups & Files pane is one way to import a file into an Xcode project.*

When you let go of the mouse button or select the file to be imported, a sheet will appear (Figure 2–21), allowing you to specify how you want to import the file. The main item to be concerned with on this sheet is the checkbox at the top, which asks you if you want to copy the object into the project folder. If this checkbox is turned on, Xcode will create a copy of the file in your project's folder and then import that copy into your project. If that box is not selected, then it will add the file to the project by linking to the original file.

Most of the time, you will want to do copy the file into your project folder, as it keeps all the resources for your project together. However, if you share resources among more than one project, then you may want to leave this checkbox turned off, which will cause Xcode to reference the file from its original location.

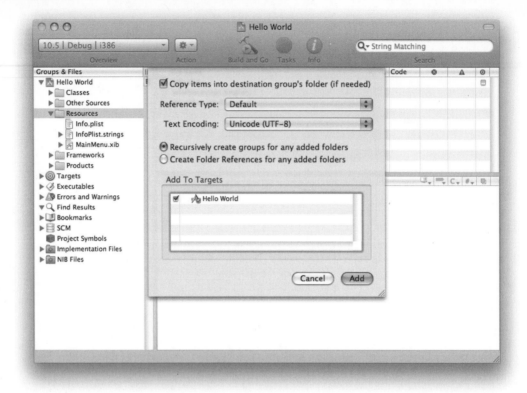

Figure 2–21. *Xcode asks you how you want to import the object.*

Make sure the box is selected, as in Figure 2–21, and then press the *Add* button. That will add this file to your Xcode project and also copy it into the project folder. Now, whenever you build your project, Xcode will include this file when it builds your application. That's not enough to make the file your application's icon, however. An application could potentially contain more than one icon file, so you have to explicitly tell Xcode which file to use for the application's main icon.

To do that, single-click on the file *Info.plist* under the *Resources* group in the *Groups & Files* pane, which will open that file up in the editing pane (Figure 2–22). *Info.plist* contains a variety of information about your application. One of the items of information it holds is the name of the application's icon file.

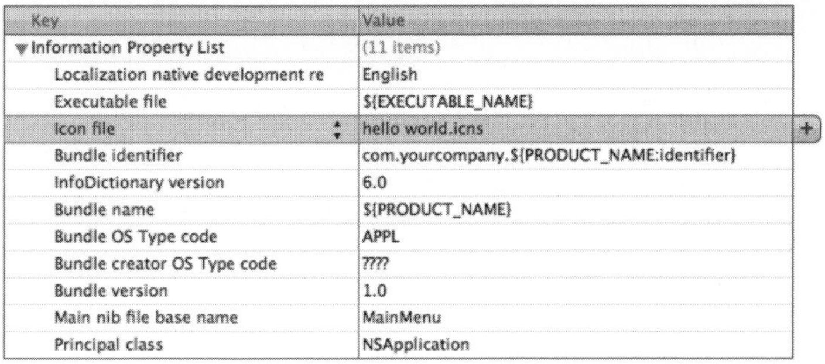

Key	Value
▼ Information Property List	(11 items)
Localization native development re	English
Executable file	${EXECUTABLE_NAME}
Icon file	hello world.icns
Bundle identifier	com.yourcompany.${PRODUCT_NAME:identifier}
InfoDictionary version	6.0
Bundle name	${PRODUCT_NAME}
Bundle OS Type code	APPL
Bundle creator OS Type code	????
Bundle version	1.0
Main nib file base name	MainMenu
Principal class	NSApplication

Figure 2–22. *Info.plist opened in the editing pane so you can specify the name of this application's icon file*

Property Lists

Info.plist is a special kind of file known as a property list. Property lists are used extensively throughout OS X. Although end users rarely see them, they are used in many parts of Cocoa development, so you will see them a lot.

Property list files are made up of a list of entries. Each entry is made up of a **key** and a **value**. Figure 2–22 shows Xcode's built-in property list editor, editing the file *Info.plist*. Each row represents a single entry. As you can see, the property list consists of two columns. The left column is labeled *Key* and the right column is labeled *Value*.

> **NOTE:** Property lists also have the ability to store multiple values under a single key. It is possible to store either an array (or list) of items under a single key, or even to store another whole set of keys and values under one key. It'll be a while before we need that functionality, but we figured you should know it was possible.

In Figure 2–22, the entry with the key *Icon file* is highlighted. The value associated with that key, shown in the right column, should be blank. Double-click the empty column to the right of the *Icon file* key, and type *hello world.icns*. Now press ⌘S to save the property list.

Are you ready to write some code? Well, guess what? There's none to write. We're done with our application.

Running Your Application

Build and run your application by selecting **Build & Run** from the **Build Menu** or by typing ⌘R. Xcode will build your application, which may take a bit, then run your application. A window should appear containing your centered, colored label. If you look in the Dock at the bottom of your Mac's main screen, you should see your application represented by the icon you imported into your project. But wait: there's more!

Select **About Hello World** from the **Hello World** menu (Figure 2–23). Not only do you get an About box for free, but it includes your icon.

Figure 2–23. *Your application uses your icon in a variety of places, including the about box.*

We're still not done. Move your mouse over the words "Hello World" in your application's main window. Your cursor should change from an arrow to a text-cursor. Because you made the label selectable, Cocoa automatically changes the cursor as a hint to the user that they can select this text. Go ahead and double-click the word *Hello*, and it will highlight. Now if you select the **Edit** menu, you'll see that the **Copy** menu item is not grayed out. If you choose it, your program will copy the word "Hello" to the pasteboard and you can then paste it into any other application that accepts text. With *Hello* still selected, select the **Edit** menu, then select the **Speech** submenu, and select **Start Speaking**. Your application will say "Hello" using your Mac's text-to-speech capabilities.

Without writing a single line of code, your application supports copying text to the pasteboard, and text-to-speech. With almost no work, your application behaves like a real Mac application, with windows and a menu bar, and it responds to the common key commands, like ⌘Q to quit. Your application's main window can be moved around, minimized to the Dock, and even closed. You can hide your application, or hide all the other applications. All of this functionality is yours for three easy payments of nothing, including shipping and handling. That is the power of Cocoa. If your computer already knows how to do something, you probably won't have to write very much code to do that thing, and sometimes you won't have to write any code at all.

Sharing Your Creation With the World

Quit *Hello World*. There's one last thing we want to show you. You've now created your application, but where is it? What if you want to give (or sell) your application to others so they can run it on their machine?

First of all, you need to compile your application a little differently if you want to let others use it. Back in Xcode, if you look in the upper left part of the project window (Figure 2–24), you'll see a large drop-down menu labeled *Overview*.

Figure 2–24. *The left side of Xcode's toolbar contains a multi-segmented drop-down menu that lets you specify the Mac OS X version to build for, build configuration, and target architecture.*

This drop-down menu works differently from most other controls of its kind. Rather than letting you just pick one item from the menu, the Overview drop-down menu lets you make several choices that affect the compilation of your app, all from a single control. Figure 2–25 shows what you'll see if you click on this control. There are several sections, and in each section you can select an item to change some aspect of the compilation process. In this case, the only things we can change are the *Active Configuration* and the *Active Architecture*.

Figure 2–25. *Peering inside the Overview drop-down list*

The second section of the drop-down menu is labeled *Active Configuration*, and that's what you need to change so you can build a version of your application to distribute. By default, when you're working in Xcode, you're working in the debug configuration. When you build an application this way, Xcode builds it with extra stuff to make it easier to troubleshoot your application. These debug symbols allow you, for example, to examine and change the values of different variables while the program is running, or to step through your source code line-by-line using the debugger. In this chapter, we're not doing anything that needs those symbols, but it's generally good to develop using the debug configuration, switching out of it only to create a distributable version of your application.

An application built using the debug configuration is going to be a bit bigger and slower than one built for distribution. On the other hand, building for distribution is typically a bit slower than building the debug version, because the compiler is doing more work to try to optimize the resulting code, and usually building for multiple platforms (Intel and

PowerPC) as well. In any case, in order to distribute your application, you have to switch to the other configuration, called the release configuration. Do that now.

Once you've selected that, select **Build** from the **Build** menu or press ⌘B to build your application. Once Xcode reports that it has successfully built the project, right-click on the top-most item in the *Groups & File's* pane. The item is named *Hello World* and represents your project.

> **NOTE:** In several places in the book, we will tell you to right-click on something. If you have an older one-button mouse, you can achieve the same thing by holding down the control key on your keyboard then clicking with the mouse's one button.

Select **Reveal in Finder** from the contextual menu that appears. This will take you to the *Hello World* project folder in the Finder. Inside the window that opens up, you'll find another folder called *build*. Inside *build*, you'll find three more folders. The folder called *Hello World.build* holds temporary files that Xcode generates during the build process. The other two are named after the configurations that we've used to build the project: *Debug* and *Release*.

Inside *Release*, and you will find two files. One, called *Hello World* or *Hello World.app* (depending on your Finder preferences) is your brand-spanking-new application.

Congratulations. You're a developer. That's a full-fledged application you're looking at, just like all the ones in your *Applications* folder. You can e-mail it to your Aunt Bessie or your best friend to show off the fact that you are now a bona fide Mac OS X application developer. Don't worry about the other file in this folder. It's something called a symbols file, and it's used in some more advanced debugging scenarios that are beyond the scope of this book.

Here's a common "gotcha" you should be aware of: if you switch to the release configuration, then go back to do more development on your application, be sure you remember to switch back to the debug configuration. In our case, now that your application has been successfully built, you should do just that: switch back to the debug configuration in case you decide to do more development on this program.

Goodbye, Hello World

In this chapter, you were introduced to Xcode and Interface Builder, the dynamic duo of Cocoa software creation tools. You designed a full-fledged application without writing a single line of code. You learned how to add a text label to your application's main window, changed the label attributes, changed your application's menu, gave your application an icon, and you even saw how to build a distributable version of your application.

In this chapter, you got your first taste of the power of Cocoa by seeing what you can do without writing any code. In the next chapter, you'll see how powerful things start to get when you actually do write some code.

Chapter 3

Lights, Camera... Actions! (and Outlets, Too)

It really is amazing all the stuff you get free with Cocoa, as you saw in the last chapter. But there was something very important missing in the last chapter's application that most applications will need: the ability to interact with the user. When you were in Interface Builder, in the last chapter, you saw that there was a whole library filled with objects like text fields and buttons that you can use to assemble your interface, but those user interface objects are no good if we can't tell when they're used or change the data they contain. In this chapter, you'll see how those objects can be used to let users interact with your application.

In this chapter, you'll first learn a little about the way OS X is organized so that you'll know where the functionality you'll be using resides. Then you'll learn about the Model-View-Controller design pattern, which was the guiding principle used by the architects of Cocoa, and which should also be your guiding principle when writing your own applications. After that, we'll discuss actions and outlets, which allow your code to interact with the stuff you build in Interface Builder. Finally, you'll dive in and build another Cocoa application, but this time you'll build one that gets information from the user and then responds to it.

A WORD ABOUT LEOPARD AND OBJECTIVE-C 2.0

Mac OS X Leopard (10.5) introduced some very big changes into the world of the Cocoa developer. With the release of Leopard, we saw the first major upgrade to Objective-C ever. Objective-C 2.0 brings a whole bunch of new features that make your life easier, including:

- **Garbage Collection**, which automatically handles memory management for you.

- **Properties,** which free you from having to write accessor and mutator methods.

- **Dot Notation**, which lets you use accessors and mutator methods similar to the way Java and C++ work.

■ **Fast Enumeration**, which provides a way to iterate over collections of objects quickly and with fewer lines of code.

Using Objective-C 2.0 in a Cocoa application makes the application only work on Mac OS X Leopard (10.5), Mac OS X Snow Leopard (10.6), or later versions. At the time of writing, however, the Leopard install base is large enough that if you're learning Cocoa now you should learn the new stuff. These new features will make developing software faster and result in better code that's easier to maintain.

Therefore, all the examples in this book assume that you are running Leopard or later, and the applications you'll be writing in this book will run only on Leopard or later. Also, although the iPhone allows for most of the new features of Objective-C 2.0, garbage collection isn't one of them, so some of what you learn in this book will not really apply to the iPhone at this time.

This Chapter's Application

After we get through a bit of theory, we're going to build an application. Our application will have a single window with three buttons. When one of the buttons is clicked, the application will display a label identifying which button it was (Figure 3–1).

Figure 3–1. *The Buttons application presents three buttons to the user. When a button is clicked, text is displayed identifying which button it was.*

The application is simple, but the mechanisms you will use to create it are the same ones that you will use in nearly all user interaction in Cocoa, so it's important that you understand what we're doing in this chapter.

Frameworks, Frameworks Everywhere

In Mac OS X, Apple has grouped code and supporting files together in special folders (or **bundles**) called **frameworks**. Frameworks are like the libraries used on most platforms, but they are more flexible because they are folders rather than flat files. Frameworks can contain images, sounds, and movies. They can even contain other frameworks.

Although OS X supports traditional Unix libraries, much of the functionality of the operating system, and nearly all of the functionality that makes OS X unique, is contained in these frameworks. There are literally dozens of frameworks that make up the core operating system, and these are generally grouped by function.

TIP: You can see the frameworks that make up Mac OS X by looking in the folder `/System/Library/Frameworks`. These frameworks should never, ever be touched, so look only, then quietly back out of the folder so they don't hear you. Frameworks can be nasty little buggers if you try and touch them. You can also see what third-party and optional frameworks have been installed in your system by looking in `/Library/Frameworks`. This is where the frameworks that are needed by programs you have installed on your Mac typically reside. Again, look, but don't touch, or you could mess up something important.

Although there are many frameworks, you'll spend the vast majority of your programming time in Cocoa using objects from just a handful. In fact, most of the objects you'll use come from a single framework called (surprise!) the Cocoa framework.

Remember how we told you that frameworks can contain other frameworks? Well, the Cocoa framework is, in fact, just a wrapper around three other frameworks that hold the bulk of the functionality you will use when writing Cocoa applications: the **Foundation framework**, the **AppKit framework**, and the **Core Data framework**.

You will periodically use functionality from other frameworks. For example, you might use the **Core Animation framework** to do some spiffy animation with your user interface, or you might use the **Core Image framework** to do some heavy-duty image manipulation. But, the vast majority of the objects you will be using will be from the three frameworks that make up Cocoa. We'll talk about the Core Data framework starting in Chapter 7, but let's take a second to briefly look at the other two, which we'll be working with in this chapter.

The Foundation Framework

The Foundation framework is aptly named. It holds the objects that pretty much everything else is built upon. The Foundation framework is shared between Cocoa and Cocoa Touch. Although the Foundation framework has evolved, many of the objects it contains have been around since the early days of NeXTStep, and their basic usage hasn't changed all that much. Foundation contains objects such as `NSString`, which is the class used to represent text in Cocoa, as well as the collection classes like `NSArray` and `NSDictionary`. You should already have some familiarity with the Foundation framework from having learned Objective-C.

The AppKit Framework

Look at your Mac's screen. Pretty much everything you see there is the domain of AppKit, which is an abbreviation of "application kit." This framework contains all the objects used to create or manage a user interface. There are objects that create buttons, windows, text fields, tab bars, and more. Any user interface element that you've seen in more than one application is probably part of the AppKit framework. All that cool stuff you got for free last chapter? Yep, all AppKit.

The Cocoa Way: Model-View-Controller

Before diving in and seeing how we use these frameworks, we need to discuss a very important bit of theory. The designers of Cocoa were guided by a concept called **Model-View-Controller** (**MVC**), which is a very logical way of dividing the code that makes up a GUI application. These days, almost all object-oriented application frameworks pay a certain amount of homage to MVC, but there are few that are as true to the MVC model as Cocoa, or that have been using it as long.

The MVC model divides up all functionality into three distinct categories:

- Model: The classes that hold your application's data.

- View: Made up of the windows, controls, and other elements that the user can see and interact with.

- Controller: Binds the model and view together and contains the application logic that determines how to handle the user's inputs.

The goal of MVC is to make the objects that implement these three types of code as distinct from one another as possible. Any object you write should be readily identifiable as belonging to one of the three categories, with little or no functionality within it that could be classified within either of the other two. An object that implements a button, for example, shouldn't contain code to process data when that button is clicked; and code that implements a bank account shouldn't contain code to draw a table to display its transactions.

MVC helps ensure maximum reusability. A class that implements a generic button can be used in any application. A class that implements a button that does some particular calculation when it is clicked can only be used in the application for which it was originally written.

When you write Cocoa applications, you will primarily create your view components using Interface Builder, although you will sometimes also modify your interface from code, or you might subclass existing view and control classes to create new ones.

Your model will be created using something called Core Data or crafting Objective-C classes to hold your application's data. We won't be creating any model objects in this chapter's application, because we're not going to store any data; but we will introduce very simple model objects starting next chapter, and move on to full-fledged model objects when we start using Core Data in Chapter 7.

Your controller component will typically be comprised of classes that you create and that are specific to your application. Controllers can be completely custom classes (NSObject subclasses), which was the traditional way of doing things in Cocoa. A few years ago, Apple began to introduce generic controller classes into the AppKit framework that handle certain basic tasks for you, such as handling an array of objects to be displayed in a list.

As we get deeper into Cocoa, you will quickly start to see how the classes of the AppKit framework follow the principles of MVC. If you keep this concept in the back of your head as you develop, you will create cleaner, more easily maintained code.

Outlets, Actions, and Controllers

Obviously, a user interface isn't much use if you can't get data in and out of it or change its appearance from code. In Cocoa, we use things called **actions** and **outlets** to interact with the user interfaces we design in Interface Builder.

- Actions are methods we write that can be executed directly as a result of user interaction, such as at the click of a button.

- Outlets are pointers to objects in our nib file. Outlets allow us to access objects in the nib from our code.

Actions and outlets are typically contained in your controller classes (although they are sometimes used elsewhere).

Declaring Outlets

Outlets are Objective-C instance variables that are declared using a special keyword: IBOutlet. An outlet is really nothing more than an object pointer that can be linked to an object in your user interface. So, for example, your controller class might declare an outlet to an editable text field like this:

```
@property IBOutlet NSTextField *nameField;
```

In this example, as far as your code is concerned, nameField is a pointer to whatever text field you link it to in Interface Builder. It will behave exactly the same way as a pointer to an object that you allocated and initialized yourself. Once an outlet is linked to an object, you can retrieve or set its value, hide it, disable it, or do anything else that the object supports. We'll see how to make the link between an outlet and an object in a nib file in a moment.

OUTLET CHANGES

Prior to Objective-C 2.0, the IBOutlet keyword was placed in the instance variable declaration, like this:

IBOutlet NSTextField *nameField

Since the release of Objective-C 2.0, Apple's sample code has been moving toward placing the IBOutlet keyword in the property declaration, like this:

```
@property IBOutlet NSTextField *nameField;
```

Both mechanisms are still supported and, for the most part, there is no difference in the way things work based on where you put the keyword. There is one exception to that, however: if you declare a property with a different name than its underlying instance variable (which can be done in the @synthesize directive), then you have to put the IBOutlet keyword in the property declaration, not in the instance variable declaration, in order for it to work correctly. Although both work, we're going to follow Apple's lead and put the IBOutlet keyword on the property declaration, for the most part. In some of our applications, we'll have outlets to objects without any matching properties, and in those cases we'll put the IBOutlet keyword in front of the instance variable declaration.

You can read more about the new Objective-C properties in the second edition of *Learn Objective-C on the Mac*, by Mark Dalrymple and Scott Knaster (Apress, 2008), and in The Objective-C 2.0 Programming Language available from Apple's developer site at:
http://developer.apple.com/documentation/Cocoa/Conceptual/ObjectiveC/ObjC.pdf

Declaring Actions

Actions are Objective-C methods that can be invoked directly from your application's user interface. They are methods just like any other Objective-C methods you've written, but they get executed when a user interface item is utilized. If you link a button to an action method, for example, the code in your action method will fire any time that button is clicked. If you link a text field to an action, its action method will fire any time the user tabs out of that text field or otherwise moves to another control. Exactly what will cause the method to fire depends on the type of object that is linked to it and, sometimes, how the attributes of that object are set. A slider, for example, may cause your action method to fire once after the user releases the mouse button, or it may repeatedly cause your method to fire as the slider is used, depending on how you set up the slider instance in Interface Builder.

Actions are created exactly the way other Objective-C methods are, except that they must be declared using a special return type: IBAction. Actions must take a single argument (typically declared as type id). This argument is used to tell the method which interface item is calling it. Action method declarations have to look like this:

```
-(IBAction)doSomething:(id)sender;
```

The name of the method can be anything you want, but the return type has to be IBAction, and the method has to take one argument of type id, which will be a pointer to the object that triggered the action. If this method gets called as the result of the user clicking a button, then sender will be a pointer to the button pressed.

CAUTION: Action methods are one area where Cocoa and Cocoa Touch are different. In Cocoa Touch, action methods can have one of three different method signatures, taking either zero, one, or two arguments. This is not the case for actions in Cocoa, which must take one and only one argument.

BUT WHAT ARE THEY?

You might be wondering just what `IBAction` and `IBOutlet` are. Are they part of the Objective-C language?

Nope. They're good old-fashioned C pre-processor macros. If you go into the *AppKit.framework* and look at the *NSNibDeclarations.h* header file, you'll see that they're defined like this:

```
#ifndef IBOutlet
#define IBOutlet
#endif

#ifndef IBAction
#define IBAction void
#endif
```

Confused? These two keywords do absolutely nothing as far as the compiler is concerned. `IBOutlet` gets entirely removed from the code before the compiler ever sees it. `IBAction` resolves to a `void` return type, which just means that action methods do not return a value. So, what's going on here?

The answer is simple, really: `IBOutlet` and `IBAction` are not used by the compiler. They are used by Interface Builder. Interface Builder uses these keywords to parse out the outlets and actions available to it. Interface Builder can only see methods that are prefaced with `IBAction` and can only see variables or properties that are prefaced with `IBOutlet`. Also, the presence of these keywords tells other programmers, looking at your code in the future, that the variables and methods in question aren't dealt with entirely in code. They'll need to delve into the relevant nib file to see how things are hooked up and used.

Outlets and Actions in Action

That's enough theory, let's get our hands dirty by writing another Cocoa application. If you're not still in Xcode, open it back up. Now, press ⌘⇧N or select **New Project...** from the **File** menu. Select the *Cocoa Application* template again (if you're running Snow Leopard, make sure the checkboxes for Core Data and Document-based application are turned off), and when prompted for a project name, type "Buttons."

Enabling Garbage Collection

We mentioned earlier that Objective-C 2.0 includes support for garbage collection (usually abbreviated "GC"). By using GC, you'll be able to write your applications more quickly and maintain them more easily, because you won't have to worry about managing the memory your objects occupy. We're going to use GC in nearly every application in this book, so try to dedicate the following steps to memory as you perform them. In the *Groups & Files* pane in Xcode, double-click the top-most item called *Buttons*. Double-clicking the root node in the *Groups & Files* pane brings up the Project Info window (Figure 3–2). This is where we can set a whole bunch of project-wide configuration options.

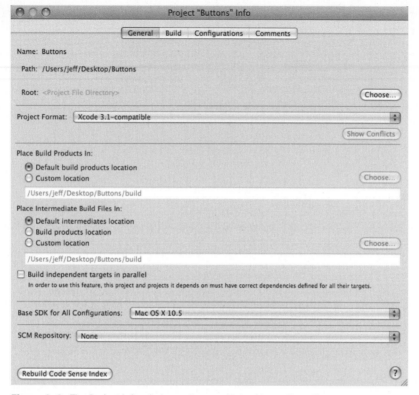

Figure 3–2. *The Project Info window, where project-wide configurations can be set.*

Select the tab labeled *Build*. Choose All Configurations from the Configuration popup list, so that the change we're about to make will be applied to every way we might build our application (with or without code optimizing, and so on). Scroll down until you see a heading that reads *GCC 4.0 – Code Generation*. If you're running Snow Leopard, it will instead refer to GCC 4.2. Underneath that heading, you should see an entry in the left-hand column that reads *Objective-C Garbage Collection*. Set the value next to it to *Required*. As of this writing, the default value for this setting is *Unsupported*, though that may change at some point.

We just turned on garbage collection for our project. Garbage collection is a relatively new feature in the Objective-C language that frees you from having to worry about most aspects of memory management, because the runtime keeps track of when objects are no longer being used and releases their memory on your behalf.

Garbage collection is not available on older versions of the Mac OS prior to Leopard (10.5), nor is it available on the iPhone. For Cocoa development that doesn't need to support legacy versions of the operating systems, though, garbage collection is the way to go. On today's powerful computer systems, the overhead associated with garbage collection is practically meaningless, and on multi-core and multi-processor machines, garbage collection can actually result in applications that perform better than those requiring manual memory management, because the garbage collector will take advantage of unused cores or processors for recovering memory. Additionally, you'll save time from not having to worry about or debug memory-related issues.

> **NOTE:** Garbage collection in Objective-C is a topic not without some controversy. Some developers have been resistant to using garbage collection, preferring to do manual memory management. With the improvements to the multi-processing architecture and garbage collector that arrived with Snow Leopard, however, the case for garbage collection has become very compelling, and it should be used unless you have a very good reason not to.

Creating Our Controller Class

Now that we've got our project set up to use garbage collection, it's time to create our controller class. Expand the *Classes* folder in the *Groups & Files* pane. If you're running Snow Leopard, you'll see a pair of files called *ButtonsAppDelegate.h* and *ButtonsAppDelegate.m* that define your application's main controller class. They were created for you when you created the Xcode project, and you can skip on down to the "Declaring an Outlet and Action" section. However, if you're still running Leopard, your version of Xcode doesn't create that class for you, so that folder will be empty. The disclosure triangle will expand, but nothing else will change. That's because there are no classes in your project yet. Our application is going to need a single controller class, however, so we're going to create that class now. Single-click the *Classes* folder to select it and select **New File...** from the **File** menu, or press ⌘N. This will bring up the new file assistant (Figure 3–3).

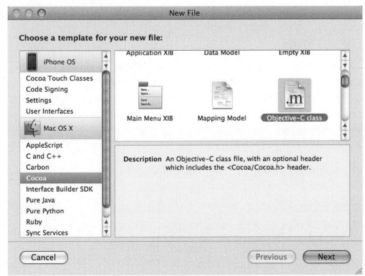

Figure 3.3. *The New File assistant allows you to choose from a large number of different file templates. This assistant looks somewhat different in Snow Leopard, where selecting the Objective-C class icon reveals a popup, letting you choose one of several classes to subclass. But for the most part they are pretty similar.*

In the list on the left-hand side of the new file assistant, under the *Mac OS X* heading, select *Cocoa*. In the upper-right pane, you'll now see a bunch of icons representing different file templates commonly used in Cocoa applications. Look for one called *Objective-C class*, and select it. When prompted for a name, call it *ButtonsAppDelegate.m*, and make sure the checkbox called *Also creates "ButtonsAppDelegate.h"* is checked. Click the *Finish* button, and your *Classes* folder in the *Groups & File* pane should now have two items in it. These files define the class that we will use as the controller for our application's main window.

> **NOTE:** If you've programmed in Cocoa Touch, you may be surprised that we're subclassing NSObject rather than a provided view controller class. Cocoa, like Cocoa Touch, does have generic controller classes, and you'll see them and learn when to use them in later chapters. Cocoa Touch was built from the ground up around the concept of generic view controllers, but Cocoa had been around for many years when they were first implemented, so Cocoa doesn't have an equivalent class to Cocoa Touch's UIViewController. As a result, the main controller classes in Cocoa are typically subclasses of NSObject.

Declaring an Action and Outlet

Now we need to edit one of those new files to declare our outlets and actions. Because you just created the two files, they are probably both selected. Single-click the *Classes* folder to deselect them, and then click on *ButtonsAppDelegate.h*. This should bring up that file in the editing pane. We need to add declarations for an outlet and an action method. Interface Builder only looks at the header (*.h*) file when it looks for the IBOutlet and IBAction keywords, so once we've declared the action and outlet in this file, Interface Builder will be able to find them.

If you look back at Figure 3–1, you'll notice that there are three buttons and one text field. When the user presses one of the buttons, the value of the text field is updated. Because we need to change the text displayed by the text field, we'll need an outlet to it. We'll also need an action method for the buttons to trigger. Because action methods receive a pointer to the object that triggered them, we can use a single action method for all three buttons. Let's declare our outlet and action now.

In the editing pane, add the following code (for brevity, the comments at the top of the file are excluded):

> **TIP:** When we want you to add code to an existing file, we will make the new code **bold**, and leave the existing code in the normal code font.

```
#import <Cocoa/Cocoa.h>
@interface ButtonsAppDelegate : NSObject {
    NSTextField    *label;
}
```

```
@property IBOutlet NSTextField *label;
- (IBAction)buttonPressed:(id)sender;
@end
```

This is pretty straightforward. First, we declare an instance variable (`label`) that is a pointer to an `NSTextField`. This pointer is what will actually hold the address of the text field object use for the label in Interface Builder. Then we declare a property based on that instance variable. This property uses the same name as the underlying instance variable, and includes the `IBOutlet` keyword, which will allow `Interface Builder` to find our outlet and make it available to us in Interface Builder. We also declare a single action method called `buttonPressed:`, which is the action method that will be triggered by the application's three buttons.

Back to Interface Builder

Expand the *Resources* folder in the *Groups & Files* pane and double-click *MainMenu.xib* to launch Interface Builder. Because Interface Builder parses outlets and actions only from the header file, we do not need to write the implementation of `buttonPressed:` before we can begin designing our interface in Interface Builder.

> **TIP:** Once Interface Builder opens, feel free to change the menu so that the items labeled *NewApplication* have the correct name. If you don't remember how to do it, refer to Chapter 2. We won't be walking you through updating the menu items in future chapters.

The very first order of business is to create an instance of the controller class we just created. Defining a class in Xcode, as we just did, creates the class, but it doesn't create any objects. In order for our class to do its job, there has to be an instance of that class when the application launches. Without an instance of the class, none of the code we write can ever get called.

You're probably familiar with creating object instances in Objective-C. Typically, you do something like this:

```
ButtonsAppDelegate *controller = [[ButtonsAppDelegate alloc] init];
```

And that's a perfectly valid way of creating an instance of an object. It's not the only way, however. If you look at the window labeled *MainMenu.xib* in Interface Builder (Figure 3–4), you'll notice that there are several icons in it. With the exception of the first three icons, each represents an instance of an object that will get created automatically when this nib file is loaded into memory. Because *MainMenu.xib* gets loaded when the application launches, adding an icon to this window here automatically results in an object instance getting created when the application launches. Let's use that feature to add an instance of `ButtonsAppDelegate` to this nib now, which will ensure that there is an instance of our controller class when our application is launched.

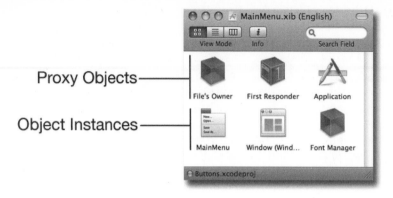

Figure 3–4. *The MainMenu.xib*

Proxy Objects

Before we do that, though, let's take a moment to look at the first three objects in the nib. These icons will always exist in Cocoa nib files. You can't delete them and, unlike the other icons, they don't cause object instances to get created when the nib is loaded. These three are called **proxy objects**, and they are here to allow connections from objects in this nib to certain objects that already exist.

The first icon in any nib file is called **File's Owner**. This icon is a proxy that points to the object instance that loaded the nib from disk or, in other words, the object instance that "owns" the nib. In an application's *MainMenu.xib* file, such as we have here, the *File's Owner* icon will always point to an instance of NSApplication, which is the class that represents the entire application, which receives input and makes sure the appropriate code gets called as a result of that input. For other nib files, *File's Owner* could be a different class, such an instance of a document class, or the class that represents a plug-in.

The second icon in this and any other nib file is called **First Responder**. We'll talk more about responders in Chapter 10, but the first responder is the object with which the user is currently interacting. If, for example, the cursor is typing in a text field, that text field is the current first responder. The first responder changes as the user interacts with the interface and the *First Responder* icon gives you a convenient way to interact with whatever control or view currently has the focus without having to write code to determine which control or view that is.

The third icon, called **Application** (or the **application proxy**) is a relatively new addition to Cocoa nib files. This object points to this application's one and only instance of NSApplication. In a *MainMenu.xib* file, the application proxy, and the *File's Owner* proxy will always point to exactly the same thing. The application proxy gives you access to your application's NSApplication instance from any nib file, even ones whose *File's Owner* is not NSApplication. For this chapter, we can forget about the application proxy, because this nib's *File's Owner* already gives us access to that object.

Creating the Controller Instance

In the library, look under *Objects & Controllers* for an object called *NSObject*. Drag that from the library to the nib's main window. As your cursor gets over the window, it will change so it has a plus icon on it (Figure 3–5) indicating that letting go of the mouse now will add this object to the nib. Let go of the mouse button to put a new object instance into the nib.

Figure 3–5. *As you drag an object from the library over to the nib, if the nib can accept the dragged object, the cursor will get a green plus sign on it to indicate that fact.*

At this point, we've added an instance of NSObject to our nib. That's not exactly what we want, but the library doesn't contain an instance of ButtonsAppDelegate, the class that we just created, so we have to grab the closest match (in this case, our class' superclass), and then change the underlying class to be correct. We can do that by single-clicking the new icon called *Object* and pressing ⌘6 to bring up the identity inspector (Figure 3–6).

The identity inspector allows us to specify the underlying class for this object instance. Because what we want is to create an instance of ButtonsAppDelegate, we need to change the value in the *Class* field from *NSObject* to *ButtonsAppDelegate*, as in Figure 3–6. Once you change the class, you should see the action and outlet we declared earlier in the *Class Actions* and *Class Outlets* sections of the inspector.

Once you hit return to commit the change, look back in the nib's main window, and you'll notice that the new icon's name has changed from *Object* to *Main Window....* Interface Builder automatically changed the name of the icon to reflect the new underlying class. The new name is longer than can be displayed in the current view, so Interface Builder has truncated it and placed an ellipsis at the end to let us know that it isn't displaying the full name. If you hold your cursor over the icon for a few seconds, a tool tip will appear with the full name.

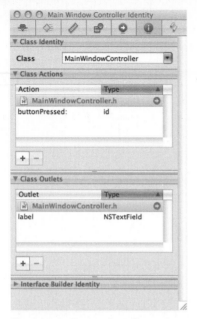

Figure 3–6. *The identity inspector is where you can change the underlying class of an object in your nib. This window is somewhat different in Snow Leopard, where the sections for actions and outlets have been moved to a different part of the GUI, namely the Library panel. We think Apple does this just to keep book authors on their toes.*

The name of the icon here in the nib can be changed to anything we want. If we had three instances of the same class, it would be very hard to tell them apart if they all had the same name. Let's change the name to something that fits by single-clicking the *Main Window Controller* icon, waiting a second, then single-clicking the text below the icon. The icon's name should become editable. Change it to read *Main Controller*, which still identifies what this instance is, but also fits in the space provided.

Setting Up the Window

Our next order of business is to design our application's interface. In the main nib window, double-click the window's icon to open our application's main window. Press ⌘1 to open up the *Attributes Inspector*. We're going to make some changes, so the attributes match what you see in Figure 3–7.

Figure 3–7. *The attributes inspector lets you configure piles of options for many kinds of objects in your nib files. Configure your window to match the settings shown here.*

Change the window's title from *Button* to *Press a Button*. The field below *Title* is labeled *Autosave*. If we provide a value in this field, our application will automatically save the location, size, and other information about the window in our user preferences so that when the user launches the application again, he or she will find the window exactly where it was left. It doesn't matter what value you put here, as long as it is unique. If you use the same autosave name for any two objects, one of them will fail to save. Type in *mainWindow* here.

Right under the *Autosave* field are three checkboxes that control some of the fundamental behavior of the window. The *Close* checkbox enables or disables the ability to close the window. In a utility application with only one window, you might want to uncheck this box so that the window can't be closed. If this box is unchecked, both the red close button in the window's title bar and the **Close** menu item will be disabled. If you allow the window to be closed, you should provide a way to make the window visible again. Alternatively, if your application is a utility that consists of only one window, it is acceptable to have the application quit when the window is closed. Later on in this chapter, we'll configure our application to quit when this window is closed, so leave the *Close* checkbox as it is. In later chapters, you'll learn how to make closed windows visible again.

The *Minimize* checkbox controls whether the window can be minimized to the dock using the yellow button in the window's title bar or from selecting **Minimize** from the **Window** menu. As a general rule, windows should be able to be minimized. There are exceptions to this, such as utility windows that are only visible when your application is front-most, but the vast majority of the time you should leave this checked.

The third box is called *Resize*, and it controls whether the user can change the size of the window by dragging the lower right corner. For this application, we're going to disable resizing of this window, so uncheck *Resize*. You'll learn how to handle controls in windows that resize later in the book.

Leave the rest of the attributes unchanged for now. The class that represents windows is a very flexible class, and the other attributes give you a tremendous amount of control over the appearance of your application, but for most windows, the default settings are what you want.

Now, press ⌘3 to bring up the size inspector (Figure 3–8). This is where we can set the size and size-related attributes of the selected object. As you saw in the last chapter, objects can be moved and resized using the mouse, but this inspector gives you more precise control over the size and position of an object.

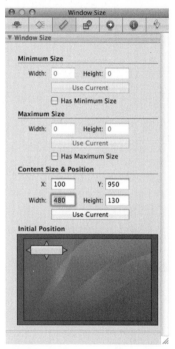

Figure 3–8. *The size inspector allows you to set the size and position of an object with pixel-level precision. This is the size inspector for a window; the size inspector for other objects looks a little different. This is the Leopard version. Appearance differs slightly in Snow Leopard.*

Set the width of your window to 480 pixels, and the height to 130 pixels. Set the x value of the window to 100, which indicates that we want the window's initial position to be on the left side of the screen. The y value can be a little more problematic. The coordinate system on your Mac's screen has 0 at the lower-left corner of the screen, with the y value getting higher as you move up toward the top of the screen. The problem here is that not everybody has the same size monitor, so any given y value will be different relative to the top of the screen on different size monitors.

Fortunately, Cocoa will automatically adjust the window's position so that the window always starts on the screen, even if the location you specify would otherwise place it offscreen somewhere, and because we gave the window an autosave name, every time the user launches the application after the first, the window will be where it was when he last quit the application. But, sometimes it's important that a window start in a particular position relative to the top of the screen.

Do you see the little diagram at the bottom of the size inspector? It gives you a visual representation of the window's initial position based on your own screen's size. The little white box represents the window, and the big box represents the screen minus the menu bar. The little grey triangles on all four sides of the white box let you lock the position of the window relative to the sides of the screen. Clicking a triangle toggles it between being extended, harpoon-like, to the edge of the mini-screen, or retracted to the edge of the window. You can place the window where you want it on your screen, then use those triangles to lock the position relative to the let and top of the screen. Let's do that now.

You need to set a y value that places the window near the menu bar, but not abutting it. The easiest way to do this is to simply move your application's main window to where you want it, then press the *Use Current* button on the size inspector, which will set the initial size and location to the current size and location of the window. You can then tweak the sizes numerically if you need to. Once you have the initial position of the window where you want it on your screen, configure the little "harpoons" so that they are extended on the left and top sides of the white box, and retracted at the right and bottom sides, leaving the inspector looking like Figure 3–9.

Figure 3–9. *The gray triangles extend out like little harpoons and anchor the window's position relative to the side of the screen they extend to.*

Designing the Window's Interface

In the library, expand the *Cocoa* node if it's not already expanded, then expand the *Views & Cells* node and click *Buttons*. This will present you with a bunch of different buttons (Figure 3–10) that you can use. The first item in the bottom list should now be *Push Button*, which is a standard OS X button. Grab one of those and drag it over to your window's interface. Use the blue guidelines to place the button in the lower right part of the window (Figure 3–11).

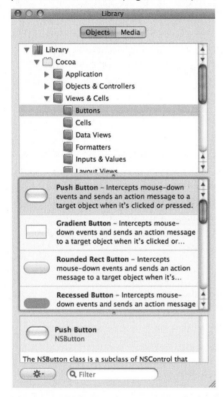

Figure 3–10. *Finding the push button in the library.*

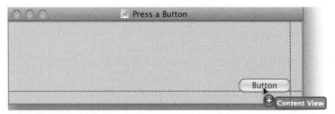

Figure 3–11. *Placing a push button into our application's main window, using the blue guidelines to place the button the correct distance from the window's edges.*

Once the button is in the right location, release the mouse, and you'll have a button on your window. Double-click the button now, which will allow you to edit the button's title. Change its title from *Button* to *Right*.

Drag a second button over from the library and place it on the lower left of the window, again using the blue guidelines. After you place this button, double-click it and change this button's title to *Left*.

> **TIP:** Instead of dragging a new button over from the library, you could have held down the option key and dragged the existing button to the left. When you hold down the option key and move an object in Interface Builder, it creates a copy of the object and moves that, leaving the original object untouched.

Bring one more button over, and use the bottom blue guideline to place the button the correct distance from the bottom of the window. Try and place it roughly in the horizontal center of the window, but don't worry placing it exactly in the center. Once it's placed, double-click the third button and change its label to *Center*. Hit return to commit the change, which should leave the center button still selected. From the **Layout** menu, select the **Alignment** sub-menu, and select **Align Horizontal Center in Container**, which will center the button in the window. Your window should not look like Figure 3–12.

Figure 3–12. *Our application's main window with the three buttons placed.*

Next, we need a label so that we can tell the user which button was clicked. A label is a GUI object that can display a piece of text, in the font and size of our choosing. From within our application code, we can programmatically change the label's text any time we want. Grab a label from the library. Remember, the label is under **Cocoa➤Views & Cells➤Inputs & Values** or you can just use the search box. Drag the label to the upper left of the window and use the guides to place it properly against the top and left margins.

Click the resize handle on the right of the label, and drag it to the right until you get to the blue guidelines on the right side of the window and let go. With the label still selected, press ⌘1 to bring up the attribute inspector, and center the text using the text alignment button. Then press ⌘T to bring up the standard font window and change the font size to 36. Your application window should now look like Figure 3–13. All that's left is to double-click the label, which will put it in editing mode, then hit the delete key to delete the text. We don't want this label to say anything until a button has been pressed.

Figure 3–13. *Our application's interface is nearly complete.*

Connecting the Outlet

Back in Xcode, we declared an outlet called `label`. It's now time to connect that outlet with the label we just added to our interface. The way we do that is to hold down the Ctrl key and click on the *Main Controller* icon in the nib's main window. Keep the Ctrl key and mouse button pressed down and move the cursor away from the icon. You should see a line from the icon to your cursor (Figure 3–14). This is called a "Ctrl-drag," and it is the primary mechanism we use to connect outlets and actions in Interface Builder. Keep dragging toward our application's main window, until your cursor is over the label. You won't be able to see the label because we deleted the text it contains, but it's still there and when your mouse is over it, it will highlight (Figure 3–15).

Figure 3–14. *Ctrl-dragging from an icon in the nib's main window to an object on the user interface is how we connect an outlet to an object on the user interface.*

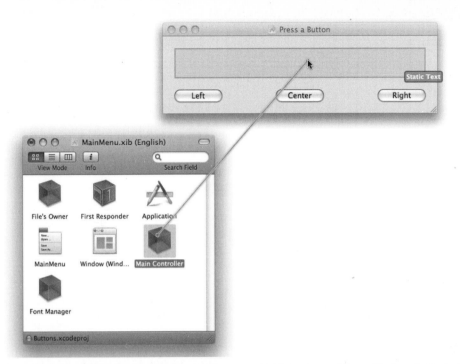

Figure 3–15. *As you Ctrl-drag over an item, it will become highlighted, even if it would otherwise be invisible.*

Once your mouse is over the label (your screen should look similar to Figure 3–15), let go of the mouse button and you will be presented with a small grey menu showing the outlets that are available for this particular object (Figure 3–16). There should only be one available outlet, called *label*. Select it.

Figure 3–16. *After Ctrl-dragging, if there are one or more outlets that are appropriate for the object you dragged to, they will be presented in a gray popup menu.*

Now, your outlet called `label` points to this label on our interface. If you call any methods on this pointer it will affect the appearance of this particular label.

Connecting the Buttons to Our Action

We also need to indicate that each of the three buttons we just added to our interface will trigger the action method called `buttonPressed:`. We accomplish this in a very similar manner to connecting outlets, but instead of Ctrl-dragging from the controller class to the interface, we're going to Ctrl-drag from the buttons down to the controller. Hold down the Ctrl key and click on the button labeled *Right*. Drag from that button to the *Buttons_App...* icon in the nib's main window. When you release the mouse button, another grey popup menu should appear. Because our controller class has only one action, a popup with one item appears (Figure 3–17). Select *buttonPressed:* by clicking on it. Repeat with the other two buttons. Now, all three of these buttons will trigger the action method called buttonPressed:.

Figure 3–17. *Connecting actions is very similar to connecting outlets. Ctrl-dragging to the controller class brings up a popup menu with all available actions.*

That is all we need to do in Interface Builder, so save the nib by pressing ⌘S and then close it and go back to Xcode.

NOTE: When linking outlets, you always Ctrl-drag from your controller class instance icon to the interface item to which you wish to link it. Each outlet can be linked to only a single interface item. When linking actions, on the other hand, you Ctrl-drag to your controller class instance icon from the user interface item, and multiple interface items can be connected to the same action method.

Implementing the Action Method

The only task remaining before we can try out our program is to actually write the code that will get called when a button is clicked. This code will look at the sender argument to determine the title of the button that was called, use that title to create a string, and then use our label outlet to display that string. Single-click on *ButtonsAppDelegate.m* and add the following code.

```
#import "ButtonsAppDelegate.h"

@implementation ButtonsAppDelegate
```

```
@synthesize label;
- (IBAction)buttonPressed: (id)sender {
    NSString *title = [sender title];
    NSString *labelText = [NSString stringWithFormat:@"%@ button pressed.", title];
    [label setStringValue:labelText];
}
@end
```

First we synthesize the accessors and mutators for our one property. Synthesizing these methods means that we don't have to provide implementations for them. They're created for us! We'll discuss this issue a bit more in Chapter 4. Then we implement the `buttonPressed:` action method. This method first grabs the title of the button that called it. It then uses that button to create a new string, and then uses that string to update the label.

Press ⌘R or select **Build & Run** from the **Build** menu to compile this source code into an application and launch it. If you press the center button, your application should look exactly like Figure 3–1.

NESTING MESSAGES

Some Objective-C developers nest their message calls pretty deeply. You may come across code like this in your travels:

```
[label setStringValue:[NSString stringWithFormat:@"%@ button pressed.",
  [sender title]]];
```

This one line of code will function exactly the same as the three lines of code that make up our `buttonPressed:` method. For the sake of clarity, we won't generally nest Objective- C messages so deeply in the code examples in this book, with the exception of calls to `alloc` and `init`, which, by longstanding convention, are almost always nested.

Click all three buttons, and notice how our one action method handles all three buttons appropriately. Move the window to a new location and quit out of the application. Press ⌘R to launch the program again, and the window should come up in exactly the same position it was in when you quit the program. If you click the yellow minimize button in the title, the window will shrink down into your dock (click it in the Dock to maximize it), and if you click ⌘W or click the red close button in the window, the window closes. Unfortunately, the application is still running, but there's no way to get the window back open. Let's address that now by configuring our application to quit when the window is closed. To do that, we'll have to use something called the **application delegate**.

The Application Delegate

Every Cocoa application has one and only one instance of a class called `NSApplication`. You don't need to interact with `NSApplication` directly very much. It's created for you and handles the event loop (the part of your application that notices user input from the mouse and keyboard, and handles the input by sending messages to the appropriate objects) and most of the lower-level stuff without you having to give it much thought.

Expand the *Other Sources* folder in the *Groups & Files* pane, and single-click on *main.m*. In that file is our application's `main()` function, which is the function that gets called when our application is launched. This function contains only one line of code, which calls a function named `NSApplicationMain()`. That function, which is part of Cocoa, automatically creates an instance of `NSApplication` for us. That instance of `NSApplication` goes into a loop and continuously polls for **events** from the keyboard, mouse, operating system, and other applications and responds to those events (don't worry about the specifics for now, you'll learn more about events later in the book). When it detects an event that signifies that the application should quit, the event loop stops and the application's execution ends.

`NSApplication` allows you to specify an optional object to act as its **delegate**. Simply put, a delegate is a class that handles certain tasks on behalf of another class. The application delegate allows our application to take actions at certain points in the lifecycle of the application so that we can avoid the messiness of having to subclass `NSApplication`.

The application delegate can be of any instance of any class, but only one object can be the application delegate. Because we already have one instance of a `ButtonsAppDelegate` that gets created when our application is launched, we can have that class do double-duty as our application delegate. We could also create a separate class to act as the application delegate and add an instance of that class to the nib, but it's fairly common practice to have the application's main window controller do double-duty as the application delegate. In fact, if you're using Snow Leopard, the `ButtonsAppDelegate` class that was created for you is already configured, in the nib file, to be the application delegate, so you can skip the next paragraph.

Double-click *MainMenu.xib* to open up Interface Builder again. Once it's open, Ctrl-drag from *File's Owner*, which for this nib, represents our application's one instance of `NSApplication`, and drag to the icon labeled *Main Controller*. When the grey popup menu comes up, select *delegate*. `NSApplication` has an instance variable called `delegate` which is an outlet, just like the ones we created in our controller class. We just connected that delegate outlet to our instance of `ButtonsAppDelegate`, which makes it the application delegate. Save the nib and go back to Xcode.

Configuring the Application to Quit on Window Close

Single-click on *ButtonsAppDelegate.m* and add the following method:

```
#import "ButtonsAppDelegate.h"
@implementation ButtonsAppDelegate
@synthesize label;
- (IBAction)buttonPressed: (id)sender {
    NSString *title = [sender title];
    NSString *labelText = [NSString stringWithFormat:@"%@ button pressed.", title];
    [label setStringValue:labelText];
}
```

```
- (BOOL)applicationShouldTerminateAfterLastWindowClosed:(NSApplication *) theApp; {
    return YES;
}
@end
```

This new method is one of those special application delegate methods. At certain predefined times during the application's run, NSApplication will look to see if its delegate has implemented a particular method. If the delegate has, NSApplication will call that method. This method we just implemented exists to let us change the behavior of NSApplication without subclassing it. The default behavior is for NSApplication to keep running until it is specifically told to quit, even if there are no windows open. It is acceptable for applications to quit when their last (or only) window is closed, however, and this method is provided specifically to let the delegate alter this behavior.

Run your application again, and close the application's main window when it comes up. The application should now quit because the application's only window has been closed.

Using the Documentation Browser

You might be wondering how we know what these application delegate methods are. It's hard to implement methods if you don't know what they are. Fortunately, they're easy to find. If you look at the method we just added, it takes one argument, which is a pointer, to the NSApplication instance that called the method. Hold down the option key (if you're running Leopard) or both the option and command keys (if you're running Snow Leopard) and double-click on the word NSApplication in the editing pane. This will open up the Documentation Browser to the definition of the word we just clicked, which is NSApplication (Figure 3–18).

If you look down through the navigation pane (to the right of the blue-shaded area), you'll see several headings, including one that reads *Delegate Methods*. If you click that, it will expand out to show you all the delegate methods that NSApplication supports. If you implement any of these methods in ButtonsAppDelegate, they will get called at the documented time.

It's worth your time to spend a few minutes looking over the application delegate methods so you'll know what's there. The Documentation Browser is your friend. You're going to spend a lot of time in here as you learn Cocoa, so get comfortable with it. If you're running Snow Leopard, there's also a more compact way to view documentation. Option-double-clicking on a class or method name will bring up a small documentation popup that gives you a brief summary of what you clicked on, and links to related documentation. Altogether, the documentation contained within Xcode is the ultimate encyclopedic reference to Cocoa, Xcode, and all other Apple development technologies. RTFM! You'll be glad you did.

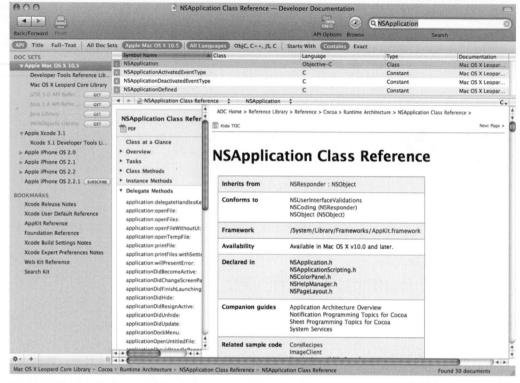

Figure 3–18. *Xcode's Documentation Browser can be brought up by option double-clicking an object, function, or method name in your source code. This is a fast and handy way to get to the documentation. This is yet another area where the GUI was reworked pretty drastically for Snow Leopard, but you should be able to find your way in either case.*

Bring It on Home

The application you just built might not seem like much of an application, but the tasks you just executed to make it, such as declaring outlets and actions, designing your interface, connecting your outlets and actions, and writing action methods are some of the most fundamental building blocks of all Cocoa applications.

So, pat yourself on the back, grab a beverage of your choice, and turn the page when you're ready to find out about the V in MVC as we take a look at several of Cocoa's most common user interface elements, and see how to use them from your code.

Chapter 4

GUI Components

In Chapter 3, we covered some of the basics involved in creating a user interface in Interface Builder and using target/action to connect it to application code written in Xcode. We've really only scratched the surface so far, but you should be happy to know that the target/action system you learned to use in the last chapter is used by almost all of the user interface objects in Cocoa. If you're not quite sure what's so great about that, you might need to review Chapter 3 just one more time to be sure you've grasped the target/action concept.

By now, you've surely noticed the wide variety of user interface objects listed in Interface Builder's Library window. Now it's time to dig deeper into Cocoa's bag of tricks, and explore some of these classes. The user interface classes available in Cocoa cover a wide range of uses, and wherever possible provide consistent APIs for their functionality, so that once you've learned how to do something with one class, you'll often be able to quickly guess how to achieve similar results with another class.

In this chapter, we'll cover some of the most common user interface classes that Cocoa provides, showing their basic usage and how you can tailor them to your needs where appropriate. Along the way, we'll also touch on some of the auxiliary Cocoa classes that may not always have a tangible screen presence, but still provide important services for your applications. We'll be focusing on the following classes (see Figure 4–1 for a sampling of what these objects can look like onscreen):

- NSTextField: The basic text input method for many applications. Responds to key-presses and renders text. Allows a great deal of editing flexibility for the user.

- NSButton: The basic mouse-triggered GUI component. Despite their differences in operation and appearance, radio-buttons, checkboxes, and plain old buttons are all instances of NSButton.

- NSPopUpButton: When you have a set of strings you want the user to choose from, an NSPopUpButton is often the way to go.

- NSComboBox: Similar to an NSPopUpButton, but with the added advantage of allowing the user to enter a value that wasn't already in the list.

- NSMatrix: An NSMatrix lets you group a series of similar controls into a single unit.

- NSLevelIndicator: Instances of this class are normally used for displaying a numeric value from a predefined range, but we'll show how they are just as useful for entering data.

- NSImageView: Users can easily bring an image into your application by dragging any image from the Finder or another application and dropping it onto one of these.

- NSTextView: This is nearly a complete text editor rolled into a single object, letting the user edit text with multiple fonts, formatting, rulers, and more.

NOTE: Throughout this book, we will sometimes use Cocoa class names (e.g. "NSButton") and other times their casual, common names (e.g. "button"). Normally we'll use the class names when discussing the code, and their casual names for most other situations, but in both cases we're really talking about the same things.

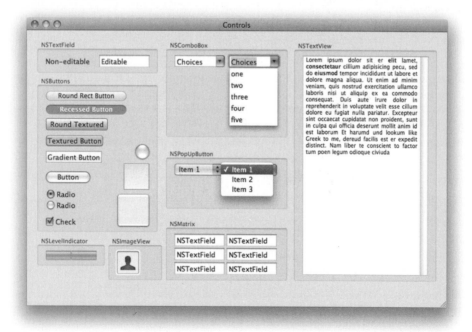

Figure 4–1. *A sampling of Cocoa UI elements*

We'll use these classes to create a simple application that *pretends* to be a sort of database application. The user will be able to edit and create some objects by using some simple GUI controls, but the results of the editing won't be saved in any way (that's where the *pretending* comes in). In later chapters, you'll learn how to use Core Data to save your objects to disk, but for now, we're going to focus on the GUI.

Creating the VillainTracker Application

The application we'll be creating in this chapter is called VillainTracker. It's a simple application for keeping track of super-villains, their last known whereabouts, special abilities, and so on. This is the sort of application that any superhero team worth its salt will have installed on their computer systems, and is therefore an obvious first app for a hero such as yourself. We'll split the development of VillainTracker into two iterations: in the first iteration, we'll create a simple app that enables us to edit information for a single villain, and in the second, in Chapter 5, we'll add the ability to manage a whole list of villains. This will demonstrate the basics of how developers have been creating applications based on the Model-View-Controller (MVC) design pattern for years. Whether you have experience with this pattern or it's new to you, it's important that you get a sense of how MVC is typically implemented in Cocoa applications, because it's a really a cornerstone of good application design in Cocoa.

We'll start by creating a new application project in Xcode. We'll lay the foundations for our user interface by creating some "stub" code in a controller class, consisting mainly of outlets and actions declared in a header file, so that we have a controller object ready to connect to some views. Then we'll switch over to Interface Builder to create the GUI and connect it to the controller. Then we'll go back to Xcode, where you'll learn how to write the code to set and retrieve values the values shown in your GUI controls, one class at a time, so you'll start to get a feel for how each of them works.

NOTE: Sometimes, when discussing GUI issues, you'll see that we use the terms "views" and "controls" almost interchangeably. Most of the Cocoa user interface classes are, technically, both views and controls, at least in the Cocoa sense; NSView is a class that allows drawing on the screen, and NSControl is a subclass of NSView that extends it by responding to user events, triggering an action in a target, and so on. So, a large part of the view layer in your application will consist of objects that are "controls," which of course you don't want to confuse with the controller layer. If this seems puzzling, just try to remember that a "control" is a particular kind of view, whereas a "controller" is an object in the controller layer that coordinates between view and model objects. After a while, it will all make perfect sense, we promise.

So, let's create a new application project. Launch Xcode, or switch to it if it's already running, and select **File▸New Project** from the menu. You'll now see the New Project assistant; under Mac OS X on the left, click Application, and then in the large pane on the right, click *Cocoa Application*, then click the *Choose...* button.

You'll now see a standard *Save Panel* that lets you navigate to a directory of your choice and create a new project there. Use the controls to navigate to a suitable spot in your home directory or your desktop, then enter the name "VillainTracker" and click *Save*. Now Xcode creates a new folder called *VillainTracker* in the location you specified, with some default content including the `VillainTracker.xcodeproj` project file, and opens a new window showing you your project.

Creating the VillainTrackerAppDelegate Class

We'll start off this project by creating a controller class. For more intricate applications, you're likely to have several controller classes, but for a simple app like this, which interacts with a single window and the application itself, one controller is all we'll need. This controller will have outlets to all the objects in our GUI (so that it can set and retrieve values in the view objects any time it needs to), and action methods for those objects to inform the controller every time a user edits a value.

Navigate into your project's *Classes* group by first expanding the top-level *VillainTracker* disclosure triangle if it's not already open, then doing the same for the *Classes* group inside of it. If you're running Snow Leopard, you'll see that Xcode has created a class called `VillainTrackerAppDelegate` for you, represented by the two files `VillainTrackerAppDelegate.h` and `VillainTrackerAppDelegate.m`. In the version of Xcode available for Leopard, however, the Classes group is empty, so you'll need to create this class. Right-click (or control-click) on *Classes*, and in the contextual menu that comes up, navigate into **Add** and choose **New File...**, which will bring up the New File wizard. On the left, under *Mac OS X,* choose *Cocoa*; and on the right, choose *Objective-C class*, then click *Next*. Now you'll be prompted for the name of your new class file. Enter `VillainTrackerAppDelegate.m`, make sure the checkbox instructing Xcode to also create a matching .h file is checked, and click *Finish*. Xcode will create the new files, and bring up an editor window showing you the header file.

Now let's start paving the way for the model class we'll be using for this application. In a "real application," we'd have a proper model class for our villain objects, something that would incorporate saving and loading from a file or a database, and in later chapters you'll see how to do just that using Core Data. But for this application, where we're mostly interested in seeing how GUI components are hooked up and used, we'll keep it simple and use an `NSMutableDictionary` to represent each of our villain objects. `NSMutableDictionary` is really quite suitable for this task, because it enables us to easily store and retrieve values of any kind, and doesn't need any predefined methods for each value, because the values are accessed using simple strings representing keys.

Start by declaring a new instance variable called `villain`, and declaring it as a property. The header file should now look something like this (the code you're adding right now is shown here in bold):

```
#import <Cocoa/Cocoa.h>
@interface VillainTrackerAppDelegate : NSObject {
  NSMutableDictionary *villain;
}
@property (retain) NSMutableDictionary *villain;
```

@end

The first line we added (between the curly braces) tells the compiler about our new instance variable, while the second line we added (starting with @property) tells the compiler that our class will contain getter and setter methods (called villain and setVillain: respectively) for the villain property, as well as hinting at the semantics of the setter (in particular, retain means that the value passed into setVillain: will be retained).

Now let's add the getter and setter in the simplest way possible, by using the @synthesize keyword to let the compiler automatically generate them for us. This is done in the class's implementation, so switch to VillainTrackerAppDelegate.m and add the line seen in bold here:

```
#import "VillainTrackerAppDelegate.h"
@implementation VillainTrackerAppDelegate
@synthesize villain;
@end
```

In case you've forgotten, this @synthesize declaration creates a pair of methods for getting and setting the villain property, following the semantics defined in the header. In this case, the @property declaration included retain within parenthesis as part of its declaration, which means that in the setter method, the incoming value will be sent a retain message, while at the same time the previous value will be sent a release. In this book, we're focusing on using GC (garbage collection) wherever possible, so we won't strictly need to use the retain specifier for properties, but it's good to know what it means anyway, because you'll see it in a lot of other places (system frameworks, and the like).

> **NOTE:** This business of property-izing instance variables, a new feature in Objective-C 2.0, is a pretty nice way of dealing with instance variables that are likely to change while the application is running. If you choose to @synthesize the getters and setters like we just did, then you know that you're accessing your instance variables in a way that is standardized and future-proof.

Now would be a good time to press the *Build* button in Xcode and make sure you haven't made any errors so far. If you've entered everything correctly, your application should compile without any warnings or errors. If not, take a look at the error messages displayed by Xcode, and try to fix the problems they refer to. In general, compiling Objective-C is a *lot* faster than compiling C++ or Java code, so you don't have much to lose by compiling frequently. During the rest of this chapter, we'll be asking you to frequently compile your app and then run it, so we can make sure that each feature we code actually works as intended before going on to the next.

Planning for the GUI

Soon we'll get started with laying out our GUI. Before we get to that however, let's add the outlets and actions for each of our GUI controls to our controller class. Remember, an outlet is nothing more than a specially-marked instance variable, and an action is simply any method that matches a specific signature, taking a single parameter of type id and returning void. Note that in source code, the return type for an action is typically marked as IBAction instead of void. IBAction is actually defined to be the same as void, so as far as the compiler's concerned it makes no difference. This is done only to provide a "hint" to Interface Builder, so that it knows which methods are meant to be action methods. Now, let's say we have some sort of design document that specifies several villain attributes and their types. Based on their types and usages, we could map each attribute to a suitable GUI class. See Table 4–1.

Table 4–1. *Villain Attributes Mapped to GUI Classes*

Attribute Name	Type	View Class
name	string (freeform)	NSTextField
lastKnownLocation	string (freeform)	NSTextField
lastSeenDate	date	NSDatePicker
swornEnemy	string (freeform, but with list to choose from existing)	NSComboBox
primaryMotivation	string (from predefined list)	NSMatrix (containing radio buttons)
powers	array of strings (from predefined list)	NSMatrix (containing checkboxes)
powerSource	string (from predefined list)	NSPopUpButton
evilness	number (0-10)	NSLevelIndicator
mugshot	image	NSImageView
notes	string (perhaps lengthy)	NSTextView

Based on this specification, we'll add one outlet and one action for each GUI control. The outlet will let us access the control to set and retrieve its value whenever necessary, and each control will call the appropriate action method to inform us when its contents have changed. Now modify the controller class's interface (in VillainTrackerAppDelegate.h), adding all the lines shown in bold here:

```
#import <Cocoa/Cocoa.h>
@interface VillainTrackerAppDelegate : NSObject {
  IBOutlet NSTextField *nameView;
  IBOutlet NSTextField *lastKnownLocationView;
  IBOutlet NSDatePicker *lastSeenDateView;
  IBOutlet NSComboBox *swornEnemyView;
  IBOutlet NSMatrix *primaryMotivationView; // matrix of radiobuttons
  IBOutlet NSMatrix *powersView; // matrix of checkboxes
  IBOutlet NSPopUpButton *powerSourceView;
  IBOutlet NSLevelIndicator *evilnessView;
  IBOutlet NSImageView *mugshotView;
```

```
    IBOutlet NSTextView *notesView;
    NSMutableDictionary *villain;
}
@property (retain) NSMutableDictionary *villain;
- (IBAction)takeName:(id)sender;
- (IBAction)takeLastKnownLocation:(id)sender;
- (IBAction)takeLastSeenDate:(id)sender;
- (IBAction)takeSwornEnemy:(id)sender;
- (IBAction)takePrimaryMotivation:(id)sender;
- (IBAction)takePowerSource:(id)sender;
- (IBAction)takePowers:(id)sender;
- (IBAction)takeMugshot:(id)sender;
- (IBAction)takeEvilness:(id)sender;
@end
```

You may notice that one thing seems to be missing here: there is no action method defined for the NSTextView used for editing our notes attribute. The reason for this is that NSTextView doesn't actually work with the target/action paradigm. Instead, it informs its delegate when changes are made to its content. We'll implement that delegate call later, when we also implement all these action methods.

You may also wonder why we didn't declare these outlets to be properties of our VillainTrackerAppDelegate class, as we did for the villain instance variable. One of the biggest reasons for using properties is to properly handle instance variables that change at run-time, by ensuring that the getters and setters in a object are correctly implemented using the @synthesize keyword. The outlets that point to our GUI controls will not change after the nib file is loaded, so there's no point going through the motions of making those into properties as well.

Later we'll implement each of the action methods to make their callers' changes propagate back to our villain object. For now, just for the sake of having a compilable application, we'll just put in some empty method implementations, like these, in VillainTrackerAppDelegate.m:

```
#import "VillainTrackerAppDelegate.h"
@implementation VillainTrackerAppDelegate
@synthesize villain;
- (IBAction)takeName:(id)sender {}
- (IBAction)takeLastKnownLocation:(id)sender {}
- (IBAction)takeLastSeenDate:(id)sender {}
- (IBAction)takeSwornEnemy:(id)sender {}
- (IBAction)takePrimaryMotivation:(id)sender {}
- (IBAction)takePowerSource:(id)sender {}
- (IBAction)takePowers:(id)sender {}
- (IBAction)takeMugshot:(id)sender {}
- (IBAction)takeEvilness:(id)sender {}
@end
```

Now that the code is stubbed out, it would be a good time to once again compile VillainTracker and make sure you get no warnings or errors. There's still no point in running the app to test it out, because we haven't made a GUI yet, but we're about to take care of that!

Building Your Interface

Now it's finally time to create the GUI for VillainTracker, using Interface Builder to edit the project's main nib file. You'll add GUI controls to match each of the outlets in the controller class, and see how to give them logical groupings and make them reposition themselves correctly when their window is resized. Finally, you'll add an instance of our controller class to the nib, and connect everything together.

Start by locating the `MainMenu.xib` in Xcode's navigation pane. You'll find it in the *Resources* group, which is inside the top-level *VillainTracker* group. Double-click `MainMenu.xib`, and Interface Builder will launch and show you the contents of the nib file. In addition to the window labeled "MainMenu.xib," which shows all the top-level contents of this nib file, you'll see an empty window labeled "VillainTracker" (or "Window" if you're running Leopard or an earlier version of Mac OS X), and a special window labeled just "MainMenu" which contains the application's menu items.

If you're running Snow Leopard, the default contents of `MainMenu.xib` are set to include the name of your application in several key spots, and you can skip to the next paragraph. If you're still running Leopard, however, you'll need to change some default values to make your app show its proper name when it runs. Go through the menu items available in the *MainMenu* window, and change all occurrences of "NewApplication" to "VillainTracker." We went through all this in Chapter 3; if you've forgotten, look there for more details on just which menu items need to be changed.

Then, take the empty window (the one labeled either "VillainTracker" or "Window," depending on your OS version) and make it bigger by dragging the resize control in the lower right. Make it about one-third the size of the screen, and leave enough room to still see the *Library* (⇧⌘L to open it) and the *Inspector* (⇧⌘I) at the same time. Don't worry about the exact size; we'll fine-tune it later.

Bringing Out Your Text Fields

Now it's time to start building the GUI. We'll do this one little piece at a time, but let's start with a look at the completed version of the window after it's all laid out, just so you can see what we're shooting for (see Figure 4–2).

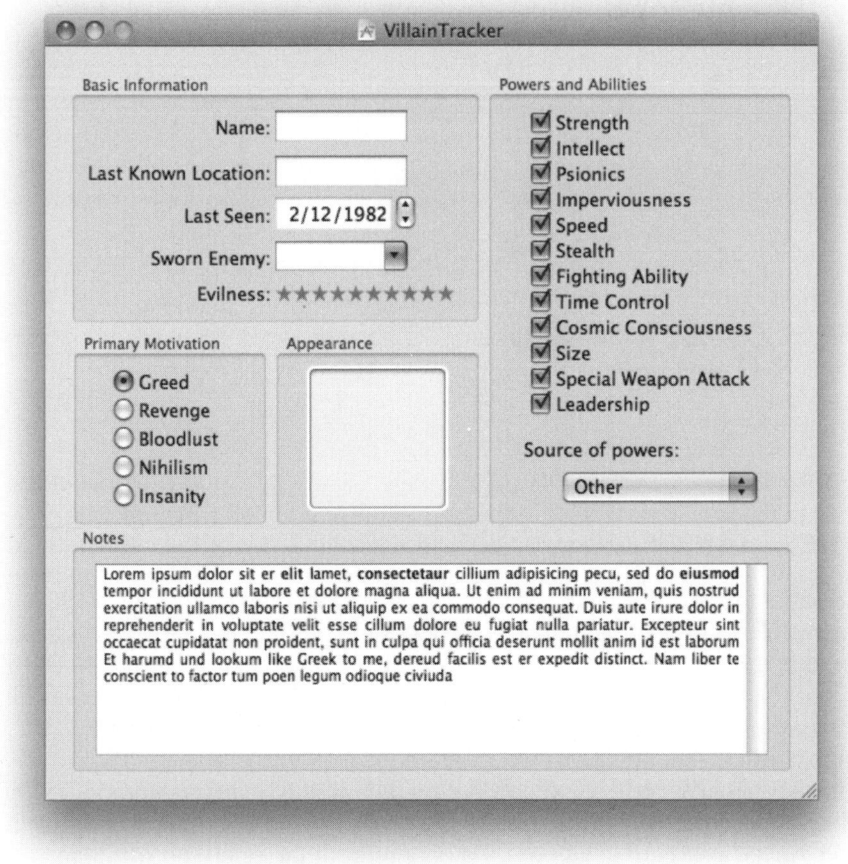

Figure 4–2. *This is how the complete VillainTracker window will look.*

The first controls we're going to set up are a couple of NSTextFields. NSTextField is a marvelously useful class that provides text-editing capabilities worthy of a full-fledged text editor, even in spots where you are just entering a few characters. In the *Library* window, make sure the *Objects* tab is selected at the top, and inside that select either *Library* or its child *Cocoa*. Then click in the search field at the bottom of the window and type in "text field." You'll see that the list of available objects in the *Library* is whittled down to just a few, including one called *Text Field*. Drag one of those (*Text Field*, not *Text Field Cell*, which is a slightly different beast that you'll encounter in Chapters 5 and 6) over to your empty "Window" window, and drop it somewhere in the upper-left portion of the window. Now, while the new text field is selected, make a duplicate of it by pressing ⌘D. A new textfield appears, overlapping the previous one. Drag the new one down a bit, and you'll see that some blue guidelines appear in the window, helping you guide it into alignment below the previous one. Let go of it when it looks roughly like what you see in Figure 4–3.

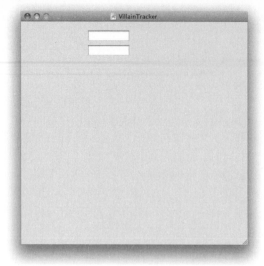

Figure 4–3. *VillainTracker's first two text fields*

Now we need to label these objects, so the user can see what they represent. Back in the *Library* window, click on the search field (deleting the text that was already there, if need be) and type in the word "label." Now you should see an object called *Label*. Drag one of those out to your window, dropping it to the left of the first text field you created. Again, you'll notice the blue lines that pop up when you drag near another object, helping you guide it into place. This label will resize horizontally to match its content when you edit it within IB. That's fine, except that by default the text is centered horizontally, which means that while you are editing it will expand in both directions and start overlapping the NSTextField to its right. To counteract that, open the *Attributes Inspector* (⌘1) and find and click the *align right* button (hint: it looks just like the corresponding button found in most word processors). Doing so will make the label retain its right-side margin even when you change its content.

Edit the text in the label to say "Name:" and then make a copy of this label by pressing ⌘D. Drag the new label down a bit so that it lines up with the lower text field, and then edit it to say "Last Known Location:" and you're done!

Letting them Pick Dates

The next GUI object we want to prepare is a date picker, which will let the user specify the date of the villain's last sighting. A date picker overcomes the ambiguities and competing standards for date formatting that can be a chore to deal with when parsing and presenting dates, and we've got access to a great built-in one in Cocoa, so let's roll with it.

In the *Library* window's search field, type "date picker" and see what comes up. You should see an entry called *Date Picker*. Grab that, drag it into your window, and drop it below the NSTextFields you created earlier, once again using the blue guidelines that pop up as you drag near the spot you're looking for. The default width for this control is smaller than the default width for the NSTextFields above it, so it won't take up the same amount of horizontal space, but that's okay. Just make it line up with the left edge of the other controls. Now click on one of the labels you created earlier and make another copy of it by pressing ⌘D. Drag it down to line up with your date picker, and change the text to "Last Seen:". Figure 4–4 shows what your window should look like now.

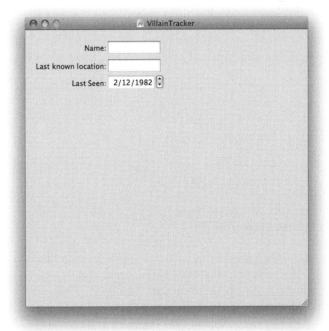

Figure 4–4. *We're off to a good start adding controls and labels to our window.*

Creating the Combo Box

Now it's time for a combo box. This control is great if you have a predefined set of valid string values to choose from, but also want to allow the user to enter a value of their own. This is perfect for the villain's swornEnemy property. We can provide some default superhero names to choose from, while still allowing the user to enter one that we don't anticipate.

Go to the *Library* window and type "combo" into the search field, and you'll see a *Combo Box* appear in the list. Drag it out into your window, below the NSTextFields and the NSDatePicker. Use the blue guidelines once again, lining it up with the left edge of the controls above it. Once more, make a copy of one of the existing labels, position it to the left of the combo box, and rename this one "Sworn Enemy:".

Now, let's populate the combo box with some default values. We want the user to be able to specify any superhero at all, even ones we don't know about (that's why we chose the combo box), but for the sake of convenience we should preload this control with names of some popular superheroes, since the popular ones also seem to be the ones who attract the most enemies.

Click on the combo box you just added, and open the *Attributes Inspector* (⌘1). In the upper section, you'll see a spot labeled *Items* where you can add items that will appear in the combo box. Figure 4–5 shows this part of the *Inspector* in action. Use the + button to add a new item, then double-click the "New Item" text that appears, and change it to "Superman." Now repeat this process, using the + button to add several items, each time editing the "New Item" text and changing it to the name of one of your favorite superheroes.

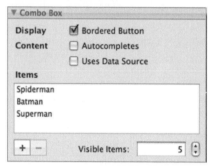

Figure 4–5. *Configuring an NSComboBox in Interface Builder*

After adding a list of superheroes, test your interface by selecting **File ▶ Simulate Interface** from the menu, or by pressing ⌘R. You'll see your window appear, and you can verify that the items you created for the combo box appear when you click on it. When you're done, press ⌘Q to return to Interface Builder.

Indicating a Rating with a Level Indicator

The next control we're going to create is an NSLevelIndicator, which we'll use to display and specify the evilness of the villain we're displaying. We'll let the user specify a "star rating" from 0 to 10 for this value, and the NSLevelIndicator will actually display it as a row of stars.

Go back to the *Library* window, and type in "level" in the search field at the bottom. One of the classes you'll see is NSLevelIndicator, which you should drag out and put into your window, once again using the blue guidelines to line it up with the left edge of the previous controls, just below the combo box you added in the previous step.

Now we need to configure this new object a bit. The NSLevelIndicator class has a number of built-in display styles, suited for different purposes. The default style for a new instance created in Interface Builder is called "Discrete", but we're going to change this to match what we're displaying, which is a sort of a rating. Bring up the *Attributes Inspector* (⌘1), and you'll see that one of the first options is a popup labeled *Style* (see Figure 4–6). Click on the popup and select *Rating* instead. You'll see that the level indicator immediately changes to a view showing a few stars.

Figure 4–6. *Configuring an NSLevelIndicator to show a star rating*

We also need to specify the maximum and minimum values that are valid for this control, so that it knows how to display the value it's given. Still in the *Attributes Inspector*, you'll see a section labeled *Values*, containing controls to set the minimum and maximum values. Set the minimum to 0 and the maximum to 10, either by typing numbers into these fields or using the small up/down buttons. A bit below those text fields is another labeled *Current*. Set that to 10, so that we can see the full range of stars in our control, and click the *Editable* checkbox so that the user can actually edit this value themselves, not just look at the pretty stars.

You may now notice that the control isn't showing you 10 stars. As of this writing, the default size of a new NSLevelIndicator dragged from the *Library* is wide enough to show just over 7 stars, and no more. Fortunately, Interface Builder provides a handy short cut that can help you "right-size" a view to make it snugly fit around its content. Select **Layout Size To Fit** from the menu or press ⌘= to make the level indicator expand to just the right size to show all 10 stars.

Finally, it's time once again to duplicate one of the existing labels in your window. Drag it into place to the left of the level indicator, and change the text to "Evilness:".

This might be a good time to once again test your interface by pressing ⌘R. You should be able to click anywhere along the line of stars and cause the control to start highlighting just that amount.

Adding Radio Buttons in a Matrix

Next, we'll create the GUI for the primaryMotivation attribute. Years of careful study of comic books have taught us that every villain has a primary motivating factor that causes them to do their evil deeds, and this motivation can always be reduced to one of these five things: greed, revenge, bloodlust, nihilism, or insanity. Of course some villains may have several of these evil-making forces at work, but we'll settle for picking the main one for each villain we're tracking.

We're going to use a set of radio buttons to let the user pick the primary motivation. Radio buttons are generally grouped in a set that works together, so that pressing one button to select it simultaneously deselects all the other buttons. If "radio button" seems like a terribly obscure name for this, then perhaps you're too young to remember the old car-radio tuner controls, prevalent up until the 1980s, which would let you select a radio station by pushing a mechanical button that would adjust the tuner to a particular station, and at the same time cause the previously-pushed button to pop back to the "out" position. In any case, radio buttons are here to stay, and are a good choice when you have a small, predefined list of things to choose from, and you'd like to keep the whole list onscreen at all times.

In Cocoa, radio buttons are normally a group of NSButtonCell instances aligned inside an NSMatrix. You can find these preconfigured in the *Library* window by typing "radio" into the search field. This will show you a *Radio Group*. Drag this out and drop it in your window, below the other controls. The default radio button matrix contains just two radio buttons, but for this example we want five. Simply resizing the matrix, by dragging one of the resize handles, won't help us here; that just stretches the existing buttons. Instead, try holding down the **option** key while dragging the bottom-center resize handle downward. That will simultaneously resize the matrix, and add new buttons inside to fill the empty space. Drag down until you can see five buttons, then release the mouse button.

> **TIP:** You may notice at some point that many of Cocoa's GUI classes seem to have a "shadow" in the form of a Cell class: NSButton has NSButtonCell, and so on. This division stems from performance issues in the past. In order to speed up drawing, some of the drawing duty was taken out of view classes, and put into special "cell" classes instead. So in an NSMatrix full of buttons, instead of having a bunch of full-fledged NSButton instances, there is a bunch of simpler NSButtonCell instances.

Now it's time to fill in the values that will be displayed in each button's title. Start with the top-most button; Double-click to select the word "Radio," then type in "Greed." Do the same for the rest of the buttons, typing in "Revenge," "Bloodlust," "Nihilism," and "Insanity," as shown in Figure 4–7. You'll see that this view doesn't expand horizontally to contain the text you typed, so do it yourself by dragging the center-right resize handle and dragging to the right until all the text you entered is visible.

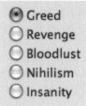

Figure 4–7. *What's your primary motivation in life?*

Before we're done, we need to assign a "tag" to each cell. We can use any integer as a tag for each cell, giving us a way to reference a cell through the matrix that contains it, without needing to have an outlet for each individual cell. We want to give a unique tag to each cell in the matrix we just created, and for the sake of convenience we want them to start at zero for the uppermost cell and increment by one each step of the way down. Besides being a simple pattern to follow, this will also allow us to create an array of strings later on, whose indexes in the array perfectly match their respective cell-tags (since an NSArray uses zero-based indexing, where the first item is at index 0, the second at index 1, and so on).

Start with the first button, "Greed." Selecting a cell in a matrix generally requires multiple clicks. The first click selects the matrix, then a second click tells the matrix that you want to focus on its insides, and the third click actually selects the cell. Once the cell is finally selected (you can tell by the highlighting), open the *Attributes Inspector* (⌘1) and look for the *Tag* field at the very bottom. Set this to 0. Now select the "Revenge" button, and set its tag to 1. Continue down the length of the matrix, ending with setting the tag for "Insanity" to 4.

Now the radio buttons for letting the user specify a villain's primaryMotivation are done! As you've done before, duplicate one of the labels, drag it down and place it above and slightly to the left of the radio button group, and change its title to "Primary Motivation:". You should now have something similar to Figure 4–8.

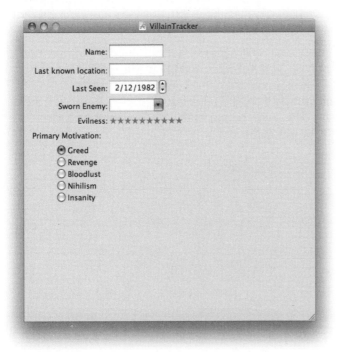

Figure 4–8. *More villain attributes than you can shake a stick at*

Adding an Image View

No villain-tracking application would be complete without a way to display the villain's cruel visage. In VillainTracker, we'll use an instance of the NSImageView class both to display a picture of the villain, and to receive a picture as input via the Mac's drag-and-drop mechanism.

Go back to the *Library* window, and type "image" in the search field. One of the results is listed as an *Image Well*, and this is in fact an instance of NSImageView. Drag one of these over to your window, and place it a bit to the right of the matrix of radio buttons from the last section.

Now, that image well is pretty tiny, so let's make it bigger. Bring up the *Size Inspector* (⌘3), and you'll see in a pair of text fields that the image well's width and height are both 48. Edit each of those, changing them to 104, and you'll see the control's size in the window change. We want to let the user drag an image into this view, so you'll also need to bring up the *Attributes Inspector* (⌘1) and click to enable the *Editable* checkbox,

Now adjust the position of the image well by dragging it a little within its window. You should see the blue guidelines pop up, and notice as you bring it near the radio buttons from the last step that this that control is now the same vertical height as the matrix of radio buttons to its left; Put them side by side, then duplicate another label, put it a bit above and to the left of the image view, and change its title to "Appearance:". See Figure 4–9 for a rough idea of the layout at this point.

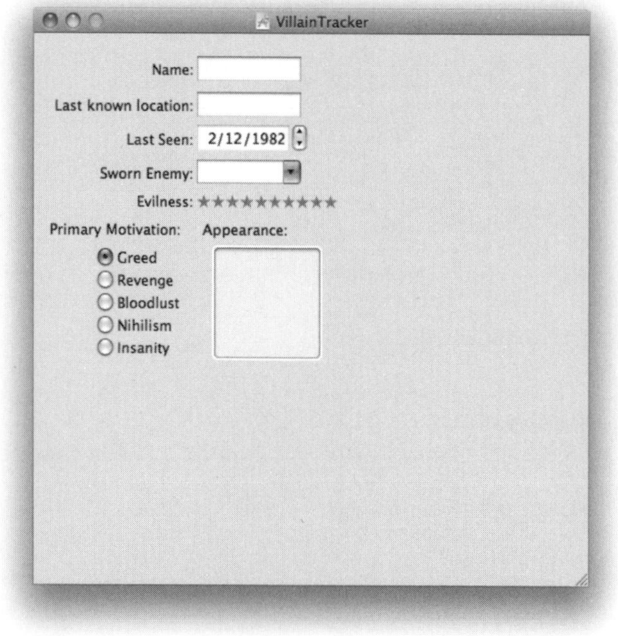

Figure 4–9. *An image well is now in place.*

Adding Checkboxes in a Matrix

The next controls we want to add are a series of checkboxes to let the user check off all the powers and abilities that the villain has (stored in the powers attribute). As in the case of the villain's primary motivation, we have come up with a classification system in which all types of supervillain powers can be pigeonholed into a category. Once again, we will use a matrix, but this time filled with checkboxes instead of radio buttons.

Go the *Library* window again, and this type "check" into the search field. One of the results will be labeled *Check Box*. Grab one of those and pull it into your window. This places an NSButton, configured to work as a checkbox, into the window. We're going to need 12 of these, lined up in a matrix, but right now we've only got this single one. Time for you to learn about a handy shortcut in Interface Builder that lets you automatically take any object that can appear in an NSMatrix, such as an NSButton, and replace it with a new NSMatrix containing a cell configured the same as your original object. Simply select your object (the checkbox), then in the menu choose **Layout ➤ Embed Objects In ➤ Matrix**. Your checkbox is now wrapped up in a matrix, and you can use the same resizing trick you learned for the matrix containing the radio buttons: hold down **option**, click on the bottom-center resize handle, and drag downwards until you see 12 checkboxes.

Next, let's configure this new matrix to work correctly with a group of checkboxes. Select the matrix itself (not one of the checkboxes inside of it), and open the *Attributes Inspector* (⌘1). At the top of the Inspector window, you'll see a popup button labeled "Mode", probably showing "List" as its value. Change that to "Highlight" instead, so we get the correct behavior.

Now fill the checkbox titles with the following: *Strength, Intellect, Psionics, Imperviousness, Speed, Stealth, Fighting Ability, Time Control, Cosmic Consciousness, Size, Special Weapon Attack, Leadership*. While clicking around to set these values, you may inadvertently turn checkboxes on and off. Don't worry about that; the states of all those checkboxes will be set from the code itself.

Just like with the matrix of radio buttons, you'll need to make the matrix a little wider so that the full text of the buttons can be seen. Drag the center-right resize handle out until all the text is visible.

Now it's time to set tags for all of these checkboxes, just like you set tags for all the radio buttons for choosing the primaryMotivation. Click to select the "Strength" cell, then open the *Attributes Inspector* (⌘1), and set the tag to 0. Then click the "Intellect" cell, and set its tag to 1. Continue through the rest of the checkboxes, ending by giving the "Leadership" checkbox a tag of 11.

At this point, you should now have something similar to Figure 4–10.

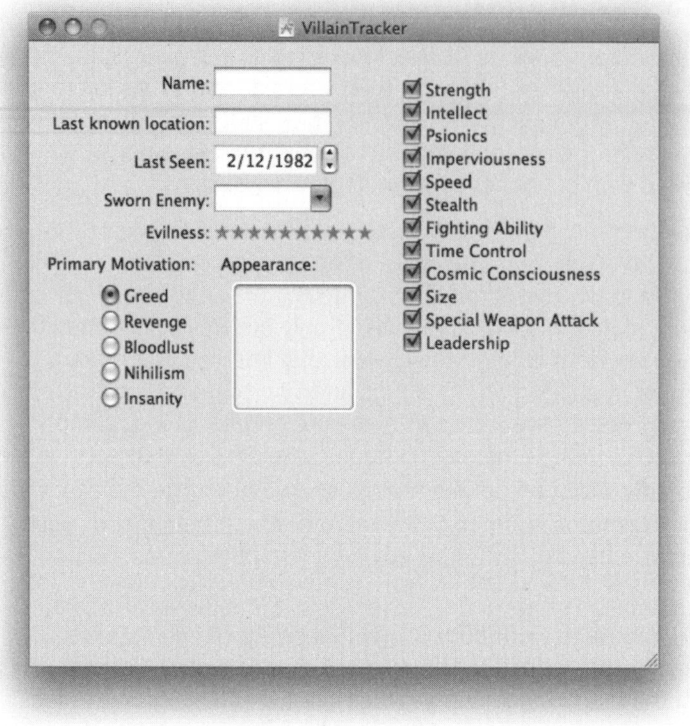

Figure 4–10. *Preparing for the worst of the worst*

Configuring a Popup Button

Now we'll deal with the villain's powerSource, using a popup button to let the user select from a predefined list in order to specify how the villain got his powers. Once again we've narrowed it down to a few choices: *Innate* (the villain was born with it), *Freak Accident* (some "act of god" such as a lab explosion, meteor strike, or similar, caused a transformation), *Superhero Action* (a superhero in the course of their heroics accidentally empowers someone else), and *Other*.

Go to the *Library* window again, and enter "popup" into the search field. Grab a Pop Up Button from the search results, and drag it into your window, placing it a bit below the checkbox matrix from the previous section. By clicking and then double-clicking on the new popup button, you can see the default list of values that can be selected. Double-click on the first one to edit its text, changing it to "Innate." Continue for the rest of the titles, entering the names mentioned previously. After entering the third one, you'll see that you're out of button values; the default popup button only has three values. Click on one of the three values, duplicate it by pressing ⌘D, and then enter the final value. Now grab another label, put it in place to the left of this popup button, and change its title to "Source of Powers:".

Inserting a Text View

Now it's time for the final control, a text view for editing free-form notes about the villain in question. We'll be using NSTextView, a powerful class for text display and editing that is used throughout the Mac OS X interface. In the *Library* window, enter "text view," and drag the resulting text view into your window, below all the other elements. Resize it to fill most of the available space. Your window layout should now look something like Figure 4–11.

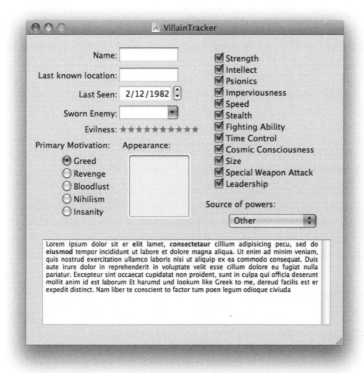

Figure 4–11. *All the controls are now in the window.*

Making Logical Groupings

Now that all the controls we need are laid out in the window, let's take a step back and see where we stand. Figure 4–11 is probably similar to the interface you have right now.

That may be functional, and clearly labeled, but it's not going to win us any design awards, that's for sure. Our interface exposes a lot of functionality, but the controls are all sort of jammed together, and it's hard to see any logical groupings of all these editable attributes. We can improve things a bit by grouping related controls inside of "box" views; Cocoa provides us with a class called NSBox that can contain several other objects and draw a nice border around them.

Interface Builder contains a nice shortcut that lets us put existing views into a box perfectly sized to contain them all precisely within its borders, so it's really easy to add this enhancement to our interface. To start, select the first five controls (in the upper left-hand of your window) and all of their labels. The easiest way to do this is to click in the upper left corner of your window, just below the window's close/minimize/maximize controls, and drag a selection box around all the views you want to select. Then, choose Layout➤Embed Objects In➤Box from the menu, and you'll see that a nice box surrounds them, with a darker gray background color and rounded corners. At the top of the box is a text label ("Box") that can be edited to something descriptive of the box's contents. Double-click that text, and change it to "Basic Information."

Go on and do the same thing for the *Primary Motivation* section. First, delete the label by selecting it and pressing *Backspace* or *Delete*. Because there's only one set of controls in the box we're going to create, we can just use the box's title instead. Now select the matrix of radio buttons, and once again select Layout➤Embed Objects In➤Box from the menu. Your radio buttons are now contained within a box. Change the box's label to "Primary Motivation."

Repeat those steps for the mugshot, once again deleting the existing label first, then creating the box via the menu, and finishing up by setting the box's label to "Appearance."

Now move on to the powers and abilities. Select the popup button and its label, along with the matrix of checkboxes. Once again, the easiest way to do this is probably to "draw a box" by clicking in the background near the window's top-right corner, and dragging down and to the left until all the relevant items are selected. Use the menu to put these views in a box, and title the box "Powers and Abilities."

Finally, select the text view created for the villain's `notes` property, and put that into a box of its own, entitled "Notes."

Now you've got a bunch of boxes created, but they're probably overlapping and generally not very well laid out relative to each other, like you see in Figure 4–12.

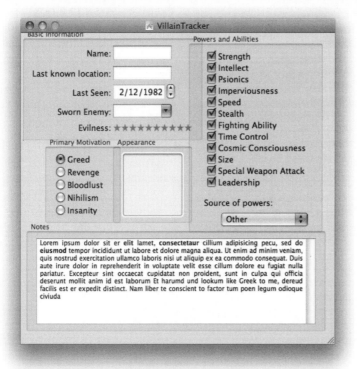

Figure 4–12. *Not the prettiest box layout you've ever seen*

Don't worry, Interface Builder's blue guidelines will help us get this straightened out in no time. Start with the first box, in the upper left-hand corner. Click anywhere in the dark background of the box (but not on a control or label) and you will be able to start dragging the entire box. As you move it around a bit, you'll see the blue guidelines appear. The guidelines can help you position views relative to one another, or relative to the window itself. You can always tell what a guideline is lining up with by following it to its end, and seeing what it connects with. When it runs all the way to the edge of the window, then you know it's setting you up for the recommended distance from the window's edge.

Now move on to the *Primary Motivation* box, lining it up with the left edge of the box above it, and a few pixels below it, again using the guidelines to help get it just right. Then take the *Appearance* box and line it up with the vertically with the *Primary Motivation* box, and horizontally with the right edge of the *Basic Information* box.

Continue with the other boxes, lining up the *Powers and Abilities* box to the right of the ones you've already done, then the *Notes* box below everything else. If you run out of space during all this movement, or if your window is much larger than the combined size of all your other views, resize your window a bit in order to fit everything.

Finish this step by resizing the width of the *Notes* box to match the combined widths of the elements above it, and resizing the NSTextView inside of it to fit its new boundaries and margins, and perhaps tweaking the sizes of some of the other boxes to make them all fit together in a uniform way. Figure 4–13 shows the kind of result you should be aiming for.

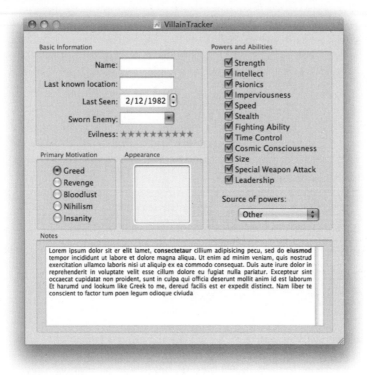

Figure 4–13. *Finally, a window layout to be proud of!*

Resizing

We've got a nice-looking window now, but there's a bit more work to be done here to make everything behave properly when the user resizes a window. Interface Builder lets you specify each view's resizing behavior relative to its enclosing view, which means that if the size of a view's parent view changes, you can specify that the inner view should resize proportionately (or not), have fixed distances to one or more edges (or not), and so on.

To understand why that's even necessary, test your interface in Interface Builder by pressing ⌘R. Now resize the window and see what happens. Oops! No matter how you resize the window, all the views seem to be "stuck" to the bottom left-hand corner.

In order to fix things, we need to make a few changes. We'll specify a minimum window size, we'll configure most of our boxes to stick to the top edge of the window instead of the bottom, and we'll configure the text view to resize itself along with the window, because it's the only view we have here that can actually benefit from additional screen real estate.

First, let's constrain the size of the window a bit. You may have noticed when testing your interface that you could make the window so small that not all GUI objects could fit inside. We don't want to deal with that possibility in this simple application, so we'll set the window's current size to be the minimum allowable size. Select your window by clicking in its title bar, then bring up the *Size Inspector* (⌘3). In the upper part of the inspector window, you'll see a section labeled *Minimum Size*. First click on the *Has Minimum Size* checkbox, then click the *Use Current* button to make sure the window can't be resized below its current size. If you test your interface now, you should see that this works.

Now, we want to make sure that most of the boxes in our interface (all except the one containing the text view) will stick to the top edge of the window when resizing, instead of the bottom. Click on the upper left-hand box labeled *Basic Information*, and you'll see that the *Size Inspector* now shows us attributes for this box, including an animated thumbnail display of how it will resize. Next to the animation, inside the *Autosizing* section, you'll see a control that resembles a set of crosshairs, with a central black square and some horizontal and vertical red lines, some solid and some dashed (See Figure 4–14).

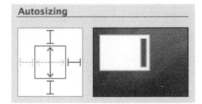

Figure 4–14. *The Autosizing control in the Size Inspector*

Basically, the black square represents the selected view. Outside the black square, a solid line indicates a margin that is fixed (relative to the parent view's boundaries) and will be preserved as the parent view is resized, and a dashed line indicates a margin that is flexible and will automatically change when the parent view is resized. Inside the black square, a solid line indicates a dimension that is flexible and will resize along with the parent, while a dashed line indicates a dimension that is fixed and won't change. This is one of those things that sounds more confusing that it really is. Trial and error, in combination with the animated preview and the "test interface" feature, will advance your grasp of this more than anything you read in a book.

For each of the upper boxes, you should configure the autosizing control so that the top and left red lines are solid, and all other red lines are dashed. Configure each of those boxes that way, test your interface, and you'll see as you resize the window that they will stick to the upper left.

The last bit of resizing configuration we want to do is for the box containing the text view, at the bottom of the window. Select the box labeled *Notes*, and edit the autoresize control so that **all** the lines are solid. That means that as resizing occurs, this box will retain the same distance to each side of its parent view (the window itself, basically), and will resize itself to match that constraint. Now do the same configuration for the text view itself, contained inside the box, so that it will resize along with the box.

Now you can test your interface, and you should see that the upper boxes hold their positions relative to the upper left corner, while the box containing the text view resizes along with the window. The layout for all our controls and other views is finally complete!

Time for the Controller

Now it's time to finally bring in the `VillainTrackerAppDelegate` that we created earlier in this chapter, and make all the necessary connections between it and the views in our window.

Go to the *Library* window's search field and type in "object." One of the search results, titled *Object*, is a generic object that starts out its life in Interface Builder as an `NSObject`, but we can easily change it to anything we want. Drag an *Object* to your main nib window, and then open the *Identity Inspector* (⌘6). The combo box at the top of this inspector lets you set the class of the selected object. Type in "VillainTrackerAppDelegate," and the new object you created is now an instance of `VillainTrackerAppDelegate`. You will even see that the "name" of the object, as shown in the nib window, has magically changed to "App Controller" to reflect the change.

If you now open the *Connections Inspector* (⌘5) you will see a list of all the outlets and actions that we previously defined in the header file, placed conveniently in alphabetical order. Now let's hook it up.

Making All the Connections

You'll need to connect each of the `VillainTrackerAppDelegate` outlets to the correct object in the window, connect each control's action back to the correct method in `VillainTrackerAppDelegate`, and make a few delegate connections to `VillainTrackerAppDelegate`. Let's start with the `VillainTrackerAppDelegate` outlets.

Leave the *Connections Inspector* open, so you have a nice view of all the `VillainTrackerAppDelegate`'s connections and can see on the fly which outlets are already hooked up. Start with the first outlet in the list (`evilnessView`, unless you've named things differently than we've described), and drag a connecting line from `VillainTrackerAppDelegate` to the correct view in the window, either by holding down *ctrl* while you click or by clicking using the right mouse button instead of the left. While dragging the line around, you'll see that it highlights as you drag it over each object in the window. Actually, it doesn't highlight over *every* object, but only over the objects for which the source of the drag (`Villain_Tracker_AppDelegate` in this case) has an outlet of the same type. This is a handy feature that lets you home in on just the objects that might be relevant.

When you finish dragging to the `evilnessView` and release the button, a small contextual window appears, showing you the outlets that can be connected to the target object. In this case, since we only have one outlet for a level indicator, that outlet (`evilnessView`) is the only one in the list; Click on it to make the connection.

Continuing going through the `VillainTrackerAppDelegate`'s remaining outlets one by one, connecting each to the correct object in the window. You shouldn't encounter any surprises along the way; The only thing to watch out for is that when you're making a connection for an outlet whose type is represented more than once in the class declaration (for example, `powersView` and `primaryMotivationView`, both of which are pointers to an `NSMatrix`), make sure you click on the correct item in the contextual window after dragging. Figure 4–15 shows a view of Interface Builder running with the `VillainTrackerAppDelegate` selected, and displaying all its connections in the *Connection Inspector*.

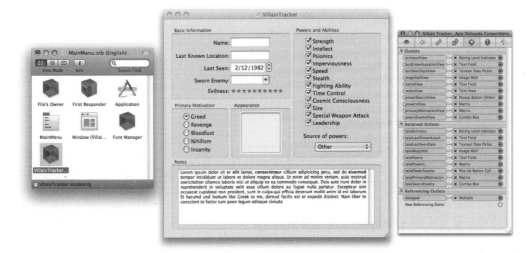

Figure 4–15. *The completed GUI and all its connections*

Now that the `VillainTrackerAppDelegate`'s "outbound" connections are done, it's time to set up its "inbound" connections. You'll do this by dragging a connection from each control back to the `VillainTrackerAppDelegate`, and then selecting the appropriate action method. Start with the first text field, the one labeled *Name*. Drag a connecting line from the text field to the `VillainTrackerAppDelegate` in the nib window, and release the mouse button. You'll see the contextual window again, but now with more items in it, and you'll see that it's split up into two sections, *Outlets* and *Received Actions*. Text fields and some other objects have a `delegate` outlet that can be used to extend their functionality in certain ways, but we're going to skip that for now and just connect to the `takeName:` method listed under *Received Actions*.

Now go on to the *Last known location* text field, and connect it to the `VillainTrackerAppDelegate`'s `takeLastKnownLocation:` method. Go on to connect the *Last seen* date picker to the `VillainTrackerAppDelegate`'s `takeLastSeenDate:` method, and continue connecting each of the controls in the upper part of the window (basically everything except for the large text view) to its corresponding action method in the `VillainTrackerAppDelegate`.

The text view is somewhat of a different beast. Unlike the other editable objects in our window, NSTextView is *not* a subclass of NSControl, which means that it doesn't know anything about the target/action pattern. However, it does expose a lot of functionality through calls to methods in its delegate. Later on, you'll implement some delegate methods inside VillainTrackerAppDelegate in order to get updated when the value of the text view changes; For now, just connect the text view's delegate outlet to our VillainTrackerAppDelegate. This is slightly complicated by the fact that the text view you dragged out from the *Library* earlier is automatically contained inside an NSScrollView, which it turn is contained in the NSBox we created earlier, so you may need to click and double-click once or twice in order to actually select the text view itself and be able to draw a connection from it.

Finally, we're going to make one additional connection for the sake of our controller class. We want to be notified when the nib is loaded and the application itself is initialized and ready to interact with the user, so that the initial display can be prepared. This is done through the use of NSApplication's delegate methods, so drag a connection from the *Application* object in the nib window to the VillainTrackerAppDelegate, and select delegate from the contextual menu.

Now we've made all the connections necessary for our application code to display values in the GUI, and to receive updates in response to user actions. Time to start writing our application!

Getting Started with Coding

Now that the GUI layout is done, it's time to switch over to Xcode. You're going to implement the "guts" of the application, which in the case of VillainTracker will all be contained in the VillainTrackerAppDelegate class. You'll learn how an NSApplication delegate (such as our controller class) can be made to react when the application launches, you'll see the basic APIs for displaying values in the GUI objects we've created, and you'll see how to implement methods that will respond to user actions by grabbing values from the relevant controls.

Standardizing Key Names

Before we start writing actual code, it's a good idea to come up with a way of standardizing the names of the keys that will be used for accessing attributes from the model objects. Whether in a case like ours, where the villain is stored in a dictionary whose attributes are only accessible by keys, or in a more complex situation using real model objects, standardizing key names is critical to ensure that you're correctly accessing the attributes in your model objects.

The technique we're using here is a simple one: we use standard C preprocessor macros to define names that are replaced with NSString instances at compile time. This eliminates the potential problem of mistyping a key name, and also adds the nice touch of working with the code-completion features in Xcode.

The following code listing includes key names for all the villain attributes that we are using in our application. With these in place, instead of using an NSString literal in your code to reference an attribute by its key name, you can (and should) use the defined name instead. Put the following code somewhere at the top of your VillainTrackerAppDelegate.m file.

```
#define kName @"name"
#define kLastKnownLocation @"lastKnownLocation"
#define kLastSeenDate @"lastSeenDate"
#define kSwornEnemy @"swornEnemy"
#define kPrimaryMotivation @"primaryMotivation"
#define kPowers @"powers"
#define kPowerSource @"powerSource"
#define kEvilness @"evilness"
#define kMugshot @"mugshot"
#define kNotes @"notes"
```

Creating the Default Villain

Now it's time to create a new villain object containing all the attributes that users can edit in the application. As mentioned earlier, we're not creating a "real" model class to contain a villain, instead going with the simpler option of using an NSMutableDictionary. We'll create it inside an NSApplication delegate method called applicationDidFinishLaunching:.

> **NOTE:** You may be wondering why we choose to put initialization code for an NSApplication's delegate into the applicationDidFinishLaunching: method, instead of into the init method. Objects that are loaded from the application's main nib file are always in a special predicament: they are being initialized as a substep in the application's own initialization routine, which means that at the time init is called on any object in the main nib file, the NSApplication itself may not be fully initialized! This has lots of repercussions, especially where the user interface is concerned, so often it's best to postpone our initialization until everything is truly ready. Because our VillainTrackerAppDelegate is set up to be the delegate of NSApplication, we have a handy way to notice when the application is really ready by implementing the applicationDidFinishLaunching: method.

Here's the code, to be entered somewhere inside the @implementation block in VillainTrackerAppDelegate.m:

```
- (void)applicationDidFinishLaunching:(NSNotification *)aNotification {
    self.villain = [[NSMutableDictionary alloc] initWithObjectsAndKeys:
                    @"Lex Luthor", kName,
                    @"Smallville", kLastKnownLocation,
                    [NSDate date], kLastSeenDate,
                    @"Superman", kSwornEnemy,
                    @"Revenge", kPrimaryMotivation,
                    [NSArray arrayWithObjects:@"Intellect",
                        @"Leadership", nil], kPowers,
```

```
        @"Superhero action", kPowerSource,
        [NSNumber numberWithInt:9], kEvilness,
        [NSImage imageNamed:@"NSUser"], kMugshot,
        @"", kNotes,
        nil];
}
```

As you can see, this code sets up all the attributes for a default villain that most people
are familiar with. The `initWithObjectsAndKeys:` method takes a `nil`-terminated list of
paired values and keys to fill the dictionary with. For the sake of legibility, we've put
each value/key pair on a line of its own. Note that the "mugshot" attribute is being set to
a pre-existing `NSImage` instance, one of several that are included in Cocoa and are
available for anyone to use in their applications. Now is a good time to once again
compile the app in Xcode just to make sure we've got everything right so far, but there's
still no point in actually running the app just yet. The GUI has been created, but
nothing's actually working just yet.

Paying Attention to Detail

The previous code listing created a villain object, but if you were to build and run your
app right now, you wouldn't see any sign of the villain. All the controls on the window
would be blank, because we haven't populated any of them with values from our villain's
attributes. Now it's time to change that. In our `VillainTrackerAppDelegate` class, we're
going to create a new private method called `updateDetailViews`, which sets up all the
GUI objects to display the attributes of the current villain. We're putting this functionality
into a method of its own (as opposed to setting things up right inside of
`applicationDidFinishLaunching:`) so that we can refresh our views whenever
necessary, not just when the application launches. We'll take you through the process of
displaying the villain's attributes, and you'll gain some familiarity with the basics of
interacting with the various classes in our GUI.

Let's start off by creating a simple "stub" of the new method. We want this method to be
accessible from anywhere in our class, but not from the outside. One way to do this is to
declare the method as part of a category, with the interface declaration made "private"
by virtue of its presence in `VillainTrackerAppDelegate`'s .m file, rather than its .h file.
So, just above the existing `@implementation VillainTrackerAppDelegate` line in the .m
file, insert the following code:

```
@interface VillainTrackerAppDelegate (privateMethods)
- (void)updateDetailViews;
@end
@implementation VillainTrackerAppDelegate (privateMethods)
- (void)updateDetailViews {
}
@end
```

We've named our `VillainTrackerAppDelegate` category "privateMethods," but we could
have called it anything, as long as it makes sense for our purposes. Before we begin
implementing the new method, make sure we're already set up to call it by inserting the
following line at the end of `applicationDidFinishLaunching`:

```
// insert this at the end of applicationDidFinishLaunching:
[self updateDetailViews];
```

Do a quick compile to make sure that what we have so far compiles cleanly. Now it's time to start implementing the updateDetailViews method, and finally see some villain data in our window!

Setting Simple Values

The first two controls we're going to set up for display are the two NSTextFields containing the villain's name and last known location. NSTextField can directly accept numbers and other sorts of input as well, but we're just passing along a simple string for each of these, using setStringValue:. Place these lines at the start of updateDetailViews, which we defined with an empty set of brackets just a few paragraphs ago:

```
[nameView setStringValue:[villain objectForKey:kName]];
[lastKnownLocationView setStringValue:
            [villain objectForKey:kLastKnownLocation]];
```

Note that we're reusing the preprocessor macros we defined earlier, so we don't have to worry about mistyping a string value. Now you should be able to compile your app, run it, and actually see some data in the window's text fields!

Next we'll set the NSDateView's value. Add this to the end of updateDetailViews:

```
[lastSeenDateView setDateValue:
            [villain objectForKey:kLastSeenDate]];
```

This is obviously quite similar to what we did for the NSTextFields: similar use of preprocessor macros, calling the relevant method for the target object (setDateValue: in this case), and so on. Once again you should compile and run after entering this code, to make sure that it works and that the correct date (today's date) is shown in the date view.

Now that you've seen the pattern here, let's take a bigger step forward, and see how to set values for all the remaining "simple" controls at once. You can either compile and run after each of these to check your work as you go, or if you're feeling a little lucky, just enter all of them and then compile and run at the end. Add these lines to the end of the updateDetailViews method:

```
[evilnessView setIntegerValue:
            [[villain objectForKey:kEvilness] integerValue]];
[powerSourceView setTitle:[villain objectForKey:kPowerSource]];
[mugshotView setImage:[villain objectForKey:kMugshot]];
[notesView setString:[villain objectForKey:kNotes]];
```

The only complication here is for the evilnessView. The view expects a C integer with which to set its value, but our villain has its evilness value stored as an NSNumber inside a dictionary, so we have the added step of converting the object into a plain old int.

Values in Complex Controls

Of the remaining attributes we're going to display, two of them are simple values (swornEnemy and primaryMotivation), while the third, powers, is a "compound value;" an array of strings. All of them are being displayed in more complex views than the previous attributes were, so we'll take a little more time with each of them.

First let's tackle the swornEnemy attribute, which is displayed in an NSComboBox. A combo box maintains a list of items that we must manually edit if we want to add new values to it. We'll need to do that any time we're displaying a villain whose swornEnemy is someone we didn't anticipate back when we were setting up the combo box in Interface Builder. In the following code, we first check to see if the combo box contains an item matching the name we want to display. If it doesn't, we add one. After that, we tell the combo box to select the appropriate item. Add this to the end of the updateDetailViews method:

```
if ([swornEnemyView indexOfItemWithObjectValue:
        [villain objectForKey:kSwornEnemy]] == NSNotFound) {
  [swornEnemyView addItemWithObjectValue:
      [villain objectForKey:kSwornEnemy]];
}
[swornEnemyView selectItemWithObjectValue:
    [villain objectForKey:kSwornEnemy]];
```

Now compile and run, and you should see that the combo box shows the correct value, in this case "Superman." You can verify that this will also work for items that aren't included in the combo box in the nib file by changing the relevant line in the applicationDidFinishLaunching: method to refer to some other superhero name that isn't present in the nib, then compiling and running again.

Next let's deal with the primaryMotivation attribute, displayed in a matrix of radio buttons. The NSMatrix class lets us select a single cell by specifying its tag, and because these are radio buttons, the others will be automatically deselected. The first thing we'll do is define a method that returns an array of strings containing all the motivations we're considering for our villains. These will be arranged in the same order as the cells in the matrix of checkboxes in the nib file, so that their index values match the tags specified for each cell. This method will be added to the privateMethods category that we created earlier.

```
// add to "@interface VillainTrackerAppDelegate (privateMethods)" section:
+ (NSArray *)motivations;
// add to "@implementation VillainTrackerAppDelegate (privateMethods)" section:
+ (NSArray *)motivations {
  static NSArray *motivations = nil;
  if (!motivations) {
    motivations = [[NSArray alloc] initWithObjects:@"Greed",
      @"Revenge", @"Bloodlust", @"Nihilism", @"Insanity", nil];
  }
  return motivations;
}
```

There are a few noteworthy things about this new method, each of which may give you some insight into the design patterns and philosophies used throughout Cocoa.

- This is a class method instead of an instance method (indicated by an initial "+" instead of "-"), so everything that happens in here applies to the whole class, no matter how many instances we may create. This is appropriate in many situations where the method doesn't deal with anything specific to an instance (for example, instance variables).

- We are using a locally-defined static variable to point to an object we create. The initial assignment to nil only occurs the first time the method is called. This is identical to the use of static local variables in standard C functions, and lets us define a chunk of code (everything inside the if clause) that will be executed only the first time this method is called.

- We are following a principle called "lazy loading." Instead of creating the array when the class is initialized, we only create it the first time it's needed. That way, in case no one ever calls this method, the array is never created.

At first glance, it may seem like overkill to be following these principles. After all, we're only going to have one instance of this controller class, so why make it a class method? And we know we're going to need to initialize that array, so why be lazy about it?

Of course in our contrived example, we could choose to follow the "simpler" route. We could just take the NSArray creation code and plop that into our code wherever we need to see the list of motivations! However, in the long run, doing things the "simple" way often backfires, and ends up not being simple at all. Remember that the systems we build may grow and be extended in the future, in ways we can't always anticipate today. Doing things the "right" way is a good way to future-proof your code, so that someone looking through the code later on (for example, trying to find where to add to the list of motivations) can figure out what's happening and find the one spot they need to change, instead of doing a manual search and replace to find every spot where an identical array is being created.

With our motivations method in place, we'll now be able to harvest from it an index number to identify the tag of the cell we want to select in the GUI. Here's one way to do this, ready to be added to the end of updateDetailViews:

```
[primaryMotivationView selectCellWithTag:
  [[[self class] motivations] indexOfObject:
    [villain objectForKey:kPrimaryMotivation]]];
```

Okay, we realize that looks like a bit of a mess if you're not used to it, and may give some of you flashbacks to the Lisp or Scheme you had to learn in your computer science education and have spent years trying to forget (These feelings are normal, and will subside over time). For the sake of clarity, we're going to unpack this a bit and show you an alternate version of the above, where some intermediate values are assigned to variables.

```
NSArray *motivations = [[self class] motivations];
id primaryMotivation = [villain objectForKey:kPrimaryMotivation];
int motivationIndex = [motivations indexOfObject:primaryMotivation];
[primaryMotivationView selectCellWithTag:motivationIndex];
```

Pretty straightforward, so you may wonder why we showed you the first version, where everything is all packed together. Basically, the first version is a kind of Objective-C code that you're likely to encounter in the wild at some point, so it's good to be able to try to eyeball it a little. Not because it's technically superior in some way (it's not), but simply because some people consider the highly nested version to be more readable in some ways, and just prefer to write their code that way. The position of the brackets, combined with features of Xcode's text editor, lets you easily do some things with the former version that take a bit more time with the latter. For example, double-clicking on a bracket in Xcode selects the entire bracketed expression, including the brackets themselves, which means you can easily select an entire method invocation, including the receiver, the method name, and all arguments, in a single double-click. This can be a huge help both when editing code and also browsing/reading code.

On the other hand, the second form we showed you can be helpful when debugging your application. Just set a breakpoint, and you've got a full complement of intermediate variables ready to divulge their contents to you. Ultimately, which style you lean toward is a matter of personal taste and practicality. Use whatever works best for you in the situation at hand. Until you've gotten a bit more Cocoa experience under your belt, you're probably better off sticking with the latter style, which shows more clearly the sequence of execution. For now, either of the alternatives shown above should work at the end of the updateDetailViews method. Compile and run, and verify that the correct primary motivation, "Revenge," is shown in the GUI.

Finally, it's time to display the powers attribute. Like the primaryMotivation, the villain's powers are shown in a matrix of button cells. This time, however, the button cells are checkboxes, and any number of them can be selected (or "checked"). Instead of a single string, the powers attribute is an NSArray containing all the relevant strings for the villain we're looking at.

We'll start off with something very similar to what we added for the primaryMotivation attribute: a new class method called powers:

```
// add to "@interface VillainTrackerAppDelegate (privateMethods)" section:
+ (NSArray *)powers;
// add to "@implementation VillainTrackerAppDelegate (privateMethods)" section:
+ (NSArray *)powers {
  static NSArray *powers = nil;
  if (!powers) {
    powers = [[NSArray alloc] initWithObjects:@"Strength",
      @"Intellect", @"Psionics", @"Imperviousness", @"Speed",
      @"Stealth", @"Fighting ability", @"Time control",
      @"Cosmic consciousness", @"Size", @"Special weapon attack",
      @"Leadership", nil];
  }
  return powers;
}
```

Like the motivations method, this method creates an array of strings whose indexes in the array correspond to the tags defined in a matrix in the nib file. Now we just have to add a bit of code to selectively "check" all the appropriate checkboxes. Add this code to the end of the updateDetailViews method:

```
[powersView deselectAllCells];
for (NSString *power in [[self class] powers]) {
  if ([[villain objectForKey:kPowers] containsObject:power]) {
    [[powersView cellWithTag:
      [[[self class] powers] indexOfObject:power]]
      setState:NSOnState];
  }
}
```

That bit of code should be pretty easy for you to grasp by now. First it deselects all the cells, so we start off with a clean slate of "unchecked" checkboxes. Then it goes through each named power from our "master list" of powers, checks to see if our villain's powers attribute contains a matching string, and if so, sets that cell's state to NSOnState, which means the checkbox is "checked." The one new thing to notice here is the special for construct. This is something called *fast enumeration*, an addition to the latest version of Objective-C that works unlike any form of for in C. It basically takes a collection (typically an NSArray) on the right side of the in, and iterates through it, assigning each object in the collection to the variable specified on the left side of the in, one at a time, then executing the subsequent curly-brace-wrapped code.

Now compile and run your application, and you should see the relevant checkboxes selected in the display: "Intellect" and "Leadership" in the case of Lex Luthor.

Responding to Input

Now that we're able to display all these villain attributes, it's time to turn things around and write the code that will let us notice changes the user makes to these fields. You previously created empty action methods which are triggered by the various GUI controls; now it's time for us to fill up those methods and make them do something useful! Also, we'll implement a delegate method to let us get the edited value for the one view in our window that doesn't work with target/action, the NSTextView.

Let's start off with the NSTextField for displaying and editing the villain's name, which triggers the takeName: method. Change the method to look like this:

```
- (IBAction)takeName:(id)sender {
  [villain setObject:[sender stringValue] forKey:kName];
  NSLog(@"current villain properties: %@", villain);
}
```

This method starts off by grabbing the string value from the sender, which is the textfield itself, and passing it along to the villain object to set its name. We end up by doing a bit of logging to show all the villain's current attributes. This can help in debugging, and also serves as a bit of a test for our code at runtime, so we can see that it's actually doing what it's supposed to do. The NSLog function takes as its first parameter an NSString used to define an output format, and one additional parameter for each formatting tag (a special sequence starting with a % sign) in the string. This is very similar to the standard printf function in C, with the addition of the %@ tag which prints a description of any Objective-C object. The output from NSLog shows up in Xcode's

Console window, which normally appears automatically when you launch an application from within Xcode.

> **TIP:** Action methods always pass along a "sender" object, which is normally the object that the user clicked or edited, triggering the method call. If your action method may be triggered by more than one GUI object, you can determine which object it came from by examining sender, comparing it to your instance variables, and so on.

Compile and run your app, and then select the text field containing Lex Luthor's name. Change the name in some way, press tab (or click on another control in the window), and you should see the output specified in the code printed to the output pane in Xcode. If you don't see any output window in Xcode when you run your app, switch to Xcode and open the console window by pressing ⇧⌘R. The villain dictionary output is formatted so that you can see each key alongside its associated value. You should be able to find the "name" key and see that its value has changed to the new value you entered.

Most of the rest of our action methods are similar to the takeName: method, and should be self-explanatory. Each of them simply does the inverse of the work we did in the updateDetailViews method, taking values from the GUI and applying them to our model object. Here's the code for all the "simple" action methods:

```
- (IBAction)takeLastKnownLocation:(id)sender {
    [villain setObject:[sender stringValue] forKey:kLastKnownLocation];
    NSLog(@"current villain properties: %@", villain);
}
- (IBAction)takeLastSeenDate:(id)sender {
    [villain setObject:[sender dateValue] forKey:kLastSeenDate];
    NSLog(@"current villain properties: %@", villain);
}
- (IBAction)takeSwornEnemy:(id)sender {
    [villain setObject:[sender stringValue] forKey:kSwornEnemy];
    NSLog(@"current villain properties: %@", villain);
}
- (IBAction)takePrimaryMotivation:(id)sender {
    [villain setObject:[[sender selectedCell] title]
        forKey:kPrimaryMotivation];
    NSLog(@"current villain properties: %@", villain);
}
- (IBAction)takePowerSource:(id)sender {
    [villain setObject:[sender title] forKey:kPowerSource];
    NSLog(@"current villain properties: %@", villain);
}
- (IBAction)takeEvilness:(id)sender {
    [villain setObject:[NSNumber numberWithInteger:[sender
        integerValue]] forKey:kEvilness];
    NSLog(@"current villain properties: %@", villain);
}
- (IBAction)takeMugshot:(id)sender {
    [villain setObject:[sender image] forKey:kMugshot];
    NSLog(@"current villain properties: %@", villain);
```

}

Enter all this into VillainTrackerAppDelegate's main @implementation section, and compile and run your app. You should now be able to edit all the fields we've dealt with so far, and see their values change in the output log. To set an image for the mugshot, just drag any image from anywhere else on your Mac; an image file from the Finder, a photo from iPhoto, a picture from Safari, and so on; and drop it into the mugshot view.

Note that for the swornEnemy combo box and the primaryMotivation radio button matrix, which had somewhat complicated procedures for setting their values, retrieving the values from them is simple enough to easily fit on a single line.

The remaining complex view, the powers checkbox matrix, is also a bit more complicated to retrieve values from, since we have to find all the checked boxes and get their associated strings. This should do the trick:

```
- (IBAction)takePowers:(id)sender {
  NSMutableArray *powers = [NSMutableArray array];
  for (NSCell *cell in [sender cells]) {
    if ([cell state]==NSOnState) {
      [powers addObject:[cell title]];
    }
  }
  [villain setObject:powers forKey:kPowers];
  NSLog(@"current villain properties: %@", villain);
}
```

Compile and run the app, click around in the powers matrix, and you should see the output log update accordingly.

Finally, we need to implement a method to retrieve the value from the notes view, an instance of NSTextView. NSTextView provides a lot of delegate methods that allow us to do many different things in response to the user's actions while editing the text. We will take a very simple approach, grabbing a copy of the value each time the user edits the text, which means after every single keypress! This would be an extreme thing to do for a large document view, where we might have performance consequences to consider, but for a smaller text view intended to hold a few notes, we shouldn't encounter any trouble with this simple approach:

```
- (void)textDidChange:(NSNotification *)aNotification {
  [villain setObject:[[notesView string] copy] forKey:kNotes];
  NSLog(@"current villain properties: %@", villain);
}
```

You may notice one unusual thing happening here: We're creating a copy of the result we get from notesView's string method. The reason for this is that internally, an NSTextView hangs onto a string of its own for editing and display, and its string method actually returns a pointer to that internal string object. If we don't make a copy we're going to end up with that string being referenced directly by our villain, which can lead to confusion later on, when we are switching between different villains being displayed by these GUI objects. We'd end up assigning the same string to several villains, and editing any villain's notes would simultaneously edit all of them! NSTextField doesn't cause us these sorts of problems, since its `stringValue` method already gives us a copy instead of passing along its internal string object.

One other thing to point out is that the `NSTextView` delegate method that we implemented has a curious method signature, and we are passed an `NSNotification` as a parameter. Here you're seeing a bit of the generic notification system that is part of Cocoa. Using a class called `NSNotificationCenter`, it's possible to configure any object to receive notifications from any other object when certain events occur. When you set up a delegate for an `NSTextView` (just to name an example; this pattern occurs for some other classes as well), some of the delegate methods you can choose to implement are specific to the delegate and can only be implemented there, but some of them are these kind of notification methods that can, in principle, also be implemented in any other class that has access to the `NSTextView` and is set up to receive notifications from it. You'll see more about this topic later in the book.

In Conclusion

We've covered a lot of material in this chapter. You've learned some of the basics that are vital to any Cocoa application: how to execute your own initialization code when your app launches; how to use Interface Builder to lay out views in a window, including specifying resizing behavior; the basics of using a variety of Cocoa's GUI classes; and more. In the next chapter we're going to build on what we've done so far, extending the VillainTracker application to be able to handle an array of villains listed in a table.

Chapter 5

Using Table Views

In Chapter 4, you learned a bit about some of Cocoa's most common GUI components, from buttons and simple input fields to full-fledged text editors. We haven't yet talked about one of Cocoa's biggest, most complex view classes, NSTableView. In this chapter, you'll learn how to use an NSTableView to display data for whole collection of components, how to respond when the user changes the table's selection by clicking a row, and how to edit values right in the table.

You'll learn how to use a table view by extending the VillainTracker application from Chapter 4. The new version of VillainTracker we create in this chapter will maintain an array of villains, display them all in a table, and let the user edit all the attributes of the selected villain when they click on its entry in the table. We'll start by using Xcode to extend the AppController class's interface to include an array of villains, some new outlets for connecting to the new table view and the window itself, and action methods for adding and deleting villains. Then we'll prepare the GUI layout in Interface Builder, and then we'll go back to Xcode to implement the changes to our controller's implementation for handling the table. Figure 5-1 shows you the end-result we're shooting for.

Preparing AppController for Multiple Villains

In Xcode, open the project you created in Chapter 4, and navigate to AppController.h so we can update the class's interface to accommodate our upcoming changes. First, we'll add the new instance variables we need. Because we're going to maintain a list of villains, we'll create an NSMutableArray called villains to contain them all. We also add an outlet called villainsTableView in order to access the NSTableView where we're going to present the list of villains. While we're at it, we'll also add an outlet called window for connecting to the NSWindow containing all of our GUI components. We'll put this to good use a little later.

For the sake of completeness, we also add a @property declaration for the new villains instance variable, to allow other code (including code in AppController's implementation) to easily and safely access and change this value.

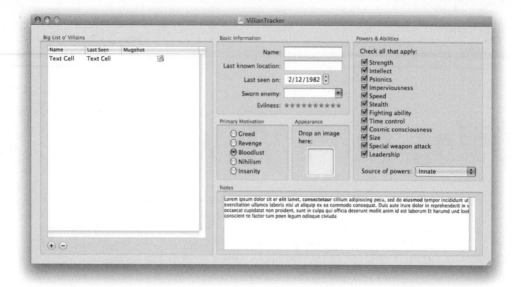

Figure 5–1. *The completed app window*

We'll also add declarations for newVillain: and deleteVillain:, our two new action methods. The following code listing shows the state of AppController.h after making these changes (new lines are in bold):

```
#import <Cocoa/Cocoa.h>

@interface AppController : NSObject {
  IBOutlet NSTextField *nameView;
  IBOutlet NSTextField *lastKnownLocationView;
  IBOutlet NSDatePicker *lastSeenDateView;
  IBOutlet ComboBox *swornEnemyView;
  IBOutlet NSMatrix *primaryMotivationView; // a matrix of radiobuttons
  IBOutlet NSMatrix *powersView; // a matrix of checkboxes
  IBOutlet NSPopUpButton *powerSourceView;
  IBOutlet NSLevelIndicator *evilnessView;
  IBOutlet NSImageView *mugshotView;
  IBOutlet NSTextView *notesView;
  IBOutlet NSTableView *villainsTableView;
  IBOutlet NSWindow *window;

  NSMutableDictionary *villain;
  NSMutableArray *villains;
}

@property (retain) NSMutableDictionary *villain;
@property (retain) NSMutableArray *villains;

- (IBAction)takeName:(id)sender;
- (IBAction)takeLastKnownLocation:(id)sender;
- (IBAction)takeLastSeenDate:(id)sender;
- (IBAction)takeSwornEnemy:(id)sender;
```

```
- (IBAction)takePrimaryMotivation:(id)sender;
- (IBAction)takePowerSource:(id)sender;
- (IBAction)takePowers:(id)sender;
- (IBAction)takeEvilness:(id)sender;
- (IBAction)takeMugshot:(id)sender;
- (IBAction)newVillain:(id)sender;
- (IBAction)deleteVillain:(id)sender;
```

@end

Now complete the @property definition of villains by adding a matching @synthesize in *AppController.m.* You'll also need to add two new method implementations (just empty shells for now) for the new action methods. Add these lines to the @implementation AppController section:

```
@synthesize villains;
- (IBAction)newVillain:(id)sender {}
- (IBAction)deleteVillain:(id)sender {}
```

Now we've added all that we need to AppController's interface, and some empty stub methods to the implementation. Hit the Build button just to make sure it compiles cleanly, and we'll move on to adjusting the GUI to make room for the table.

Making Way for the Table View

In Xcode's project navigation panel, double-click MainMenu.xib to open it in Interface Builder. You're going to make the window bigger, add a table view and a few buttons, and adjust the resizing characteristics of all the NSBoxes so that the table view will resize fully in both dimensions, and the other boxes will move accordingly.

Start by resizing the window, making it about 400 pixels wider (about half again as wide as it was to begin with), but the same height as before. We're going to follow the conventions of the western, left-to-right world, and arrange things so that the selection on the left (in the table view) determines what is presented on the right (all the other views), so you should also drag all the existing views to the right side of the window. See Figure 5-2 to get an idea of what to aim for.

Now bring up the *Library* window and type "tableview" into its search field. Drag the resulting NSTableView into to the empty space in the window. The default size for the table view is quite a bit smaller than the space you're putting it in, but don't bother with resizing it to fill the available space just yet, we'll get to that in a bit. For now, let it just sit there in the middle of the empty space.

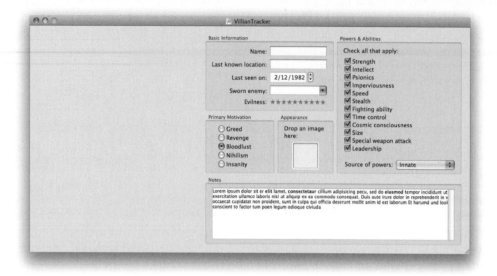

Figure 5–2. *Make your window look like this in preparation for the table view.*

The first thing we're going to do with this table view is configure its columns. By default, a new table view has two columns, but we'd like it to have three, so that we can show the name, date of last sighting, and mugshot for each villain in our list. To add a column, you have to sort of "drill down" through a few layers of views. Open the *Attributes Inspector* to help guide your way; it will always show you a bit of info about the selected object, most critically the class name. The first time you click on the table view in your window, you'll see that the *Attributes Inspector* shows you "Scroll View Attributes." That's because the table view you dragged out from the *Library* is actually contained inside an NSScrollView. Click again, and the inspector will show "Table View Attributes;" you're getting closer! Click again, this time in the large blank space of the table (below the column headers) and the inspector will show "Table Column Attributes," which is what we were looking for. Now that you have a column selected, Choose Edit➤Duplicate from the menu, and you'll see that your table now has three columns.

We want to configure these table columns to correspond to the name, lastSeenDate, and mugshot values in our villain objects, and we'll do that by supplying each of them with an identifier that is the same as the key-name for the attribute we want to show. Later on, you'll see how we use this identifier in our code to easily prepare values for display. Select the first column, and then in the Attributes Inspector, type "name" into the Identifier field. While you're there, type "Name" into the Title field; this determines what will appear in the text of the column's header. Repeat this process for the second column, entering "lastSeenDate" as the Identifier and "Last Seen" as the Title, and again for the third title, entering "mugshot" for the Identifier and "Mugshot" for the Title.

That final column needs a little extra configuration, because it's going to display an image instead of text. Fortunately, Cocoa provides a class that makes this easy. You may remember from Chapter 4 that whenever we had an NSMatrix full of controls, those controls were actually instances of a subclass of NSCell, a class that is more lightweight than NSView or NSControl. NSTableView also draws its content using cells, and by default it uses NSTextFieldCell for displaying and editing string values. We'll change this to make it use an NSImageCell instead, so that the third column can display an image. Once again go to the Library window, and enter "imagecell" into the search field, which will bring up NSImageCell. Drag this over to your table view, into the space where the mugshot column should be. The column will highlight and your mouse pointer will acquire a green "+" badge when you're over a drop-ready spot. Release the button, and voila! That table column is now ready to display an image.

Now we're going to add a pair of buttons, one for adding a new villain to the list, and one for deleting the selected villain. Back in the Library window, type "button" into the search field, and you'll see a surprisingly large list of buttons show up in the results. Someone at Apple really likes to design buttons! Despite their differences in appearance, just about everything in this list is just an NSButton, which at its core always does the same basic thing. Some of them are pre-configured in different modes to work as a checkbox or disclosure triangle, but otherwise they all do the same basic thing: call an action method in a target object when clicked.

Pick one of the first few buttons you see in the list (maybe *Push Button* or *Rounded Rect Button*) and drag it to your window, dropping it just below the table view. This will be our "Add Villain" button. Instead of titling the button with the text "Add Villain" however, we'll use one of Cocoa's built-in graphic images to make it resemble "add" buttons in other applications. While the button is still selected, bring up the *Attributes Inspector*, and locate the *Image* combo box. Click on the small triangle at the right end of the combo box, and start typing "nsaddtemplate." When you see that it's filled in the full text as "NSAddTemplate," press Enter and you'll see that your new button now has a "+" image. Resize the button horizontally so that it is just wide enough to contain the image, then duplicate the button (with ⌘D) to make another button. Select this second button, go back to the *Image* combo box in the *Attributes Inspector* again, and begin typing "nsremovetemplate," which will provide you with a "-" image in your button.

Now, take the "add" button, and drag it to a point just below the bottom edge of the table view, using the blue guidelines to make its left edge line up with the left edge of the table view, and its top edge the recommended distance from the table view's bottom edge. Drag the "remove" button into location just to the right of the "add" button. Then, select both buttons and the table view by dragging a selection rectangle over all of them, and choose **Layout➤Embed Objects In➤Box** from the menu, then set the title of the new box to "Big List o' Villains". Your newest views are now all contained inside an NSBox, just like the rest (except that it's not yet properly sized or aligned with anything). Figure 5-3 shows what you should be seeing at this point.

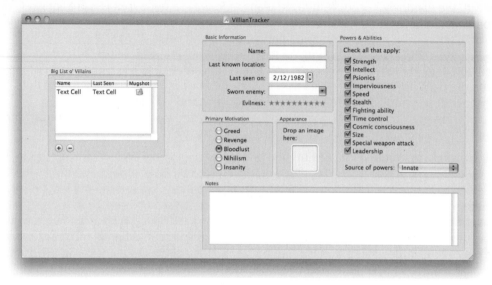

Figure 5–3. *The table view and its buttons are in place, but not yet resized.*

Tweaking the Autosizing Characteristics

Now let's make the table view and its surrounding box fill up that space. Grab the new box and position it so that its bottom edge is aligned with the bottom of the Notes box, and its left edge is the correct distance from the left edge of the window. Then grab its upper right-hand resize handle, and drag it up and to the right so that its upper and right-hand edges are the correct distances from the top of the window and the boxes to its right, respectively. As usual, the blue guidelines will help make this happen.

Now select the table view inside its box, and resize it using the upper-right resize handle so that it fills the box to the top and the right. See Figure 5-4 to get an idea of what you're shooting for.

In Chapter 4, we configured our boxes so that the Notes box would resize fully with the window, while everything else remained stuck to the upper left. Now that we have a table view on the left, we're going to reconfigure the resizing behavior of our boxes so that the table view resizes fully with the window, the Notes box resizes vertically (while keeping the same width), and everything else sticks to the upper right.

Start by selecting the table view. Open the Size Inspector (⌘3), and in the *Autosizing* section, click on each of the dashed red lines (both inside and outside the black box) to make them solid. The solid lines inside the black box configure it to resize in both dimensions, and the solid lines outside the black box make sure that its external margins (relative to the view it's in) will remain the same. In other words, the table view will resize fully in both dimensions as its parent view is resized. Next, select the "Big List o' Villains" box itself by clicking its title, and give it the same treatment, so that it will resize fully with the window. Figure 5-5 shows what this configuration looks like in the *Autosizing* section of the *Attributes Inspector*.

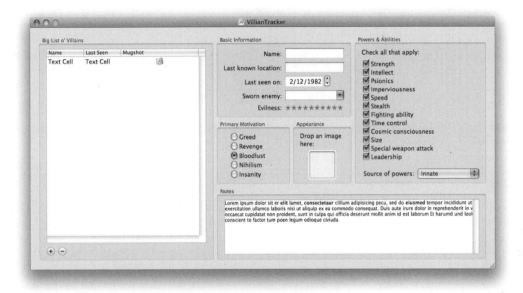

Figure 5–4. *This is how we want the window to look.*

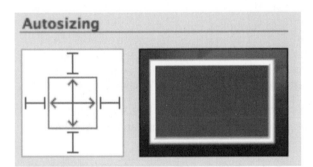

Figure 5–5. *These Autosizing settings for both the table view and its enclosing box will allow them to resize fully with the window.*

Now select the "Notes" box, and change its *Autosizing* configuration so that it still resizes vertically, but no longer resizes horizontally, and allows its left-hand margin to be flexible (to leave room for the resizing table view). Do this by making the inner horizontal line and the left margin red line dashed, while leaving the other red lines solid, as shown in Figure 5-6.

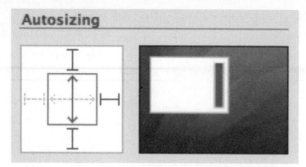

Figure 5–6. *These Autosizing settings for the box containing the "notes" text-view will make it resize the way we want it to.*

Now it's time to take care of all the other boxes on the right side (everything above the Notes box). For each box, first click to select the box, then edit its Autosizing behavior by make sure that the red lines for its upper and right margins are solid, and all other red lines are dashed, just like you see in Figure 5-7.

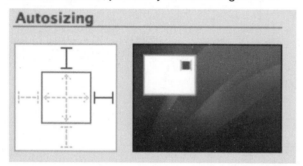

Figure 5–7. *These Autosizing settings should be applied to all the remaining boxes, making them "stick" to the upper-right corner of the window.*

Do that for each of the remaining boxes, then choose File▶Simulate Interface. Resize the window, and you should see that all the views resize as planned.

For the rest of this book, we're going to skip any further discussion of the autosizing features, and leave it up to you to determine the autosizing options for your layouts as you see fit.

Making Some New Connections

Before we get into the code for this app, there's one last step that we need to do in Interface Builder: connect AppController's new actions and outlets. Click on the *AppController* icon in the main nib window, then open the *Connection Inspector* (⌘5), and you'll see that our two new outlets, villainsTableView and window, now appear in the list. Ctrl-drag from AppController to the window (either to its icon in the main nib window, or to the title bar of the actual window), release the button, and select window.

Then Ctrl-drag from `AppController` to the table view, release the button, and select `villainsTableView`.

Now it's time to connect a couple of outlets from the table view to our `AppController`. These two outlets let us specify which object will be able to respond to `NSTableView`'s `delegate` methods (called, for example, when the table view's selection changes) and its `dataSource` methods (used to populate the table with data). In our case, we are using `AppController` to handle both of these duties. Ctrl-drag from the table view to the `AppController` and click on `dataSource`, then repeat the drag and click `delegate`. If dragging from the table view to `AppController` doesn't bring up a menu of outlets to choose from, you're probably dragging from the `NSScrollView` instead. Click it again to select the table view inside the scroll view, and try again.

The last step is to connect the new "add" and "remove" buttons to the relevant action methods in `AppController`. First ctrl-drag from the "add" button to the *AppController* icon and select the `newVillain:` action, then ctrl-drag from the "remove" button to the *AppController* icon and select the `deleteVillain:` action.

With those connections out of the way, our GUI layout is done for now, and we can get back into writing the code.

Making Way for the Table View: Code Edition

With the groundwork we already laid in Chapter 4, adding support for an array of villains is surprisingly simple. Basically, we have to create an array, tell the table view when we want it to display its content (whenever its content has changed), implement a few `dataSource` methods to give the table view its content, and implement a `delegate` method that will be called when the table view's selection changes (so that we can update all the other views to match the selected villain). Then we'll add a pair of methods to add and delete villains from the array, and we'll be done!

Let's start off by initializing an array to hold our villains, and telling the table view that it should load its content. We do this by adding just a few lines to `applicationDidFinishLaunching:`, as seen in bold in the following listing. First we create an array to hold all villains (which initially contains just the first villain we created in code earlier) and assign it to our `villains` instance variable. Then we tell the table view to load its content, and then to select its first row.

```
- (void)applicationDidFinishLaunching:(NSNotification *)aNotification {
    self.villain = [NSMutableDictionary dictionaryWithObjectsAndKeys:
                @"Lex Luthor", kName,
                @"Smallville", kLastKnownLocation,
                [NSDate date], kLastSeenDate,
                @"Superman", kSwornEnemy,
                @"Revenge", kPrimaryMotivation,
                [NSArray arrayWithObjects:@"Intellect",
                  @"Leadership", nil], kPowers,
                @"Superhero action", kPowerSource,
                [NSNumber numberWithInt:9], kEvilness,
                [NSImage imageNamed:@"NSUser"], kMugshot,
                @"", kNotes,
```

```
                                  nil];
     self.villains = [NSMutableArray arrayWithObject:self.villain];
     [villainsTableView reloadData];
     [villainsTableView selectRow:0 byExtendingSelection:NO];
     [self updateDetailViews];
}
```

You'll also need to add the [villainsTableView reloadData] call to the end of each of the takeName:, takeLastSeenDate:, and takeMugshot: methods, so that when the user edits the controls for those attributes, the table view will be updated accordingly. Just copy that line and paste it into the end of each of those methods. It may seem like overkill to call a method that looks like it's going to reload the entire table of data just because a single value has been changed, but don't worry: NSTableView uses "lazy loading," and normally only requests content for a given row when that row is about to be displayed. You might have a million rows of content, but if you never scroll past the first 30, no more than the first 30 are likely to be loaded by the table view. Likewise, telling a table view to reload its data will only make it load the visible rows immediately, the rest will only be reloaded when they scroll into display.

At this point, you should be able to compile and run your app, and you should see roughly the same thing you saw at the end of chapter 4, plus a big empty table view and a couple of buttons that have no effect. Time to fill that table view with villains!

The Table View Needs Your Help

We've told the table view to load its content, but it can't do anything until we implement some methods from the NSTableDataSource protocol in the object we connected to the table view's dataSource outlet: our AppController. NSTableDataSource is an informal protocol, similar to most delegate protocols, which means that you don't have to declare that your class conforms to the protocol. As a result, implementing the NSTableDataSource methods is, as far as Objective-C is concerned, optional. In spite of that, there are a few methods that are in fact required for the table view to display anything: numberOfRowsInTableView:, and tableView:objectValueForTableColumn:row:, both of which are used by the table view to prepare content for display. Here's how these should be implemented in AppController.m:

```
- (NSInteger)numberOfRowsInTableView:(NSTableView *)aTableView {
    return [villains count];
}
- (id)tableView:(NSTableView *)aTableView
 objectValueForTableColumn:(NSTableColumn *)aTableColumn
    row:(NSInteger)rowIndex {
    return [[villains objectAtIndex:rowIndex]
           objectForKey:[aTableColumn identifier]];
}
```

The first method should be self-explanatory: we just return the size of the array so that the table view knows how many rows it needs to display. The second method is called by the table view each time a cell is going to be displayed in the table. We're given a pointer to the column that the cell is in, and an index number indicating which row it's in.

The row index number is the same as the index number for the relevant object in our content array, so calling [villains objectAtIndex:rowIndex] returns the relevant model object from villains. As you may recall, the model objects we're using are in fact just NSMutableDictionary instances, with all their values accessible by keys. When we configured the identifier attribute of each column in our table view, we used the same key names that our model objects use, so we retrieve that key from the table column, and use that to get the relevant value from the model object.

For example, when the cell in the top row under the "Name" column is about to be displayed, this method will be called with a rowIndex of 0, and a TableColumn pointing to the "Name" NSTableColumn. We use the 0 to specify which villain to grab from our villains array, then we use value returned by the table column's identifier method, @"name", to retrieve a value from the chosen villain.

If that's not quite sinking in, here's a slightly longer (in terms of lines of code, not run-time) way to implement the same method, which may clarify it for you:

```
- (id)tableView:(NSTableView *)aTableView
 objectValueForTableColumn:(NSTableColumn *)aTableColumn
  row:(NSInteger)rowIndex {
  NSMutableDictionary *villain = [villains objectAtIndex:rowIndex];
  id keyName = [aTableColumn identifier];
  return [villain objectForKey:keyName];
}
```

Now you should be able to compile and run VillainTracker, and see that the default villain is displayed both in the controls and as the only row in the table view. Furthermore, if you edit the villain's name, last seen date, or mugshot in the controls, you should see those new values reflected in the table view. You still can't edit anything directly in the table view, but let's change that right now. We're going to implement one more dataSource method, tableView:setObjectValue:forTableColumn:row:, which will allow the user to edit values directly in the table view, and push the changes down into the model objects. This is basically the inverse of the last method you saw, and is nearly as simple in its implementation:

```
- (void)tableView:(NSTableView *)aTableView
   setObjectValue:(id)anObject
   forTableColumn:(NSTableColumn *)aTableColumn
   row:(NSInteger)rowIndex {
   [[villains objectAtIndex:rowIndex] setObject:anObject
     forKey:[aTableColumn identifier]];
   [self updateDetailViews];
}
```

Here you see that we're looking up the relevant villain in the same way as before, and this time instead of returning a value, we're using the column's identifier to set an attribute of the villain object. We end the method by calling updateDetailViews, so that any editing we do directly in the table view will be displayed in the other controls as well.

At this point you should be able to compile and run your app, and see that you can edit the value in the *name* column in the table view, and see your change register in the dedicated Name control as soon as you press tab or enter.

Now it's time to implement a delegate method that is called whenever the table view's selection changes. This lets us notice which row the user has selected, change our villain instance variable to point at the relevant row in the villains array, and redisplay all the other controls to match the new selection. Add this method to the @implementation section in AppController.m:

```
- (void)tableViewSelectionDidChange:(NSNotification *)aNotification {
 if ([villainsTableView selectedRow] > -1) {
  self.villain = [self.villains
          objectAtIndex:[villainsTableView selectedRow]];
  [self updateDetailViews];
  NSLog(@"current villain properties: %@", villain);
 }
}
```

You'll see that the meat of this method is wrapped inside an if-clause. That's necessary, because it's possible for a table view to tell us that it currently has no selected row at all, which it does by returning -1 from its selectedRow method. Beyond that, you should be able to understand what's happening in there by now. Compile this to make sure that no errors have crept in, but you don't need to run it just now: we haven't added the code for creating or deleting a villain yet, so there's no use trying to make sense of the table view's selection (since it can't really change while the table only has one entry).

Adding and Deleting Villains

Finally, let's implement the newVillain: and deleteVillain: methods, both of which we provided as "stubs" earlier. The newVillain: method adds a new "empty" villain object to our array of villains, tells the table to reload, and tells the table view which row to select (the last one, since that's the one we just added).

```
- (IBAction)newVillain:(id)sender {
 [window endEditingFor:nil];
 [villains addObject:[NSMutableDictionary
  dictionaryWithObjectsAndKeys:
          @"", kName,
          @"", kLastKnownLocation,
          [NSDate date], kLastSeenDate,
          @"", kSwornEnemy,
          @"Greed", kPrimaryMotivation,
          [NSArray array], kPowers,
          @"", kPowerSource,
          [NSNumber numberWithInt:0], kEvilness,
          [NSImage imageNamed:@"NSUser"], kMugshot,
          @"" , kNotes,
          nil]];
 [villainsTableView reloadData];
 [villainsTableView selectRow:[villains count]-1
  byExtendingSelection:NO];
}
```

The only new thing you might see in here is [window endEditingFor:nil], which simply tells the window that it's time to end whatever other editing behavior the user is currently engaged in, such as typing in a text field. We need to call this method so that the edited value can be "saved" to its underlying villain object, because later in newVillain: we're going to change the table view's selection, which would in turn wipe out the values shown in the various controls!

Now you should be able to compile and run your app, and see that the "+" button now actually makes something happen. Furthermore, you should be able to click back and forth between all of the villains in the table view and see the values in the other controls change accordingly.

Next we have the deleteVillain: method, which you see here. We've added comments to show the different sections, which will be described after the code.

```
- (IBAction)deleteVillain:(id)sender {
 //
 // Section 1:
 //
 [window endEditingFor:nil];
 int selectedRow = [villainsTableView selectedRow];
 //
 // Section 2:
 //
 [villains removeObjectIdenticalTo:villain];
 [villainsTableView reloadData];
 //
 // Section 3:
 // if (selectedRow >= [villains count]) {
  selectedRow = [villains count]-1;
 }
 // Section 4:
 if (selectedRow > -1) {
  // deselect all rows to ensure that the tableview sees the
  // selection as "changed", even though it might still have
  // the same row index.
  // Section 5:
  [villainsTableView deselectAll:nil];
  [villainsTableView selectRow:selectedRow byExtendingSelection:NO];
  [self updateDetailViews];
 }
}
```

This method is a bit more complicated than most of the code we've shown you in this book so far, so a little additional explanation is in order.

In Section 1, we tell the window to finish up any editing that's going on, then we grab the index of the table's currently selected row; that is, the row that's going to be deleted. Note that we already know which villain is selected, because it's stored in an instance variable, but having the row index is important for making sure the post-delete selection makes sense (later, in Section 4).

In Section 2, we delete the selected object (pointed at by the villain instance variable) from the villains array, then we tell the table view to reload. Note the method for removing the villain from the array, removeObjectIdenticalTo:. This method makes the NSMutableArray scan itself for the object by comparing its actual memory address with the memory addresses of the objects it contains, so that it only finds and removes exactly the object we pass in. Otherwise, if we had gone with the more commonly used removeObject: method, it would be comparing objects by sending the isEqual: method, which in turn compares values. In that case, any other villain objects we had entered with attributes identical to those of the selected villain would run the risk of being deleted as well.

In Section 3, we make a small adjustment: If the previous selected row index was the last in the array, now that we've removed an object from the array, that index is out of bounds. In that case, we reset it to point at what is now the last object.

Next, Section 4 checks to see if selectedRow is 0 or higher. This check is important, because there's a real chance that Section 3 set it to -1! Consider the case where we only have one object in the array, and click the "remove" button: At the outset, selectedRow would be 0 (the index of the only row in the array), but after Section 3 it would be -1, which Section 4 handles by just skipping the rest of the method.

Finally, Section 5 deselects everything in the table view, then selects what we now want for the selected row, and finally updates all the views based on the current selection. It may not seem obvious, but it's important to first deselect all rows in the table view, otherwise the tableViewSelectionDidChange: delegate method may not always be called (because often, after deleting a row, the selected row index itself will be the same number, and the table view has no way of knowing that we've deleted an object from our content array, making the row index number now refer to a different object).

Now you should be able to compile and run your app, and see that you can now also delete the selected villain, and the values in the controls will change to match the new selection.

In Conclusion

You've now seen a simple demonstration of how to maintain a list of items, display them in a table view, and edit the details for the selected item in a separate set of controls. You've learned a bit about how NSTableView uses its dataSource to access items for display and editing, and seen how it informs its delegate when the selection changes, allowing you to manually update the content in views that are dependent on the table view's selection.

If you're familiar with other desktop GUI development environments, some of this may have seemed a bit foreign to you, but hopefully you can see some of the advantages included in the approach that Cocoa supports, such as providing a clean division between code and GUI layout. However, at this point it's time for a confession: the way we've been doing things in Chapters 4 and 5 isn't necessarily the best way to do these sorts of things in Cocoa. As simple as it's all been so far, we've actually been showing you the *hard* way to solve these problems! During the past few years, a new approach to GUI programming has taken root in the Cocoa community, and is becoming more prevalent all the time; it's a technology called Cocoa Bindings, and it's the topic of Chapter 6.

Cocoa Bindings

In Chapters 4 and 5, you learned about how to connect a controller object to various kinds of view objects, both to display values and to retrieve new values in response to user actions. In our examples, we typically had one small action method for each view (triggered when the user edited the value displayed in the view), plus one large updateDetailViews method that updated the contents of all the views at once (called whenever the selection changed). That's fine for a simple project, but there are some problems with that approach. First of all, there's a scalability issue. Imagine having not ten, but a hundred views. Following our approach, you'd end up with a controller having a hundred small action methods, and one *huge* method to push values into all of the views!

Plus, we really have some tight coupling between our controller and its associated views. For example, what if you start off with an NSDatePicker for displaying and editing a date, but later decide you want to use an NSTextField? Besides modifying the GUI, you'd also have to change the outlet, the corresponding action method, and the updateDetailViews method.

Fortunately for us, Apple recognized this problem some time ago, and since Mac OS X 10.3 it has included a technology called Cocoa Bindings that solves many of these problems. Cocoa Bindings lets you use Interface Builder to configure a view so that it retrieves its value and passes changes back to a model object more or less automatically. All you do is tell it which controller object to deal with, and which string it should use as a key for getting and setting a value. You can access model objects through your own controller classes, or using generic controller classes provided by Apple.

This results in an architecture where your own controller class often doesn't need to know anything specific about any of the view objects in use. You don't need to have instance variables pointing at them, and you don't need to implement action methods to get their input! Your controller ends up as little more than a simple channel between a model object and a bunch of view objects, and from the controller's point of view it doesn't make a difference if there are ten views or a hundred.

In this chapter, you'll learn how to use Cocoa Bindings with simple controls such as checkboxes, sliders, and text fields, as well as with complex controls such as table views. You'll create bindings that connect to model objects through a couple of Apple's included controller classes. You'll also get an introduction to using NSUserDefaults and its bindings-ready friend NSUserDefaultsController to deal with preferences in your application.

Binding to Simple Controls

The example application for this chapter is something that could be used by a Game Master in a role-playing game to randomly create characters, monsters, and dungeons. The main window will contain buttons that create random game objects when the user clicks them, and text fields to display the result. We'll also make a Preferences window where the user can specify some parameters for the creation of the game objects. We won't do the actual "rolling" of these random objects. We'll just display a summary of the parameters used each time the user clicks one of the buttons. The random game object creation is a bit too far afield for this book, and could be a fun "exercise for the reader" if you are so inclined!

Create the DungeonThing Project

Launch Xcode, and select **File➤New Project** from the menu. Choose Cocoa Application, then navigate to the directory where you want to create your new project, and name it DungeonThing. Now create a DungeonThingAppDelegate class, as you've done in the earlier projects (if you're running Snow Leopard, it's already created for you). The DungeonThingAppDelegate class interface is pretty simple; we're going to create quite a lot of options that the user can select in the Preferences window, but our controller doesn't need to know about any of those GUI controls, because they'll all store their values directly into the app's preferences via NSUserDefaultsController, one of Cocoa's bindings-ready controller classes. All we need to add are three action methods, one for each "create" button to call when it's clicked, as well as outlets for three text fields in the GUI, where we'll display the results. In the second half of this chapter, even those three outlets will go away, because those text fields will also be handled using Cocoa Bindings. For now, make your *DungeonThingAppDelegate.h* look like this (new parts are in bold):

```
#import <Cocoa/Cocoa.h>
@interface DungeonThingAppDelegate : NSObject {
  IBOutlet NSTextField *characterLabel;
  IBOutlet NSTextField *monsterLabel;
  IBOutlet NSTextField *dungeonLabel;
}
- (IBAction)createCharacter:(id)sender;
- (IBAction)createMonster:(id)sender;
- (IBAction)createDungeon:(id)sender;
@end
```

Then switch over to *DungeonThingAppDelegate.m*, and add the code shown in bold. As before, we provide empty method definitions for each action, for the sake of having code that actually compiles.

```
#import "DungeonThingAppDelegate.h"
@implementation DungeonThingAppDelegate
- (IBAction)createCharacter:(id)sender { }
- (IBAction)createMonster:(id)sender { }
- (IBAction)createDungeon:(id)sender { }
@end
```

After entering this code, compile your application just to make sure there are no syntax errors. We'll come back and fill in the code for those action methods later.

Create a Preferences Window

Now find the *MainMenu.xib* in Xcode (you'll find it in Resources in the navigation pane) and double-click to open it in Interface Builder. This starts off as a standard empty application GUI which you should be familiar with by now. As before, you'll probably want to edit some items in the menu, changing every occurrence of "NewApplication" to "DungeonThing."

This nib file already contains a main window, which we'll get to a little later on, but first we'll get to the heart of the matter by creating a *Preferences* window, whose GUI controls will be configured exclusively with Cocoa Bindings. In the *Library* window, type "window" and drag out the Window object you see in the result list. This window will be our *Preferences* window. Use the *Attributes Inspector* (⌘1) to set the window's title to "DungeonThing Preferences," and you'll see that the label under the corresponding icon in the nib window also changes. In the same *Inspector* window, click to turn off the *Resize* checkbox, because there's no reason to allow the user to resize the window. You should also click to turn off the *Visible at Launch* checkbox, so that the window doesn't appear on-screen as soon as the nib loads. We only want the *Preferences* window to appear when the user selects the appropriate menu item.

Make the window a bit wider than its default size, in order to accommodate the controls we're about to add. Press ⌘3 to bring up the *Size Inspector*, and make sure that your new window is selected by clicking its title bar, then type 530 into the *Width* field.

The final step is to hook things up so that a user can open this window by accessing the **Preferences** item in the menu. Double-click the *MainMenu* object in the main nib window, and navigate to the **Preferences** item. This object will connect to the *Preferences* window with target/action, so Ctrl-drag from the menu item to the *Preferences* window (either drag to the icon representing the window in the main nib window, or to the title bar of the real window), and select the makeKeyAndOrderFront: action. That's a method that will make any window become the front-most window in its application, and also become the "key" window, ready to receive events in response to the user pressing keys on the keyboard (hence the "makeKey" in the method name).

Add a Tab View

We're going to split up the application preferences into different three different groups, one for each of the three game objects the user can create. We'll separate the groups by placing the controls an NSTabView, which lets the user switch between different views by selecting from a list of tabs along the top. In the *Library* window, type in "tab," then drag the resulting *Tab View* into your empty window. Resize it so that it nearly fills the window (as shown in Figure 6–1), leaving the standard margin that the blue lines will happily show you.

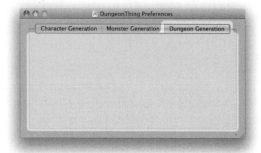

Figure 6–1. *The preferences window for DungeonThing looks like this after the creation and naming of the tabs*

When you drag out a new tab view from the *Library*, by default it has two tabs, but we want ours to have three. Click the tab view, and open the *Attributes Inspector* (⌘1). There you will see a *Tabs* field. Click the tiny up-arrow to change its value from 2 to 3, and you'll see that there are now three tabs. Double-click on the title of each tab, and change their titles to "Character Generation," "Monster Generation," and "Dungeon Generation," respectively. Figure 6–1 shows what your window should look like at this point.

Character Generation Preferences

Now let's start populating these tabs with some controls. First up is the *Character Generation* tab, so click on that tab to select it. By now you should be comfortable enough finding views and controls in the *Library* that we won't hold your hand and tell you every single step of grabbing these objects and dragging them into your window. It should be just about enough for you to look at Figure 6–2 and know that we're using a slider, a matrix of radio buttons, a matrix of checkboxes, and a handful of text fields for labels, including the small one out to the right of the slider.

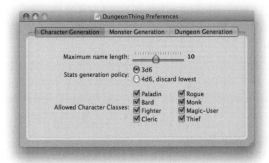

Figure 6–2. *Here are the preferences for character generation in DungeonThing.*

Drag out each of these objects from the *Library* and align them roughly as you see in Figure 6–2. The only class there that you may not have used already is NSSlider, which works a lot like the NSLevelIndicator that we used in Chapter 4. To make it look and act like the one seen in the image, select it and open the *Attributes Inspector* (⌘1). Give it 19 tick marks, check the box to make it stop only on tick marks, set its minimum and maximum values to 2 and 20, and its current value to 10. A bit further down, click to turn on the *Continuous* checkbox (so the slider will report its value continuously while the user is dragging it), and you're all set. Figure 6–3 shows you how it's done.

Figure 6–3. *Configuration of an NSSlider for selecting an integer between 2 and 20*

One other adjustment that needs to be made, but can't be seen from the screenshot, is to make the matrix containing the checkboxes behave appropriately in response to mouse clicks. Because NSMatrix is designed to contain a variety of controls, it has multiple ways of interacting with its cells when the user clicks on one of them. Select the matrix of checkboxes, and in the *Attributes Inspector*, set the *Mode* popup to *Highlight*. This mode makes the matrix handle a click in a cell by toggling the clicked cell's selected state between zero and one, which switches the checkbox on and off.

The last configuration required for this tab is to set the tags for the two radio buttons, so we can tell them apart later (the checkboxes don't need to have their tags set, because they will be dealt with a little differently when we get to the bindings). Do this by keeping the *Attributes Inspector* up, then click on first one radio button and then the other, typing in new tag values for each of them in the *Inspector*. Set the tag for the first radio button cell to 1, and set the second to 2.

Monster Generation Preferences

The next tab contains controls that let the user specify preferences for random monster generation, which you can see depicted in Figure 6–4.

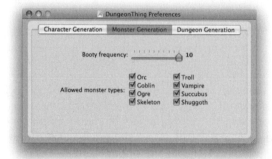

Figure 6–4. *Monster Generation preferences*

Here we have a slider, a matrix of checkboxes, and a couple of text fields as labels. The slider should be configured similarly to the one used in the *Character Generation* tab, but with a few different attributes: minimum value of 1, maximum value of 10, and showing 10 tick marks.

Dungeon Generation Preferences

Finally, we'll create the GUI for the *Dungeon Generation* preferences. This is a simple one, with just sliders and text fields, as seen in Figure 6–5.

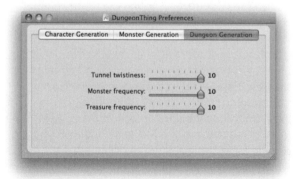

Figure 6–5. *Dungeon Generation preferences tab*

These sliders should be configured just like the one in the *Monster Generation* tab, with a range from 1 to 10, and showing 10 ticks.

Binding to NSUserDefaultsController

At this point, we have all these GUI controls in a window, but we have no outlets to connect to them, and no action methods for them to call when the user clicks on them. So, now what? Now it's time to create your first bindings! We're going to use a class called NSUserDefaultsController, which is a bindings-ready generic controller class that is included in Cocoa. A bindings-ready controller like this lets us bind view objects to an underlying model object right within Interface Builder. One nice thing about this class is that it maintains its own storage in the form of NSUserDefaults, which is the standard class used in Cocoa applications for saving and retrieving a user's application preferences. This will let us bind each view object's value to a uniquely keyed value in the application's preferences. These preferences are automatically saved before a user exits the application, and reloaded the next time the user launches the application again.

Bindings for Character Generation

Go to the Preferences window we're building, and switch back to the *Character Generation* pane. Click on the slider, then bring up the *Bindings Inspector* by pressing ⌘4. In this *Inspector*, you can see all the attributes of a view object that can be bound to a value in a model object. Most often, you'll be binding the *Value* to something, but each view class offers its own set of attributes available for binding. The slider, for instance, can have its *Max Value* and *Min Value* attributes bound to something, which would allow you to vary those extremities based on values in a model object. Some other view objects can bind text colors and fonts to model values, and most of them can have their *Hidden* and *Enabled* states bound to model values. For now, we're going to bind this slider's *Value* attribute, so click the *Value* disclosure triangle to see its configuration options. Figure 6–6 shows the default settings.

To establish a binding, you need to configure at list three things: the controller object to bind to, the controller key, and model key path (all the rest are optional settings that allow you to refine the binding's behavior in special situations, some of which we'll cover later). You pick the controller object from the *Bind to:* popup list, which contains all controller objects that are present in your nib file, including any controllers of your own, any generic controllers you've dragged over from the Library, and special controllers like NSUserDefaultsController, which is available automatically in every nib file (and shows up as *Shared User Defaults Controller* in the popup list). The controller key lets you choose different "aspects" of the model object or objects that a controller provides. For example, NSArrayController, which provides binding access to an array of objects, has different controller keys to provide access to the entire sorted array, or just the current selection. The model key path is a string that is used as a key to get and set a value in the model object.

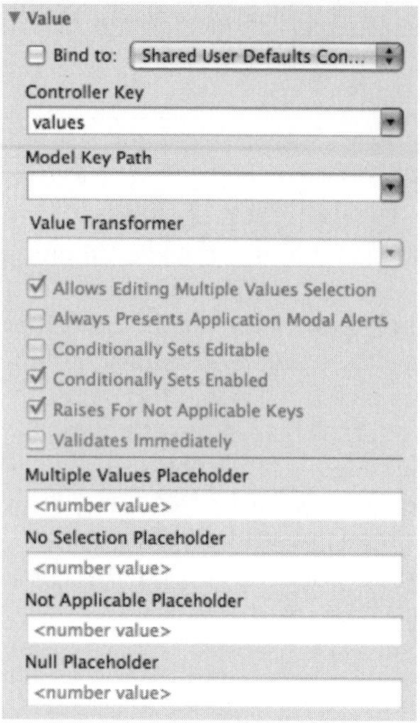

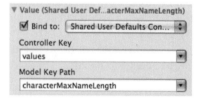

Figure 6–6. *The default "unbound" state for an NSSlider's Value binding options*

So, for your first binding, start off by picking the *Shared User Defaults Controller* from the popup list. This controller is automatically available in any nib file, though you can't see it anywhere until you use it in a binding, at which point it appears in the main nib window. Now check the *Controller Key* combo box, and make sure it's set to "values." Then click on the *Model Key Path* combo box, and type "characterMaxNameLength." This string defines the key that will be used to store the slider's value in NSUserDefaults—the user's application preferences. Press Enter or tab out of the field, and you'll see that the *Bind to:* checkbox at the top of the *Inspector* gets checked. That's it! We don't need to worry about any of the remaining controls for now, their default values are fine for our purposes. Figure 6–7 shows what the relevant configured bits in the *Inspector* should look like when this binding is configured.

Figure 6–7. *The completed binding for the first slider*

Now select the small text field to the right of the slider, and configure the exact same binding you did for the slider: *Shared User Defaults Controller*, "values," and "characterMaxNameLength." That will make it pull its display value from the same place (the value for "characterMaxNameLength") in the same model object (the user's

application preferences). To see a little Cocoa Bindings magic in action now, select
File▶Simulate Interface from the menu, click and drag the slider, and watch the value in the
small text field update simultaneously. While you're dragging the slider, its value is being
pushed into your application preferences by the NSUserDefaultsController, which also
passes the value along to the other object that's bound to the same key: the little text
field. Pretty neat trick! But it's not a trick at all. It's a simple example of the dynamic
nature of Cocoa Bindings. Using this technology, you can eliminate a lot of boring code
from your controller classes, and sometimes get rid of your controller classes entirely,
using only Cocoa's included controller classes instead.

Let's move on to the next GUI control, the matrix of radio buttons in the middle. Click on
the matrix, and then look at the *Bindings Inspector*, where you'll see that there is no
Value option. For this control, instead of binding a *Value*, we'll be binding the *Selected
Tag* attribute, which means that when a user selects a cell, that cell's tag will be pushed
down to the model, and when the Preferences window is brought up next time, that
saved tag will determine which radio button is selected. Open up the *Selected Tag*
section of the *Inspector*, and again make sure that *Shared User Defaults Controller* is
selected, and that the *Controller Key* is "values," but this time type
"characterStatsGenerationPolicy" into the *Model Key Path* and press Enter.

Next, let's tackle the *Allowed Character Classes* checkboxes. For each of these, we'll
make up a new key name, and use it to bind the *Selected* status to a value in the user's
application preferences. Click on the first cell, *Paladin*. You should see that the *Inspector*
title changes to *Button Cell Bindings*. If not, click on the button again until you get there.
Now bind this button cell's *Value* attribute to the "characterClassAllowedPaladin" key.
Repeat these steps for each of the remaining button cells, binding each of them via
Shared User Defaults Controller with the appropriate key name. *Bard* should be bound
with the "characterClassAllowedBard," *Fighter* with "characterClassAllowedFighter,"
and so on. When you get to Magic-User, for the sake of consistency, use the key name
"characterClassAllowedMagicUser," leaving out the "-" symbol.

Bindings for Monster Generation

Now switch over to the *Monster Generation* tab. Bind the *Value* of the slider to
"monsterBootyFrequency," and do the same for the small text field to the right. Then
configure the checkboxes, the same way you did on the *Character Generation* tab. Click
on the *Orc* checkbox until the checkbox itself is selected, and bind its *Value* to
"monsterTypeAllowedOrc." Continue through the rest of the checkboxes, binding the
Value for each of them to the appropriate key name: "monsterTypeAllowedGoblin,"
"monsteryTypeAllowedOgre," and so on.

Bindings for Dungeon Generation

Finally, switch to the *Dungeon Generation* tab, which contains just three slider and text
field pairs. To the right of the *Tunnel Twistiness* label, configure the *Value* bindings for
both the slider and the text field to "dungeonTunnelTwistiness." Bind both of the

Monster Frequency controls' *Values* to "dungeonMonsterFrequency," and both of the *Treasure Frequency* controls' *Values* to "dungeonTreasureFrequency."

Create the Main Window

Now it's time to pay some attention to our main window, which will contain buttons the user can click to generate the characters, monsters, and dungeons, and text fields to display the results. Click the main window's title bar (or double-click its icon in the main window if it's not already visible) and bring up the *Size Inspector* (⌘3). Change the window size to 731 by 321, then switch to the *Attributes Inspector* (⌘1) and click to turn off the *Resize* checkbox, which will give us one less thing to worry about. This application displays a limited data set, so there's no reason for the user to make the window any bigger. We're now going to create three sets of GUI components, one set for each of the three types of data we're dealing with. We'll manually lay out the first set, then duplicate it for the other two.

First we'll create a text field inside a box for displaying results. Go to the *Library* window and enter "nsbox" into the search field. Look for the *Box* in the results, and drag one of these out to your window. While the new box is selected, switch back to the *Size Inspector*, and set the box's size to 227 by 247. While you're at it, go ahead and set each of its X and Y values to 20. This puts the box in the lower-left corner of the window, in the position it would be in if you dragged it to the lower left and let it sit where the blue guidelines recommend. Then switch back to the *Attributes Inspector*, and set the *Title Position* to "None" so that the title won't be shown.

Now, go back to the *Library* and search for "label." One of the results is *Wrapping Label*; grab that, drag it so that it is directly overlapping the box you created, and let go. Doing this puts it "inside the box." Once it's there, expand the label to fill the box, by first dragging its bottom left corner down to the lower left, then dragging its top right corner to the upper right. In both cases, the blue guidelines will show up when you're just the right distance from the edge of the box. Finally, triple-click to select the text ("Multiline Label") in the text field, and press Backspace or Delete to clear out the text.

Let's top this box off by adding the button that will eventually put some text into the text field we just created. Find a button in the *Library* (a *Push Button* will do nicely), and drag it out to a spot just above the box. During the drag, the blue lines will appear, showing you the correct distance from the top of the window, and also showing you when the button is lined up directly above the center of the box. That's where you want to drop it! Then double-click the button to edit its title, and change it to "Generate Character." Figure 6–8 shows what you should be seeing at this point.

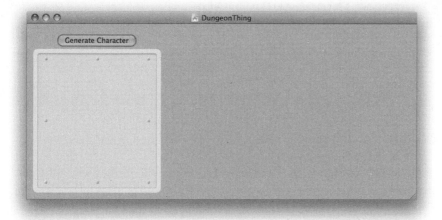

Figure 6–8. *We've created the first of three sets of views for the main window. The text field inside the box is highlighted, just so you can see where it is.*

Now select all the views you just created, by clicking anywhere in the window and then pressing ⌘A to select all objects in the window. Duplicate them by pressing ⌘D, which will show you a new set of identical objects, overlapping and slightly position-shifted from the originals. Drag this cluster to the center of the window, using the blue guidelines to make sure that they are at the same vertical position at the originals, and with just the right horizontal spacing between the boxes. Then press ⌘D again, and drag the third cluster of objects to the right side of the window, again using the blue guidelines to help position them properly. Finally, double-click on the two new buttons, changing their titles to "Generate Monster" and "Generate Dungeon" respectively. Figure 6–9 shows what the window should look like now.

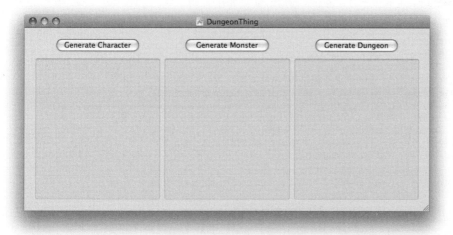

Figure 6–9. *Here's what the completed main window for DungeonThing looks like.*

Set Up the DungeonThingAppDelegate

Now that the initial set of bindings are out of the way and the main window is all set up, we can go ahead and create an instance of our DungeonThingAppDelegate. Go the *Library* window, search for "nsobject," and drag the resulting *Object* to your main nib window. Then bring up the *Identity Inspector* (⌘6) and change the new object's *Class* to "DungeonThingAppDelegate." If you're running Snow Leopard, you can skip that step, since the app delegate is already included in the nib file that's created for you.

One at a time, Ctrl-drag from the DungeonThingAppDelegate to each of the three labels (actually NSTextFields) in the three boxes, connecting them to the characterLabel, monsterLabel, and dungeonLabel outlets. Then Ctrl-drag from each of the three buttons back to DungeonThingAppDelegate, connecting each to the relevant DungeonThingAppDelegate action methods, createCharacter:, createMonster:, and createDungeon:.

Define Your Constants

At this point, the GUI is completed, and the relevant bindings are all configured so that the controls in the Preferences window will all have their values saved in the user's application preferences. All that's left is for us to write the action methods that will use NSUserPreferences to retrieve the preferences values, and display them. Like we mentioned before, we're stopping short of actually *using* the values to generate game item descriptions, but feel free to make that enhancement later on, if you'd like.

Let's start off by defining some constants, just like we've done in previous examples (if it's slipped your mind, see Chapter 4 for a discussion of the benefits of doing this). Here are the constants to match all the values you've already set in for the preferences' key names in the nib file. Insert these somewhere at the top of *DungeonThingAppDelegate.m*:

```
#define kCharacterMaxNameLength @"characterMaxNameLength"
#define kCharacterStatsGenerationPolicy \
  @"characterStatsGenerationPolicy"
#define kCharacterClassAllowedPaladin @"characterClassAllowedPaladin"
#define kCharacterClassAllowedBard @"characterClassAllowedBard"
#define kCharacterClassAllowedFighter @"characterClassAllowedFighter"
#define kCharacterClassAllowedCleric @"characterClassAllowedCleric"
#define kCharacterClassAllowedRogue @"characterClassAllowedRogue"
#define kCharacterClassAllowedMonk @"characterClassAllowedMonk"
#define kCharacterClassAllowedMagicUser \
  @"characterClassAllowedMagicUser"
#define kCharacterClassAllowedThief @"characterClassAllowedThief"

#define kMonsterBootyFrequency @"monsterBootyFrequency"
#define kMonsterTypeAllowedOrc @"monsterTypeAllowedOrc"
#define kMonsterTypeAllowedGoblin @"monsterTypeAllowedGoblin"
#define kMonsterTypeAllowedOgre @"monsterTypeAllowedOgre"
#define kMonsterTypeAllowedSkeleton @"monsterTypeAllowedSkeleton"
#define kMonsterTypeAllowedTroll @"monsterTypeAllowedTroll"
#define kMonsterTypeAllowedVampire @"monsterTypeAllowedVampire"
```

```
#define kMonsterTypeAllowedSuccubus @"monsterTypeAllowedSuccubus"
#define kMonsterTypeAllowedShuggoth @"monsterTypeAllowedShuggoth"

#define kDungeonTunnelTwistiness @"dungeonTunnelTwistiness"
#define kDungeonMonsterFrequency @"dungeonMonsterFrequency"
#define kDungeonTreasureFrequency @"dungeonTreasureFrequency"
```

> **NOTE:** In order to fit the confines of the book format while still showing valid code, we've "wrapped" some of these lines by putting a backslash as the *very last character* of a line, which makes the C preprocessor just tack on the content of the next line, as if it were all on the same line to begin with. Feel free to omit this manual wrapping in your own code, making each of those #defines into a one-line declaration.

Specify Default Preferences Values

With the constant definitions in place, we're ready start coding. Before we implement our action methods, you need to learn a bit about NSUserDefaults. As we've mentioned, this class lets you store and retrieve a user's application preferences as a sort of hash or dictionary, keyed off strings of your choosing. One thing that every application should do is create a set of default values for NSUserDefaults, which it will use as a "fallback position" in case the user hasn't set a value for a given key. For example, say you want to store an integer whose relevant range is a number between one and ten, using the key @"greatness". Setting a default value of 1 for the @"greatness" key ensures that the first time a user runs the application, and NSUserDefaults tries to retrieve the @"greatness" value, it finds the default value (1) that you specified in code. Without taking this step, retrieving any numeric value that hasn't already been set by the user will get you a zero, and retrieving any unset object value will get you a nil.

It's common practice to set up these values in a method that is called early in the application's startup phase, typically in a class that is included in the main nib. The initialize class method is a good place for this, since it's called exactly once for each class, the first time a class is accessed. Let's create such a method in our DungeonThingAppDelegate:

```
+ (void)initialize
{
  [[NSUserDefaults standardUserDefaults] registerDefaults:
   [NSDictionary dictionaryWithObjectsAndKeys:
    [NSNumber numberWithInt:1], kMonsterBootyFrequency,
    [NSNumber numberWithBool:YES], kMonsterTypeAllowedOrc,
    [NSNumber numberWithBool:YES], kMonsterTypeAllowedGoblin,
    [NSNumber numberWithBool:YES], kMonsterTypeAllowedOgre,
    [NSNumber numberWithBool:YES], kMonsterTypeAllowedSkeleton,
    [NSNumber numberWithBool:YES], kMonsterTypeAllowedTroll,
    [NSNumber numberWithBool:YES], kMonsterTypeAllowedVampire,
    [NSNumber numberWithBool:YES], kMonsterTypeAllowedSuccubus,
    [NSNumber numberWithBool:YES], kMonsterTypeAllowedShuggoth,
    [NSNumber numberWithInt:7], kCharacterMaxNameLength,
    [NSNumber numberWithInt:1], kCharacterStatsGenerationPolicy,
```

```
        [NSNumber numberWithBool:YES], kCharacterClassAllowedPaladin,
        [NSNumber numberWithBool:YES], kCharacterClassAllowedBard,
        [NSNumber numberWithBool:YES], kCharacterClassAllowedFighter,
        [NSNumber numberWithBool:YES], kCharacterClassAllowedCleric,
        [NSNumber numberWithBool:YES], kCharacterClassAllowedRogue,
        [NSNumber numberWithBool:YES], kCharacterClassAllowedMonk,
        [NSNumber numberWithBool:YES], kCharacterClassAllowedMagicUser,
        [NSNumber numberWithBool:YES], kCharacterClassAllowedThief,
        [NSNumber numberWithInt:3], kDungeonTunnelTwistiness,
        [NSNumber numberWithInt:7], kDungeonMonsterFrequency,
        [NSNumber numberWithInt:1], kDungeonTreasureFrequency,
        nil]];
}
```

This method calls NSUserDefaults' registerDefaults: method, passing in a dictionary of default values for our application. We're setting a default value for every key-name that we're using in our application, so that we know that when we ask for a value, we'll always get something relevant.

Create the Action Methods

Now we can start implementing our action methods. Let's start with createCharacter:, which will display a summary of all the preferences values related to character creation. We start off by grabbing the shared instance of NSUserDefaults, then create an empty string to hold the summary text, and then we actually create the summary, one preferences entry at a time. At the end, we put the summary text into the relevant NSTextField. Note that at the beginning of this method, we create an NSMutableString with a particular capacity, but this is not an upper size limit; NSMutableString is smart enough to "grow" if necessary. The method looks like this:

```
- (IBAction)createCharacter:(id)sender {
  NSUserDefaults *ud = [NSUserDefaults standardUserDefaults];
  NSMutableString *result = [NSMutableString stringWithCapacity:1024];
  [result appendString:
    @"Generating a character within these parameters:\n"
     "----------------\n"];    // protip: split strings across lines like this!
  [result appendFormat:
    @"Maximum name length: %d\n",
    [ud integerForKey:kCharacterMaxNameLength]];
  [result appendFormat:
   @"Stats generation policy: %d\n",
   [ud integerForKey:kCharacterStatsGenerationPolicy]];
  [result appendFormat:
   @"Allows Paladin: %@\n",
   [ud boolForKey:kCharacterClassAllowedPaladin] ? @"YES" : @"NO"];
  [result appendFormat:
   @"Allows Bard: %@\n",
   [ud boolForKey:kCharacterClassAllowedBard] ? @"YES" : @"NO"];
  [result appendFormat:
   @"Allows Fighter: %@\n",
   [ud boolForKey:kCharacterClassAllowedFighter] ? @"YES" : @"NO"];
  [result appendFormat:
   @"Allows Cleric: %@\n",
```

```
      [ud boolForKey:kCharacterClassAllowedCleric] ? @"YES" : @"NO"];
    [result appendFormat:
     @"Allows Rogue: %@\n",
     [ud boolForKey:kCharacterClassAllowedRogue] ? @"YES" : @"NO"];
    [result appendFormat:
     @"Allows Monk: %@\n",
     [ud boolForKey:kCharacterClassAllowedMonk] ? @"YES" : @"NO"];
    [result appendFormat:
     @"Allows Magic-User: %@\n",
     [ud boolForKey:kCharacterClassAllowedMagicUser] ? @"YES" : @"NO"];
    [result appendFormat:
     @"Allows Thief: %@\n",
     [ud boolForKey:kCharacterClassAllowedThief] ? @"YES" : @"NO"];
    [characterLabel setStringValue:result];
}
```

After entering that code, try compiling and running your application. If all goes well, you should be able to see the main window, hit the *Generate Character* button, and see a result something like Figure 6–10.

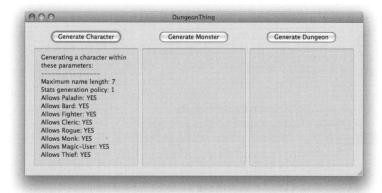

Figure 6–10. *The first run of DungeonThing*

The next step is to open the *Preferences* window, and start making some changes in the *Character Generation* tab. Disable some checkboxes, drag the slider, etc. After each change, click the *Generate Character* button in the main window again, and the displayed parameters should change to reflect the contents of the *Preferences* window.

Now that that's working, let's fill in the method bodies for `createMonster:` and `createDungeon:` as shown below. These methods both work just like the `createCharacter:` method already shown.

```
- (IBAction)createMonster:(id)sender {
  NSUserDefaults *ud = [NSUserDefaults standardUserDefaults];
  NSMutableString *result = [NSMutableString stringWithCapacity:1024];
  [result appendString:@"Generating a monster within these parameters:\n----------------
-\n"];
  [result appendFormat:
   @"Booty frequency: %d\n",
   [ud integerForKey:kMonsterBootyFrequency]];
```

```
        [result appendFormat:
         @"Allows Orc: %@\n",
         [ud boolForKey:kMonsterTypeAllowedOrc] ? @"YES" : @"NO"];
        [result appendFormat:
         @"Allows Goblin: %@\n",
         [ud boolForKey:kMonsterTypeAllowedGoblin] ? @"YES" : @"NO"];
        [result appendFormat:
         @"Allows Ogre: %@\n",
         [ud boolForKey:kMonsterTypeAllowedOgre] ? @"YES" : @"NO"];
        [result appendFormat:
         @"Allows Skeleton: %@\n",
         [ud boolForKey:kMonsterTypeAllowedSkeleton] ? @"YES" : @"NO"];
        [result appendFormat:
         @"Allows Troll: %@\n",
         [ud boolForKey:kMonsterTypeAllowedTroll] ? @"YES" : @"NO"];
        [result appendFormat:
         @"Allows Vampire: %@\n",
         [ud boolForKey:kMonsterTypeAllowedVampire] ? @"YES" : @"NO"];
        [result appendFormat:
         @"Allows Succubus: %@\n",
         [ud boolForKey:kMonsterTypeAllowedSuccubus] ? @"YES" : @"NO"];
        [result appendFormat:
         @"Allows Shuggoth: %@\n",
         [ud boolForKey:kMonsterTypeAllowedShuggoth] ? @"YES" : @"NO"];
        [monsterLabel setStringValue:result];
    }
    - (IBAction)createDungeon:(id)sender {
        NSUserDefaults *ud = [NSUserDefaults standardUserDefaults];
        NSMutableString *result = [NSMutableString stringWithCapacity:1024];
        [result appendString:@"Generating a dungeon within these parameters:\n----------------
-\n"];
        [result appendFormat:
         @"Tunnel twistiness: %d\n",
         [ud integerForKey:kDungeonTunnelTwistiness]];
        [result appendFormat:
         @"Monster frequency: %d\n",
         [ud integerForKey:kDungeonMonsterFrequency]];
        [result appendFormat:
         @"Treasure frequency: %d\n",
         [ud integerForKey:kDungeonTreasureFrequency]];
        [dungeonLabel setStringValue:result];
    }
```

With those methods in place, you should be able to compile and run DungeonThing, modify all the values under every tab in the *Preferences* window, and see the modified values reflected in the output text fields. The first version of DungeonThing is now complete!

Binding to a Table View

DungeonThing is fine for what it does (aside from the fact that it doesn't really generate the game objects, of course), but if you started using such a system "in production" (say, while playing Dungeons and Dragons or a similar game), you'd quickly encounter one major problem: the random game objects aren't retained in any way! As soon as you click to create a new random character, for example, the previous character is just wiped out, and you have no way of ever seeing it again.

For the next iteration of DungeonThing, we're going to add some table views to show lists of all created game objects. Clicking on a game object in a table view will show its values in the relevant text field. Unlike Chapter 5, where we showed you how to handle the table view in your own code, here we're going to show you how to use the NSArrayController class, a generic controller class included with Cocoa, to manage the display of these table views with no custom code of your own, thanks to Cocoa Bindings. We'll need to add a few outlets and other instance variables to our DungeonThingAppDelegate class, for three instances of NSArrayController and three arrays (one for each type of game object). We'll also remove the NSTextField outlets, because those will also be configured with bindings to display their contents. Finally, we'll change the action methods just slightly, to insert each created object into the relevant array. When we're done, the source code will be almost identical in size, because all configuration of the table views is done right in the nib file.

Make the Code Bindings-Ready

Let's start by making the necessary changes in the header file. In order to maintain lists of generated objects, our DungeonThingAppDelegate needs three new NSMutableArray instance variables, one for each kind of game object. Each array will be managed by an NSArrayController in the nib file, so we'll also add three outlets to connect to those. We'll also change the labels in the window, so that they access their content through the NSArrayControllers as well. This means that we can remove the three existing outlets to NSTextFields, because we never need to deal with them from the code now. Finally, we declare the three NSMutableArrays as properties, so that they are readily available for the NSArrayControllers to access them. The changes you need to make in *DungeonThingAppDelegate.h* are shown below. Note that in addition to adding the lines shown in bold, you should delete the old outlet declarations pointing at NSTextFields.

```
#import <Cocoa/Cocoa.h>
@interface DungeonThingAppDelegate : NSObject {
  NSMutableArray *characters;
  NSMutableArray *monsters;
  NSMutableArray *dungeons;
  IBOutlet NSArrayController *characterArrayController;
  IBOutlet NSArrayController *monsterArrayController;
  IBOutlet NSArrayController *dungeonArrayController;

  IBOutlet NSTextField *characterLabel;
  IBOutlet NSTextField *monsterLabel;
  IBOutlet NSTextField *dungeonLabel;

}
@property (retain) NSMutableArray *characters;
@property (retain) NSMutableArray *monsters;
@property (retain) NSMutableArray *dungeons;
```

```
- (IBAction)createCharacter:(id)sender;
- (IBAction)createMonster:(id)sender;
- (IBAction)createDungeon:(id)sender;
@end
```

Now it's time for the changes in the implementation file. Here, we need to complete the @property declarations for our NSMutableArrays by creating accessor methods using @synthesize, initialize the NSMutableArrays themselves, and modify the action methods to push the created values into our arrays, instead of just displaying the values directly in the text fields.

First, let's add the code for synthesizing accessors for our arrays, and implement a new init method to contain the initialization for the arrays. Place the following code near the top of the @implementation DungeonThingAppDelegate section:

```
@synthesize characters;
@synthesize monsters;
@synthesize dungeons;
- (id)init {
  if ((self = [super init])) {
    characters = [NSMutableArray array];
    monsters = [NSMutableArray array];
    dungeons = [NSMutableArray array];
  }
  return self;
}
```

THE CANONICAL INIT METHOD

The preceding code snippet shows an example of an init method that creates values for our class's instance variables. The form of this init method is fairly standard, and you're likely to see something similar in most Objective-C classes you see, but it does some things that seem strange at first glance, and is worth explaining a bit. The method starts off with this peculiar if statement:

```
if ((self = [super init])) {
```

That if-statement is really killing two (or more) birds with one stone. First, it's calling the superclass's implementation of init, and assigning its return value to the special variable self. Then it checks the value of the assignment itself (that is, the value of self after it's been assigned), and only executes the following block of code if it's not something that evaluates as false, e.g. a nil pointer value.

This usage of self, assigning a value to it, is really unusual. In fact, the only time you're ever likely to see code assigning a value to self is within an init method such as this. The reason for doing it this way is to allow for the possibility, however slight, that the superclass's init method will return a different value than what was pointed at by self from the outset. On the one hand, the superclass may find that it fails to initialize itself properly for some reason, and signal this by returning nil from the init method, which is the "standard" way of dealing with an object initialization failure (rather than, say, raising an exception). In this case, the class will notice the nil value, and skip the block following the if statement, dropping down to the end where it returns the value pointed at by self, which is now nil.

The other possible alternate return value for the superclass's init method is a different instance altogether. The idea is that the superclass might have a smart scheme for recycling objects in a private pool instead of constantly deallocating and creating new ones, and a part of that scheme would be that the init method would sometimes return an old, second-hand object instead of the shiny new one you just tried to create. The question of whether or not this situation is a realistic one is a subject of occasional debate among Cocoa programmers. Here, we're erring on the side of caution by writing our init method to allow for this possibility.

Next, we're going to change a single line at the end of each action method. Instead of putting the summary text created by the method directly into a text field, we'll add each summary to an array, using NSArrayController to do this so that all dependent views (any views that have bindings through the same NSArrayController) will be automatically updated as well. Rather than inserting the bare string into the array, we're creating an NSMutableDictionary containing the created object and the current time, using the dictionary as the simplest sort of model object, containing two keyed values. Implement this change at the end of createCharacter: by changing this:

```
[characterLabel setStringValue:result];
```

to this:

```
[characterArrayController addObject:[NSMutableDictionary dictionaryWithObjectsAndKeys:
    result, @"createdObject",
    [NSDate date], @"timestamp",
    nil]];
```

Similarly, at the end of createMonster: change this:

```
[monsterLabel setStringValue:result];
```

to this:

```
[monsterArrayController addObject:[NSMutableDictionary dictionaryWithObjectsAndKeys:
    result, @"createdObject",
    [NSDate date], @"timestamp",
    nil]];
```

Finally, change the end of createDungeon:, changing this:

```
[dungeonLabel setStringValue:result];
```

to this:

```
[dungeonArrayController addObject:[NSMutableDictionary dictionaryWithObjectsAndKeys:
    result, @"createdObject",
    [NSDate date], @"timestamp",
    nil]];
```

There you have it, all the code changes we need to make! Note that unlike our example in Chapter 5, the code here doesn't have to do anything at all regarding the table views. No delegate or dataSource methods to implement, no outlets pointing to the table views, nothing. Thanks to bindings and NSArrayController, the table views will really take care of themselves.

Show History in Tables

Now it's time to go back to Interface Builder, create some table views, and set up their bindings to the new arrays we added to DungeonThingAppDelegate. We'll also configure the existing text fields to get their data through bindings. Switch over to Interface Builder, or if you've closed your nib file, open it again by double-clicking it in Xcode's navigation pane.

Dealing With Inconsistencies in Nib Files

The first time you bring this nib file to the front after making the changes described in the last section, you may notice a small yellow triangle at the bottom of the main nib window. This warning triangle turns up whenever inconsistencies arise that Interface Builder can't resolve without your help. Click the warning triangle to show what the problems are. In this case, Interface Builder has noticed that its internal idea about DungeonThingAppDelegate no longer matches the reality described in the header file: The nib file contains connections for outlets that no longer exist! To resolve these problems, select DungeonThingAppDelegate in the main nib window, then bring up the *Connections Inspector* (⌘5). At the top of the Inspector, you'll see all the current outlet connections, including the ones for the missing outlets (each of them marked with an exclamation point). Eliminate the bad connections by clicking the small "X" control on each of them. Figure 6–11 shows all the parts you'll see while fixing this.

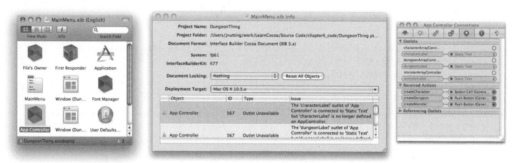

Figure 6–11. *The main nib window shows a warning triangle after you remove outlets from a class. Clicking the triangle reveals details about the problems, and the Connections Inspector lets you remove the obsolete connections.*

Configuring the Table Views and Text Views

Now it's time to get to work on the main application window. Start off by making the window larger. We're going to create three "history" table views, one below each of the existing sets of views, so we need to make the window taller (but we can keep the current width). Use the window's resize control in the lower right to make the window about twice its current height. The blue guidelines will help you maintain the current width.

In the *Library* window, search for "table" and drag the resulting table view out into the window. Position it so that its upper left corner is just below the lower left corner of the left-most box, then grab the table view's lower right resize handle, and drag it down until the table fills most of the available space down to the bottom of the window, with its right edge lined up with the right edge of the box above it. Figure 6–12 shows you the idea.

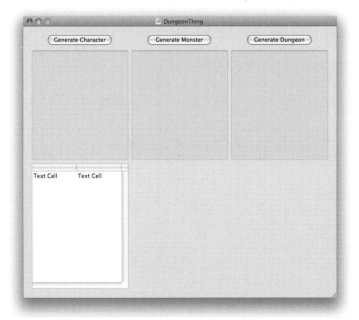

Figure 6–12. *We've begun adding tables to the window.*

In our history tables, we're only going to display the time that the object was created. The user can then click on a row to see the relevant object displayed in the text field above the table. This means that we only want to have one column in the table, so select the column on the right side by clicking in the empty space where the column's data would appear (if there were any), below the header. You may need to click 3 or 4 times in order to drill down into the table until you see the column highlighted. Once it's highlighted, then press Backspace or Delete to get rid of it.

Next, resize the remaining column so that it fills the width of the table. Do this by clicking in the table header until the entire table header is selected. Then mouse over the vertical line marking the edge of the table column header, and drag it to the right until the column fills the whole table.

Finally, let's disable editing in the remaining column, since we don't want the user to change the timestamp of a created object. Click on the table column until it's selected, then bring up the *Attributes Inspector* (⌘1) and click to turn off the *Editable* checkbox. While you're at it, click to turn off the *User Resizable* checkbox as well, as there's no reason to let the user resize the table view's only column.

At this point, the table view and its column are graphically laid out, and everything is configured except its bindings. This is a perfect time to duplicate the table you've just made for displaying characters, so that we can use the exact same configuration for monsters and dungeons. Click the window background, then click once on the table view to select it (along with its enclosing NSScrollView). Now press ⌘D to duplicate the table view, and drag it the new one into place at the bottom of the center view group. Then press ⌘D once again, and drag the final table view into place in the window's bottom right corner. For both of those, you'll of course use the blue guidelines to help you line them up properly. Figure 6–13 shows the final layout.

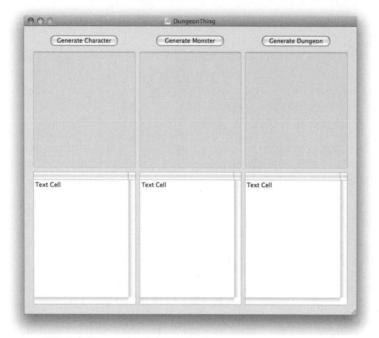

Figure 6–13. *The final DungeonThing window layout*

Create and Configure an Array Controller

Now it's time to create an NSArrayController so that we can configure some bindings for the first set of objects, the characters. In the *Library* window, search for "array," and you'll see NSArrayController appear in the results. Drag one of these out to the main nib window, and immediately change the name shown under the new object's icon in the main window by clicking first on the icon, then the text itself. We'll be using this controller to provide access to the characters array, so name it "characters." Giving this top-level nib object a unique name of its own will help a bit later on, when we'll be adding two more array controllers to this nib.

You may recall that we added some NSArrayController outlets to DungeonThingAppDelegate. Now's the time to connect DungeonThingAppDelegate's characterArrayController outlet to our new array controller. Ctrl-drag from DungeonThingAppDelegate to the new "characters" array controller, and choose characterArrayController from the resulting menu.

Next, click on the array controller again and bring up the *Attributes Inspector* (⌘1). You'll see some options at the top that let you fine-tune the behavior of the array controller, but for now we'll leave them all as they are. What you do need to configure is the lower portion of the *Inspector*, in the *Object Controller* section. Make sure that *Mode* is set to "Class," and that *Class Name* is "NSMutableDictionary." This configuration tells the controller that the model objects it's dealing with are instances of NSMutableDictionary, a "normal" class (rather than an *Entity*, which we'll cover as a part of Core Data in Chapter 7). Below that you'll see a table view that lists the attributes that the array controller should be able to access in the model objects. Click the "+" button below the table view, and type in "createdObject," then click "+" again and type in "timestamp." Figure 6–14 shows the completed attributes configuration for the array controller.

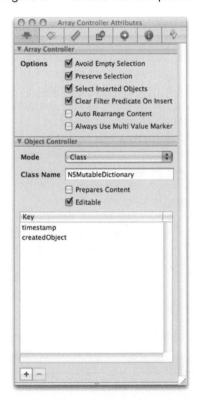

Figure 6–14. *The configured attributes for our first NSArrayController*

You may recognize these as the keys that we used in the code for creating an NSMutableDictionary each time the user clicks a button. These keys are what we'll now use to creating bindings for our GUI objects.

The next thing you have to do is configure a binding, not for a GUI object, but for the array controller itself! It just so happens that NSArrayController is not only a "provider" of bindings-ready access to model objects. It's a "consumer" as well, retrieving its content array from another object via Cocoa Bindings. In our case, it will get its content from DungeonThingAppDelegate's characters array. With the array controller still selected, bring up the *Bindings Inspector* (⌘4). Click on the disclosure triangle next to *Content Array* to open it up, and set up the desired binding by choosing "App Controller" from the popup list, typing "characters" into the *Model Key Path* field, and pressing Enter. Note that our DungeonThingAppDelegate required no special preparation in order to be "bindings-friendly." All we have to do is expose an instance variable as a property (as we've done for our three content arrays), and we can immediately use it to bind other objects to!

Now we've added an NSArrayController and configured it to access the right data from our DungeonThingAppDelegate. It's time to bind some GUI objects to this new controller.

Bind Table Display via the Array Controller

First we'll set up a single binding for the table view. In fact, it's not the table view but the table column itself that needs a binding. We're going to bind the table column's displayed value to the characters array (through the array controller), grabbing the timestamp attribute from each model object. Here's how: click on the table column until it's selected, then open the *Value* binding configuration section in the *Bindings Inspector*. Choose "characters" from the popup list, then "arrangedObjects" in the *Controller Key* combo box, then "timestamp" in the *Model Key Path*, and click the *Bind* checkbox. We mentioned earlier that the *Controller Key* combo box lets you choose different aspects of the controller object you're binding through. In this case, binding through "arrangedObjects" means that we're binding to the entire sorted array of objects. This sort of binding is usually only appropriate for view objects that can display an entire array of content, such as a table column. Choosing "timestamp" for the *Model Key Path* tells the table column which value it should pull from each model object it gets access to.

Bind a Text Field via the Array Controller's Selection

The final binding that needs to be done for the characters section is for the text field that displays the value. This binding will also be done through the array controller, grabbing the createdObject attribute from the controller's selected object.

Click to select the text field in the box on the left. Your first click probably selects the box itself, and clicking again will then select the text field. Now look again at the *Bindings Inspector*, and find the *Value* binding configuration. Select "characters" from the popup list, "selection" from the *Controller Key* combo box, and "createdObject" from the *Model Key Path* combo box, then click to turn on the *Bind* checkbox. Note that by choosing "selection" for the *Controller Key*, we specify that the array controller will only make the selected object available to this control, rather than a whole array of them as it does with the table column.

Making Sure it Works

Now switch back to Xcode, and build and run your application. You should be able to create a new character, and see it appear in the text field along with a timestamp entry in the table below. Modify some preferences, then make another character, and you should see the new parameter summary in the text field, and a new timestamp in the table view. Switch between the rows by clicking on them, and you should see the value in the text field change accordingly.

If any of those things don't work, go back to Interface Builder and double-check the configuration of your bindings, as well as DungeonThingAppDelegate's connection to the array controller.

Rinse, Repeat, Rinse, Repeat

Now that we're dealing with characters entirely with bindings, we can go back and do the same things for monsters and dungeons. Create a new NSArrayController by duplicating the "characters" array controller (thereby keeping its existing configuration, including the key names we already entered), name it "monsters," connect DungeonThingAppDelegate's monsterArrayController outlet to it, configure its *Content Array* binding to connect to the "monsters" attribute in DungeonThingAppDelegate, and configure the two relevant GUI objects (the table column and the text field) through the "monsters" array controller, all as described previously. Build and run the app and make sure it's all working, then repeat all this once more for dungeons.

Okay, But How Did That Work?

Now that you've gotten your feet wet with Cocoa Bindings, you may have the distinct feeling that you've just witnessed some sort of magic show, and find yourself wondering how the tricks actually work! That's a completely understandable feeling. We programmers are accustomed to being required to spell out every movement of a chunk of data and every update to the screen in excruciating detail, and suddenly we find that simply setting a value somewhere causes some unseen forces to propagate the value to other views on the screen. This section will attempt to clarify the process for you, by explaining the Cocoa concepts of Key-Value Coding and Key-Value Observing, and how Cocoa Bindings uses these to do its magic.

Key-Value Coding

First let's talk about Key-Value Coding. The idea behind KVC is to allow us to refer to an object's attributes by using strings that match attribute names, or that match the names of some getter and setter methods. Say, for instance, that you have a class called Person, which has the concept of a firstName, either in the form of an instance variable called firstName, or a pair of methods called firstName and setFirstName:. Using KVC, you can access a person's firstName attribute using the following incantation:

```
[myPerson setValue:@"Barack" forKey:@"firstName"];
```

Given the key name firstName, this method call first checks to see whether the object has a method called setFirstName:, and if so, invokes it to set the value. If that doesn't work, it checks to see if there's an instance variable called firstName, and tries to set it directly.

You can also retrieve a value in a similar manner:

```
myNameString = [myPerson valueForKey:@"firstName"];
```

A similar sequence occurs in this case. It first looks for a method called firstName, and if there isn't one, it tries to find an instance variable with the same name.

The result of all this is that KVC gives us a way to talk about an object's attributes in an extremely generic fashion. Not only is the object's storage of its attributes transparent to us, even the way to access an attribute from the outside is something that we don't need to worry about. It could change, perhaps even inside a running a program, and we wouldn't notice the difference.

The setValue:forKey: and valueForKey: methods are defined in NSObject (with some additional extensions for collection classes like NSArray and NSSet) to try to determine, on the fly, the best way to access the value, based on the name of the key. This means that they are ready to use on every class in Cocoa.

One additional point to make about KVC is that the strings used as keys can actually be used as a sort of path, to traverse relationships between objects. For example, let's imagine that our Person class also contains a property called mother, which is a pointer to another Person. If you want to set the firstName of myPerson's mother, in normal code you would likely do it one of these ways:

```
myPerson.mother.firstName = @"Anne";
[myPerson.mother setFirstName:@"Anne"];
[[myPerson mother] setFirstName:@"Anne"];
Using KVC, you have an additional way to accomplish this:
[myPerson setValue:@"Anne" forKeyPath:@"mother.firstName"];
```

The KVC methods are smart enough to look at the key string, split it apart by paths, and traverse any object relationships mentioned in the path, so the previous line ends up calling something like this:

```
[[myPerson valueForKey:@"mother"] setValue:@"Anne" forKey:@"firstName"];
```

While neither of the KVC options are really appealing for regular use in your own code (because the "normal" versions all read a bit more nicely), it can be used to great advantage in situations requiring more flexibility, such as, say, an interface that lets you configure which values will be displayed in a view object just by typing in the name of the path to the attribute, without requiring compilation of any source code or anything. Sound familiar?

Key-Value Observing

The next piece of the puzzle is Key-Value Observing. With KVO, an object can register with another object to be informed of changes as they occur. For instance, continuing with the last example, I can tell myPerson to notify me whenever the value of its firstName attribute changes like this:

```
[myPerson addObserver:self forKeyPath:@"firstName" options:nil context:NULL];
```

In return, myPerson will call a method called observeValueForKeyPath:ofObject:change:context: in the observer whenever the firstName attribute changes, whether that change occurs via the setValue:forKey: method or by someone calling the setFirstName: method. The way this is implemented is quite clever, and involves some meta-programming deep inside Cocoa, creating a subclass of Person at runtime that overrides the setFirstName: method, and passes along a message to all observers after the value changes. This is done so smoothly that you would never suspect the existence of the hidden Person subclass unless you went looking for it, and really dug deep in just the right places. As a result, you don't really need to know about these implementation details. Just be glad you're entering into the world of Cocoa programming at a time when this particular technology has matured as much as it has, because it was a little rough around the edges when it first came out!

At the end of the day, you probably won't need to deal with KVO directly at all. Almost everything you'd ever want to do with KVO can be done more cleanly and easily with Cocoa Bindings, which is built on top of it and provides a higher-level interface. That's why we've focused on the functionality of Cocoa Bindings, and aren't doing any direct programming with KVO.

Cocoa Bindings: How It Works

While a complete and accurate description of the implementation of Cocoa Bindings is outside the scope of this book, it may be useful for you to get a fuller picture of how it uses KVC and KVO to do its work. Now that you've gotten a brief intro into KVC and KVO, let's take a look at how these bits fit together.

When you establish a binding in Interface Builder, like you've done numerous times in this chapter already, you're actually defining a sort of contract. You're declaring that when this nib is loaded and these objects are set up, a sequence of events will occur to establish some KVO relationships between the objects, using a key path string (using KVC) to define which attribute is in focus for each binding, along with other information to identify which aspect (e.g. the displayed value, the enabled state, and the like) of the "receiving end" (typically a GUI control) should be affected by changes in the underlying value. At runtime, then, Cocoa will set things up so that the control (or any other object you've established a binding on) will be set up to observe changes in the controller based on the relevant key, and the controller will be set up to observe changes in the control's chosen aspect.

In Conclusion

Bindings are a really powerful technology, and in retrospect you can probably see that's it's possible to implement nearly everything shown in Chapters 4 and 5 using Cocoa Bindings, creating an app with almost no custom code whatsoever! This doesn't in any way diminish the usefulness of the techniques shown in previous chapters, however. The fact is that sometimes you will want to access values in the GUI manually, in methods called by target-action. A general rule of thumb is that if you're in a situation (a simple app, or a subcomponent of a larger app) where you don't have any apparent model objects to work with, you may be best served by doing things "the old way," but, in general, Cocoa Bindings are the preferred method for developing Mac apps from here on out.

In the next few chapters, we'll show you how to do even more with bindings using Core Data. Core Data's functionality is orthogonal to Cocoa Binding's; whereas Cocoa Bindings lets you eliminate some boring controller code, Core Data takes care of a lot of the "plumbing" that you'd otherwise have to write for your model classes, giving you a storage back-end, built-in Undo/Redo support, and much more. Together, Cocoa Bindings and Core Data can get you building so much software, so effectively, you'll be making other people's heads spin!

Chapter 7

Core Data Basics

In earlier chapters, we've shown you various ways that Cocoa lets you display data in view objects, from manually getting and setting values based on the contents of model objects to having the data automatically synchronized between model and view objects using Cocoa Bindings, which eliminates the need for a lot of boring controller code. Now it's time to learn about Core Data, a powerful framework that gives your model objects a complete set of built-in capabilities. We'll start by telling you a bit about what Core Data is and how it fits in with the other parts of Cocoa. Then you'll use Core Data to create a full-featured database application called MythBase, including a GUI that allows you create, search, edit, and delete entries, all without writing a single line of code (see Figure 7–1 for a shot of MythBase in action). Then we'll explore some of the code resources that are created for you automatically when you create a Core Data project, and finally we'll show you how to add functionality ("business logic") to your model objects.

What You've Been Missing

All of our examples in previous chapters have used instances of NSMutableDictionary in the place of real model objects. What do we mean by "real model objects?" Well, besides just being able to hold onto pieces of data, which are accessible using field names or keys (something that NSMutableDictionary does well enough), real model objects should include some of the following features:

- **Archiving**. Model objects should have access to a built-in mechanism for being saved to disk, and later reloaded.

- **Business Logic**. There should be a way to give a model object custom behavior that operates in response to input values.

- **Validation**. Each model object should be able to automatically validate input values.

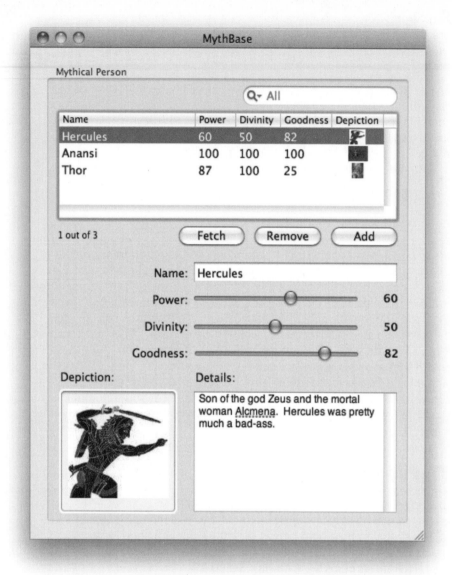

Figure 7–1. *The MythBase application, in all its glory*

In the past, Mac application developers following MVC principles would typically have to roll their own solutions for these common needs, but Core Data provides all of this and more. Besides the features listed previously, Core Data also provides additional key features:

- **Undo/redo support**. Core Data's mechanisms for handling values are tied into the standard Undo facility in Mac OS X. Having this built in to your model classes saves you the additional effort of implementing this common functionality yourself.

■ **Integration with Cocoa Bindings**. Together with Cocoa Bindings, Core Data provides you with a mechanism for connecting views to models using generic controller objects, thereby eliminating a lot of boring glue code.

Taken together, all of these features provide the core of your application with some sturdy infrastructure. You can use Core Data to build GUI apps (with or without Cocoa Bindings), command-line tools, games, or any other sort of software system that can be specified using traditional object modeling techniques. In other words, almost any application at all.

Creating MythBase

Now, let's get started creating MythBase, a GUI application that lets us maintain a database of mythological figures. We'll use Core Data for the model layer, and Cocoa Bindings to handle most of the controller functionality. There will be some new concepts and terminology to tackle, and we'll cover each piece as we get to it.

In the first iteration, we'll define a model for our application using a special tool inside Xcode, and create a simple GUI using an assistant in Xcode. In the second iteration, we'll refine the GUI to improve the user experience a bit. Then, after explaining some other aspects of the application, we'll take a third pass at the functionality, adding some business logic to the application's model layer.

Start by creating a new application project. In Xcode, choose **File➤New Project**, then select *Application* on the left side of the window. Click to turn on the *Use Core Data for storage* checkbox (see Figure 7–2), and then click *Choose.* This procedure is slightly different for Xcode versions prior to 3.2, on Mac OS X 10.5 and earlier, where Core Data Application appears as a separate project type. Navigate to the directory where you want to save your new project, and enter MythBase as the project's name.

Now that the project is created, we need to prepare it for garbage collection in the usual way. Select the top-level MythBase group in the navigation pane, and open the *Info* window by pressing ⌘I. Switch to the *Build* tab, select *All Configurations* in the *Configuration* popup, then start typing "garbage" in the search field to the right. When the *Objective-C Garbage Collection* item is shown, click the popup containing its value on the right and change it to *Required*.

Figure 7–2. *Creating a new application project, and turning on the Core Data option*

Defining the Model

At this point, you'll have a brand-new project, similar to the ones you've created before. Choosing to use Core Data causes Xcode to use a slightly different project template, so this project will have a thing or two you haven't seen in your old projects. In Xcode's navigator pane, you'll find a new top-level group called *Models*; inside that, you'll see the project's default empty model file, called MythBase_DataModel.xcdatamodel. A model file contains metadata about your application's model layer. You create the model file using a graphical tool built into Xcode, and your application reads the model file at runtime.

MODELING: WHAT?

From this point, we're going to assume that you have some idea of what object modeling or database modeling is. But on the offchance that you're totally perplexed by this, here's a *very* brief summary. The idea is that the things your application is dealing with, the content that your application is "about," can be split into independent chunks and organized into a reasonable structure through modeling techniques. Using Core Data, you'll want to figure out how to organize your data along the following lines:

- **Entities**: An entity is used to describe a uniquely identifiable "thing" in your application, something that can exist and be described and identified on its own terms. Entities are usually the big "nouns" of your system. People, companies, and monetary transactions are all entities. Eye color, market capitalization, and transaction amounts are not.

- **Attributes**: Anything that seems like a descriptive feature of an entity, without referring to anything else, is probably an attribute of that entity. Eye color, market capitalization, and transaction amounts are all likely to be attributes of the aforementioned people, companies, and monetary transactions. A person's current account balance, a company's CEO's phone number, and a transaction recipient's email address are *not* attributes of the entities we mentioned. Each of these is better modeled by traversing a *relationship* to another entity and accessing an attribute found there.

- **Relationships**: Use relationships to establish linkages between entities. Relationships can be one-to-many (one person may be the recipient of many transactions), many-to-one (many people can be employed by the same company), one-to-one (each person can have exactly one spouse), or many-to-many (a company can have many people as customers, and at the same time a person can be a customer of many companies).

The model file contains information that should be familiar to anyone who's ever done any sort of object modeling, database modeling, or really any sort of entity-relationship modeling at all. First of all you have the concept of an *entity*, which corresponds roughly to a class in object modeling or a table in database modeling. Each entity consists of several *attributes*, and entities can be joined together with *relationships*. Within Xcode and the documentation, attributes and relationships are referred to collectively as *properties*, and this reuse of the same term in Objective-C 2.0 is no coincidence. Within a model object, each attribute and each relationship can be accessed through an Objective-C property, named the same as the property defined in the model file. In the model we're going to build for MythBase, we'll create a single entity with several attributes. We'll cover relationships in Chapter 8.

Using Xcode's Model Editor

Start by double-clicking the `MythBase_DataModel.xcdatamodel` file in Xcode's navigation pane. This opens up the model file in Xcode's built-in model editor, which resembles a blank sheet of graph paper topped by a couple of table views and some other controls, as seen in Figure 7–3.

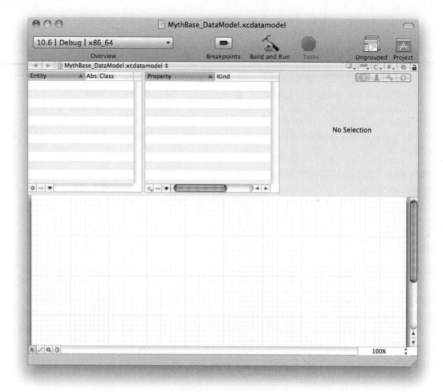

Figure 7–3. *A new model file, before creating any entities*

The graph paper area is a sort of workspace, where the entities you create will be shown, along with all their attributes and relationships. The area at the top, above the graph paper, shows a list of all entities on the left, the selected entity's properties in the middle, and detailed information about the selected entity or property (whichever was clicked last) on the right. You can edit all the model file's important details in the upper portion, while the lower portion lets you graphically reorganize the display as you wish, so that you can visually group the entities together in a way that make sense to you.

Creating an Entity

For MythBase, we're going to create a single entity, called MythicalPerson, with a handful of attributes. To start, create a new entity by clicking the "+" button that appears near the window's center-left point, just below the *Entity* tableview. This places a new entity, called simply *Entity*, in the upper-left-hand table view, as well as in the middle of the graph paper area. With the new entity selected, its details are visible in the upper right. Go change the new entity's name to "MythicalPerson," and leave the rest of the controls in their default states. Note that the class name for the entity is NSManagedObject, a generic class included in Core Data that provides all the basic functionality for Core Data's model objects. Later we'll need to write some code for this entity, at which point we'll create a custom subclass of NSManagedObject, but for now the generic class will do just fine.

Now let's create our entity. We've done some object modeling and have come up with a few characteristics that a mythical person may have.

The MythicalPerson entity will have six attributes. These are shown in Table 7–1, which includes a general description of the type of each attribute, and the corresponding Core Data storage type.

Table 7–1. *MythicalPerson Attributes*

Attribute Name	General Type	Core Data Type
name	string	String
details	string	String
divinity	integer (0-100)	Int 16
goodness	integer (0-100)	Int 16
power	integer (0-100)	Int 16
depiction	image	Transformable

Core Data includes String and Date types, as well as a selection of numeric types: Int 16, Int 32, Int 64, Float, Double, Decimal, and Bool. In addition, it includes a Binary type which allows generic storage of any sort of data you may want to attach to an entity (which you pack into a binary chunk on your own), and a special Transformable type which allows many otherwise unsupported Cocoa classes, such as NSImage, to be stored with Core Data. More on that later. Note that the Core Data storage types have different names from the value classes in Cocoa (NSString, NSNumber, and the like). When Core Data attributes are read into a running application, they are converted into the nearest Cocoa equivalent, which means, for example, that all the numeric types end up as NSNumber in an application, and are converted back into the underlying storage format for saving.

Creating Attributes

Let's start creating MythicalPerson's attributes. Click to select the MythicalPerson entity, then click the small "+" button underneath the *Property* table view to add a new property. A small menu of choices pops up. Click Add Attribute and an attribute will appear in the table view. On the right, you'll see all the settings that are available for this attribute; set its name to "name," then press Enter.

Now look at the checkboxes just below the *Name* field, labeled *Optional*, *Transient*, and *Indexed*. The meaning of *Optional* is clear enough. Having it checked means that users can choose to not enter a value for that attribute when creating or editing an object. As for the others, checking *Transient* configures things so that this attribute isn't saved along with the other data, while checking *Indexed* turns on indexing for the attribute, enabling speedy search of a Core Data storage back-end based on this attribute. For the name attribute, make sure that *Indexed* is checked, and that the others are not.

Below the checkboxes, you specify the attribute's type using a popup list. Select *String* from the popup list, and you'll see some additional options appear in the space just below it, where you can specify simple validation rules such as the string's length. Here you can also specify the default value, which will appear whenever a new MythicalPerson instance is created. Enter "Name" for the default value, leaving the other fields blank.

Now let's move on to the details attribute, which is meant to hold a textual description of the MythicalPerson in question. Click the "+" button below the *Property* table view, choose Add Attribute, and change the new attribute's name to "details." We're going to configure this one a little differently than the name attribute. It should be a String (chosen from the popup list), and the *Indexed* checkbox should be checked, but in this case the *Optional* checkbox should also be checked, so that users can choose to leave this field empty if they want. Also, we'll leave the default value blank.

Now we'll tackle MythicalPerson's numeric attributes: divinity, goodness, and power. Make a new attribute and name it "divinity," and this time configure the checkboxes so that it's optional, but neither transient nor indexed (because we don't anticipate any real need to search for MythicalPersons using the divinity value as a search parameter). Then click the *Type* popup list, and choose Integer 16, the smallest integer type support by Core Data. You'll see the display change to show some additional configuration that applies to the chosen type. Here we can set up some automatic validation rules by specifying min and max values, and also specify the default value for this attribute.

In Table 7–1, we defined divinity as an integer value from 0 to 100, the idea being to place the character somewhere on a scale between human and godlike. For example, the Greek god Zeus would have a divinity value of 100, his son Hercules (whose mother was a normal human) would have 50, and a normal human (like, again, Hercules' mother) would have 0 divinity. By specifying min and max values for the attribute, we let Core Data help us out, ensuring that no invalid values for these attributes can be saved. Enter 0 for the min value, 100 for the max value, and 50 for the default value. See Figure 7–4 to see some entity/attribute editing in progress.

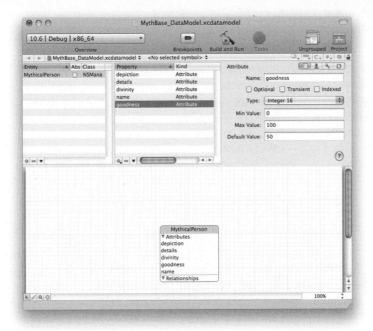

Figure 7–4. *This is what editing an entity in a Core Data model file looks like.*

Now we're going to create the other two numeric values, goodness and power. These also express characteristics of each `MythicalPerson` on a scale from 0 to 100, and will have the exact same configuration as divinity (except, of course, for the name of the attribute itself). The easiest way to make these, giving them the exact same options, is to select the divinity attribute by clicking on it in the table view, then copy it (⌘C), then paste it (⌘V) twice, resulting in two new attributes named "divinity1" and "divinity2." Rename those "goodness" and "power", and that's it; those two new attributes will have the same min and max values as the original.

Attributes for Unsupported Types

The last attribute left to configure is the depiction attribute. As we mentioned earlier, the depiction attribute is meant to store an image, and Core Data doesn't know anything about the `NSImage` class normally used in Cocoa. Fortunately, Core Data's *Transformable* type provides a simple way to store an image anyway. Create a new attribute, and name it "depiction." Then turn the *Optional* checkbox on (and the others off), and choose Transformable from the *Type* popup list. The view changes to show the configuration for the Transformable type: a single text field labeled *Value Transformer Name*. The idea is that a Transformable attribute holds a chunk of data that Core Data doesn't really understand; when Core Data reads this chunk of data from storage, it puts it into an `NSData` object (an object that can hang onto any old chunk of data, acting as an Objective-C "wrapper" for it), which it then passes through a *transformer*, a special class that knows how to take an object of one kind and transform it into something else. In the other direction, when an object is going to be saved to storage, Core Data takes the new value and passes it through the same transformer, however this time doing the transformation in the reverse direction.

In this case, we're going to use a transformer called NSKeyedUnarchiveFromData, which knows how to produce an object of any kind, given an NSData object containing a key-archived version of the object. That surely leaves you wondering what keyed archiving is. We won't go into it in detail here, but basically keyed archiving is a way of archiving or serializing all of an object's instance variables in a dictionary-like format, making it possible to reconstruct the object later. This technology is used in a variety of ways in Cocoa, and all of Cocoa's classes have this functionality built in. This means that you can take an NSImage, or an instance of any other Cocoa class, and stuff it into an NSData object using NSKeyedUnarchiveFromData's reverse transformation. And if you implement the NSCoding protocol in your own classes, saving and loading their instance variables in a keyed fashion, you can archive your own objects in the same way.

Getting back to the depiction field, the idea is to write the name of the transformer class into the *Value Transformer Name* text field. As it turns out, keyed archiving is so widespread that in this situation, specifying a transformer for an attribute in Xcode's modeling tool, it's used as a default. If you just leave the field blank, the entity will be configured to use NSKeyedUnarchiveFromData to transform model attribute values to and from NSData for storage.

You've now defined the entire model for this chapter's MythBase application, so let's move on to creating the GUI.

The Automatic GUI

The developer tools have special support for Core Data, allowing you to quickly make a feature-rich GUI application for accessing your model objects through Core Data. This auto-generated GUI will let you create new objects, edit them, search for them, and delete them. And not only can you get that far without writing any code, you can even get a rough version of the GUI up and running with little more than a drag of the mouse. The GUI created by this process works entirely through Cocoa Bindings, using an NSArrayController just like you used for creating DungeonThing in Chapter 6. The key difference is that the NSArrayController created here will access its data through Core Data instead of through your own controller's array (like we used in DungeonThing). In this section we'll show you how to do this, and then in the next section we'll show you how to tweak your GUI to make it even better.

Start by going back to Xcode's navigation pane. Go into the *Resources* group and double-click MainMenu.xib to open it in Interface Builder. This brings up a nib file much like you've seen in earlier, including a menu and an empty window. Bring the empty window to the front (double-click on its icon in the main window if the window isn't showing), and make it a bit bigger; somewhere about 500 × 600 will do nicely.

Now go back to Xcode, and bring up your model file if it isn't still showing. What you're going to do is ⌥-drag the MythicalPerson entity from the graph paper workspace over to the blank window in Interface Builder. Start by holding down ⌥, then click and hold on the box representing the `MythicalPerson` entity. Keep holding the mouse and drag away, and you'll see a translucent copy of the entity box being pulled along with your mouse pointer. Once the drag is started, you can release the ⌥ button. Now drag the entity over the empty window in Interface Builder. If you can't see it, use ⌘Tab to switch back to Interface Builder (while still holding down the mouse button!), drag over the middle of the empty window, and release the mouse button.

Now you'll be presented with the *New Core Data Entity Interface* assistant (see Figure 7–5). This assistant lets you choose from a few different GUI templates, each with some options of its own. Select *Master/Detail View* from the popup list, and click to enable each of the *Search Field*, *Details Fields*, and *Add/Remove* checkboxes.

Figure 7–5. *Making choices in the New Core Data Entity Interface assistant*

Then click *Next*, and the assistant will ask you which attributes should be included in the GUI. We want to show all of the entity's attributes in our GUI, so leave them all checked and click *Finish*. Now the assistant will automatically create an `NSArrayController` in your nib file, and add several views to the window where you dragged the entity. The new `NSArrayController` will be pre-configured using Cocoa Bindings to retrieve its content through the Core Data entity you dragged, and the controls in the window will be configured with Cocoa Bindings to access their values through the `NSArrayController`. Figure 7–6 shows the new content of your window.

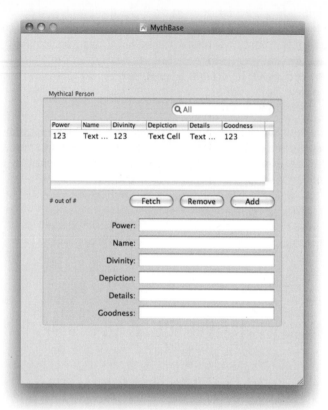

Figure 7–6. *The automatic GUI, created entirely by the assistant*

At this point, you can save the nib file, switch back to Xcode, and compile and run your app. You'll see the GUI that the assistant created for you, now connecting to real data storage (a file accessed via Core Data, which we'll explain in more detail later in this chapter), and almost fully functional. You can add new mythical people, set their name, details, power, divinity, and goodness values. You can save the objects by selecting File▸Save from the menu (or by pressing ⌘S), and you can delete them, edit them, and search for them right in the window's search field. Note that the numeric values honor the limits you configured in the data model file. If you try to save an object whose divinity exceeds 100, for example, the app will show you a warning panel and the save will be cancelled. The one part of the app that doesn't actually work is the depiction attribute. Trying to set a value for the depiction attribute in either the table column or the text field won't actually work until we configure things a bit more in the next section.

MythBase is obviously not very polished at this point. There's a lot that needs fixing, but as you can see it's pretty functional already, and we haven't even written a line of code, or touched a single control in Interface Builder.

Refining the GUI

Now it's time for us to fix some of the obvious problems with the GUI, and also satisfy the urge to dig deeper that any programmer *has* to feel (don't tell me you didn't) when too many things start to work "magically" with just a few button clicks.

Go back to Interface Builder, and bring up the *Bindings Inspector* (⌘4). While you're editing the GUI, it can be instructive to keep an eye on this *Inspector*, which will show you the bindings for each object you click on. Most of the bindings you'll see here are similar to the bindings you configured in Chapter 6; the one that differs the most is the binding for the *Mythical Person Controller* in the main nib window, through which the controller accesses model objects. In DungeonThing, the array controllers we created always had their *Content Array* bound to a property of our controller. If you click on the *Mythical Person Controller*, you'll see that here, instead of the *Content Array*, the array controller's *Managed Object Context* is bound to a property of our app's controller called managedObjectContext. The *Managed Object Context* is, as you may have guessed, an object that lets an array controller (or, for that matter, your own code) tap into a source of model objects (instances of NSManagedObject or a subclass) through Core Data. You'll see how our app controller provides this a little later, when we examine the controller code that was put in place automatically when we created this project.

Now let's start working on the table view. We want to lose the *Details* column (it will typically contain a lot more text than the table view will show anyway), reorder the columns so that the numeric values are displayed side-by-side, and make the *Depiction* column show an image. Figure 7–7 shows what we're aiming for.

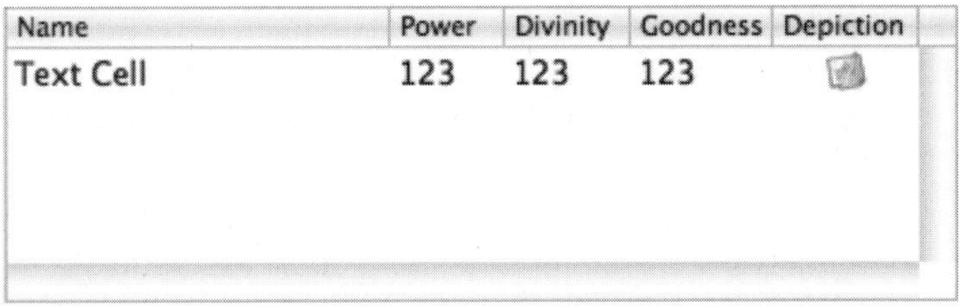

Name	Power	Divinity	Goodness	Depiction
Text Cell	123	123	123	

Figure 7–7. *This is what your table view should look like after it's fully configured.*

First, click on the *Details* column (not the column header, but the space below it) until it's selected, and then press delete or backspace. That takes care of the unwanted column.

Next, let's reorder the remaining table columns. Click on the table header until the entire table header area is highlighted with a lightly colored, round-cornered "focus area," leaving the rest of the window dark. At that point, you can click and drag the table columns to reorder them. Put *Name* on the left, followed by *Power*, *Divinity*, *Goodness*, and finally *Depiction*. While you're at it you'll want to shrink most of the columns by dragging the small vertical lines that separate the column headers from each other, making each column small enough to just hold the title and no more. Do that for every column except the *Name* column, for which you should do the opposite: widen it so that it fills up all available space.

Now we're going to use an `NSImageCell` to display an image in the *Depiction* column, similar to what we did with the VillainTracker table view in Chapter 5. Go to the *Library* window, and type "imagecell" into the search field. Drag the resulting *Image Cell* over to your window, dropping it on the *Depiction* table column.

We now need to configure one more thing in order to make the *Depiction* column actually display images. Remember our earlier discussion about transformers, and the Transformable type used by Core Data? Because depiction is a transformable attribute, its value needs to be converted between what we see in the GUI (an `NSImage`), and something that Core Data is capable of storing (`NSData`). We'll do this by adding `NSKeyedUnarchiveFromData` to the Cocoa Bindings configuration for this table column. Bring up the *Bindings Inspector* (⌘4), and make sure that the table column, not the image cell, is selected by clicking in the white space of the column. You'll see a binding, pre-configured by the assistant that created all these controls, for the column's *Value*. Click on the *Value Transformer* popup list, and choose `NSKeyedUnarchiveFromData`. That's it! The *Depiction* column is now ready to show images.

Now let's do something about the text fields at the bottom, where the details of the selected `MythicalPerson` are shown. Currently they're not in any particular order, so we'll want to change that. We'll also want to have something bigger than a text field for the details attribute, and of course we need to have an image view for the depiction attribute. To accommodate a larger text view and an image view, make the `MythicalPerson` view taller, by first dragging the whole view to the top of the window, then dragging the bottom-center resize handle down to the bottom of the window.

To start off fixing up the lower part of the window, select the text fields for details and depiction, and delete them. We can reuse the labels though, so drag each of them to the bottom of the view to get them out of the way. Now you're going to rearrange the remaining text fields so that they're in the order we want. The idea is to select text fields and their labels in pairs, and move them around together, so that they're in the same order as in the table view: Name, Power, Divinity, Goodness, as shown in Figure 7–8.

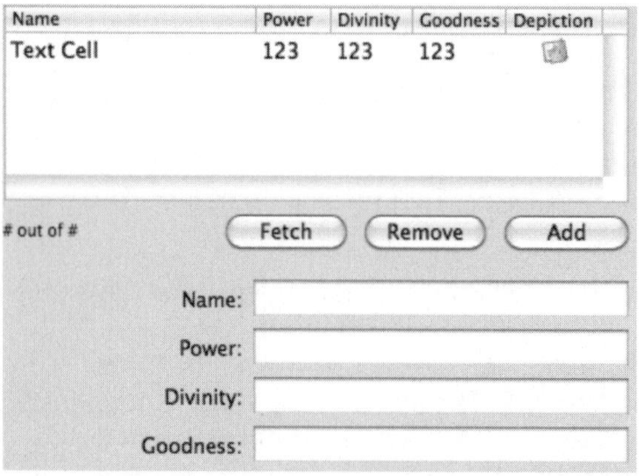

Figure 7–8. *The text fields, after putting them in the right places*

You can select these pair-wise either by "drawing a box" around them, or by first clicking on the text field, and then **Shift**-clicking on its corresponding label. While dragging things around, you're bound to inadvertently drag something where you didn't want to put it. Remember that Edit▶Undo (⌘Z) is your friend!

Now let's set up the image view for the depiction attribute, and the text view for the details attribute. Find an NSImageView in the *Library* and drop it just below the text fields, then find an NSTextView and put it next to the image view. Drag the old *Depiction* and *Details* labels up above their views, and resize the views so that your window looks something like Figure 7–9.

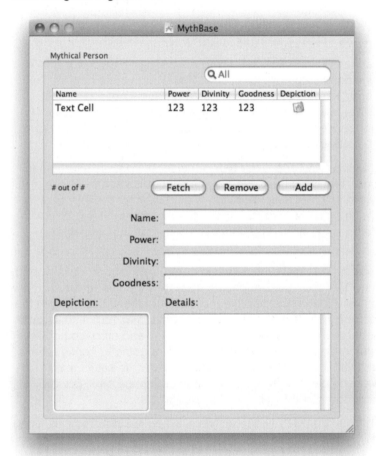

Figure 7–9. *Our window is starting to shape up!*

Now we just have to configure the new controls so that they'll actually display something. Select the image view, and in the *Bindings Inspector* open up the *Value* binding configuration. Choose *Mythical Person Array Controller* in the popup list, *selection* in the *Controller Key* combo box, *depiction* in the *Model Key Path* combo box, and NSKeyedUnarchiveFromData in the *Value Transformer* combo box. Now switch to the

Attributes Inspector (⌘1), and click to turn on the *Editable* checkbox (so that a user can drag an image into the image view).

Next, select the text view. NSTextView is able, by default, to display rich text, which is a great feature but comes at a price: In Cocoa, rich text is represented by instances of NSAttributedString, a class that's a lot more complicated than NSString, and not something we want to get into here and now. In order for the text view to be able to bind its display value to a plain old string, we have to turn off rich text handling. So, in the *Attributes Inspector*, click to turn off the *Rich Text* checkbox (if you don't see that, you've probably selected the text view's superview, an NSScrollView. Click the text view once more to select the NSTextView inside). Now, switch to the *Bindings Inspector* again, and open the configuration for the *Value* binding. Choose *Mythical Person Array Controller*, *selection*, and *details* in the relevant popup and combo boxes.

Now save your work in Interface Builder, switch back to Xcode, and hit the *Run* button. If all goes well, your interface comes up, fully functional! You can create a new Mythical Person (or select one you created earlier), drag an image (from the Finder, or a web page, and the like) into the image view, and the image will appear in the table view immediately. When you choose File▶Save from the menu, or quit the application, the image you dragged in will be saved to the data store along with the rest.

The last thing that isn't quite satisfying about our GUI is the set of controls for entering numeric values. Sure, you can type a number into a text field, but it's somewhat error-prone (since a user can type in any text they want) and is generally not the way people expect to enter numbers much of the time these days. Let's replace each text field with a slider and label combo, like we did in the *Preferences* window for DungeonThing in Chapter 6.

Back in Interface Builder, select and delete the text field controls for power, divinity, and goodness. Leave the labels where they are though, because they'll point right at the new controls. Now, find a horizontal slider in the *Library*, and drag it to the window. Open the *Attributes Inspector*, and set the slider's min and max values to 0 and 100. Also, click to turn on the *Continuous* checkbox. Now find a label in the *Library*, and drag it out to the right of the slider, all the way to the right edge of the view. We're going to configure this label with a binding so that it will display the value set by the slider, so set its text to "100" in the nib file; that way you can see the largest amount of space it will take up. Then resize the slider to fill up most of the gap.

Before going on, there's an issue that we need to address. When NSSlider passes along its value (to the underlying MythicalPerson), it sends a floating-point value instead of an integer. When the object is saved to storage later, this value is converted to an integer, but before that, it's kept as a float value. This means that when the value is passed along via Cocoa Bindings to other controls (such as the small label to the right of the slider), the floating-point value is passed along, and that's what's displayed in the text field. Fortunately, Cocoa has a solution for this problem in the form of a class called NSFormatter. A formatter is an object that can change the display of a value, formatting it in any way you like. We're going to attach a formatter to the label so that we can force it to always display an integer, regardless of the value it receives.

In the Library, search for "numberformatter," and drag the resulting NSNumberFormatter (a subclass of NSFormatter) to the small label, which highlights when you're right on top of it. Then select the formatter by first selecting the small label in the window, then clicking on the tiny icon that appears below it. That icon represents the formatter, which is attached to the control, and clicking on it lets you edit the formatter's attributes. Now bring up the *Attributes Inspector*, and see what the options for NSNumberFormatter look like. You get a whole host of options for defining how the formatter will display numbers, including how many digits to display after a decimal point, what the decimal and thousands separators look like, currency symbols, and so on. You don't actually need to configure anything in there right now, since the default values for an NSNumberFormatter are just right for our purposes: By default, NSNumberFormatter will round any value to the nearest integer.

Now select both the slider and the small label and duplicate them twice, once for divinity and once for goodness, placing the new sets in line with the labels. Figure 7–10 shows what you should be seeing at this point.

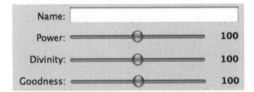

Figure 7–10. *Replacing text fields with sliders*

Now for the final step: binding the new controls to the selected MythicalPerson's values. One at a time, select each of these six objects (three sliders and three labels), and bind its *Value* so that the *Mythical Person Array Controller* is the controller, *selection* is the *Controller Key*, and the appropriate attribute—*power*, *divinity*, or *goodness*—is selected in the *Model Key Path* combo box.

Save your work, switch to Xcode, and click the *Build & Run* button. Running the app, you should see the sliders and text fields update as you select objects in the table, and dragging a slider should update both the corresponding text field and the matching cell in the table view. If you play around with the app a bit more, trying out the search field above the table view, you may be in for a rude awakening, and find that your app hangs or crashes, and dumps a lot of strange output into the console log in Xcode. The problem lies with the search field that the assistant creates: it's automatically bound up with several search predicates, one for each attribute. These search predicates (which you'll be seeing more of in Chapter 9) are used to try to match up the value that the user types in with objects in the data store. The assistant-created GUI includes a search predicate for every attribute, including the binary depiction attribute. Unfortunately, binary and transformable attribute are inherently *not* searchable, and Core Data tries to deal with the mess up as well as it can, but unfortunately it doesn't help. The search functionality is inoperable with a search predicate for the depiction attribute in place.

Fortunately, you can make searching work for your project by removing the offending search predicate. Use the Bindings Inspector to examine the search field's bindings. In the "Search" category, you'll see a bunch of numbered Predicate bindings. Open each one until you find the one for "depiction," then just deactivate that binding. Unfortunately, even though we wrote that paragraph as if it what we described actually works, it doesn't quite work if you're running Leopard. Turning off the checkbox for Predicate5 (containing the search predicate binding for the depiction attribute) in a list of 8 predicates (the last one being empty, ready to add a new one if need be) actually eliminates Predicate7 instead! This is clearly a bug in Interface Builder. You could work around it by eliminating the last three predicates, and then re-adding in the last two, but for our purposes, it's enough to just eliminate the last three predicates and not bother putting the last two back in place for now.

You've now made a pretty cool-looking app entirely by defining a model, dragging an entity into Interface Builder, and then adjusting and swapping out some controls in the GUI. This is a great example of the kind of visual programming model that Cocoa has always enabled, and with the addition of Cocoa Bindings and Core Data in the past few years it's become even more complete. Of course, underlying all this stuff are frameworks and APIs that enable all this "magic" to happen in Xcode and Interface Builder, and there are times when you will want or need to access Core Data functionality from code. The rest of this chapter will introduce you to some aspects of programming (in the traditional, code-based sense) with Core Data.

Exploring the Template Code

When you created the MythBase project, an application delegate class called MythBase_AppDelegate was created for you. This class contains code to load the model information from the Core Data model files contained within your application. It also opens up the on-disk storage where Core Data reads and writes its model objects, or creates this storage if it doesn't already exist. And finally, it provides access to the data storage via an NSManagedObjectContext, which other objects can in turn bind to (such as the array controller in our nib file) in order to read from and write to storage.

All the code shown here has been reformatted to better fit the format of this book, so your version may look slightly different, but should be syntactically identical.

The App Delegate Interface

Let's jump right in and take a look at the header file, MythBase_AppDelegate.h, shown in the following listing. This is the autogenerated code created by the version of Xcode available for Snow Leopard. The version created by Leopard's Xcode may be slightly different, and if you like you can change it to match the version shown here:

```
#import <Cocoa/Cocoa.h>
@interface MythBase_AppDelegate : NSObject
{
    NSWindow *window;

    NSPersistentStoreCoordinator *persistentStoreCoordinator;
    NSManagedObjectModel *managedObjectModel;
```

```
        NSManagedObjectContext *managedObjectContext;
}
@property (nonatomic, retain) IBOutlet NSWindow *window;
@property (nonatomic, retain, readonly) NSPersistentStoreCoordinator
    *persistentStoreCoordinator;
@property (nonatomic, retain, readonly) NSManagedObjectModel
    *managedObjectModel;
@property (nonatomic, retain, readonly) NSManagedObjectContext
    *managedObjectContext;
- (IBAction)saveAction:sender;
@end
```

As you can see, this declares a simple class with four instance variables, all of them declared as properties. The `window` variable also features `IBOutlet` in its property declaration which makes it into an outlet, available for connecting to a window in Interface Builder. The other three variables are instances of some important Core Data classes:

- `NSManagedObjectModel` loads information about entities and their properties from one or more model files (normally contained inside your application bundle), and acts as a sort of metadata repository containing the structure of your application's managed objects. Many applications will never need to interact with this directly.

- `NSPersistentStoreCoordinator` manages the back-storage, giving access to one or more instances of `NSPersistentStore`, which each represent a storage location (in a file, or in memory). The purpose of the coordinator is to let the application access several persistent stores as if they were one. Some applications may want to use this to partition application data across multiple stores. For example, you may want to distinguish between normal entities, whose objects that are saved to disk, and transient entities, whose objects that are only held in memory, and will disappear when the user quits the app. Even though they're not saved to disk, the transient objects will still benefit from the other features of Core Data (simple undo support, integration with Cocoa Bindings, and the like).

- `NSManagedObjectContext` is responsible for dealing with the life-cycle of all managed objects (the model objects that we're storing via Core Data). It accesses the objects themselves through an `NSPersistentStoreCoordinator`, and provides high-level functionality for creating, reading, updating, and deleting objects. Most applications will use an `NSManagedObjectContext` at some time or another, for creating objects, saving changes, and so on.

You'll see how each of those objects is used when we look at the implementation file. The final declaration in the header file is for the `saveAction:` method, which is called with the user selects **File▶Save** from the MythBase menu. You'll see how that works in the next section.

The App Delegate Implementation

Now let's switch over to `MythBase_AppDelegate.m`, and see what it does. Besides implementing the `saveAction:` method declared in the interface, it also needs to make sure that the appropriate accessors for its declared properties are all implemented. That includes both a getter and a setter for `window`, and just a getter for the others (which were declared `readonly`).

As with the header file, this code was auto-generated using Xcode 3.2 running on Snow Leopard. The Leopard version looks slightly different. However, all classes and methods used in this version are also available in Leopard, so if you're still using Leopard and want to make use of the latest versions of these default files, feel free to change your auto-generated code to match what you see here.

The applicationSupportDirectory Method

The file starts out like this:

```
#import "MythBase_AppDelegate.h"
@implementation MythBase_AppDelegate
@synthesize window;
/**
 Returns the support directory for the application, used to store the
 Core Data store file.  This code uses a directory named "MythBase"
 for the content, either in the NSApplicationSupportDirectory location
 or (if the former cannot be found), the system's temporary directory.
 */
- (NSString *)applicationSupportDirectory {
  NSArray *paths =
    NSSearchPathForDirectoriesInDomains(NSApplicationSupportDirectory,
    NSUserDomainMask, YES);
  NSString *basePath = ([paths count] > 0) ? [paths objectAtIndex:0] :
    NSTemporaryDirectory();
  return [basePath stringByAppendingPathComponent:@"MythBase"];
}
```

The first thing shown in the class's implementation is `@synthesize window`, which takes care of the getter and setter for `window`. After that comes the implementation of a method called `applicationSupportDirectory`, which returns a string containing the name of a directory where the application can save its data–in our case, the location where Core Data should save its persistent store. Normally this method returns the full path of a subdirectory of the *Application Support* directory, which is located inside the *Library* directory in the user's home directory (`/Users/somebody/Library/Application Support/MythBase`). If that directory doesn't exist, it returns the path to the system temporary directory (`/tmp`) instead.

The `applicationSupportDirectory` method is sort of a "helper" method, called elsewhere in the class's implementation. Note that this method is not declared in the header file, nor in a private category or anything of the sort. In an Objective-C implementation block, code can call any methods that appear earlier in the same implementation block, even if they're not declared anywhere. This is sometimes a handy shortcut when you want to refactor your code a bit, extracting some functionality into a method of its own, but don't need to make it accessible anywhere outside the current class implementation.

The managedObjectModel Accessor Method

Next, we see the managedObjectModel method. This method serves as the getter for the managedObjectModel property.

```
/**
 Creates, retains, and returns the managed object model for the
 application by merging all of the models found in the application
 bundle.
 */
- (NSManagedObjectModel *)managedObjectModel {
  if (managedObjectModel) return managedObjectModel;
  managedObjectModel = [[NSManagedObjectModel
    mergedModelFromBundles:nil] retain];
  return managedObjectModel;
}
```

The method simply checks to see if the managedObjectModel has already been created. If so, it returns it, and if not, it creates it by reading all model files contained within the application, via a convenient class method in NSManagedObjectModel (mergedModelFromBundles:). The managedObjectModel method may be called by any piece of code that needs access to metadata about the model. In particular, it's called when we create the NSPersistentStoreCoordinator, which will need to either read from, or create storage for our model, so it needs the gritty details.

ERROR HANDLING WITH NSERROR

Some of the code being shown here makes use of NSError objects to handle errors that may occur. We haven't yet covered NSError, but offer a brief explanation here.

The basic idea behind NSError is that some methods need to be able to inform the caller about potential errors that may occur, without using the return value for this purpose. To make this work, you pass in a pointer to a pointer (sometimes called a "handle" in C parlance) to an NSError, so that the method may create an NSError object and point your pointer at it, something like this:

```
NSError *error = nil;
[someObject doSomething:&error];
if (error) {
  // handle the error somehow!
}
```

For more details about NSError, see Chapter 12.

The persistentStoreCoordinator Accessor Method

Next up is the considerably longer persistentStoreCoordinator method:

```
/**
Returns the persistent store coordinator for the application.  This
implementation will create and return a coordinator, having added the
store for the application to it.  (The directory for the store is
created, if necessary.)
*/
- (NSPersistentStoreCoordinator *) persistentStoreCoordinator {
  if (persistentStoreCoordinator) return persistentStoreCoordinator;
  NSManagedObjectModel *mom = [self managedObjectModel];
  if (!mom) {
    NSAssert(NO, @"Managed object model is nil");
    NSLog(@"%@:%s No model to generate a store from", [self class],
      _cmd);
    return nil;
  }
  NSFileManager *fileManager = [NSFileManager defaultManager];
  NSString *applicationSupportDirectory = [self
    applicationSupportDirectory];
  NSError *error = nil;
  if (![fileManager fileExistsAtPath:applicationSupportDirectory
    isDirectory:NULL] ) {
    if (![fileManager
      createDirectoryAtPath:applicationSupportDirectory
      withIntermediateDirectories:NO attributes:nil error:&error])
    {
      NSAssert(NO, ([NSString stringWithFormat:
        @"Failed to create App Support directory %@ : %@",
        applicationSupportDirectory,error]));
      NSLog(@"Error creating application support directory at %@ : %@",
        applicationSupportDirectory,error);
      return nil;
    }
  }
  NSURL *url = [NSURL fileURLWithPath:[applicationSupportDirectory
    stringByAppendingPathComponent:@"storedata"]];
  persistentStoreCoordinator = [[NSPersistentStoreCoordinator alloc]
    initWithManagedObjectModel:mom];
  if (![persistentStoreCoordinator
    addPersistentStoreWithType:NSXMLStoreType
    configuration:nil
    URL:url
    options:nil
    error:&error])
  {
    [[NSApplication sharedApplication] presentError:error];
    [persistentStoreCoordinator release], persistentStoreCoordinator =
      nil;
    return nil;
  }
  return persistentStoreCoordinator;
}
```

This method starts by looking for an existing object in the `persistentStoreCoordinator` instance variable, returning it if there is one. Otherwise, it needs to initialize the coordinator itself, so it goes on to look for a `managedObjectModel` by calling the method of the same name. If it doesn't exist, then the application contains no model, and this method logs an error and returns nil. Otherwise, it goes on to check for the existence of a directory (specified by the value returned by the `applicationSupportDirectory` method) where the app's Core Data storage should be loaded. If the directory doesn't exist, it tries to create it; and if that doesn't work, it logs an error and returns nil.

If we get past all those edge cases (and we usually will), then the method builds a URL pointing at where the storage file should be located, creates an `NSPersistentStoreCoordinator`, and tells the coordinator to add a new store, given the URL. The coordinator is smart enough to look at the URL, figure out if there's already a persistent store there, and if not, create one for us. If it encounters any error along the way, it tells us so, and the application reports an error to the user.

A few points of interest about this method: for one thing, this is where the actual filename for your app's data store (currently *storedata*, though under Leopard it defaulted to `MythBase.xml`) is specified. If you wanted to name your file something else, this is where you'd change it. Also, this is where the type of the backing store is specified. It's currently set to `NSXMLStoreType`, which means that the stored data will be in an XML-formatted file. This sort of storage is nice while you're developing your app, since the resulting file is easy to parse with other tools, or for that matter read with your own eyes. However, before delivering a final application, you may want to consider changing your data store to another type, for the sake of size, speed, and other considerations. The other choices you have are `NSBinaryStoreType`, which saves its data in a binary format that takes less disk space and is faster to read and write, and `NSSQLiteStoreType`, which in addition to the advantages of `NSBinaryStoreType` also frees the persistent store from the burden of holding the entire object graph in memory at once; it only loads objects as they're accessed. That difference becomes crucial when dealing with a large data set. Because of this advantage, we recommend changing from `NSXMLStoreType` to `NSSQLiteStoreType` before releasing your application. There's an additional store type, `NSInMemoryStoreType`, which can be used for maintaining an in-memory object graph that's never saved to disk. The default Core Data application template does a pretty good job of tucking away the data storage for you so that you don't have to give it too much thought, but at some point before shipping your app you will have to decide which of these formats to use for your app's storage. We've given our recommendations, but you might want to consult the documentation in Xcode (search for "core data programming guide" to gain more understanding before deciding how to tackle this issue.

The final thing to point out about `persistentStoreCoordinator` is that if you want to partition your data into different stores (for example one that's on disk and one that's only in memory, disappearing when the app terminates) this is where you'd need to make the changes, adding each of your persistent stores to the coordinator.

The managedObjectContext Accessor Method

Now let's look at the managedObjectContext method, which is the getter for the read-only property of the same name:

```
/**
 Returns the managed object context for the application (which is
 already bound to the persistent store coordinator for the
 application.)
 */
- (NSManagedObjectContext *) managedObjectContext {
  if (managedObjectContext) return managedObjectContext;
  NSPersistentStoreCoordinator *coordinator = [self
    persistentStoreCoordinator];
  if (!coordinator) {
    NSMutableDictionary *dict = [NSMutableDictionary dictionary];
    [dict setValue:@"Failed to initialize the store"
      forKey:NSLocalizedDescriptionKey];
    [dict setValue:@"There was an error building up the data file."
      forKey:NSLocalizedFailureReasonErrorKey];
    NSError *error = [NSError errorWithDomain:@"YOUR_ERROR_DOMAIN"
      code:9999 userInfo:dict];
    [[NSApplication sharedApplication] presentError:error];
    return nil;
  }
  managedObjectContext = [[NSManagedObjectContext alloc] init];
  [managedObjectContext setPersistentStoreCoordinator:coordinator];
  return managedObjectContext;
}
```

Like the other methods we've seen acting as a getter for a property, this method first checks to see if the instance variable has been set, and if so, returns it. Otherwise, it checks for the existence of a persistent store coordinator by calling the persistentStoreCoordinator method. If that returns nil, then the method reports an error and returns nil itself. If not, it simply creates a managed object context, sets its persistent store coordinator, and returns the context.

This code is pretty straightforward, and is probably nothing you'll ever pay much attention to, except perhaps to customize the error reporting.

An NSWindow Delegate Method

Next up is an NSWindow delegate method called windowWillReturnUndoManager:

```
/**
 Returns the NSUndoManager for the application.  In this case, the
 manager returned is that of the managed object context for the
 application.
 */
- (NSUndoManager *)windowWillReturnUndoManager:(NSWindow *)window {
  return [[self managedObjectContext] undoManager];
}
```

This method lets us specify the object that handles undo/redo actions for the window containing our GUI. We'll discuss the undo/redo system in Chapter 11, but for now all you need to know is that this method tells the system to use Core Data's undo manager, which is accessed through the managed object context.

The saveAction: Action Method

Next up, the saveAction: method, which is called when the user clicks the relevant menu item. As before, the note about different versions of code generated by different versions of Mac OS X and Xcode applies here as well. This is the Snow Leopard version; the Leopard version may be slightly different.

```
/**
 Performs the save action for the application, which is to send the
 save: message to the application's managed object context.  Any
 encountered errors are presented to the user.
 */
- (IBAction) saveAction:(id)sender {
  NSError *error = nil;
  if (![[self managedObjectContext] commitEditing]) {
    NSLog(@"%@:%s unable to commit editing before saving",
      [self class], _cmd);
  }
  if (![[self managedObjectContext] save:&error]) {
    [[NSApplication sharedApplication] presentError:error];
  }
}
```

This method is pretty straightforward. It first tells the context to ensure that any pending edits are committed to the underlying model objects, and prints a warning in case the commit fails. Whether the commit succeeds or fails, it then proceeds to tell the context to save all model objects to storage. If that fails, it shows the user an error.

An NSApplication Delegate Method

Now we come to this class's longest method, the NSApplication delegate method applicationShouldTerminate:. This method is called by the application when the user selects Quit from the menu, and gives the delegate a chance to save changes, inspect its state, ask the user if they really want to quit, and so on. The value returned by this method determines whether the application will really terminate or not. Here's the code:

```
/**
 Implementation of the applicationShouldTerminate: method, used here
 to handle the saving of changes in the application managed object
 context before the application terminates.
 */
- (NSApplicationTerminateReply)applicationShouldTerminate:
    (NSApplication *)sender {
  if (!managedObjectContext) return NSTerminateNow;
  if (![managedObjectContext commitEditing]) {
    NSLog(@"%@:%s unable to commit editing to terminate",
      [self class], _cmd);
    return NSTerminateCancel;
  }
  if (![managedObjectContext hasChanges]) return NSTerminateNow;
```

```
      NSError *error = nil;
      if (![managedObjectContext save:&error]) {
        // This error handling simply presents error information in a
        // panel with an "Ok" button, which does not include any attempt
        // at error recovery (meaning, attempting to fix the error.)  As a
        // result, this implementation will present the information to the
        // user and then follow up with a panel asking if the user wishes
        // to "Quit Anyway", without saving the changes.
        // Typically, this process should be altered to include
        // application-specific recovery steps.
        BOOL result = [sender presentError:error];
        if (result) return NSTerminateCancel;
        NSString *question = NSLocalizedString(
          @"Could not save changes while quitting.  Quit anyway?",
          @"Quit without saves error question message");
        NSString *info = NSLocalizedString(
          @"Quitting now will lose any changes you have made since the last successful
save",
          @"Quit without saves error question info");
        NSString *quitButton = NSLocalizedString(@"Quit anyway",
          @"Quit anyway button title");
        NSString *cancelButton = NSLocalizedString(@"Cancel",
          @"Cancel button title");
        NSAlert *alert = [[NSAlert alloc] init];
        [alert setMessageText:question];
        [alert setInformativeText:info];
        [alert addButtonWithTitle:quitButton];
        [alert addButtonWithTitle:cancelButton];
        NSInteger answer = [alert runModal];
        [alert release];
        alert = nil;
        if (answer == NSAlertAlternateReturn) return NSTerminateCancel;
      }
    return NSTerminateNow;
}
```

First it checks to see whether there really is a managedObjectContext to worry about. If not, it just returns NSTerminateNow immediately, and the application terminates. Then, it tells the context to commit any pending changes. If that fails, it logs an error message and returns NSTerminateCancel, which makes the application abort the current termination procedure and just continue about its business. Then, it checks to see whether the managedObjectContext actually has any pending changes, and if it doesn't, it returns NSTerminateNow.

Finally, it does the big step of telling the context to save its changes. If the save fails, then the final big conditional block is triggered. That block constructs an NSAlert, a special type of window that appears in front of all other application windows and forces you to make a choice by clicking a button (you'll learn more about NSAlert and other windows in Chapter 10). In this case, it's telling the user that their changes were not saved, and asking them to choose whether to quit the app anyway, or cancel the termination and go back to normal. Depending on the return value from this request, it either returns NSTerminateCancel, or "falls through" and returns NSTerminateNow.

Time to point out a small bug in this method: near the end, when the method checks to see if the Cancel button was pressed, it's actually comparing answer to the wrong value. It should be NSAlertSecondButtonReturn instead of NSAlertAlternateReturn. Not such a big deal perhaps, but this error in the logic makes it impossible to avoid quitting when the app is in a particular invalidate state. Oops!

One interesting thing to note is the use of NSLocalizedString in this method. NSLocalizedString is a simple way to let your code use localized resources if present. It's a C function that takes two arguments: a default string and a key used for looking up a localized string. For instance, in a call like NSLocalizedString(@"Cancel", @"Cancel button title"), NSLocalizedString will first check to see which language the user prefers, then check to see if there exists a localized string for that language, keyed off @"Cancel button title", and if so, returns it. Otherwise, it will just return the first parameter, @"Cancel".

The Obligatory Dealloc Method

Finally, the last method is a simple dealloc, shown here:

```
- (void)dealloc {
  [window release];
  [managedObjectContext release];
  [persistentStoreCoordinator release];
  [managedObjectModel release];
  [super dealloc];
}
```

No surprises here. This is the standard way to release instance variables in a dealloc method. However, keep in mind that in an app using garbage collection, the dealloc method is never actually called.

Adding Business Logic

Now that you've seen the basic idea of constructing an application with Core Data, including defining the model, configuring the GUI, and knowing your way around the template-provided code in your project, it's time to learn a bit about how to use Core Data to actually implement something "interesting" in your model objects: Your application's "business logic."

Some amount of business logic is specified right in the model file, such as an integer's min and max size, while some things require a bit of code. Fortunately NSManagedObject provides several "hooks" into spots where you can test your objects' attributes to validate them and make sure they're okay.

Validating Single Attributes

Let's say we want to add a special constraint to MythBase to ensure that no MythicalPerson can be named "Bob." To do this, we just have to add the method shown here to the @implementation section of MythicalPerson.m:

```
-(BOOL)validateName:(id *)ioValue error:(NSError **)outError {
  if (*ioValue == nil) {
    return YES;
  }
  if ([*ioValue isEqualToString:@"Bob"]) {
    if (outError != NULL) {
      NSString *errorStr = NSLocalizedString(
        @"You're not allowed to name a mythical person 'Bob'. "
        " 'Bob' is a real person, just like you and me.",
        @"validation: invalid name error");
      NSDictionary *userInfoDict = [NSDictionary
        dictionaryWithObject:errorStr
        forKey:NSLocalizedDescriptionKey];
      NSError *error = [[[NSError alloc]
        initWithDomain:@"MythicalPersonErrorDomain"
        code:13013 userInfo:userInfoDict] autorelease];
      *outError = error;
    }
    return NO;
  }
  return YES;
}
```

Note the name of this method, validateName:error:. Attribute validation in Core Data works through the use of methods named validate<*attribute name*>:error:, which are called (if they exist) on each managed object when it's time to save changes to the data store. Within this method, you should check the proposed value and return YES if it's okay. If not, you return NO, and should also create an NSError object describing the error, setting the passed-in NSError** to point at it. Note that when creating the error, you need to specify a string identifying the error name, and an integer specifying just which error it was. In a larger application, it's a good idea to standardize these values in some way. Doing so can help you track down errors that users may report, and can also give you a way to catch some recurring errors and handle them individually (for instance, in the app controller's saveAction: method). We'll talk about this more in Chapter 12.

At this point, you can compile and run MythBase, and everything will work the same as before, up until you change a MythicalPerson's name to "Bob" and try to save your changes, at which point you'll be warned that it's an invalid value.

Validating Multiple Attributes

Sometimes, you'll need to be able to validate several attributes at once, making sure that they make sense together. For example, let's say that we decide on a new constraint for each MythicalPerson: the value of the power attribute can only exceed 50 if the value of the divinity attribute is 100 (meaning that only a person operating in full "god mode" can have a power level above 50). Rather than check for this condition in validatePower:error: or validateDivinity:error:, the recommended procedure is to check for this in two other validation methods that are called whenever a new managed object is created, or edited: validateForInsert:, and validateForUpdate:. Because we're going to check for the same internal consistency problem (where power > 50 and divinity < 100) in both spots, we'll put that check into a method of our own, validateConsistency:, which is called by the other two. First, let's implement the two Core Data validation methods:

```
- (BOOL)validateForInsert:(NSError **)error
{
  BOOL propertiesValid = [super validateForInsert:error];
  BOOL consistencyValid = [self validateConsistency:error];
  return (propertiesValid && consistencyValid);
}

- (BOOL)validateForUpdate:(NSError **)error
{
  BOOL propertiesValid = [super validateForUpdate:error];
  BOOL consistencyValid = [self validateConsistency:error];
  return (propertiesValid && consistencyValid);
}
```

These methods both work in the same way. First, they call the superclass's version of the same method; that's very important, because that's the method that actually calls all of the validate<*attribute name*>:error: methods for each changed attribute. Then our own validateConsistency: method is called. If the return values for both of these calls return YES, then the method itself returns YES, otherwise it returns NO.

Now let's see what validateConsistency: looks like:

```
- (BOOL)validateConsistency:(NSError **)error
{
  int divinity = [[self valueForKey:@"divinity"] intValue];
  int power = [[self valueForKey:@"power"] intValue];
  if (divinity < 100 && power > 50) {
    if (error != NULL) {
      NSString *errorStr = NSLocalizedString(
        @"Power cannot exceed 50 unless divinity is 100",
        @"validation: divinity / power error");
      NSDictionary *userInfoDict = [NSDictionary
        dictionaryWithObject:errorStr
        forKey:NSLocalizedDescriptionKey];
      NSError *divinityPowerError = [[[NSError alloc]
        initWithDomain:@"MythicalPersonErrorDomain" code:182
        userInfo:userInfoDict] autorelease];
      if (*error == nil) {
        // there was no previous error, return the new error
        *error = divinityPowerError;
      }
      else {
        // combine previous error with the new one
        *error = [self errorFromOriginalError:*error
          error:divinityPowerError];
      }
    }
    return NO;
```

```
  }
  return YES;
}
```

Be sure to enter that method somewhere above the `validateForInsert:` and `validateForUpdate:` methods, so the compiler knows how to deal with it properly. This method is a little more complicated than the single attribute validation method. We do the same sort of checking for a problem, returning YES if it's okay, and otherwise constructing an NSError, setting the error parameter to point at it, and returning NO. However, in order to "play nice" with Core Data, we have to check for the existence of a pre-existing error, and if there is one, combine it with our own into a special kind of error. This lets Core Data eventually report back *all* the errors it finds when it tries to save. This error combining is done using another method of our own, `errorFromOriginalError:error:`, which we should add to our class:

```
- (NSError *)errorFromOriginalError:(NSError *)originalError
   error:(NSError *)secondError
{
  NSMutableDictionary *userInfo = [NSMutableDictionary dictionary];
  NSMutableArray *errors = [NSMutableArray
    arrayWithObject:secondError];

  if ([originalError code] == NSValidationMultipleErrorsError) {
    [userInfo addEntriesFromDictionary:[originalError userInfo]];
    [errors addObjectsFromArray:[userInfo
      objectForKey:NSDetailedErrorsKey]];
  }
  else {
    [errors addObject:originalError];
  }
  [userInfo setObject:errors forKey:NSDetailedErrorsKey];
  return [NSError errorWithDomain:NSCocoaErrorDomain
                            code:NSValidationMultipleErrorsError
                        userInfo:userInfo];
}
```

Basically, this method checks the `originalError` parameter to see if it already contains multiple errors, and if so, just adds the new one to the list. Otherwise, it combines the two single errors into a new multiple error object.

With all that in place, you should now be able to compile and run, select a MythicalPerson, set their power above 50, their divinity below 100, and try to save. You'll see an error telling you about the problem. You can also make sure that reporting of multiple problems works, by leaving this power/divinity inconsistency in place, changing the name to "Bob," and trying to save. You should see a warning panel telling you that multiple validation errors occurred, but you don't see details about any of them. This suggests a good idea for a future expansion of the app delegate's `saveAction:` and `applicationShouldTerminate:` methods: come up with a way to display multiple errors instead of just calling `presentError:` as is currently done. There's something to tackle on a rainy day!

Creating a Custom Attribute

Another common sort of simple "business logic" calls for the creation of custom attributes that are based on the values contained in an object's attributes. For example, if you have an entity with `firstName` and `lastName` attributes, you might want to make a custom attribute called `fullName` that combines the two together.

This sort of thing is a piece of cake with Core Data. In our case, let's say we want to add an attribute to `MythicalPerson` called `awesomeness`, which will be calculated from the `MythicalPerson`'s power, divinity, and goodness. We start off by defining a method called `awesomeness` in `MythicalPerson`'s implementation:

```
- (int)awesomeness
{
  int awesomeness = [[self valueForKey:@"divinity"] intValue] * 10 +
    [[self valueForKey:@"power"] intValue] * 5 +
    [[self valueForKey:@"goodness"] intValue];
  return awesomeness;
}
```

With that in place, you can call the awesomeness method on any `MythicalPerson` and get the result. This also works with Cocoa Bindings of course, so we can easily bind a GUI control's value to this new property. Go back to Interface Builder, make the window and box a little bigger, and add a label and a level indicator from the Library window, something like you see in Figure 7–11.

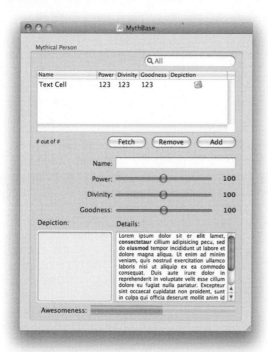

Figure 7–11. *MythBase, now with added Awesomeness!*

Now select the *Awesomeness* control, and bring up the *Attributes Inspector*. Set the *Style* to *Continuous*, and the *Minimum* and *Maximum* to 0 and 1600, respectively. Now switch to the *Bindings Inspector*, and bind the level indicator's *Value* via the *Mythical Person Array Controller*, with the controller key *selection* and the model key *awesomeness*. Note that Interface Builder doesn't know anything about awesomeness, so you'll have to type it in yourself instead of just picking it from the combo box; we're sure you'll agree that's a small price to pay for awesomeness.

Save your changes, switch back to Xcode, *Build & Run*, and off you go. Switch between different rows in the table view, and you'll see the bar of awesomeness change. Drag a slider and, now wait a minute; the awesomeness value doesn't change! The reason for this is that no part of Core Data, not our model file, not our `MythicalPerson` class, not the controller we're using, knows that awesomeness depends on other values, and needs to be recalculated if they change. This is fixed by implementing one more small method in `MythicalPerson`:

```
+ (NSSet *)keyPathsForValuesAffectingAwesomeness {
  return [NSSet setWithObjects:@"divinity", @"power", @"goodness",
    nil];
}
```

This is another method name that's constructed dynamically based on an accessor name. We saw this pattern when validating a single attribute as well. In this method, we return a set of attribute names that our awesomeness attribute is dependent on. With this in place, Core Data will automatically call this method at some point, and sort things out so that changes made to any attributes in the set will also trigger controllers to update any objects with bindings to the awesomeness attribute.

Build and run your app, and now the green bar changes when you drag one of the other sliders. Awesome!

In Conclusion

In this chapter, we've covered a pretty wide range of material about Core Data. You've learned about creating a model file in Xcode, and about using the combo of Core Data and Cocoa Bindings to quickly put together a decent GUI. You've also gotten some idea of the underpinnings of how Core Data stores its data, and learned some basics about implementing your own business logic. In Chapter 8 you'll build on this knowledge, learning how to complete your data models by adding relationships.

Core Data Relationships

In the last chapter, you learned a lot of the basics about how Core Data works, but worked with an extremely simple data model, which contained just a single entity. In this chapter, we're going to show you how to extend your data model to contain multiple entities, and how to define relationships between those entities. You'll also see how to create a GUI that shows these relationships and lets you edit them. Along the way, you'll catch your first glimpse of how Core Data deals with multiple, incompatible versions of your data model, and how it can migrate a data store from one model version to the next.

We'll show you all of this while extending the MythBase project from Chapter 7 to include some data that's often overlooked with discussing mythical heroes and gods: the legendary bands they performed in! The night that *Achilles and the Grecian Formula* shook the Old Parthenon Ballroom to the ground is the stuff of legends, and who could forget *The Four Norsemen*'s farewell concert at the Clontarf Supper Club? The enhancements we'll make to MythBase in this chapter (see Figure 8–1) will help you keep track of this crucial information.

We'll start out by adding all the new entities and relationships we want to our data model, then go on to setting up the GUI that will let us edit everything.

To prepare for the rest of this chapter, go the Finder and make a copy of the last chapter's final MythBase project directory, then go into the new directory and double-click *MythBase.xcodeproj* to open it in Xcode.

Figure 8–1. *The new and improved MythBase application we'll create in this chapter*

Modeling New Entities and Relationships

We're going to be adding three new entities to MythBase: `MythicalBand`, `MythicalGig`, and `MythicalVenue`. We'll also add relationships between several of them. When we're done, our data model will look like Figure 8–2.

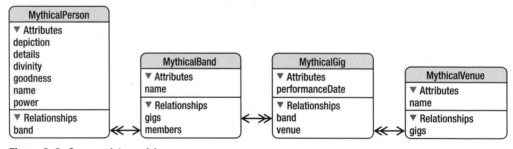

Figure 8–2. *Our new data model*

Model Versioning and Migrations

Before we get started making changes to the data model, there's one important issue that needs to be addressed: migration. We're not talking about people moving from one country to the next, or birds flying south for the winter. We're talking about your data. If you've ever developed a database application, you'll be familiar with the concept of "migrating" data from one deployment version to the next. This typically involves writing some sort of script that makes changes to the database structure itself (adding, deleting, or altering tables and columns) and populates new fields with appropriate values. With Core Data, you don't exactly write a script, but the same idea is in use. In your data store, Core Data saves some metadata about the structure of the data model. When your app runs, Core Data tries to read from the data store. If it determines that the app has a new version of the data model with a different structure, it will automatically update the data store to match the latest data model. Let's see how this works.

Preparing for Multiple Model Versions

The first thing we need to do is convert our current model to a special multi-versioned format. This will allow us to store multiple versions of our data model within our Xcode project as well as within MythBase itself. In Xcode's navigation pane, open the *Models* group and select *MythBase_DataModel.xcdatamodel*. Now select **Design➤Data Model➤Add Model Version** from the menu. You should now see, in the navigation pane, that *MythBase_DataModel.xcdatamodel* has become *MythBase_DataModel.xcdatamodeld*, and has acquired a small disclosure triangle to the left of the name.

Click the triangle to open the contents, and you'll see that it contains two versions of your model file. The one with a "2" tacked onto the end of the filename is the new one where we'll make some changes. Select this new model file, then select **Design➤Data Model➤Set Current Version** from the menu. The next time you build MythBase, this new compound model, containing multiple versions of the model, will be copied into the app, and the app will try to use what you've set as the "current version." Here, a problem can arise: if you just hit build at this point, it will simply copy the new multi-version model into your app, leaving the old, single-version model file there as well! This leads to an error when we run the app and it tries to load all the model files in the bundle, because it will encounter multiple models with the same version metadata (the pre-existing model, and the "version 1" in the multi-version model). The simplest way to get rid of the old model is to select **Build➤Clean** from the menu. Then, the next time you do a normal build (a little later on), you'll be all set.

Adding New Entities

We've decided that we want to be able to keep track of not just the bands that some of our mythical people played in, but also the venues they played at, and even dates of specific gigs, so we're going to add three new entities: MythicalBand, MythicalVenue, and MythicalGig (see Figure 8–3 for an overview).

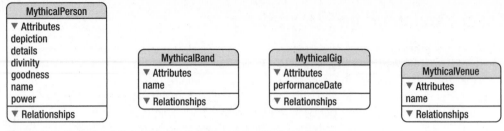

Figure 8–3. *Here are all the entities we'll define, along with their attributes.*

Make sure that the new model file is selected, then create a new entity and name it MythicalBand. Give this entity a new attribute, called "name," set its type to *String*, and click to turn off the *Optional* checkbox and turn on the *Indexed* checkbox.

Now create another new entity named MythicalVenue, also with a single *String* attribute called "name," which should also be *Indexed* but not *Optional*.

Finally, create an entity called MythicalGig. Unlike the other entities we've added, gigs don't have names. The only distinguishing characteristics of a MythicalGig are its relationships to a band and a venue (which we'll get to in a bit) and the date of the performance. Add a new attribute, name it performanceDate, and change its type to **Date**. You can leave the performanceDate set to be *Optional* (since the exact dates of some ancient gigs may have gone down the memory hole), and there's no need to turn on *Indexing* for it either.

Add Relationships

Now it's time to add relationships, so that each object can be attached to other relevant objects. We're going to define a one-to-many relationship from MythicalBand to MythicalPerson, a one-to-many relationship from MythicalBand to MythicalGig, and finally another one-to-many relationship from MythicalVenue to MythicalGig. See Figure 8–4 for an overview.

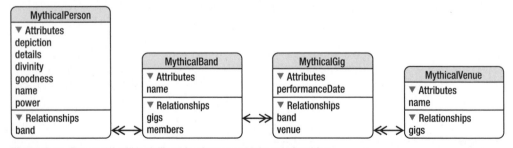

Figure 8–4. *The model will look like this after you add the relationships.*

At this point we should clarify our terminology a bit. In Core Data, each relationship is actually a one-way affair, and they're not defined in terms like "one-to-many," "one-to-one," "many-to-many," and so on. Instead, each Core Data relationship is either "to-one" or "to-many." In order to create what in normal usage (if you accept the notion that any form of computer programmer jargon is "normal") is called a "one-to-many relationship" in Core Data, you actually have to create two relationships: a "to-many" relationship rooted at the first entity and ending at the second, and a "to-one" relationship rooted at the second entity and ending at the first. You then tell specify in your model that these two are inverse relationships, and Core Data then understands the bidirectional nature of what you've configured. This setup allows you, if you wish, to create a relationship that is truly unidirectional, though in practice it's questionable whether that's ever really desirable. The examples in this book all use bidirectional relationships.

So, let's create these relationships, starting with a one-to-many relationship from `MythicalBand` to `MythicalPerson`. Select `MythicalBand`, and click the "+" button below the `Property` table, just as you would for creating an attribute, but this time select **Relationship** from the popup menu. This creates a new relationship, whose configuration options (see Figure 8–5) look a little different than what you've seen when creating attributes.

Figure 8–5. *Configuration options for a new relationship*

You'll see a *Name* field, and checkboxes for *Optional* and *Transient*, but otherwise it's all different. The *Destination* popup lets you choose where the other end of the relationship goes, and after setting that the *Inverse* popup lets you choose which other relationship (if any) should be used to create a bidirectional relationship. A checkbox lets you specify that this is a to-many relationship, and if that's checked, two fields are enabled that let you put handy constraints and the minimum and maximum number of objects may be attached on the other end. Finally, the *Delete Rule* popup lets you decide what should happen to objects at the other end of the relationship if the "source" of the relationship is deleted. The most common choices are *Nullify* (which means that the "source" is removed from any inverse relationship in the "destination" element), *Cascade* (which means that the "destination" object or objects are also deleted), and *Deny* (which means that if this relationship is present, the "source" object will refuse to be deleted at all). A fourth alternative, *No Action*, leaves the inverse relationship intact, leaving the developer with the task of taking care of it (or risk ending up with data integrity problems). We won't use that option at all.

Name the relationship you've just created "`members`," and set its destination entity to `MythicalPerson`. Click to turn on the *To-Many Relationship* checkbox, and leave the *Delete Rule* set to *Nullify* (which is the default value). Congratulations, you've just made your first unidirectional relationship! Doing this simple step gives the `MythicalBand` entity a new `members` property with a whole set of new features. Each band can now provide an array of `MythicalPerson` objects, and that array will be automatically maintained in line with the options you configured. In the graph paper area, you'll see a unidirectional arrow, with a sort of double head, from `MythicalBand` to `MythicalPerson`.

Now let's create the inverse of this relationship. Select the `MythicalPerson` entity, and add a new relationship. Set its destination entity to `MythicalBand`, and then set its inverse to `members`. The rest of the default values can be left as they are. You'll now see a bidirectional arrow between `MythicalPerson` and `MythicalBand`, with a single head at the band end.

Let's move on to the one-to-many relationship between `MythicalBand` and `MythicalGig`. Select `MythicalBand`, create a new relationship named "gigs," with `MythicalGig` as its destination, and the *To-Many Relationship* checked. Because a gig without a band doesn't do us any good, set the *Delete Rule* to *Cascade*. That way, if a band is deleted, all its gigs will be deleted, too. Now select `MythicalGig` and make a new relationship called "band," with `MythicalBand` as its destination, and select `gigs` as its inverse relationship. Here, we can leave the *Delete Rule* set to its default value, *Nullify*. This simply means that if a gig is deleted, any trace of the gig on remaining end of the relationship to the band will be wiped out, but the band itself will be left intact.

Finally, it's time for the one-to-many relationship between `MythicalVenue` and `MythicalGigs`. Select `MythicalVenue`, create a new relationship named "gigs," with `MythicalGig` as its destination, and the *To-Many Relationship* checked. Because a gig without a venue is just as meaningless as a gig without a band, here we'll also set the *Delete Rule* to *Cascade*, so deleting a venue will also delete all its gigs. Now select `MythicalGig` and make a new relationship called "venue," with `MythicalVenue` as its destination, and select `gigs` as its inverse relationship.

You've now created all the relationships we're going to need for the new version of MythBase, and your model should look similar to what you saw in Figure 8–4, a couple of pages ago.

Creating a Simple Migration

Assuming that you've previously gone through Chapter 7, and used that version of MythBase to save some data, running the new version at this stage will give you some problems. You'll see some error messages about mismatched data store versions when you start up, and you'll get nothing but an empty table view where the `MythicalPerson` objects you created previously should be. And if you add some new objects and try to save them, you'll just get more errors! The reason for this is that the current version of your app's data model differs quite a bit from the version that was used to save the data previously, and Core Data is smart enough to detect this, let our app delegate know about it, and prevent us from overwriting the old version with new data. Not only that, but it's also smart enough to automatically "upgrade" an existing data store to work with our new model version, but only after we create a migration.

Core Data migrations are centered around files called *mapping models*, which are created and configured right in Xcode. For simple things like adding new empty tables and optional attributes, no particular configuration is necessary, we just create a mapping model and its default configuration does all the work. If you're creating a required attribute, or new tables that need to be populated with existing data, you can define some mappings in Xcode that will populate values for you. For more complex data manipulations, you can write Objective-C code to handle aspects of your migration, and this code will be automatically run when the migration occurs. In this example, we'll get by with just a simple mapping model without any extra configuration at all.

Right-click (or control-click) the *Models* group in the Xcode navigation pane, and select **Add▸New File** from the contextual menu. In the window that comes up, choose *Mapping Model* from inside the *Cocoa* section, and click *Next*. Name your new mapping model *MythBase_1_to_2.xcmappingmodel* and click *Next*. The next window shows you an overview of your project's groups and files, similar to the main navigation pane, and asks you to set the source and destination models. Click your way into your multi-version model file (inside the *Models* group), select the first version and click *Set Source Model*, and then select the new version and click *Set Destination Model* (see Figure 8–6).

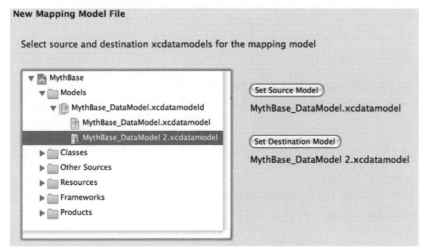

Figure 8–6. *We've specified the versions we want to migrate between.*

Then click *Finish*, and you'll be taken back to your Xcode project window, with the new mapping model selected in the navigation pane. The editor for the mapping model is a complicated-looking set of views that we're not really going to explore at this point. It gives you a set of views that are somewhat reminiscent of the upper part of the Xcode data model editor (see Figure 8–7). On the left you have a table showing all entities, to the right of that you have a table showing all the selected entity's properties, both attributes and relationships, and a third view shows the details for the last selected entity or property.

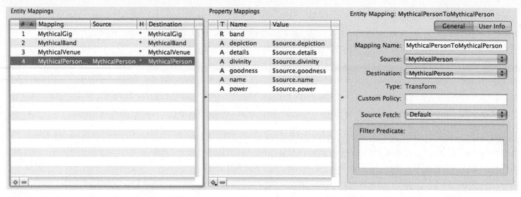

Figure 8–7. *Xcode's view of a mapping model, showing mapping details for the MythicalPerson entity*

Feel free to click around on the various entities and properties to see what the configuration GUI looks like, but stop short of editing any of the configuration options! The default values here are just what we need.

Time to Run

Before we're ready to go further, we need to make one small change to the application's source code. In the current version, the app tries to load data from its data store, and if the structure of the stored data doesn't match the structure described in the latest version of the data model, problems will occur, and the app will show the user an error. To fix this, and make the application upgrade the data store, all we need to do is pass in a configuration option to the method that loads the data store. Open up *MythBase_AppDelegate.m*, and locate the persistentStoreCoordinator method. Toward the end of that method, you'll see a group of lines that look like this:

```
if (![persistentStoreCoordinator addPersistentStoreWithType:NSXMLStoreType
    configuration:nil
    URL:url
    options:nil
    error:&error]){
```

What we're going to do is create a dictionary of options to pass along in that method call. This dictionary contains a single key-value pair, which tells the store coordinator that it should try to update existing data to match the current data model. Replace the lines shown above with the following:

```
NSDictionary *optionsDictionary =
    [NSDictionary dictionaryWithObject:[NSNumber numberWithBool:YES]
    forKey:NSMigratePersistentStoresAutomaticallyOption];
if (![persistentStoreCoordinator addPersistentStoreWithType:NSXMLStoreType
    configuration:nil
    URL:url
    options:optionsDictionary
    error:&error]){
```

With the above in place, you should be able to build and run your application, and it will "just work!" You'll see the old data that you had previously stored with the Chapter 7 version of MythBase, now converted to our app's newest data model. Of course, you won't see any of the new entities we've created in the model—in fact, if all goes according to plan, you won't *see* anything different from Chapter 7 at all—but the underlying structure has now been modified to include the new entities and relationships.

So how did that happen? You may recall, from Chapter 7, the following method call in MythBase_AppDelegate's persistentStoreCoordinator method:

```
[persistentStoreCoordinator addPersistentStoreWithType:NSXMLStoreType
                            configuration:nil
                            URL:url
                            options:optionsDictionary
                            error:&error]
```

It may not be obvious, but that method call is what triggers the data migration to occur. When the code shown previously is executed, what normally happens is that the data store is opened up and prepared for use. However, if the structure of the data store doesn't match the structure of the coordinator's data model (which is the current version we specified in Xcode), then a whole different chain of events takes place. Core Data will look for the existence (within the app's bundle) of a mapping model that can convert the data store from the old structure to the new structure. In our case, MythBase now contains that mapping model, so the migration is performed automatically, with the old data file first being backed up in case something goes terribly wrong. Thanks to this automatic procedure, our users don't need to worry about importing or converting data. When they run a new version of our app, their previously stored data is converted automatically and, except in the case of a really huge data store, quickly.

Updating the GUI

Now that we have our updated data model ready to go, it's time to move on to create the GUI. We're going to leave the existing window almost intact, and add a couple of new windows, one focused on MythicalBands, and one focused on MythicalVenues.

Create the Band Window

First, we'll create a new window to show a list of MythicalBands. Open up *MainMenu.xib* in InterfaceBuilder, and create a new NSWindow. Use the *Attributes Inspector* to name this window *Mythical Bands*. We're going to use Xcode's built-in Core Data GUI creation assistant again, so switch back to Xcode. Bring up the latest version of the data model, and ⌥drag the MythicalBand entity from the graph paper area to the new window you just created in Interface Builder (remember, if you can't see that new window after you've started dragging, you can switch back to Interface Builder by pressing ⌘Tab). When you release the entity over the window, you'll see the *New Core Data Entity Interface* assistant appear, just like when you started creating the GUI for Chapter 7. Select *Master/Detail View* from the popup list, and click to enable the *Search Field* and *Add/Remove* checkboxes (this time leaving the *Details Fields* checkbox unchecked), then click *Next*. The next window asks which attributes we want to display. Now our

MythicalBand entity has some relationships, and we don't want to display those just yet, so turn off the *members* and *gigs* checkboxes, and click *Finish*.

Now you'll have a fresh new GUI in your window, very similar to what was created for the MythicalPerson entity in Chapter 7. This window is going to be focused on the bands, and even has *Mythical Bands* as its title, so let's lose the box surrounding all the stuff that was created for us: Click on the box title (which is also *Mythical Bands*) and select **Layout▸Unembed Objects** from the menu. Then select the window by clicking its title bar, and select **Layout▸Size To Fit** from the menu, which shrinks the window to make it precisely fit the content, and finally delete the unnecessary *Fetch* button. The resulting window should now look like Figure 8–8.

Figure 8–8. *The beginnings of the Mythical Band window*

Now save your changes, switch to Xcode, and *Build & Run* the app. You'll see that the new window appears, and that you can add some bands, edit their names directly in the table view, and save your changes.

Giving Useful Names to Array Controllers

So, you now have two windows, each focused on a single entity, but so far have no way of connecting the two together. We're going to address this in a moment, but before we do, there's a change you should make in your nib file that will be helpful when configuring the new bindings we're about to create.

Each time we've created a piece of the GUI by dragging in an entity from Xcode's data modeler, the "assistant" creates an NSArrayController whose visible name (the name that appears within Interface Builder) defaults to something like *<entity name> Array Controller*, in our case *Mythical Person Array Controller* and *Mythical Band Array Controller*. As you may have noticed when connecting some of the bindings in Chapter 7, these names seem a bit longer than what Interface Builder is really designed to show. They barely fit into the popup buttons in the *Bindings Inspector*, and they make all of the summary info shown for each bound attribute overflow, with some of its text being replaced with ellipses (see Figure 8–9).

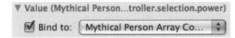

Figure 8–9. *Lengthy names for our array controllers make it harder to see what we're dealing with. This is the Value binding for one of the sliders in our GUI.*

You can improve this situation by changing the names of your controllers. Changing the names won't modify any of the bindings you've configured, or change anything for your application's users. The only one who'll see the change at all is you, but remember that you're important, too. Just as it's important to format your source code in such a way that it's easy for you to scan through it and find what you need, doing what you can to streamline your editing experience in Interface Builder will save you time and frustration.

So, go to the main nib window, make sure you're looking at the icon view (the left-most icon in the row of small icons at the upper left should be selected), and find your *Mythical Person Array Controller*. Click on its name, and change it to just *Persons*. Do the same for *Mythical Band Array Controller*, changing its name to *Bands*. Doing this will eliminate a lot of words (e.g. "Mythical," "Array," and "Controller") that are otherwise spread a bit too liberally throughout your nib file, and leave you with a display that's hopefully easier for your eyes and brain to scan and comprehend quickly (see Figure 8–10).

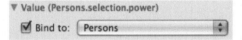

Figure 8–10. *Renaming our array controllers lets us see the information we need in a slightly more compact way. This is the same binding that was shown in Figure 8–9, after changing the array controller's name.*

Putting People in Bands

Now let's make it possible to attach a person to a band by adding a simple popup button to the MythicalPerson display, which will let you pick a MythicalBand for the selected MythicalPerson. The popup button will be connected through Cocoa Bindings, which means that besides always being automatically updated to show the correct value for the selected person (just like the other controls do), it will also be automatically updated to always show the current list of bands, changing its content automatically as the user makes changes in the *Mythical Bands* window. This will be done by configuring a few bindings on the popup button, using both the *Persons* and *Bands* controllers.

Let's start off by making a change to our original window, so that it better matches the new one. Open up the original window (the one with *MythBase* in the title), select the box (entitled *Mythical Person*) that contains all the window's controls and views, and then select **Layout▶Unembed Objects** from the menu, just like we did for the *Mythical Bands* window. Then select the window by clicking its title, and use the *Attributes Inspector* to rename it *Mythical People*. This way, the two windows have the same general appearance. Each is centered around a particular entity, but neither of them has any distinction as the "main window."

Now, select all the views in the upper part of the window (all the sliders and their labels, and everything above them) and drag them up a bit, then select everything below the sliders and drag it all down a bit. In the space between, drag out a label (name it *Member of Band:*) and a popup button from the library. Line it all up so it looks roughly like Figure 8–11.

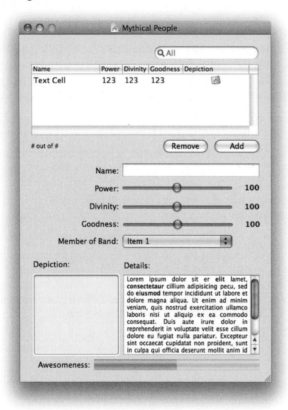

Figure 8–11. *The new and improved Mythical People window*

All that's left now is to configure some bindings for the popup button. Unlike a text field or a slider, the popup button's display needs several bindings in order to make it behave in a useful way. Consider that a popup button needs to have an array of strings to display (we're going to display all available band names here), an array of underlying objects that those strings belong to (the bands themselves), and something to indicate which item in the list is selected (through the selected person's band relationship). The first two of those will be bound via the *Bands* controller, through which we can easily bind to an array of all bands, or all band names. The third will be bound via the *Persons* controller.

Start by selecting the popup button, and opening the *Bindings Inspector*. Open the configuration for the *Content* binding at the top of the list, select *Bands* in the popup list, *arrangedObjects* for the *Controller Key*, and click the checkbox. This tells the popup button where to find the list of underlying objects.

Next, open the configuration for the *Content Values* binding. Once again select *Bands* in the popup list, *arrangedObjects* for the *Controller Key*, and this time pick *name* for the *Model Key Path*. This tells the popup button that it should populate its displayed values by grabbing the same array (*arrangedObjects*) and using the result of asking each for its *name*.

Finally, open the *Selected Object* binding configuration. Here, you should choose *Persons* from the popup list, *selection* for the *Controller Key*, and *band* for the *Model Key Path*. The popup list will automatically connect things so that when the *Persons* controller's selection changes, the popup will notice the new selection's band, look that up in the array of *Content* (which it picks up from the *Bands* controller), and display the corresponding string from the *Content Values* array (also from the *Bands* controller). Verify that this works by saving your changes, hitting **Build & Run** in Xcode, and trying it out. You should see that for each `MythicalPerson` you pick, you can select a `MythicalBand` to attach them to (see Figure 8–12).

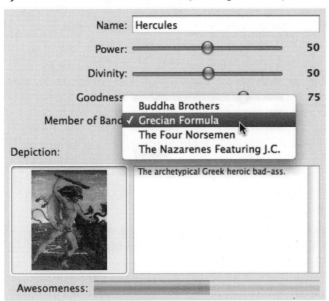

Figure 8–12. *Setting Hercules as a member of the band Grecian Formula*

Showing the Bands' Members

Now that we can add people to a band, how about being able to see a list of all the members in a band? Let's add that to the *Mythical Bands* window. We won't use any sort of assistant for this, instead we'll manually add a table view and an array controller and hook it all up.

Start by grabbing an NSArrayController from the *Library*, and dragging it to your main nib window. Just like we've done with the other array controllers, we want to give this controller a name that is short but meaningful. This controller is going to handle a list of MythicalPersons, but we've already got an array controller called *Persons*, and anyway we want to make it easy to see that there's some context to this (it will only show people that are members of the selected band), so let's name this one *BandMembers* in the main nib window.

Then, with the new array controller still selected, open the *Attributes Inspector*, and in the *Object Controller* section set the *Mode* to *Entity*, and the *Entity Name* to MythicalPerson. Click to turn on the *Prepares Content* checkbox. This ensures that the controller's content is fetched automatically when the nib loads.

Now switch to the *Bindings Inspector*, where we're going to configure two bindings that will let this controller automatically get its content based on the selected MythicalBand. First, at the very bottom, open up the configuration for *Managed Object Context*. Choose *MythBase_AppDelegate* in the popup, and *managedObjectContext* for the *Model Key Path*, which should automatically turn on the *Bind To* checkbox. This configuration is the same as for all our array controllers, and allows them to connect to the Core Data storage. Next, in the *Controller Content* section, open up the *Content Set* binding configuration, and choose *Bands* in the popup, *selection* for the *Controller Key*, and *members* for the *Model Key Path*. Doing so makes the controller's content dependent on the selected band.

Now, bring up the *Mythical Bands* window, and make it a bit taller, almost twice as high, so that we can fit another table view beneath the current content. Then drag over a table view from the *Library*, and click on it to select the table view itself (instead of the scroll view containing it, which is what is selected by default just after the drag). We're only going to show the names of the band members here, so we only need one column in this table. Bring up the *Attributes Inspector*, find the *Columns* setting and change it to 1. Then make the column heading nicer, like you've done in previous chapters, by setting its title to *Member Name* and making it fill the width of the table. Finally, top it all off with a *Band Members* label, so the users know what they're looking at. Figure 8–13 shows approximately what you should see at this point.

Now all that's left is configure a binding for that column. Start by selecting the column. Remember, you may have to click several times to drill down to just the right depth. One handy way to avoid all this extra clicking is to control-shift-click on the column. Doing so brings up a special menu, showing the list of all the view objects at the spot you clicked: the column, and each of its superviews. Now bring up the *Bindings Inspector*. Open the *Value* configuration, select *BandMembers* in the popup, *arrangedObjects* in the *Controller Key*, and *name* in the *Model Key Path*, turning on the *Bind To* check box. Then save your work, hit **Build & Run** in Xcode, and you'll see the new functionality: specifying a band for a person will add that person to the band's members array, which you'll see when you select the band in the *Mythical Band* window.

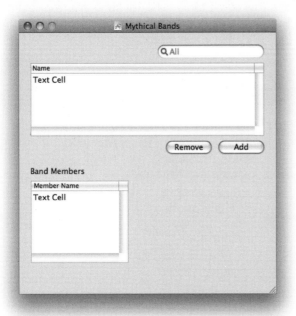

Figure 8–13. *Adding band members to the Mythical Bands window*

Create a Venue Window

Now it's time to create one more window, for displaying and editing MythicalVenues, once again using the "assistant." First go back to Interface Builder and create another empty window. Then switch back to the model file in Xcode, and ⌥-drag the MythicalVenue entity over to the new window you just created (don't forget about ⌘Tab). Once again, the *New Core Data Entity Interface* assistant appears. Select *Master/Detail View* from the popup list, and click to enable the *Search Field* and *Add/Remove* checkboxes (again leaving the *Details Fields* checkbox unchecked), then click *Next*. The next window asks which attributes we want to display. Turn off the *gigs* checkboxes, and click *Finish*.

Finish off this window by removing the labeled NSBox that contains all its content, because we really don't need it. Just select the box by clicking its title, then select **Layout**▸**Unembed Objects** from the menu. Save your work, **Build & Run** in Xcode, and verify that you can add venues and edit their names.

Adding a Gig List to the Band Window

The final piece of functionality we need to add is the ability to create MythicalGigs. MythicalGigs sit between MythicalBands and MythicalVenues, each of which may have multiple gigs. Gigs, meanwhile, each have exactly one band and one venue. We'll add another table view to contain the needed functionality, placed beside the members table view in the *Mythical Band* window. Each row of the table view will contain a text field for displaying and entering the gig's `performanceDate`, and a popup button for selecting the venue (see Figure 8–14).

Figure 8–14. *This is what the final Mythical Bands window will look like.*

Start by finding an `NSArrayController` in the *Library*, dragging it to the main nib window, and naming it *Gigs*. Open the *Attributes Inspector*, set *Mode* to *Entity* and enter `MythicalGigs` for the *Entity Name*, then click to turn on the *Prepares Content* checkbox.

Now switch to the *Bindings Inspector*. Bind the new array controller's *Managed Object Context* to *MythBase_AppDelegate*'s *managedObjectContext*, and bind its *Content Set* through *Bands*, with *Controller Key* set to *selection*, and *Model Key Path* set to *gigs*.

Next, we're going to set up the GUI itself. Drag another table view from the *Library* to the *Mythical Bands* window, along with a *Gigs* label, and lay them out as shown in Figure 8–14. This table view is going to display one column of dates, and one column of popup lists showing the selected venue for each gig. Let's start with the left column. First, change its title to *Date*, then select the column itself (below the header) and bring up the *Bindings Inspector* again. Bind the column's *Value* through the *Gigs* controller, with *Controller Key* set to *arrangedObjects* and *Model Key Path* set to *performanceDate*.

Now, this column contains dates, so it would be nice to use a date picker here, like we used in Chapter 4, but unfortunately the `NSDatePickerCell` isn't quite up to the task (it's not really meant for use in a table view). Fortunately, we can get some satisfaction here by using an NSDateFormatter. Find one of those in the *Library*, and drag it out over the *Date* column you're working on (in fact, you need to drag it precisely over the NSTextFieldCell at the top of the column). The date formatter will do the work of converting between dates and strings for you, but we want to configure it a bit. Because we're dealing with mythological events, some of the dates are BC-era, and by default the date formatter doesn't show BC or AD. To change this, click on the text field cell in the column until you see a small bronze icon appear just below it. That icon represents the formatter attached to the column. Click on it, and then open the *Attributes Inspector*.

At the top of the *Inspector*, click on the *Behavior* popup and change it to *Mac OS X 10.4+ Custom*, which will allow us to define the formatting. The format is shown as a row of pale blue "pills," each containing an element of a date (month, year, and so on), and below that are shown more date elements that can also be shown. Drag the *Era* box out to the end of the format, and that column is done.

The final column is for specifying the venue, and here we'll configure a popup button, similar to what we did for picking a band in the *Mythical Person* window. First set the column's title to *Venue*, then find an NSPopupButtonCell in the *Library* and drag it out over the column. You'll now need to configure three bindings for the column. First, bind *Content* to the *Venues* controller's *arrangedObjects*. Next, bind *ContentValues* to the *Venues* controller's *arrangedObject*, this time specifying *name* for the *Model Key Path*. And last but not least, bind the *Selected Object* to the *Gigs* controller's *arrangedObjects*, using *venue* as the *Model Key Path*.

The final step is setting up *Add* and *Remove* buttons, so the user can create and delete gigs. Duplicate the two buttons in the upper part of the window, and drag the new ones down below the table view of gigs. Control-drag from the *Add* button to the *Gigs* controller and select the add: action, then Ctrl-drag from the *Remove* button to the *Gigs* controller and select the remove: action. As a final touch, we can make these buttons automatically enable and disable themselves appropriately as the table view's content and selection change, using some simple bindings. Select the *Add* button, open the *Bindings Inspector*, and bind its *Enabled* attribute to the *Gigs* controller's *canAdd* controller key. Then select the *Remove* button, and bind it to the *Gigs* controller's *canRemove* controller key.

Now save your work, **Build & Run** in Xcode, and behold! Assuming that everything's configured correctly, you should now be able to add gigs to each band's info.

Wrapping Up Relationships

In this chapter, you've expanded the old data model, growing it from a single entity on its own to a full complement of entities, interrelated with relationships. You've also seen how each of those relationships can be expressed in a GUI (for example, using a popup list to choose the remote end of a to-one relationship, and a table view to show all the contents of a to-many relationship), configured, and managed entirely with Cocoa Bindings. Not to beat a dead horse about this "visual programming" business, but it bears repeating that everything in this chapter was done without a single line of code on our part.

NOTE: Our use of the term "visual programming" has nothing to do with Microsoft's use of the word "visual" in its development tools. The idea behind visual programming is to allow a program, or some portion of it, to be constructed using graphical components that don't require the sort of textual, procedural programming that's traditionally been used for writing software. Cocoa embraces visual programming to some extent, letting you put together application prototypes or even entire applications using just the Xcode data modeler and Interface Builder. However, it's not intended to comprise a complete visual programming system, so for every Cocoa app you build, you will out of necessity have to break down and write some code!

Furthermore, these usage patterns can be applied equally well to your own applications. Just the act of modeling your problem domain, defining entities and relationships, can often start giving you a sense of how to build your GUI. As you get farther along in the application development process, you're sure to find more ways to connect different kinds of controls to your data using Cocoa Bindings, and will sometimes find a need to supplement that by writing code to connect things and shuffle data between objects.

As you work through the rest of this book, you'll see several more examples of applications that use Core Data and Cocoa Bindings as core parts of their architectures, so you'll see even more approaches to using these technologies. The next chapter, Searching and Retrieving Core Data, is the last chapter dealing exclusively with Core Data, showing you how to limit the extent of what you're showing in your GUI, an absolute necessity for any application work with a large set of data.

Chapter 9

Search and Retrieve Core Data with Criteria

In the MythBase examples in Chapters 7 and 8, you learned the basics of how Core Data works, letting you create, retrieve, update, and delete objects from a backing store with a minimum of fuss. So far, we've been working primarily with full data sets in MythBase. For most of the entities we've used (MythicalPerson, MythicalBand, and MythicalVenue), all the objects for each entity are loaded during application startup, and kept in memory for the entire life of the application. That's okay for an application like MythBase, which maintains a small database, but what if one of your main entities consists of thousands or millions of instances in a backing store? Your app would load everything from storage when the app launches, which would probably lead to the app filling up all available memory, swapping to disk, and so on. Apart from that problem, you'd also probably end up with a bad user experience, because a GUI that's navigable when it's displaying twenty objects in a table view may become impossible to use effectively when there are thousands of entries.

The solution to this problem involves an important piece of functionality: a way to provide some search criteria so that we can limit the objects pulled out of storage by a controller. In this chapter, we'll introduce you to the use of NSPredicate to restrict searches to just a subset of all the objects for a given Entity. You'll see how to specify a "hard-coded" NSPredicate, both in Interface Builder and in your source code, and you'll also see how to let your users define the values for a predicate using NSPredicateEditor.

Creating QuoteMonger

We'll demonstrate the use of NSPredicate by creating an app called QuoteMonger, which allows you to keep track of all your favorite shows, and famous quotes from them. This will be a Core Data application with two entities, and a GUI made partly by using the assistant that appears when dragging an entity from Xcode to Interface

Builder, and partly by setting things up all on our own. Figure 9-1 shows you a view of the completed application.

Figure 9-1. *QuoteMonger's data entry and search windows*

> **NOTE:** By the time you've gotten this far in the book, you should have gained some experience with the basics of creating Xcode projects and files, so we're not going to continue giving exact click-by-click instructions for some of the things you've already done several times, instead reserving the highest level of detail for the new topics we're covering in each chapter.

Create the Project and Its Data Model

Start by creating a new Core Data project in Xcode, and naming it QuoteMonger. Then edit the *QuoteMonger_DataModel.xcdatamodel*, and add two entities called Show and Quote.

Give Show a single attribute called name, of type String. Turn off the *Optional* checkbox, and turn on the *Indexed* checkbox. Then give Quote two String attributes called quoteText and character. For each of those, turn on the *Indexed* checkbox, but only turn off the *Optional* checkbox for quoteText, leaving it on for character (because it's conceivable that you can't quite remember or determine who said something, but want to store it as a quote anyway).

Finally, make a one-to-many relationship from Show to Quote (remember, that means making two relationships: a to-many from Show to Quote called quotes, and a to-one from Quote to Show called show, and configuring them to be each other's inverse). The resulting data model should look like something like Figure 9-2.

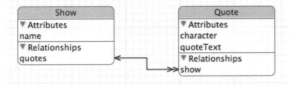

Figure 9-2. *The data model for QuoteMonger*

The Data Entry Window

With the data model in place, it's time to start building the GUI. The interesting part, which this chapter is mostly about, is the search window. But, we can't do any searching until we have some data to search, so we'll start by creating the portion of the GUI that lets us do data entry. We're going to make a very basic GUI for this, using our old friend, the *New Core Data Entity Interface* assistant, modifying things just slightly so that shows and quotes are displayed in a single window, and that only quotes that are tied to the currently selected show are displayed.

A Two-Part Autogenerated Window

Double-click *MainMenu.xib* in your Xcode project to open it in Interface Builder. This brings up the standard empty application nib you've learned to deal with before. Select the NSWindow instance in the main nib window, and use the resizing control to make it taller, about twice as tall as it started out. We'll need this space, because we're going to put two sets of views in here, one for the Show entity and one for the Quote entity.

Now go back to the data model editor in Xcode, and ⌥-drag the Show entity over to the empty window in Interface Builder (don't forget, you can ⌘Tab to switch back to Interface Builder during the drag). When you release the drag, the *New Core Data Entity Interface* assistant will appear. Choose *Master/Detail View*, click to turn on the *Add/Remove Buttons* checkbox, then click *Next*. Then, in the list of properties to include, click to turn off quotes, leaving just name enabled, and click *Finish*. In the new GUI that's created, select and delete the Fetch button. The new GUI is placed directly in the center of the window; drag it upwards, into the upper half of the window.

NOTE: If you're using Leopard, the auto-generated nib file has its *# out of #* textfield somewhat out of place, tucked away behind the table view, so you'll need to dig it out if you want to see it in the GUI. Select the table view, then select **Layout▶Send To Back** from the menu, then drag the *# out of #* textfield down to line it up with the other buttons.

Now do the same set of things for the *Quote* entity, dragging it to the window as well. When it comes time to select properties to include, turn off show, leaving character and quoteText enabled. Everything else should be done just the same. After the GUI has been created, drag the new box down a bit so you can see both sets of views. Figure 9-3 shows what the window should look like now.

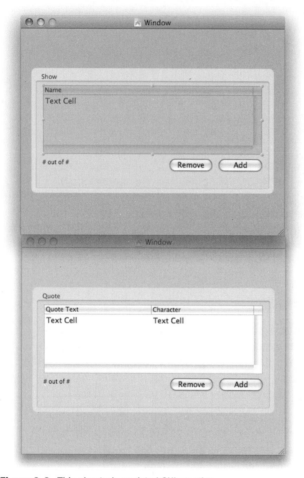

Figure 9-3. *This chapter's assisted GUI creation*

Smoothing Out the Rough Spots

Now we're going to rearrange things a bit so that our window looks a little more orderly, and configure the array controllers so that the display of quotes is dependent on the selected show. Start by dragging the NSBox labeled *Quote* from the other window into position below the *Show* box, using the blue guidelines to help align the two. Then, select the window by clicking its title bar, and make it just the right size to show its content by selecting **Layout▶Size To Fit** from the menu, ending up with the much more compact result shown in Figure 9-4.

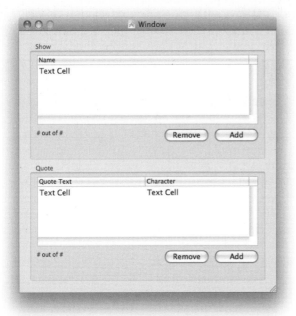

Figure 9-4. *The data entry window for QuoteMonger*

Complete the window configuration by opening the *Attributes Inspector* and setting the window's title to *Data Entry*.

Now, let's configure the array controllers a bit. Like before, our friendly assistant has given them some unwieldy names, *Show Array Controller* and *Quote Array Controller*. Edit each of those in the main nib window, changing them to *Shows* and *Quotes*, respectively. Now, select the *Quotes* controller, and open the *Bindings Inspector*. By default, each array controller will fetch all objects for the corresponding entity. We're going to change this one to only fetch quotes based on the selected Show. Open the *Content Set* binding, select *Shows* in the popup list, *selection* in the *Controller Key* combo box, and type in *quotes* in the *Model Key Path* combo box. Finally press Return to turn on the binding.

Enter Some Initial Quotes

Save your changes, switch back to Xcode, and click **Build & Run**. The app should start up and show you the *Data Entry* window. Select the Add button below the upper table view to add a show, and double-click in the highlighted space in the table view to edit the show's name. Do this a few times to create a few Show instances. Now, with one of the shows selected, add a quote in the lower table, editing the text and the names of any characters right into the table. If you add a quote that contains an exchange between two or more characters, enter the names of all involved characters in the Character field. When we later enable search based on character names, it will work with all the names you entered. Add a few more quotes, spread across a few different shows. You'll see that the list of quotes changes when you select a different show, and if you quit and restart QuoteMonger, you should see that everything you entered has been saved.

Creating the Quote Finder Window

Now it's time to lay the foundation for the search window. Once again, we'll use our friendly assistant to start things out, but from then on we'll be making lots of changes. Back in Interface Builder, find the window that was left empty after its contents were moved to the other window and bring it to the front. Then go back to Xcode again, and ⌥-drag the Quote entity back to the empty window in Interface Builder. Select *Master/Detail View* (just like we always do), but this time leave all the checkboxes turned off, and just click *Next*. In the list of properties to include, turn off show, leaving just character and quoteText, then click *Finish*. As ever, the generated view includes a # *out of* # text field, which in this case we don't want, so you should select and delete it. If you're running Leopard and can't see the text field (because it's hiding behind the table view), then select the table view, select **Layout▸Send To Back** from the menu, then select and delete the text field.

We don't want to include the NSBox in our layout, so select the box, and then select **Layout▸Unembed Objects** from the menu. Set the window's title to *Quote Finder*, and rename the new array controller in your main nib window, probably called *Quote Array Controller*, to *FoundQuotes*.

A few adjustments need to be made to the table view. First of all, we don't want any of the retrieved values to be editable here. This window is for search and display only. So bring up the *Attributes Inspector*, then select each of the table columns and click to disable the *Editable* button in the *Inspector*. We also want to display the show that each found quote belongs to, so add a column to the table view by duplicating one of the existing ones. Set the new column's title (in the *Attributes Inspector*) to *Show*, and configure its *Value* binding (in the *Bindings Inspector*) to use the *FoundQuotes* controller, with arrangedObjects as the *Controller Key* and show.name as the *Model Key Path*. Make the table view a bit wider, and resize one or more of the columns so that they all fit.

Now make the window a bit taller, drag out an NSTextView from the *Library*, line it up beneath the table view, and resize it to match (see Figure 9-5). This text view will show the full quote of the selected item. Click to select the NSTextView (not the NSScrollView that contains it), turn off the *Editable* and *Rich Text* checkboxes in the *Attributes Inspector*, then switch back to the *Bindings Inspector* and configure the text view's *Value* binding with *FoundQuotes*, *selection*, and *quoteText*.

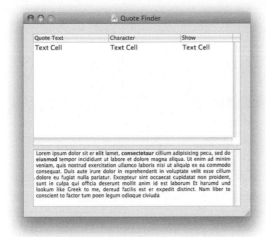

Figure 9-5. *First pass at the Query Finder window*

We also need to make one change to the *FoundQuotes* controller, so that it will correctly reload and refilter its contents whenever the user makes changes in the *Quotes* controller. Select *FoundQuotes*, and bring up the Inspector Panel. Click to turn on the *Auto Rearrange Content* checkbox to enable this option.

Now switch back to Xcode, click **Build & Run**, and you'll see that you now have two windows. The new Query Finder window simply shows all quotes you've entered with the data entry window. The rest of this chapter will show you how to change that using an NSPredicate, so that only the quotes a user searches for show up in this window.

Limiting Results with NSPredicate

As we've already mentioned, you can limit which records an NSArrayController prepares for display by using an NSPredicate. You can assign a predicate to an array controller directly in Interface Builder; from within your application code during initialization or whenever conditions change, warranting a refetch; or through Cocoa Bindings, which means that changes to a predicate can be automatically propagated to a controller. We'll explore all of these options in this chapter.

Creating Predicates

The simplest way to create an NSPredicate is by using a format string containing attribute names, comparators, and values to compare against. The definition of a predicate looks a lot like a WHERE clause in SQL, and serves much the same purpose. Predicates are not limited to just Core Data usage, and can be applied to other areas of Mac OS X such as Spotlight. In its most basic form, you can define an NSPredicate like this:

```
NSPredicate *p = [NSPredicate predicateWithFormat:
    @"(quoteText CONTAINS[cd] 'missed') OR "
    "(character CONTAINS[cd] 'kramer') OR "
    "(show.name CONTAINS[cd] 'trek')"];
```

> **NOTE:** In C, if you have multiple inline string constants in your code separated only by whitespace (including carriage returns) they will all be concatenated together into a single character array, which can help format long strings in your code. This trick works equally well for inline `NSString` constants, just put a single @-symbol before the first string, as shown previously.

In this example, we actually have three conditions, joined together by ORs, and wrapped in parentheses just like you might do in application code. Each of these conditions uses the `CONTAINS` comparator (which does exactly what you might guess), with some options specified inside square brackets. The c makes the comparison case-insensitive, while the d makes the comparison diacritic-insensitive. An equality comparison specifying both, for example, will consider "ramon" and "Ramón" to be equal.

`CONTAINS` is just one of several comparators available within the predicate. All attributes can use the =, <, >, >=, <=, !=, and `BETWEEN` comparators. (Note that ==, =>, =<, and <> are equivalent to =, >=, <=, and !=, respectively.) String attributes can use the `BEGINSWITH`, `CONTAINS`, `ENDSWITH`, `LIKE`, and `MATCHES` comparators.

> **NOTE:** These should mostly be self-explanatory, with a couple of notable exceptions: `BETWEEN` lets you specify a pair of lower and upper bounds, so the value to the right of it should be substituted in with a two-item `NSArray`; `LIKE` lets you do wildcard matching, and `MATCHES` lets you use regular expressions to do advanced comparisons. However, the last of those, `MATCHES`, doesn't work with an SQLite backend, so it's not much use when fetching values from a Core Data store.

The hard-coded option is fine if you really need a fixed query for some special purpose in your application, but sometimes you'll want to create a query based on user input or other current data. Fortunately, the `NSPredicate` class provides an easy way to interpolate values, using the same `predicateWithFormat:` method you just saw. For example:

```
// Assume these variables exist and point at valid objects
NSString *quoteInput;
NSString *characterInput;
NSString *showNameInput;
NSPredicate *p = [NSPredicate predicateWithFormat:
    @"(quoteText CONTAINS[cd] %@) OR "
    "(character CONTAINS[cd] %@) OR "
    "(show.name CONTAINS[cd] %@)",
    quoteInput, characterInput, showNameInput];
```

When that code runs, the values of the three variables will be put into the resulting predicate. Note that the %@ markers in the format string are not surrounded by single-quotes, as the bare values were in the previous example.

Specifying an NSAppController's Predicate in Interface Builder

Let's try one of the most basic ways to put a predicate to use: attaching it directly to a controller in Interface Builder. Go back to your *MainMenu.xib* file in Interface Builder, select the *FoundQuotes* controller in the main nib window, and bring up the *Attributes Inspector*. At the bottom, you'll see a text view labeled Fetch Predicate, where you can simply add some text to define a predicate. Try entering this:

```
show.name CONTAINS[cd] 'trek'
```

Then save your changes, switch back to Xcode, and click **Build & Run**. Now the search window won't necessarily show all the quotes you've entered. If you've entered some *Star Trek* quotes, it will show only those, but if you haven't entered any *Star Trek* quotes, you'll now see nothing in the search window. Of course, it's possible you've *only* entered *Star Trek* quotes, in which case this view will be just the same as it was before. In that case, enter some quotes from another show, to verify that the predicate is filtering them out (and also because, really, there's more to television than just *Star Trek*).

User-Defined Predicates

The nib-defined predicate is fine for special uses, where some part of your GUI should always show a particular subset of the data, but what we're after is the ability to let the user define the search parameters themselves. Ideally, they should be able to choose multiple parameters to search on, edit the values to compare against, and even change the comparator itself (instead of just using CONTAINS all the time). Fortunately, Cocoa provides a GUI control called NSPredicateEditor, in Mac OS X 10.5 and later, that does just that!

With NSPredicateEditor, you can make a GUI that works a lot like the Smart Playlist feature in iTunes, or the Smart Mailbox feature in Mail. Users can add and remove search criteria, and the results will update on the fly. See Figure 9-6.

Figure 9-6. *QuoteMonger's predicate editor in action*

Both NSPredicateEditor and NSArrayController can set and retrieve the value of their NSPredicate via a binding, so what we'll do is add an NSPredicate as a property of the app delegate, and make the appropriate bindings. Then, when the user makes any changes in the predicate editor, the updated predicate will automatically be passed along to the array controller.

Adding a Predicate to the App Delegate

We'll start by adding a new property to the app delegate. Open *QuoteMonger_AppDelegate.h*, which you'll see looks just like the default app delegate header that was generated for MythBase. Add a new instance variable called searchPredicate and a matching property declaration. The interface declaration should now look something like this (new lines are in bold):

```
@interface QuoteMonger_AppDelegate : NSObject {
  IBOutlet NSWindow *window;

  NSPersistentStoreCoordinator *persistentStoreCoordinator;
  NSManagedObjectModel *managedObjectModel;
  NSManagedObjectContext *managedObjectContext;
  NSPredicate *searchPredicate;
}
@property (retain) NSPredicate *searchPredicate;
- (NSPersistentStoreCoordinator *)persistentStoreCoordinator;
- (NSManagedObjectModel *)managedObjectModel;
- (NSManagedObjectContext *)managedObjectContext;

- (IBAction)saveAction:sender;
@end
```

Now switch over to *QuoteMonger_AppDelegate.m* and add the following code near the top, just after the @implementation QuoteMonger_AppDelegate line.

```
@synthesize searchPredicate;

#define DEFAULT_PREDICATE @"(quoteText CONTAINS[cd] 'missed') OR " \
                          "(character CONTAINS[cd] 'kramer')"
- (id)init
{
  if ((self = [super init])) {
    searchPredicate = [[NSPredicate
        predicateWithFormat:DEFAULT_PREDICATE] retain];
  }
  return self;
}
```

The first line synthesizes a getter and setter for the searchPredicate property, and the init method creates a default value for it.

Now let's hook up our controller to use this new predicate. Go back to Interface Builder, select the *FoundQuotes* controller, and bring up the *Attributes Inspector*. Select all the text in the *Fetch Predicate* text view and delete it, then switch to the *Bindings Inspector*. In the *Controller Content Parameters* section, open the *Filter Predicate* binding info. Select *QuoteMonger_AppDelegate* in the popup, type "searchPredicate" into the *Model Key Path* combo box, and press Return to turn on the binding.

Save your work, go back to Xcode, and click **Build & Run**. You should now see a different set of results, quotes spoken by a character named "Kramer" or containing the word "missed." If nothing is matching, add a quote with one of these characteristics in order to test out the search window.

Add a Predicate Editor to the Search Window

We now have our FoundQuotes controller fetching values based on the contents of a predicate which is "owned" by the app delegate. The next step is to add an NSPredicateEditor to the search window, and configure it to let the user edit the predicate.

In Interface Builder, bring up the *Quote Finder* window. Make the whole window a bit taller, and drag the existing table view and text view down to the bottom. Then find an NSPredicateEditor in the Library, drag it into the empty space at the top of the window, then resize it to make it fill the available space. Figure 9-7 shows the idea.

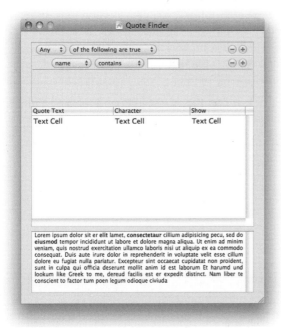

Figure 9-7. *The predicate editor is in place in our search window.*

Configuring the Predicate Editor

Now it's time to bind the editor to the app delegate's predicate instance. Select the NSPredicateEditor (don't forget the extra click to select the editor itself, not the scroll view that contains it), open the *Bindings Inspector*, and then examine the *Value* binding info. Select *QuoteMonger_AppDelegate* in the popup, then type in searchPredicate in the *Model Key Path* combo box, and press Return to activate this binding.

At this point, there's only one more thing we need to do in order to enable searching with this predicate editor: we have to tailor it to the attributes we want to search on. NSPredicateEditor is a quite complex control, and fortunately most of its interesting features can be configured directly in Interface Builder. The predicate editor displays one or more NSPredicateEditorRowTemplate objects, which can each be configured to do searching in a variety of ways. You can make row templates that allow you to specify numbers or dates to compare against object values, or to pick from a list of predefined strings. In our case, we're going to configure a row template that lets the user type a string in a text field to search by character names, show names, and quote contents. This row template can be reused, allowing the user to specify multiple search criteria simultaneously. In addition, another row template will let the user choose whether the search criteria must all be met (boolean AND) or whether it's enough that any match succeeds (boolean OR) for a quote to appear in the results.

In Interface Builder, drill down into the predicate editor by clicking on the lower of the two rows you can see (the one containing popup buttons showing *name* and *contains*). With that row template selected, bring up the Attributes Inspector. There you'll see several checkboxes that let you choose which comparators you'll allow the user to use, and popup buttons that let you choose the nature of the expressions used on either side of the comparator (*Key Paths*, *Strings*, *Constant Values*, and the like). The default setup, with *Key paths* on the left and *Strings* on the right, is perfect for our purposes, but we need to do is adjust the *Key paths* for our searching needs.

Edit the three default values that are listed below *Left Exprs Key paths*, changing them to quoteText, character, and show.name. While you're at it, click to turn on the *Case insensitive* and *Diacritical mark insensitive* checkboxes (see Figure 9-8).

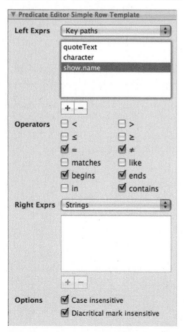

Figure 9-8. *Configuring an NSPredicateEditorRowTemplate*

Then, examine the popup button in the row template itself. This will show three entries, whose names are the same as what you just entered for key paths. Change these to more human-readable names: *Quotation*, *Character Name*, and *Show Name*.

Now click on the upper row template, the one showing "*Any of the following are true.*" The configuration for this is very simple. Checkboxes let you choose to allow boolean AND, OR, and NOT for the user to search on. Enable all of those, to allow the most utility.

Now there's just one more piece of configuration that we need to do. By default, NSPredicateEditor lets the user delete all the rows, right down to the last one, at which point there is no longer a "+" button to add any back in. Change this by selecting the predicate editor itself (not one of the row templates) and clicking to turn off the *Can Remove All Rows* checkbox in the *Attributes Inspector*.

Save your work, **Build & Run** in Xcode, and bask in the glory of QuoteMonger! You can now easily search through all saved quotes, using the three criteria we configured in the predicate editor.

Saving a Predicate

Before we call it a day, let's add one final bit of polish that will make using QuoteMonger a friendly experience for our users. Right now, each time a user launches the app, it starts up with our silly default query. Wouldn't it be nice if it instead showed the last query from the previous time it was running? It turns out that this is a piece of cake. NSPredicate has a handy method called predicateFormat that returns the predicate's value in the form of a string. So, we can save the current searchPredicate's string representation using NSUserDefaults when the user quits the app, and check for a saved string when the app launches. Open up *QuoteMonger_AppDelegate.m*, and make the following changes to the first part of its implementation (just add all the lines that appear in bold):

```
@implementation QuoteMonger_AppDelegate

@synthesize searchPredicate;

#define DEFAULT_PREDICATE @"(quoteText CONTAINS[cd] 'missed') OR " \
                          "(character CONTAINS[cd] 'kramer')"
#define STORED_PREDICATE_KEY @"storedPredicateFormat"

- init
{
  if ((self = [super init])) {
    NSString *format = [[NSUserDefaults standardUserDefaults]
        objectForKey:STORED_PREDICATE_KEY];
    if (format)
      searchPredicate = [[NSPredicate predicateWithFormat:format]
          retain];
    else
      searchPredicate = [[NSPredicate predicateWithFormat:
          DEFAULT_PREDICATE] retain];
  }
```

```
    return self;
}

- (void)applicationWillTerminate:(NSNotification *)aNotification
{
    NSString *format = [searchPredicate predicateFormat];
    [[NSUserDefaults standardUserDefaults] setObject:format forKey:STORED_PREDICATE_KEY];
}
```

We start by defining a string, which will be used as a key to store and retrieve the predicate from the user's preferences using NSUserDefaults. Then, we enhance the init method to look for a stored predicate. It first checks to see if a stored predicate string exists, and if it does, it populates the searchPredicate instance variable with a new predicate created from the format string. If there is no stored predicate, the default predicate is created instead.

Finally, we implement the applicationWillTerminate: method. This method is called automatically when the user quits the application, giving us a chance to do some final cleanup. Here, we convert the current search parameters (maintained in the searchPredicate instance variable) into a string, and save that string into the user's preferences so that the same search will pop up the next time the user runs the app.

Save, **Build & Run**, then modify the search terms. Quit the app and run it again, and you should see your previous search terms show up again.

In Conclusion

In this chapter you've learned the basics of how to use NSPredicate to narrow down a Core Data result set. You've seen how an NSPredicate can be constructed in code, or in Interface Builder, or by user interaction with NSPredicateEditor. You've even gotten a hint of how these predicates can be saved for later use, much like iTunes and Mail do with smart playlists and smart folders. These techniques can help you easily bring new levels of functionality to your own apps.

In Chapters 7 through 9, we've covered the main concepts you need to get up and running with Core Data, and now it's time to move on to other topics. We won't be leaving Core Data behind, however, as it will still play a role in some further exercises, though not to the same extent. We don't have enough space in this book to turn every example into a fully fledged application. Even in cases where we're not using Core Data, however, you might want to think about where it could fit into what we're demonstrating in the coming chapters. Now that you've got Core Data at your fingertips, you'll probably have a whole new view on some aspects of application development that you would have solved in a different way before. Speaking of views, that's where we're headed in Chapter 10, with a look at some of the most prominent and widely used view components in Cocoa and elsewhere: windows, menus, and sheets.

Windows and Menus and Sheets

For the past several chapters, we've been focusing on what could be considered the "back end" of Cocoa programming, the model and controller classes that provide functionality to help take care of your application's infrastructure. Now it's time to turn our attention to the "front end" of Cocoa, and pay more attention to the view part of the MVC architecture.

In this chapter, we're going to focus on windows (not the Microsoft kind), menus (not the restaurant kind), and sheets (not the bed kind), all of which are high-level GUI objects that practically no Cocoa application can do without. Windows provide the foundation for view objects to do their drawing. In Cocoa, these are represented by NSWindow, its direct subclass NSPanel, and several specialized subclasses. Menus provide the familiar top-of-the-screen access to system-wide and application-specific user actions that most Mac applications have, and are represented by a hierarchy of NSMenu and NSMenuItem objects. Sheets provide an alternative to the classic free-floating modal window by letting you attach a modal window as an overlay on an existing window, giving the user a more coherent interface.

We're going to explore each of these three areas in a "lab," a toy application that has no real use, and is only created for demonstrating some functionality and letting you see how these things work.

NSWindow and NSPanel

Start by creating a new Xcode project using the Cocoa Application template, and name it *WindowLab*. We'll use this project as a testbed for demonstrating a variety of window features.

In Mac OS X, nearly everything you see on-screen is presented using windows. Many windows are easily recognizable, having the standard controls along the top, drop-shadow behind it, perhaps a resizing control at the lower right.

But some windows aren't so obvious. For example, if you launch a game that takes over the whole screen for its display, even if it's presenting custom controls of its own that have nothing to do with Cocoa, that's all occurring in a window. The Dock at the bottom of the screen is surely a window. And if you drag a file icon from one Finder window to another, the icon you're dragging is actually being "carried" inside a small, transparent window!

In all of these cases, you're seeing and interacting with instances of NSWindow and its subclasses. NSWindow is a very versatile class that lets you configure several behaviors right out of the box, and lets you do even more by subclassing. In general, if you want to change the appearance of the window itself, either its "chrome" (the title bar and upper-left corner controls), its transparency, or its shape, you'll probably need to subclass NSWindow, but otherwise, you almost never will. In this book, we're going to stick to the kinds of windows that are ready to use directly and conform to Apple's Human Interface Guidelines, and won't be subclassing NSWindow to change its appearance.

> **TIP:** The Human Interface Guidelines (often shortened to "HIG") are a set of recommendations that Apple provides for application developers. The HIG acts as a sort of style guide that you can refer to when you're concerned that your application looks a little "off." It's not a strict set of rules, and no one is going to stop you from violating the HIG. In fact, many applications, including Apple's own, stray from the guidelines in all kinds of ways. However, it gives you a good baseline, describing how the various components are meant to be used.
>
> We mentioned the HIG in Chapter 2 already, but it's worth pointing out again. You can find the HIG online at http://developer.apple.com/documentation/UserExperience/ Conceptual/AppleHIGuidelines.

Figure 10–1 gives you a glimpse of the main kinds of windows that are prevalent in most Cocoa applications today. There are two included drawing styles for NSWindow, the "normal" appearance and the "textured" appearance, which somewhat resembles a shiny piece of metal. NSPanels can be configured to be in utility mode (in which case they have a smaller title bar, cast a smaller shadow, and float above the application's other windows) or to look like a normal window, and in either case the choice of normal vs. textured also applies, just like NSWindow. One additional option for NSPanel is to run in *HUD* (short for heads-up display) mode, in which case the panel's color scheme is inverted, its title bar and bottom edge are modified, and the whole window is made slightly transparent. This mode (which has no textured option) is intended to allow the user to see through a part of the interface to what's behind it, and is put to good use in applications like iPhoto, where you can bring up a HUD panel containing adjustable color settings, through which the photo you're looking at can still be seen.

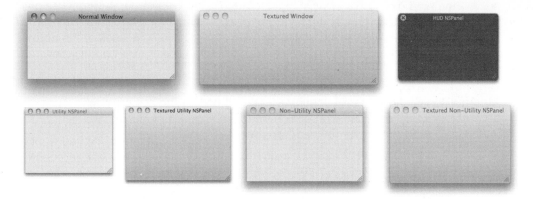

Figure 10–1. *A sampling of the main types of windows that are readily available in Interface Builder*

Unlike some other GUI toolkits, where one of the first things you do when creating a new application is to subclass some sort of Application class and some sort of Window class, Cocoa allows for true separation of the model, view, and controller portions of your application. The window only needs to know how to display itself and provide a graphics context for its views, so that's all it does. Any code that deals with what happens to a window while the application is running (e.g. it gets loaded from a nib file, or gets dragged across the screen, or gets closed by the user) can typically be dealt with by the window's delegate object (i.e. its controller).

Handling Input

In addition to providing a frame for views to display their stuff, NSWindow also handles user input from the mouse and keyboard. Any mousing action (clicking, dragging, moving, releasing, and so on) in an NSWindow will trigger a method in NSWindow that finds the appropriate view object in its contents and calls the same method in the view. This symmetry works because NSWindow and NSView both inherit from NSResponder, where the methods for handling these events are defined. Likewise, when the user presses or releases a key on the keyboard, the application calls a method in the application's "key window" (i.e. the window that currently has keyboard focus; usually the last window the user clicked in), which in turn determines which view currently has keyboard focus, and passes off responsibility, calling the same method in the focused view.

To Use a Panel, or Not to Use a Panel

Assuming you don't need to modify the basic appearance of windows, you'll be using either NSWindow or its subclass NSPanel to display the controls and other views in your application. The core elements of your application will usually be in an NSWindow, while NSPanel is used for auxiliary windows, such as the Inspector in Interface Builder. From a user's standpoint, there are just a few critical differences between NSWindow and NSPanel:

- NSPanel instances normally become invisible when another application becomes the active application, and reappear when their own application becomes active again.

- An NSPanel can be made to "float" in front of all the other windows in its application, including the main window.

- An NSPanel can be easily configured to not become the key window unnecessarily, so a user can click a button in an auxiliary panel and then continue typing in the main window.

Window Attributes

In the WindowLab project in Xcode, navigate to the *MainMenu.xib* file and double-click to open it in Interface Builder. One of the objects included in the application nib file is, as always, a window. Click to select it in the main nib window, then open the *Attributes Inspector* so that we can explore it a bit (see Figure 10–2). In earlier chapters, you've seen this inspector for setting a window's title, but of course there's more we can do here.

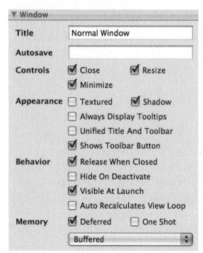

Figure 10–2. *The Attributes Inspector for an NSWindow*

You're already familiar with the *Title* text field. Just below that is the *Autosave* field, which provides a very nice bit of functionality: enter a text string in this field, and the window will use that string as a key in the NSUserDefaults system, storing and retrieving its position and location based on that key. That means that as a user rearranges the windows in your application, the window positions are saved in the user's preferences, and the windows will appear in the same locations the next time they run your app. And all you have to do to make it happen is fill in this text field for each window in your app, entering a unique value for each window.

Next, there are some checkboxes that let you turn off some of the standard window controls. Note that turning off these checkboxes won't remove the corresponding buttons from the window's title bar; it will just make them permanently grey and inactive while your app is running. Clicking to turn off the *Resize* checkbox will, however, make the resizing handle at the lower right disappear when your app runs (it's always there in Interface Builder however, so that you can still modify your window even when you won't allow the users to do so).

Below that are some checkboxes that for tweaking a window's appearance, including enabling textured mode, disabling the drop-shadow behind the window, and more. The options that mention *Toolbar* here are referring to the optional NSToolbar that can be attached to a window, which we'll explain a little later in this chapter.

The next chunk of checkboxes lets you fine-tune the window's behavior in a number of ways, most of them self-explanatory. The exception is the *Auto Recalculates View Loop* checkbox, whose name is puzzling at best. Here's the idea: each window maintains a list of all the view objects it contains, which the user can shuffle between by using the Tab key. If you turn this checkbox on, then any views that are added to the window while the app is running will automatically be inserted somewhere into this "loop."

Finally, there are options related to a window's memory usage. You should normally leave *Deferred* on, because this skips the allocation of some internal memory for the window until it's about to actually display the window. You should normally leave *One Shot* turned off. If it's on, that same internal memory is freed as soon as the window is closed, so this should only be turned on in case the window in question is a temporary window that can only be shown once per session, such as a splash screen. Finally, a popup window offers you the ability to switch the window's "backing store" from *Buffered* to *Retained* or *Unretained*. Never do that! The *Retained* and *Unretained* options are only there to support specific sorts of legacy code, and all new Cocoa applications should leave this set to *Buffered* for every window.

Now pull an NSPanel out from the *Library* window, and look again at the *Attributes Inspector*, where you'll see a few more checkboxes than you saw when inspecting an NSWindow. The most important ones here are *Utility*, which if enabled gives the panel a distinctive appearance, as well as making it float above the application's other windows; and *HUD*, which gives the window the even more distinctive "heads-up" appearance. Try out some of these checkboxes and see how they affect the panel's appearance. When you're done, you can delete the panel from the nib file.

Standard System Panels

In addition to the generic window classes that are meant for you to fill with your own views and controls, Cocoa includes some specialized window subclasses for use in your applications. These are meant to meet the needs of a wide variety of applications, so using them gives you a lot of functionality for free, and at the same time provides your users with familiar interfaces that they've probably used in other applications.

The Color Panel

First let's take a look at NSColorPanel. This panel provides an interface that allows the user to select a color. We're going to use the color panel to set the color of a piece of on-screen text, by implementing a method in our controller class that's called whenever the user selects a color in the color panel.

If you're running Snow Leopard, Xcode will have created a class called *WindowLabAppDelegate* for you. Otherwise, in Xcode, make a new Objective-C class file called *WindowLabAppDelegate.m*, along with its matching *.h* file. We're going to add an outlet called title and an action called showColorPanel:, as seen here:

```
#import <Cocoa/Cocoa.h>
@interface WindowLabAppDelegate : NSObject {
  IBOutlet NSTextField *title;
}
- (IBAction)showColorPanel:(id)sender;
@end
```

Now switch to the *.m* file, and add the following implementation for the showColorPanel: method, along with a method called changeColor:, like this:

```
#import "WindowLabAppDelegate.h"
@implementation WindowLabAppDelegate
- (IBAction)showColorPanel:(id)sender
{
  // create the color panel
  NSColorPanel *panel = [NSColorPanel sharedColorPanel];
  // bring the color panel to the front of the screen
  [panel orderFront:nil];
}
- (void)changeColor:(id)sender
{
  // in this method, the "sender" parameter is the NSColorPanel
  // itself.  We just ask it for its color, and pass it along to
  // the "title" object.
  [title setTextColor:[sender color]];
}
@end
```

The showColorPanel: method will be called by a simple button click in our GUI, which we'll configure in Interface Builder. But the changeColor: method will be called whenever the user clicks on a color in the color panel, even though there won't be any direct connection between the color panel and our code. This bit of "magic" works thanks to a Cocoa concept called the responder chain (see sidebar).

THE RESPONDER CHAIN

The responder chain is an ad hoc collection of objects, gathered on the fly when necessary during the life of an application, that can be queried to see if they implement a particular action. This lets certain actions be configured in a generic way, so that at runtime they will be invoked on the object that makes most sense at the time. The chain is arranged in order of specificity, starting with the object that is "nearest" to the action, and continuing along toward the most generic. Configuring an object to use the responder chain is done in Interface Builder by connecting to an action on the nib's *First Responder* icon, which is nothing more than a proxy for the first object in the responder chain that says, at runtime, "Yes I can" when asked if it implements a particular method.

This is all made somewhat more confusing by the fact that each window has its own notion of a "first responder," which is typically the control or view that the user last interacted with (thereby making it a likely candidate for receiving key-presses, and the like).

Let's try to clarify this with an example. Consider the case of a button whose target/action is configured to call a method called showThing: on the *First Responder*. When a user clicks the button, each of a list of objects will be asked, in order, if they implement a showThing: method, right up until one of them answers YES, at which point that object's showThing: method is called, and the responder chain's work is done. Here's an example of what the responder chain can look like:

1. The window's "first responder" (the view that's currently in focus and accepting keyboard input), its superview, the superview's superview, and so on, all the way up the view hierarchy within the window

2. The window itself

3. The window's delegate

4. The application object, NSApp

5. The application object's delegate

The responder chain may contain additional objects as well, especially if you're working on a Document-based application, in which case open documents and their controller's will have a spot in the chain as well. More on that in Chapter 11.

As soon as any one of those objects says it implements showThing:, then the method is called on that object, and the search is over.

Now go to Interface Builder, where *MainMenu.xib* is still shown. If you're using Snow Leopard, you should see an instance of WindowLabAppDelegate already set up in your nib file. Otherwise, drag a plain object from the *Library* into your main nib window, and change its class to WindowLabAppDelegate using the *Identity Inspector*. Then Ctrl-drag from the *Application* icon to the WindowLabAppDelegate instance and connect the application's delegate outlet. Now open up the empty window contained in your nib, then drag first a wrapping label and then a button from the *Library* into the empty window. Then lay the window out roughly as shown in Figure 10–3.

Figure 10–3. *A very simple window layout*

Next, Ctrl-drag from the button to the app delegate in the main nib window, and connect to its showColorPanel: action, and then Ctrl-drag from the app delegate to the label, connecting the title outlet there.

Now save your work, switch back to Xcode, and hit **Build & Run**. Your new app will appear, and clicking the button will bring up the color panel. Click around on some different colors, and the color of the selected text will immediately change to reflect the new selection.

So, considering that the color panel has no direct connection to our app delegate, it's fair to wonder: how does that work? How does the changeColor: method in our app delegate get called? The key is the use of the responder chain, as described earlier. NSColorPanel uses the responder chain to find an object that implements the changeColor: method. As the application's delegate, our little controller object is one of the last objects queried to see if it implements the method, and since it does, it gets called. Note that if the window implemented the method itself, or if it had a delegate that implemented the method, one of those methods would have been called instead.

Now we need to end this section with a reality-check. In reality, what we just did can be more easily (and more handsomely) accomplished by using an NSColorWell, a special control that launches the NSColorPanel when clicked. We'd only need to write code to declare a property in a controller class to contain an NSColor, and then use Cocoa Bindings to bind the NSColorWell's *Value* attribute and the NSTextField's *Text Color* attribute to the property in our controller. This example is included here, as-is, mainly to show you how to use the color panel from your own code, as well as give you a first look at the responder chain concept.

The Font Panel

The next special panel we're going to look at is NSFontPanel. Unlike the color panel, the font panel, does **not** have a matching control that launches it. However, it can be integrated fairly well with the contents of the system's **Format** menu, as you'll see a little later.

What we're going to do here is create an action method that opens the font panel, and another method which updates the text field. Then we'll create a button to let the user invoke this functionality. In the *WindowLabAppDelegate.h* file, add the following method declaration inside the class's @interface block:

```
- (IBAction)showFontPanel:(id)sender;
```

Then switch to the *.m* file and add the following methods to the @implementation section:

```
- (IBAction)showFontPanel:(id)sender
{
  NSFontPanel *panel = [NSFontPanel sharedFontPanel];
  NSFontManager *manager = [NSFontManager sharedFontManager];
  [manager setSelectedFont:[title font] isMultiple:NO];
  [panel orderFront:nil];
}
```

```
- (void)changeFont:(id)sender
{
  // here, 'sender' is the shared NSFontManager instance
  NSFont *oldFont = [title font];
  NSFont *newFont = [sender convertFont:oldFont];
  [title setFont:newFont];
}
```

This follows the same usage pattern as the color panel. When the user clicks on a font, the font panel uses the responder chain to look for an object that implements the changeFont: action method, and it manages to find it in our app delegate. Here, things are slightly more complicated, because in both of these methods we make use of a shared instance of the NSFontManager class. A running application's notion of the selected or current font is held within this shared instance, which we use first in showFontPanel: to indirectly tell the NSFontPanel which font it should begin displaying, and then again in changeFont: to get the new selected font. We get the new font by passing the old font to the font manager's convertFont: method, which combines characteristics of the old font with the state of the user's selection in the font panel (for example, if the old font is Lucida Grande/Bold/36, and the user selects Times New Roman, leaving the rest alone, the converted font will be Times New Roman/Bold/36).

Now, switch back to Interface Builder, where we'll hook things up. First make your window a little taller. Then duplicate the button you've already got, name the new one "Show Font Panel," and Ctrl-drag from it to the app delegate in the main nib window, connecting to the showFontPanel: action method. Save your work, go back to Xcode, and **Build & Run**. You can now change both the color and the font for the displayed text (see Figure 10–4).

Figure 10–4. *Setting a label's color and font*

A Controller With a Nib of Its Own

Next, we're going to demonstrate a simple pattern that occurs often in Cocoa development: making a controller class that loads its own nib file, becoming the "owner" of all the objects in the file. In every application we've created so far, all the GUI elements are contained inside the application's single *.nib* file. This works well enough for simple applications, but it has its limits. For one thing, we only have one instance of each window and each controller in the nib. For another thing, the entire main nib file is loaded at once, when the application is starting up, and the more stuff you have in that nib, the slower and more memory-intensive the startup phase will be. Granted, on modern computers with several gigabytes of RAM, this may not be such a huge problem, but as a programmer it's always good to try to not waste CPU and RAM recklessly. Finally, putting too many top-level objects (windows, controllers, and the like) into a single nib file makes life more difficult for you, the programmer, because it's harder to see which controllers and windows belong together.

The solution to both of these problems is to distribute some of your GUI objects into other nib files, and mediate their use with controller classes that load the nibs. This technique is used by many Cocoa applications, which commonly split windows for preferences, documents, tools, and so on into separate nib files. The following sections will demonstrate two different ways of doing this, with increasing complexity.

Loading a Nib With NSWindowController

The first and easiest way is to use Cocoa's NSWindowController class to load the nib file and be its owner. Start by going to the WindowLab project in Xcode, and adding a new method called loadEasyWindow: to the WindowLabAppDelegate class, as seen here:

```
// Add this to the @interface section in the .h file
- (IBAction)loadEasyWindow:(id)sender;

// Add this to the @implementation section in the .m file
- (IBAction)loadEasyWindow:(id)sender
{
  NSWindowController *easyController = [[NSWindowController alloc]
      initWithWindowNibName:@"EasyWindow"];
  [easyController window];
}
```

In that method, we first initialize a new controller, telling it the name of the nib file to use, then we call its window method, which is what actually loads the nib file and displays the window.

Switch over to Interface Builder, and make a brand new file. Choose the Empty template, then drag out a window from the Library, and give the window the title Easy Window. Then save the file as EasyWindow.xib, in the same directory where WindowLab's other nib file (MainMenu.xib) is located. Interface Builder will ask you if you want to add it to the WindowLab project; click the checkbox to confirm that you do.

Now switch back to MainMenu.xib in Interface Builder. Make your window a bit taller once more, and add another button below the others, this one a spaced a bit farther away so that it doesn't appear to be involved with the text field from the previous exercises. Label the new button "Easy Window," and connect it to the app delegate's loadEasyWindow: action. Save, go back to Xcode, **Build & Run**, and you'll see that your app's new button lets you create new windows with each press of the button (see Figure 10–5).

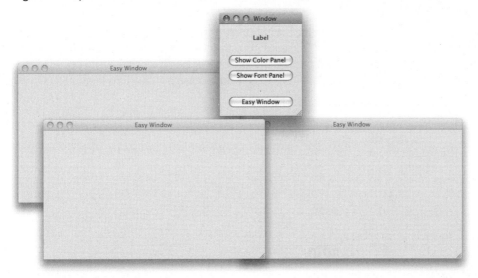

Figure 10–5. *Some easy windows*

Each time, it's actually creating a new NSWindowController instance, which loads a fresh copy of the nib file, including all objects inside of it. In this case all we have is a window, but you can put anything you like inside those nib files, including for example controller objects for accessing Core Data.

Subclassing NSWindowController

Of course, often you'll need a bit of your own code in your controller class. You can easily subclass NSWindowController to suit your needs here as well. Our next steps will be to create a subclass and create a new nib file for it to load, and set up a way to call it from our main window and controller.

In Xcode, make a new class in the WindowLab project called NotSoEasyWindowController by selecting **File▸New File...** from the menu and choosing to create an NSWindowController subclass. Because we're making our own class here, we can build in the name of the nib file so that anyone using this class only needs to know about the class, not the name of the nib file itself. We can also make things even easier for callers: assuming that anyone who creates an instance of this class wants to load the nib file, let's build the call to window right into the init method. Do this by creating the following init method:

```
- init {
  if ((self = [super initWithWindowNibName:@"NotSoEasyWindow"])) {
    [self window];
  }
  return self;
}
```

That's the recommended form of the standard `init` method, in which we call another `init` method in the superclass, do work specific to our instance if it succeeds, and finish up by returning a pointer to `self`.

With that in place, let's add a small bit of functionality to our window controller class, so that after our nib file is created, we can make sure that our window is connecting up with it as it should: A simple method that makes the computer beep when it's called. Add the following method declaration and definition to the new class's .h and .m files:

```
// add this to NotSoEasyWindowController.h:
- (IBAction)beep:(id)sender;
```

```
// add this to NotSoEasyWindowController.m:
- (IBAction)beep:(id)sender
{
    NSBeep();
}
```

While you're still in Xcode, add another method to the `WindowLabAppDelegate` class:

```
// add this to WindowLabAppDelegate.h:
- (IBAction)loadNotSoEasyWindow:(id)sender;
```

```
// add this to WindowLabAppDelegate.m:
- (IBAction)loadNotSoEasyWindow:(id)sender
{
    [[NotSoEasyWindowController alloc] init];
}
```

You'll also need to add the following `#import` directive at the top of WindowLabAppDelegate.m, so that the compiler knows about the new class when it's compiling the app delegate:

```
#import "NotSoEasyWindowController.h"
```

Now switch over to *MainMenu.xib* in Interface Builder. Once again, make your window a bit taller, duplicate the last button, and name it "Not So Easy." Then connect it to the app delegate's `loadNotSoEasy:` action method.

Still in Interface Builder, make a new empty file, and save it as *NotSoEasyWindow.xib*. Drag a window out of the *Library* and title it "Not So Easy Window," then drag a button onto the new window and title it "Beep."

Now all that's left to do is connect the button to the controller. In previous chapters, every controller we've created has been added to a nib file as a top-level object, but when you're loading a nib file yourself, you can specify an object to be its "owner," which in Interface Builder is represented by the *File's Owner* object in the main nib window. `NSWindowController`, our controller's parent class, already sets itself up as the owner of the nib file when it loads the file, but we still have to manually configure that in Interface Builder so that we can make use of it. Select the *File's Owner* icon, and open the *Identity Inspector* (⌘6). At the top of this inspector, you can set the class of the object that you expect to be the file's owner. By default it's set to `NSObject`. Change it to `NotSoEasyWindowController`, then Control-drag from the new button you added, to the *File's Owner* icon in the main nib window, and select the `beep:` method. Save your changes, switch to Xcode, **Build & Run**, and you should see that your newest button lets you create windows that beep when you press their buttons, as seen in Figure 10–6.

Figure 10–6. *These windows' buttons will beep at you.*

Modal Windows

Now we're going to move on to a special kind of GUI item, the modal window. Everyone has used modal windows at one time or another, but if you're new to desktop GUI programming, the term may be new to you. Basically, a modal window is one that puts your application in a particular "mode." Specifically, a mode where it will only accept input through the controls on the modal window itself, and clicking anywhere else in the application will just make it beep at you. Because of their disruptive nature, modal windows should be used sparingly, in cases where the application can't really move forward on its own without the user answering a question of some kinds (such as, "There are 5 open documents with unsaved changes, are you sure you want to quit?"). In cases where the information the app needs from the user is related to just a single window or document, you may be better off using a sheet, described later in this chapter, which locks down a single window instead of the entire application.

The NSAlert Functions

The simplest modal windows available in Cocoa are the alert panels, which are created and run with a single function call. The function returns when the user clicks one of the buttons, and you can then check the return value to determine which of the buttons they clicked. Depending on how you call the function, there may be one, two, or three buttons presented for the user.

The most commonly used modal alert function is NSRunAlertPanel. It has a few variants called NSRunCriticalAlertPanel and NSRunInformationalAlertPanel, which are used for specific purposes specified in Apple's user interface guidelines, but you can safely stick with NSRunAlertPanel. Each of these functions takes five or more parameters. First the title that appears at the top of the panel, then the full text to display, which presents some information or asks the user a question, then three strings (which may be nil) containing the button titles. Button titles left as `nil` will simply be undisplayed, except for the case where they're all `nil`, in which case a single *OK* button is included on the panel.

To see some alert panels in action, implement the following method in WindowLabAppDelegate.m. Be sure to put a matching declaration in the .h file as well:

```
- (IBAction)runModalAlerts:(id)sender
{
  NSRunCriticalAlertPanel(@"Basic Usage", @"This is a plain alert panel.", nil, nil,
nil);
  NSRunAlertPanel(@"Three Buttons", @"We can set button titles:",
    @"Really?", @"Oh, how delightful!", @"Whatever.");
  NSRunAlertPanel(@"Formatting Strings", @"We can also do some formatting, %@ %@",
    nil, nil, nil, @"putting values for insertion at the end,", @"after the three button
values.");
  switch (NSRunAlertPanel(@"Noticing The Selection",
            @"And of course, we can detect which button is clicked.",
            @"Default", @"Alternate", @"Other")) {
    case NSAlertDefaultReturn:
      NSRunInformationalAlertPanel(@"Result:", @"You pressed the default button",
        nil, nil, nil);
      break;
    case NSAlertAlternateReturn:
      NSRunInformationalAlertPanel(@"Result:", @"You pressed the alternate button",
        nil, nil, nil);
      break;
    case NSAlertOtherReturn:
      NSRunInformationalAlertPanel(@"Result:", @"You pressed the other button",
        nil, nil, nil);
      break;
    default:
      break;
  }
}
```

Test these out by going into MainMenu.xib, adding yet another button to your window (title it *Run Modal Alerts*), and connecting it to the app delegate's `runModalAlerts:` action. Save, back to Xcode, **Build & Run**, and give it a whirl.

Open Panels and Save Panels

The other most commonly used modal panels in Cocoa are probably the ones for opening and saving files, NSOpenPanel and NSSavePanel. Using these panels is typically more than just a one-liner. You might first need to configure various options on the panel (for instance, whether it should allow the user to select multiple files for opening, or just one), then run the panel, check the return value (which indicates whether the user eventually clicked the open or save button, or canceled out), and then grab the resulting filenames from the panel. Note that these panels don't actually do any file I/O, they just prompt the user for filenames and give you back the results.

To see an example of how this can work, consider the following method, which pretends to copy a file. This method uses an NSOpenPanel to prompt the user for the file to copy, then uses an NSSavePanel to let the user specify where the file should go:

```
- (IBAction)copyFile:(id)sender
{
  NSOpenPanel *openPanel = [NSOpenPanel openPanel];
  [openPanel setTitle:@"Select file to copy:"];
  if ([openPanel runModalForTypes:nil] == NSOKButton) {
    // get the first (and only) selected filename
    NSString *openPath = [[openPanel filenames] objectAtIndex:0];
    // pull out just the filename, without directory path
    NSString *openFilename = [openPath lastPathComponent];
    NSSavePanel *savePanel = [NSSavePanel savePanel];
    [savePanel setTitle:@"Enter destination filename:"];
    // run the save panel in its default directory, with the opened filename
    // as a suggestion.
    if ([savePanel runModalForDirectory:nil file:openFilename] == NSOKButton) {
      NSString *savePath = [savePanel filename];
      NSString *message = [NSString stringWithFormat:
        @"You've opened this file:\n\n%@\n\nand saved it here:\n\n%@\n\n",
        openPath, savePath];
      NSRunAlertPanel(@"Copying file (not really)", message, nil, nil, nil);
    }
  }
}
```

Put that method into *WindowLabAppDelegate.m*, and create the matching declaration in the *.h* file. Then go back to *MainMenu.xib* in Interface Builder, and once again add a new button (call this one "Copy File") and connect it to the new copyFile: action. Save your changes, go back to Xcode, **Build & Run**, and try out the new button. You'll see a standard Open panel appear, followed by a standard Save panel. Note that the Save panel even has built-in functionality to warn you when you're selecting an existing file, asking you if you really want to overwrite it (remember, it's perfectly safe to confirm overwriting the file in this example, since we're not actually copying anything).

It's probably worth mentioning here the not-so-obvious fact that NSOpenPanel is actually a subclass of NSSavePanel. That means that if you can't seem to find the functionality you're expecting in NSOpenPanel's documentation or header file, you may need to check out NSSavePanel as well.

System Menus

Now that you've seen some of the basics of how windows are used in Cocoa, let's spend some time dealing with another ever-present feature of Mac OS X, the application menu. Unlike most other current operating systems, Mac OS X presents its menu at the top of the screen instead of at the top of each window. This arrangement has some nice upsides: screen real estate is saved, because instead of a horizontal strip taking space at the top of every open window, you have just a single horizontal strip at the top, showing the menu for the active application. Also, the menu is easier and quicker to "hit" with the mouse, because you can just flick the mouse upwards and you know you'll hit the menu, leaving you with just fine-tuning left and right to find the top item you want to select.

This arrangement isn't without complications, however. In a typical Windows application, you might have a number of different windows, each with its own menu, containing items that are only relevant to that window's contents. While it's technically possible to do something similar in a Mac OS X application, changing the structure of the menu as different windows are selected, this usage is frowned upon, and will probably bother some users, who on the Mac are quite accustomed to applications that behave in a consistent manner. Instead, you can implement a behavior that is fully supported and recommended: Enabling and disabling menu items based on the currently selected window (or, indeed, the currently selected object inside a window). In this section, we're going to show you how to do this, but first we're going to talk a bit about the system menus that are included with Cocoa and standard across most applications.

Standard Application Menu Items

Apple's guidelines define a set of menus and menu items that should appear in most applications. Create a new application in Xcode, and name it MenuLab. This is where we'll do some experimenting with menu items. Open the freshly created *MainMenu.xib* file, and double-click the *MainMenu* object to take a look at the predefined set of menus. This set contains top-level entries for the application itself, followed by **File, Edit**, **Format**, **View**, **Window**, and **Help**, each of which contains menu items of its own. Open up the *Connections Inspector* (⌘5) so that we can examine some of these items and see what they're connected to. Just click around on each of the various menu items, and keep your eye on the *Inspector* after each click. There are a few exceptions, but most of the items are connected to the *First Responder* proxy that we talked about earlier. Soon you'll see that by connecting a menu item to the *First Responder*, not only will the item call its action method in the most relevant object, it will also be automatically enabled and disabled based on the contents of the responder chain.

Your Own Menus

The standard menus contain a lot of functionality, everything from bringing up the app's About Box to editing and formatting text, to dealing with windows, is all set up. However, many applications need some extra functionality, something that doesn't seem right to attach to a window, or just takes up too much space in a window. One common way to address this is to add one or more additional top-level menu items, usually between the **View** and **Window** menus. For instance, the Finder has a **Go** menu in there, and Xcode has, by my reckoning, no less than five additional top-level menus: *Project*, *Build*, *Run*, *Design*, and *SCM*. In our application, we'll get by with just one additional menu. In the last paragraph, we asked you to create a new Cocoa project called MenuLab. If you're running Snow Leopard, the template used to create your new application already contains an app delegate class, and you can move along to the next heading. Otherwise, if you're on Leopard, configure the app delegate as follows: create a new Objective-C class named `MenuLab_AppDelegate`. Open up the new project's *MainMenu.xib*, and set up the app delegate: Drag an NSObject out of the *Library* to the main nib window, set its class to `MenuLab_AppDelegate` using the Identity Inspector, and connect the application's delegate outlet to this new instance.

Enabling/Disabling With Bindings

The first thing we're going to do is set up a pair of menu items to control a boolean attribute in our app delegate. You could use these to control some sort of switch that affects an application-wide setting. In our case, we'll create a property called `turbo`, which presumably makes everything happen faster (easy enough in MenuLab, because it doesn't actually do anything). We'll have two menu items labeled "Turbo On" and "Turbo Off," and connect each of them to an action method in our app delegate to do the actual toggling. Then we'll use bindings to enable and disable them as appropriate, so that when `turbo` is `YES`, only the "Turbo Off" item is clickable, and when `turbo` is `NO`, only the "Turbo On" item is clickable.

Start off in Xcode, by adding the turbo property to the app delegate, along with an action method to toggle the value of the property. The changes you need to make to both *MenuLab_AppDelegate.h* and *MenuLab_AppDelegate.m* are shown here, in a somewhat compacted form, with blank lines removed. All you need to add are the lines shown in bold.

```
//
// MenuLab_AppDelegate.h:
//
#import <Cocoa/Cocoa.h>
@interface MenuLab_AppDelegate : NSObject {
  BOOL turbo;
}
@property (assign) BOOL turbo;
- (IBAction)toggleTurbo:(id)sender;
@end

//
// MenuLab_AppDelegate.m:
//
#import "MenuLab_AppDelegate.h"
@implementation MenuLab_AppDelegate
@synthesize turbo;
- (IBAction)toggleTurbo:(id)sender {
  self.turbo = !self.turbo;
}
@end
```

Now switch back to *MainMenu.xib* in Interface Builder. Open up the nib file's empty window, change its title to "Turbo Switch", and drag in a checkbox from the *Library*, changing its title to "Turbo" once it's in place. We put this checkbox there to give us a direct view of the value stored in the app delegate's turbo property, so we can easily check and see that our menu items are doing the right thing. Open the *Bindings*

Inspector, and configure the checkbox's *Value* binding, connecting it to *MenuLab_AppDelegate* using the *turbo* key path.

Next, it's time to create some menu items (Figure 10–7 shows you what it should look like when we're done). Double-click the MainMenu object in the nib window, so you can see the menu we're going to add to. If any of the submenus are open, click in the menu window's title bar to close them. Now, search for "submenu" in the *Library*, and drag the resulting *Submenu Menu Item* over to the menu, placing it between the **View** and **Window** menus. Double-click on the new top-level menu item, and change its title to *Tools*. Clicking on it again will reveal that it already contains a single item (titled "Item"). Click to select it, then press ⌘D to duplicate it, which places an identical item just below it.

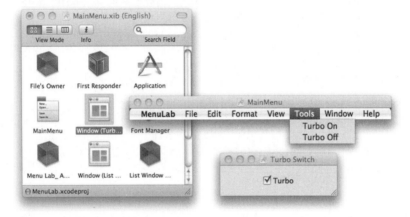

Figure 10–7. *Setting up menu items for toggling a boolean attribute*

At this point, the lower of the two new menu items should be selected. Double-click to select the title text, and rename it "Turbo Off." Ctrl-drag from it to the *MenuLab_AppDelegate* icon in the main window, and connect to the `toggleTurbo:` action. Now bring up the Bindings Inspector, and configure the menu item's *Enabled* binding, connecting to *MenuLab_AppDelegate* using the `turbo` key path. This ensures that the menu will only be enabled if the value of app delegate's `turbo` property is YES.

Now go back to the upper menu item, renaming it "Turbo On," and connecting it to the app delegate's `toggleTurbo:` action just like you did for **Turbo Off**. Because the condition for whether this menu item should be enabled or disabled is the opposite of the condition for the **Turbo Off** menu item, the binding is going to be a little different. It should also have its Enabled binding configured with *MenuLab_AppDelegate* and the `turbo` key path, but below that you also need to specify `NSNegateBoolean` as the *Value Transformer*.

Save your changes, go back to Xcode, and **Build & Run**. You should see the Turbo Switch window appear, containing a checkbox. Your app should have a **Tools** menu containing **Turbo On** and **Turbo Off** items, only one of which should be enabled at a time, and clicking the enabled item should toggle the checkbox and change the state of both menu items, so that now only the other item is enabled. Also, clicking the checkbox should affect the enabled/disabled state of each menu item appropriately.

You've now seen a simple way to enable and disable menu items through the use of bindings, but we'd be remiss if we didn't point out that this usage is sort of artificial, and not really the way that you'd normally deal with application-wide boolean values in a menu. In a case like this, instead of two menu items, one of which is always disabled, you're more likely to use a single menu item showing a checkbox to indicate a state, just like the checkbox in our window does. As it turns out, that's even easier to do than what we've already done. Go back to Interface Builder, select the **Turbo Off** item, and duplicate it with ⌘D. Rename the new item "Turbo," and configure its *Value* binding, connecting to *MenuLab_AppDelegate* using the turbo key path. That's it! Save, back to Xcode, **Build & Run**, and try it out. Note that this quick method doesn't even need the `toggleTurbo:` method, so if you want, you can delete that method along with the **Turbo On** and **Turbo Off** items.

Enabling/Disabling With First Responder

Now we're going to show you a more common way of automatically enabling and disabling menu items, which gives you more fine-grained control, so that the enabled state of each menu item can be updated automatically depending on which window is selected, which text field or other control in a window is selected, and so on. This method works using the responder chain, somewhat similar to how the color panel finds an object to pass a selected color to, as described earlier in this chapter. In this case, the method that's searched for along the responder chain is `validateUserInterfaceItem:`, whose declaration looks like this:

```
- (BOOL)validateUserInterfaceItem:
          (id <NSValidatedUserInterfaceItem>)anItem;
```

If it's implemented in the responder chain's objects, this method is called at the appropriate time to see if the user interface item (in this case, a menu item) should be enabled or not. In implementing this method, you can use `anItem` to get some information about the object that's going to be enabled or disabled; you can ask it for its action (so you can compare with one of your own methods) and for its tag (in case you'd rather compare against a control tag you've established in IB). Usually you'll just want to use the action. We'll show you how this works in just a bit, but first we should probably clarify just when this method is called.

Here's the basic idea: any time Cocoa is about to draw the menu, generally in response to the user clicking on the menu bar, some checks are made for each menu item to determine whether it should be enabled or disabled. The flowchart in Figure 10–8 gives a rough outline of the sequence of events.

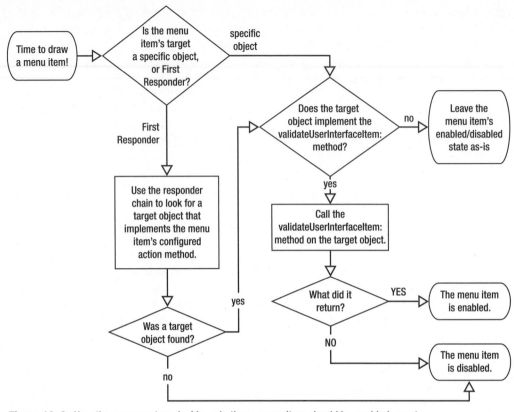

Figure 10–8. *How the menu system decides whether a menu item should be enabled or not*

The upshot of all this is that the menu item's target object, whether configured explicitly or found in the responder chain, is the one that decides whether the menu item should be enabled (at the current time) or not. This means that you have complete dynamic control over each menu item. By implementing `validateUserInterfaceItem:` in each of your classes containing methods that are called by menu items, whether directly or through the responder chain, you can define some logic that the menu system calls at the right time, and automatically enables or disables each menu item based on what you return.

Let's illustrate this with an example. We'll create a new window in our nib file, matched by a new delegate class just for that window, which will implement `validateUserInterfaceItem:` to handle the state of a menu item. In a real application, you would probably base it on the content of a model object, but for simplicity's sake, we'll enable or disable a menu item based on what's selected in the window.

Start by creating a new class in Xcode, just a plain `NSObject` subclass called `ListWindowDelegate`. In its header, define an integer property called `selectedTag`, which we'll later bind to a GUI object (add the lines that are shown in bold):

```
#import <Cocoa/Cocoa.h>
@interface ListWindowDelegate : NSObject {
```

```
    NSInteger selectedTag;
}
@property (assign) NSInteger selectedTag;
@end
```

In the matching .m file, we're going to synthesize the accessors for the selectedTag property, implement the specialAction: method that a menu item will be connected to with target/action via the *First Responder* proxy, and implement the validateUserInterfaceItem: method.

```
#import "ListWindowDelegate.h"
@implementation ListWindowDelegate
@synthesize selectedTag;
- (BOOL)validateUserInterfaceItem:
            (id <NSValidatedUserInterfaceItem>)anItem {
  SEL theAction = [anItem action];
  if (theAction == @selector(specialAction:) ) {
    if (self.selectedTag == 13013) {
      return YES;
    } else {
      return NO;
    }
  }
  // default, in case it's not the action we care about
  return YES;
}
- (void)specialAction:(id)sender {
  NSRunAlertPanel(@"Boy Howdy!",
    @"That's some mighty special action you got there!",
    nil, nil, nil);
}
@end
```

We should point out a thing or two about the validateUserInterfaceItem: method. First, you'll see that we're using the item's action to determine what method it would call if clicked. In code, an action (or any kind of method for that matter) can be referred to by the Objective-C SEL type. Technically, a SEL is not a method, but a "selector": a sort of hash of the method's name, somewhat modified for performance considerations, which the Objective-C runtime can use to look up the method's actual implementation. Besides looking up a method, a SEL can be compared to another SEL, such as that returned by the @selector(specialAction:) construct shown in the code. In our method, we test to see whether the menu item in question is targeted at the action method we care about, in which case we go deeper (if not, we fall through to the end of the method, where we just return YES, assuming the menu item is calling some other action method that we're not going to worry about validating for now). If the actions match up, we then do a simple check against some internal state, in the form of the selectedTag property, to see if we want to allow this menu item to be enabled or not.

Now let's create a GUI to put this code to work. Back in *MainMenu.xib* in Interface Builder, drag a plain NSObject from the Library to the nib window, and use the Identity Inspector to change its class to ListWindowDelegate. Then drag out a new window from the *Library*, and connect its delegate outlet to the ListWindowDelegate object you've already got. Now find a radio group in the *Library*, and drag it into the new window. Including this in the window gives us a rudimentary way to provide a sort of selection for the window and its delegate. Bind the group's *Selected Tag* to the `ListWindowDelegate`'s `selectedTag` property. That way, the delegate is informed whenever someone clicks one of the radio buttons. Now expand the radio group to contain more radio buttons by ⌥-dragging the lower resize handle until there are seven or eight buttons. Then, click on one of the buttons near the middle, and use the Attributes Inspector to change its title to "Special Selection," and its tag to 13013, the "magic number" that we looked for in the code.

All that's left is configuring a new menu item to call the `specialAction:` method via the *First Responder*. Start by selecting the *First Responder* item in the nib window, and bringing up the *Identity Inspector*. Here is where we can manually add any action methods that we want this proxy object to know about. You'll see a list of system-defined actions. Add one of your own by clicking the + button, and changing its name to `specialAction:` (don't forget the colon!). Now for the menu item: find a plain menu item in the *Library*, and drag it into the **Tools** menu you created earlier. Set its title to "Special Action," and configure its target/action by Ctrl-dragging to the *First Responder* item in the nib window, and selecting `specialAction:` from the resulting list.

Now it's time to see this in action. Save your work, go back to Xcode, and hit **Build & Run**. Your app now has a new window, where you can select one of the radio buttons. Click around on some of the radio buttons, each time clicking the **Tools** top-level menu item to see if the **Special Action** item is enabled. It should only be enabled if the *Special Selection* button is selected. If another radio button is selected, or if the app's other window (the old window with the Turbo checkbox) is selected, the menu item should be disabled.

This basic concept can be extended as far as you want. The point is that enabling and disabling menu items is really quite simple. You never have to manually enable or disable individual menu items as things happen in your app; you just write code that is called automatically when a menu item is about to be displayed, and deal with it then.

Sheets

The final topic we're going to cover in this chapter is the concept of sheets. A sheet is simply a window that is temporarily attached to another window, and run in a semi-modal way, such that the "other window" doesn't receive any events. The idea is that an application can have several windows which aren't impacted by each other's demands for user attention. For example, in the TextEdit application included with Mac OS X, you can have the Save As panel appearing as a sheet on one document, the Print panel appearing as a sheet on another, and continue typing in a third (see Figure 10–9).

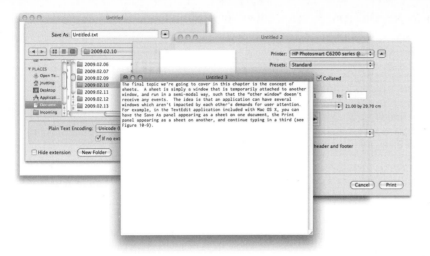

Figure 10–9. *Some standard sheets in action*

Chances are, you won't use sheets in every Cocoa app you ever build, but they are useful in situations where your application needs some sort of user input related to a particular window, and you'd rather not use a modal panel that stops input to the rest of your application. In the example just shown, for instance, without the use of sheets, that Save panel would probably run in a modal fashion, blocking input to all other windows until the user dismissed the save panel. With the use of sheets, the user can temporarily leave the ongoing Save operation and do some other interaction with the application before committing the Save.

Sheets aren't represented by a particular class in Cocoa. Rather, they are normal windows, used in a special way. Every NSWindow can have a sheet attached to it, and every window or panel that's normally used in a modal way can be used as a sheet as well.

Let's see the basics of how to use a sheet by attaching an NSSavePanel to a normal window. Create a new Cocoa application project in Xcode, and save it as SheetLab. If the new project doesn't include an app delegate (e.g. if you are running on Leopard), make a new NSObject subclass called SheetLab_AppDelegate, then open up *MainMenu.xib* and drag a new object from the Library, changing its class to SheetLab_AppDelegate, and connecting the NSApplication's delegate outlet to it.

Now, edit *SheetLab_AppDelegate.h*, adding an outlet and an action method:

```
#import <Cocoa/Cocoa.h>
@interface SheetLab_AppDelegate : NSObject {
    IBOutlet NSWindow *window;
}
- (IBAction)runSaveSheet:(id)sender;
@end
```

Then edit *SheetLab_AppDelegate.m*, adding the following method implementations:

```
#import "SheetLab_AppDelegate.h"
@implementation SheetLab_AppDelegate
- (IBAction)runSaveSheet:(id)sender {
  NSSavePanel *panel = [NSSavePanel savePanel];
  [panel beginSheetForDirectory:nil
    file:nil
    modalForWindow:window
    modalDelegate:self
    didEndSelector:@selector(savePanelDidEnd:returnCode:contextInfo:)
    contextInfo:NULL];
}
- (void)savePanelDidEnd:(NSSavePanel *)sheet
        returnCode:(int)returnCode
        contextInfo:(void *)contextInfo {
  if (returnCode==NSOKButton) {
    NSRunAlertPanel(@"Saving! (just pretending)",
      @"You chose to save in the file:\n\n%@",
      nil, nil, nil, [sheet filename]);
  }
}
@end
```

The `runSaveSheet:` method grabs the standard save panel, and tells it to run modally attached to a window (using the `window` instance variable). It also specifies what method should be called when the sheet is done, passing in the selector of the next method, `savePanelDidEnd:returnCode:contextInfo:`, which gets called at the end of the modal session, at which point it can check the `returnCode` (to see whether the user clicked *Save* or *Cancel*), access the save panel to get the chosen filename, and so on.

Now open up *MainMenu.xib* in Interface Builder, and add a new button to the empty window that's been provided for you. Label the button "Run Save Sheet," and connect it to the app delegate's `runSaveSheet:` action method. The final thing to connect here is the app delegate's `window` property, so Control-drag from the app delegate to the window you have, and select `window` from the list of choices. Save your changes, switch back to Xcode, **Build & Run**, and you should see this all working. Clicking the *Run Save Sheet* button brings up the modal save panel, attached as a sheet on top of the window you just clicked in.

Wrap-up

This chapter provided an introduction to several key parts of the Cocoa GUI experience, as well as a few examples of how the responder chain is used. These features are crucial to making a professional-quality Mac application. Mac users tend to be pretty unforgiving when applications use non-standard behaviors without a good reason, so it's important to know how to deal with windows and menus in ways that users will recognize. In the next chapter, we'll build on this knowledge as we explore Cocoa's classes for dealing with documents and their associated windows.

Chapter 11

Document-Based Applications

So far, the applications we've built in this book all have one major shortcoming in common: each of them acts in sort of an all-or-nothing way. You've either got a particular piece of data in the one backing store that the application is using (if it's using one at all), or you don't have it anywhere. None of them has any notion of letting you split your data into the discrete, unrelated storage units that we call "documents." Although having everything in a single database is good for some purposes, for others it's a huge hindrance. What if you want to share just a part of your data with someone else, or you want to be able to view details for two or more of the same kind of Core Data entity, in multiple windows beside one another, to be able to compare them? Most people are familiar with these possibilities from using almost any modern application, where multiple documents can be open simultaneously, and actions in one don't affect the others.

As it turns out, the good folks at Apple thought of this years ago, and built document support right into Cocoa, centered around the NSDocument and NSDocumentController classes. Cocoa's document architecture gives you access to a whole lot of infrastructure that you'd otherwise have to build yourself, such as managing the window and its title bar, dealing with the open panels and save panels, and more. If you're using Core Data in your application, it will even take care of the actual opening and saving all on its own, so your application code never even has to touch a document file.

In this chapter, you'll learn the basics of how to create a document-based Cocoa application, including the use of Core Data, by creating an application called ColorMix. ColorMix lets the user choose two colors using the standard system color panel, and then presents a grid of color swatches demonstrating different methods of blending the two colors together. Each set of two chosen colors (and its 15 blended colors) can be saved in a document, which is just like any other file and can be saved anywhere you like, and then reopened later on. Along with learning about how Cocoa does documents, you'll also build some simple view classes for drawing colored rectangles, and interact with Core Data in your code. Figure 11–1 shows what the ColorMix application will look like when we're all done.

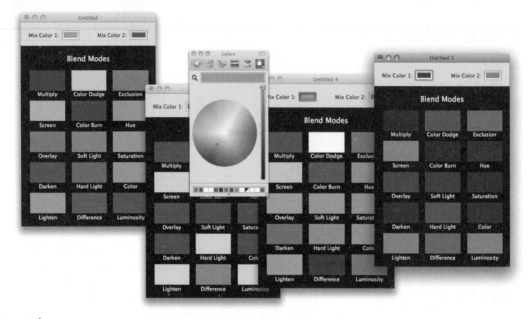

Figure 11–1. *The completed ColorMix application*

If you've used graphics software such as Photoshop or Gimp, you're probably familiar with some of these blend modes. Each of them uses a particular formula that takes the red, green, and blue components of each of the two colors and produces an output color. We won't describe the blend modes here, but you can find detailed descriptions and examples of them at http://en.wikipedia.org/wiki/Blend_modes and elsewhere. What we will do here is show you how to build an application that gives the user a hands-on way to explore all of these modes, two chosen colors at a time.

The blend modes we'll be using are all built into Core Graphics, an important part of Cocoa's graphics architecture that we'll talk more about in Chapter 13. Using this built-in functionality lets you skip doing any sort of color computation on your own; all you do is call Core Graphics functions to set blend modes, and draw rectangles.

Creating the ColorMix Application

Start by creating a new application in Xcode. The new application will use both NSDocument architecture and Core Data, so you'll want to pick the appropriate template when creating the application. If you're running Xcode 3.1 on Leopard, this means choosing the *Core Data Document-based Application* template in the *Mac OS X / Application* section of the New Project assistant; in Snow Leopard, it means choosing the *Cocoa Application* template, then making sure that the checkboxes for creating a document-based application and for using Core Data are both checked. Name the new application ColorMix. As we've done before, open the *Inspector* panel for the project, find the build setting for *Objective-C Garbage Collection*, and set it to *Required*.

The ColorMix application will have a few things you haven't seen created for you before. In particular, it has a class called MyDocument (a subclass of NSPersistentDocument, which is itself a subclass of NSDocument, both of which we'll explain a little later), and a matching *MyDocument.xib* resource. These are the two key elements that you'll extend to define the behavior and appearance of your documents. Apart from that, you'll also see a model file where we'll set up the Core Data entity and attribute information for this app.

Examining the Default Nib Files

Before we get to work on creating anything, open the *MainMenu.xib* file in Interface Builder. You might notice something different about this nib file, compared to every other *MainMenu.xib* file that's been created for you: it contains no window! The main nib window shows you various proxy objects, the menu itself, and that's it. That's another clue that we're dealing with a different sort of creature when creating a document-based application, because such an application (such as Xcode, Microsoft Office, Garage Band, and the like) usually doesn't have any notion of a "main window," and instead puts the bulk of the application into one or more document windows.

Open the Connections Inspector, and take some time to click on some of the menu items and see how they're hooked up. You'll find that many of the items in the **File** menu are connected to *First Responder*, calling actions whose names contain the word "document" (newDocument:, openDocument:, and so on). It turns out that several of these actions are implemented in the NSDocumentController class. This is a special class that has a single shared instance at runtime, for managing all the application's open documents. You won't see this shared instance, or even a proxy for it, in this nib file or anywhere else. The NSApplication creates this object during application launch, and is added to the responder chain so that it can handle these actions.

After you've taken a look around, you can close the *MainMenu.xib* for this application, and you'll never need to open it again. Remember that the only real content in there is the menu, and most of the menu items are connected to actions on *First Responder*, which means they'll find their way to the relevant window controller or the shared NSDocumentController when the time comes.

Now open *MyDocument.xib* and see what it has to offer. You'll find an NSWindow ready for you to fill in some content, and if you open the *Identity Inspector*, you'll see that the *File's Owner* is an instance of MyDocument. Apart from that, it's a blank slate, which you'll make your mark on just a little later.

Defining the Model

Before we start building a GUI of any kind, let's create the data model that will be used to represent a document. This is an extremely simple model, containing a single entity with two attributes. We'll create just a single instance of that one entity in each document, but everything you learn about documents in this chapter applies equally well to large, complex data models.

Open the *MyDocument.xcdatamodel*. Create an entity and name it *ColorSet*. With the new entity still selected, create an attribute, name it *color1*, set its type to *Transformable*, and click to turn off the *Optional* checkbox. Then create a second attribute, name it *color2*, and configure the rest just like the first: the type is *Transformable*, and *Optional* should be turned off. These attributes represent the two colors that the user will choose for each document. Each of them contains an instance of NSColor, which is not one of the supported Core Data types, hence the use of *Transformable* as we described in Chapter 7.

Save the model, and you're done with it. We told you it was an extremely simple model!

Setting Two Colors

Now it's time to start putting the GUI together. Remember that this occurs in the document window, so switch back to *MyDocument.xib* in Interface Builder. The default window contains an NSTextField ("Your document contents here"), which you should delete before going on.

In previous Core Data examples, you learned how to drag entities from Xcode's data modeling tool into Interface Builder. Now it's time to learn another way that's just as good. In the *Library* window, search for "core data," and you'll see the *Core Data Entity* appear in the results. This special object, when dragged into a window, will let you pick an Xcode project, data model file, and entity (see Figure 11–2).

Figure 11–2. *This window lets you choose a data model and entity from among all open Xcode projects.*

After clicking *Next*, it will run the same assistant that you've seen when creating the other Core Data apps. This time, choose the *Single Item View* option from the popup list, click on through the next window where you can choose which attributes should appear, and that part's done. Your nib file now contains a properly configured NSObjectController, and the window contained in the nib file now has a very minimal GUI, featuring a text field for each color.

The Simplest of GUIs

That auto-generated GUI is not only minimal, it's also inappropriate: our attributes are meant to be NSColor instances, not strings or anything else that can fit into a text field, so the first thing to do is delete those text fields. We also have everything held inside a box labeled *Color Set*, which we really don't need because that's the only entity this app has. Select the box by clicking its title, then choose **Layout▸Unembed Objects** from the menu. To underline the fact that the two colors will eventually mixed together, add the word "Mix" to the two remaining labels' titles, ending up with "Mix Color 1" and "Mix Color 2". Let's face it: that whole GUI is pretty useless for our purposes. We really only dragged in the entity from the Library window because it gives us a nice, properly configured NSObjectController to work with. Speaking of which, select that controller object in the nib window and, keeping in line with what we've done with these controllers in the past, rename it to *colorset*.

Now find an NSColorWell in the *Library* window and drag it to the document window you're building. Once it's in place, duplicate it with ⌘D, and then rearrange the labels and color wells to look something like Figure 11–3.

Figure 11–3. *The bare minimum GUI for selecting two colors*

Now select the color well on the left, open the *Bindings Inspector*, and configure its Value binding to use the *colorset* controller with the *selection* controller key and the *color1* model key path. Select the color well on the right, and configure its Value binding to use the *colorset* controller with the *selection* controller key, this time with the *color2* model key path. Save your work, switch back to Xcode, and click **Build & Run**. Our app launches, and a new, empty "Untitled" document window appears, but the color wells are unclickable! In our haste to get something onscreen, we neglected to create something pretty important: a model object!

Creating a Default ColorSet

What we need to do is write some code that will insert a new ColorSet object into the object controller whenever a new document is created. In Xcode, open the *MyDocument.h* file. Here we're going to add two instance variables. One is an outlet called objectController for pointing to the NSObjectController that the assistant put into our nib file a page or two ago. The other is a BOOL called isNew that we'll use to keep track of whether each document has just been created or was loaded from a file. Here are the changes for the .h file:

```
#import <Cocoa/Cocoa.h>
@interface MyDocument : NSPersistentDocument {
  IBOutlet NSObjectController *objectController;
  BOOL isNew;
}
@end
```

Now switch to the *.m* file. This file contains some ready-made methods, with comments showing where you can extend their behaviors. We're going to implement a bit of functionality in the init and windowControllerDidLoad: methods, as well as implementing the initWithType:error: method, which we'll explain in a bit. The predefined methods in here all come from NSDocument, which handles most of the document-related functionality for us. MyDocument's direct superclass, however, is NSPersistentDocument, which implements additional functionality for storing documents as Core Data storage back-ends. Here you see the lines you need to add:

```
#import "MyDocument.h"
@implementation MyDocument
- (id)init {
    self = [super init];
    if (self != nil) {
    }
    return self;
}
- (id)initWithType:(NSString *)typeName error:(NSError **)outError{
  if (self = [super initWithType:typeName error:outError]) {
    isNew = YES;
  }
  return self;
}
- (NSString *)windowNibName {
    return @"MyDocument";
}
- (void)windowControllerDidLoadNib:(NSWindowController *)windowController {
    [super windowControllerDidLoadNib:windowController];
  if (isNew) {
    id newObj = [objectController newObject];
    [newObj setValue:[NSColor redColor] forKey:@"color1"];
    [newObj setValue:[NSColor yellowColor] forKey:@"color2"];
    [objectController addObject:newObj];
  }
}
@end
```

The bits of bold code are executed when a new document is being created. The first, `init`, is called on every instance of `MyDocument`; here, we simply set `isNew` to `NO`. The second, `initWithType:error:`, is only called when a new document is being created from scratch. This is where we'd ideally want to initialize our model objects, but all access to the model objects is mediated through the `NSObjectController`, which is in the nib file, which at this point hasn't been loaded yet. So we just set the `isNew` flag to True, and move along. Finally, `windowControllerDidLoadNib:` is called in `MyDocument` after its nib has been loaded. Here we use the `objectController` to create a new model object, set values for its two attributes, and add the new object to the controller.

With that in place, all that's left to do is to connect `MyDocument`'s `objectController` outlet within *Interface Builder*. So switch back over there, Ctrl-drag from the *File's Owner* to the colorset object controller, and select the `objectController` outlet. Save your work, go back to Xcode, **Build & Run**. You should now see red and yellow colors in the two color wells, and clicking on one of them should bring up the color panel and let you change the color.

Not only that, but you'll now find that a full complement of document functionality is available through the menu. You can save your documents, close them, access recent documents, open documents, and so on.

Settling on a File Format

Having gotten to this point, you've probably noticed that when you save a document, a popup list lets you choose to save the file as *Binary*, *SQLite*, or *XML*, and the file extension is set accordingly. While this level of flexibility may be of some use during development, for a shipping product you should really just pick a format and stick with it, to avoid confusing your users. In general, SQLite is probably the best choice for most applications. You should also change the file extension to something that suggests the use of your app, instead of the default extension. All of these options are configured in Xcode's *Target Inspector*. Go back to Xcode, open the Targets group in the navigation pane, click on the *ColorMix* target, and press ⌘I to open the *Inspector*. Select the *Properties* tab, and the lower half of the panel shows you a table containing all three pre-configured file formats (labeled here as "Document Types"); Select and delete the *Binary* and *XML* options (by using the "-" button at the table's lower left-hand corner), leaving only the *SQLite* option. Give this remaining format a decent filename extension by editing the value shown in the *Extensions* column, changing it to *ColorMix*. Now save your work, **Build & Run**, and save a color set, verifying that you now have no choice about what kind of file format to save it as.

Adding Color

Now the document stuff is all working as it should, but we've got a really boring application that doesn't do anything interesting at all. Let's make our app do what we promised in the beginning of this chapter: display a bunch of colors made by blending the two chosen colors using all of Core Graphics' predefined blending modes.

To do this, we're going to create a new class called ColorBlendView, which will be a direct subclass of NSView. One of the primary things you typically do in an NSView subclass is override the drawRect: mode to specify exactly what should be drawn. We're going to do just that, and fill each view with a blended color. In order to do the blending, each instance of ColorBlendView needs to know which blending mode to use, and which two colors to blend. We'll set up the blending mode for each ColorBlendView by hand, but the values for the two colors will be populated using Cocoa Bindings, so that as soon as the user changes one of the chosen colors, all of the ColorBlendView objects in our window will be instantly redrawn.

The ColorBlendView Class

Start by creating a new class in your project. In the *New File* assistant, choose *Objective-C NSView subclass* from the *Cocoa* section, name your new class ColorBlendView.m, and click the checkbox to also create the *.h* file.

Now edit *ColorBlendView.h*, adding the bold lines shown in the following:

```
#import <Cocoa/Cocoa.h>
@interface ColorBlendView : NSView {
  NSColor * color1;
  NSColor * color2;
  CGBlendMode blendMode;
}
@property (retain) NSColor * color1;
@property (retain) NSColor * color2;
@property (assign) CGBlendMode blendMode;
@end
```

This gives our class two NSColor objects, which will be populated by Cocoa Bindings, and a CGBlendMode, which will be set by the MyController class when it's loading a nib file. Now switch over to *ColorBlendView.m*, where the first thing we'll do is define the methods for the properties we've declared. Most of the properties we've declared previously in this book have their methods defined entirely with the @synthesize declaration, but here we have a bit of a special case, because we want our view to redraw itself each time any of the property values changes. So we use both @synthesize declarations and explicit setter methods. Explicit methods, if present, always take the place of any synthesized methods, which means we can synthesize the getters even while explicitly coding the setters.

```
// put these at the beginning of the @implementation block
@synthesize color1;
@synthesize color2;
@synthesize blendMode;
- (void)setBlendMode:(CGBlendMode)bm {
  if (blendMode != bm) {
    blendMode = bm;
    [self setNeedsDisplay:YES];
  }
}
- (void)setColor1:(NSColor *)c {
  if (![c isEqual:color1]) {
```

```
        [color1 release];
        color1 = [c retain];
        [self setNeedsDisplay:YES];
    }
}
- (void)setColor2:(NSColor *)c {
    if (![c isEqual:color2]) {
        [color2 release];
        color2 = [c retain];
        [self setNeedsDisplay:YES];
    }
}
```

A couple of things to point out: you may have noticed that we're using release and retain here, even though we're using garbage collection. This is partly due to old authors having deeply ingrained habits that are hard to break, but there are practical reasons for doing so as well. In this case, this small class is something that one might want to port over to a platform where garbage collection isn't available, such as the iPhone. With the balanced retain/release calls in place, moving this code to the iPhone is as simple as changing a few class names (for example, NSView and NSColor become UIView and UIColor). The other thing to note is the [self setNeedsDisplay:YES] call. we'll get into this more in later chapters covering drawing in Cocoa, but the basic idea is that when you want to draw some content in an NSView, you call this method, which sets a flag, and when your application is done processing whatever event it's currently handling, it will look through the open windows to see if anyone has been flagged for redrawing, which leads to the eventual calling of the drawRect: method.

Speaking of which, the only other method we need to implement in this class is the drawRect: method itself.

```
- (void)drawRect:(NSRect)rect {
    // don't draw anything if we don't have two valid colors.
    if (!self.color1 || !self.color2) return;

    CGColorRef cgColor1 = genericRGBWithNSColor(self.color1);
    CGColorRef cgColor2 = genericRGBWithNSColor (self.color2);

    CGContextRef myContext = [[NSGraphicsContext currentContext] graphicsPort];
    CGContextSaveGState(myContext);

    CGContextSetFillColorWithColor(myContext, cgColor1);
    CGContextSetBlendMode(myContext, kCGBlendModeNormal);
    CGContextFillRect(myContext, NSRectToCGRect(rect));

    CGContextSetFillColorWithColor(myContext, cgColor2);
    CGContextSetBlendMode(myContext, self.blendMode);
    CGContextFillRect(myContext, NSRectToCGRect(rect));

    CGContextRestoreGState(myContext);

    CGColorRelease(cgColor1);
    CGColorRelease(cgColor2);
}
```

Try not to get too caught up in the details here. It's enough if you read the comments, and trust that the code is doing what the comments claim it's doing. After going through some of the later chapters where we'll be dealing with graphics, this will start to make more sense.

The final piece we need to add for this class to work is a conversion routine so that the NSColors that are picked by the user in the color panel can be converted to the CGColorRefs that are necessary for the Core Graphics functions. For some reason, Cocoa doesn't include any one-line function or method calls that do this, but the following function does the trick nicely. Insert this near the top of the .m file. Anywhere above the drawRect: method is fine, but, for the sake of keeping things structured, we'd recommend putting it just above the @implementation block, to make it clear that this function is not a part of the class.

```
static CGColorRef genericRGBWithNSColor (NSColor *color) {
  CGColorRef cgColor = NULL;

  NSColorSpace *nsColorSpace = [NSColorSpace genericRGBColorSpace];
  NSColor *deviceRGBColor = [color colorUsingColorSpace: nsColorSpace];
  if (deviceRGBColor != nil) {
    CGFloat components[4];
    [deviceRGBColor getRed: &components[0] green: &components[1]
                      blue: &components[2] alpha: &components[3]];

    cgColor = CGColorCreate([nsColorSpace CGColorSpace], components);
  }

  return cgColor;
}
```

With that in place, the ColorBlendView class is complete. Save your work and click **Build**, and it should compile cleanly. We're only asking you to click **Build** now to make sure that no typos have crept in up to this point; we haven't set up the GUI yet, so there's no point hitting **Build & Run** right now.

Adding Blended Colors to the GUI

Now it's time to add the blended color swatches to our document window. Let's start by adding an outlet for each of them to the *MyDocument.h* file. Each of the new outlets shown here will end up connected to an instance of ColorBlendView. We're also adding a line near the top with an @class declaration, which simply tells the compiler that the next token (ColorBlendView) is the name of a class. That's just enough information to let the compiler deal with instance variables and method arguments that are pointers to instances of that class, without importing the class' header itself. Using these forward declarations consistently in your header files can give you slightly better compile times, and also makes your header files less brittle, because they have fewer dependencies on one another. In your implementation files, however, where you're going to call methods on these classes, you'll need to import the header file.

```
#import <Cocoa/Cocoa.h>
@class ColorBlendView;
```

```
@interface MyDocument : NSPersistentDocument {
  IBOutlet NSObjectController *objectController;
  BOOL isNew;
  IBOutlet ColorBlendView *multiplyBlendView;
  IBOutlet ColorBlendView *screenBlendView;
  IBOutlet ColorBlendView *overlayBlendView;
  IBOutlet ColorBlendView *darkenBlendView;
  IBOutlet ColorBlendView *lightenBlendView;
  IBOutlet ColorBlendView *colorDodgeBlendView;
  IBOutlet ColorBlendView *colorBurnBlendView;
  IBOutlet ColorBlendView *softLightBlendView;
  IBOutlet ColorBlendView *hardLightBlendView;
  IBOutlet ColorBlendView *differenceBlendView;
  IBOutlet ColorBlendView *exclusionBlendView;
  IBOutlet ColorBlendView *hueBlendView;
  IBOutlet ColorBlendView *saturationBlendView;
  IBOutlet ColorBlendView *colorBlendView;
  IBOutlet ColorBlendView *luminosityBlendView;
}
@end
```

Now go back to *MyDocument.xib* in Interface Builder, and make the window bigger, about 350×500, leaving the two color pickers at the top. Find a `CustomView` (really an instance of a plain old `NSView`) in the *Library*, drag it into the window, and use the *Identity Inspector* to change its class to `ColorBlendView`. Then resize the `ColorBlendView` to about 90×50, using the *Size Inspector* to help you out. We need to see which blend mode the view represents, so drag a label from the *Library* into the window, just below the `ColorBlendView`, and use the *Attributes Inspector* to center the label's text (see Figure 11–4).

Figure 11–4. *Putting the first ColorBlendView in place*

Select both the `ColorBlendView` and the label, press ⌘D to duplicate them, and line the new ones up a bit to the right. Press ⌘D again, and line the new set up even further to the right. Now select all three `ColorBlendViews` and all three labels, press ⌘D, and line the new ones up below the old ones. Keep doing this until you have five rows of three labels, then go through all of the labels and set their titles, as shown in Figure 11–5.

Figure 11–5. *The grid of soon-to-be-blended colors*

With the layout in place, it's time for a whole lot of connecting. You need to Ctrl-drag from the `MyDocument` icon in the nib window to each of the `ColorBlendViews`, connecting each with the outlet named similarly to the label below it.

Then it's time to go back to *MyDocument.m* in Xcode. You're going to add the code that will configure each `ColorBlendView` with the right blend mode, and manually configure bindings so that each `ColorBlendView` is updated whenever the user picks a color. Start by importing the header file for the `ColorBlendView` class, so that we can call its methods. Add the following line somewhere near the top of *MyDocument.m*:

```
#import "ColorBlendView.h"
```

Next, modify the `windowControllerDidLoadNib:` method as shown here:

```
- (void)windowControllerDidLoadNib:(NSWindowController *)windowController
{
  [super windowControllerDidLoadNib:windowController];
  if (isNew) {
    id newObj = [objectController newObject];
    [newObj setValue:[NSColor redColor] forKey:@"color1"];
    [newObj setValue:[NSColor yellowColor] forKey:@"color2"];
    [objectController addObject:newObj];
  }
```

```
[multiplyBlendView setBlendMode:kCGBlendModeMultiply];
[screenBlendView setBlendMode:kCGBlendModeScreen];
[overlayBlendView setBlendMode:kCGBlendModeOverlay];
[darkenBlendView setBlendMode:kCGBlendModeDarken];
[lightenBlendView setBlendMode:kCGBlendModeLighten];
[colorDodgeBlendView setBlendMode:kCGBlendModeColorDodge];
[colorBurnBlendView setBlendMode:kCGBlendModeColorBurn];
[softLightBlendView setBlendMode:kCGBlendModeSoftLight];
[hardLightBlendView setBlendMode:kCGBlendModeHardLight];
[differenceBlendView setBlendMode:kCGBlendModeDifference];
[exclusionBlendView setBlendMode:kCGBlendModeExclusion];
[hueBlendView setBlendMode:kCGBlendModeHue];
[saturationBlendView setBlendMode:kCGBlendModeSaturation];
[colorBlendView setBlendMode:kCGBlendModeColor];
[luminosityBlendView setBlendMode:kCGBlendModeLuminosity];
NSArray *allBlendViews = [NSArray arrayWithObjects:
  multiplyBlendView, screenBlendView, overlayBlendView,
  darkenBlendView, lightenBlendView, colorDodgeBlendView,
  colorBurnBlendView, softLightBlendView, hardLightBlendView,
  differenceBlendView, exclusionBlendView, hueBlendView,
  saturationBlendView, colorBlendView, luminosityBlendView, nil];
for (ColorBlendView *cbv in allBlendViews) {
  [cbv bind:@"color1" toObject:objectController
withKeyPath:@"selection.color1" options:nil];
  [cbv bind:@"color2" toObject:objectController
withKeyPath:@"selection.color2" options:nil];
  }
}
```

The first part of that chunk of code sets the blend mode for each view, one at a time. The second part configures bindings for each `ColorBlendView`. Because the bindings are the same for all of them, we iterate through an array (created on the fly just before the `for` loop) of all the `ColorBlendViews`, and do the bindings for each of them.

This is really the first time we've asked you to do a lot of GUI configuration in code. With Cocoa's included objects, you can configure a lot of things right in Interface Builder, but it's not always so straightforward with your own classes. It is possible to write plugins for Interface Builder that will allow you to configure your own classes there as well, which can be a good idea in some situations, but would be overkill in this case.

Note that the calls to `bind:toObject:withKeyPath:` accomplish the same thing as configuring bindings in Interface Builder. Each binding you configure in Interface Builder is, in fact, more a verb than a noun. When you load a nib file containing bindings, each saved binding triggers a call just like you see here. Note also that what's represented in Interface Builder as a *Controller Key* and *Model Key Path*, at the end of the day, are merged into a single string for the `bind:toObject:withKeyPath:` call.

Okay, enough theorizing for now. It's time to save your work, **Build & Run**, and you should see something like Figure 11–6.

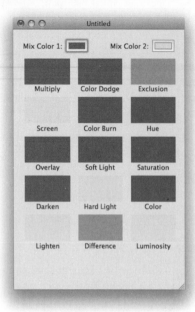

Figure 11–6. *Finally, we see the blended colors.*

Click on one of the color wells to open the color panel and start sliding things around in there, and you'll see that all 15 blended colors are updated right along with the color you're setting. Pretty slick! But the window itself still looks pretty boring.

Adding Some Background Bling

There's a simple way to spruce this window up. We'll put a black backdrop behind everything in the lower part of the window. In Xcode, make a new NSView subclass called BlackView, with the following content:

```
// BlackView.h:
#import <Cocoa/Cocoa.h>
@interface BlackView : NSView {
}
@end

// BlackView.m:
#import "BlackView.h"
@implementation BlackView
- (void)drawRect:(NSRect)rect {
  [[NSColor blackColor] set];
  NSRectFill(rect);
}
@end
```

This simple class does nothing but draw a black rectangle over its whole area. Perfect! Now go back to Interface Builder, drag an NSView from the Library to your document window, and use the Identity Inspector to change its class to BlackView. While it's still selected, resize it to cover everything below the color wells, then use the **Layout**➤**Send To Back** function in the menu to push it to the background of the window. Select all the labels in the window, and use the *Attributes Inspector* to set the foreground color for all of them to white. Finally, slide all the labels and blend views down a bit and make room for another label entitled *Blend Modes*. Make it white as well, and use the font panel to make it a bit bigger than the other labels. Save your work, go back to Xcode, and **Build & Run**. Figure 11–7 shows the completed window as it appears in Interface Builder, alongside the running app.

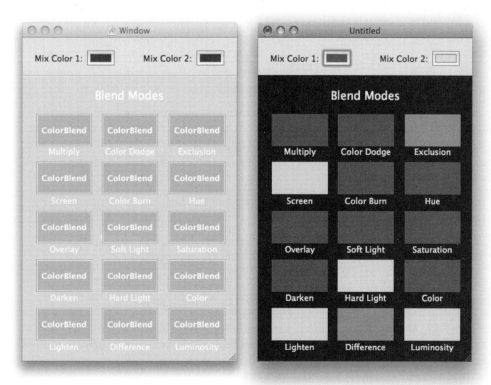

Figure 11–7. *ColorMix in its final form*

Now that the application is up and running, you can use the standard menu items to create multiple documents, specify different colors for each document, save documents, close them, manage their windows, and so on. Cocoa's document architecture takes care of the details of instantiating your documents and document controllers, loading nib files, using a Save panel, and more. All of these features can be enhanced by the developer (e.g. you can customize the process of saving documents in various ways), but you can also go quite a long way using just the basic functionally that works right out of the box.

About Undo and Redo

At this point, we should mention NSUndoManager, which handles undo/redo support in Cocoa. You may have noticed that the actions you perform in ColorMix (really just changing colors) are all undoable, and redoable, via items in the Edit menu. Also, you may have noticed that these undo and redo actions are document-specific; making changes and undoing them in one document is completely separate from whatever happens in other documents. What's probably not so clear, however, is just what's enabling that functionality; we haven't written any code to deal with undo and redo, and yet there it is. The short answer is this: in a Core Data application, basic undo/redo typically is taken care of for you, and you don't have to do anything. The managed object context that deals with the model objects is able to notice when an object is edited, and add an inverse operation to the "undo stack." The upshot of this is that, for most modern Cocoa apps, you get undo and redo for free.

However, this is a book about programming, not about listing cool features of the frameworks. At the very least, you need to know a bit about how the underlying pieces work, so you have some idea where to tweak things if necessary. So, here's a crash course in how undo/redo support works in Cocoa, and how Core Data and NSDocument conspire to make it work automatically.

The Undo Stack

Many programmers have probably never given much thought to how undo and redo are typically implemented in an application. It's one of those things that have become so universally accepted and expected that it seems like it's just part of the natural order of things. The basic premise is this: each time you edit something in your app, an item representing the reverse of the editing needs to be created. So, if the user adds the letter "X" to the end of a piece of text, a piece of code needs to create a representation of the opposite, an operation that can delete that same "X." That representation is then placed on a stack of similar items somewhere (the "undo stack"). Invoking an "undo" command consists of popping the most recent item from the top of the undo stack, and performing the action it describes. At the same time, invoking an "undo" command ends up creating yet another item, the reverse of the reversed item from the undo stack (the same as the original edit, in fact), and placing it on a "redo stack", in case the user later wants to undo the undo.

This architecture has variations, such as limited stack sizes, or just single undo items without any stacks at all, but the basic architecture is pretty similar across most platforms. One thing that's pretty special about Cocoa's way of implementing this is that, instead of representing each undo item in a special form that has to be later decoded in some way, each undo item is constructed implicitly using the target object, the method selector to be called on it, and whatever arguments are required. When the "undo" command is triggered, there's no decoding or lookups of any kind. The method is simply invoked just like any other Objective-C method.

Let's take a look at an example. Imagine the following method, placed in a class that has a settable name:

```
- (void)setName:(NSString *)newName {
    if (![newName isEqual:name]) {
        name = newName;
    }
}
```

Now imagine that we want to make setting the name an action that can be undone. This is easily accomplished by adding the lines shown in bold below:

```
- (void)setName:(NSString *)newName {
    if (![newName isEqual:name]) {
        NSUndoManager *undoManager = …
        [undoManager registerUndoWithTarget:self
                selector:@selector(setName:)
                object:name];
        [undoManager setActionName:@"Name Change"];
        name = newName;
    }
}
```

Note that we left out the part of the code where we actually acquire the undo manager. In an actual application, the undo manager can come from one of several places, depending on whether or not the app has Core Data and NSDocument support. In a Core Data app, you can always ask the shared NSManagedObjectContext object for an undo manager, and in an app with both Core Data and Document support each document has its own undo manager.

The ultimate expression of this occurs in a Core Data application, which actually implements something like the above on your behalf. If you look at the setName: method above, you can see that it's pretty formulaic. Core Data implements some magic behind the scenes so that you don't have to implement that setName: method. As soon as any edit occurs to a model object, Core Data notices and sets up the undo for you.

In Conclusion

Now you've created your first NSDocument-based application from the ground up, and learned a bit about drawing to an NSView and dealing with colors, all of which are useful skills for a variety of application areas. In later chapters, we'll build on those skills even more, especially the fun graphics programming where Cocoa really shines, but in the next chapter we have to take a break from the fun and learn what happens when things go wrong in your apps, and how to deal with them, using NSError and NSException.

Chapter 12

Exceptions, Signals, Errors, and Debugging

Anyone who's done any sort of programming knows that sometimes, things just don't work out as planned. You forget to handle a specific edge case, or a system call fails in a way that's never occurred to you, and suddenly your program blows up in your face. Every programming language and development environment has ways of dealing with these problems, and Cocoa is no exception. In this chapter, you'll learn about Cocoa's mechanisms for creating and handling exceptions and errors, two similar-sounding but conceptually very different systems. You'll learn the different ways that each of them is used, how to handle them, and how to initiate them yourself. You'll also learn how certain memory abuses can cause signals to occur, typically resulting in a crash. And, we'll take a peek at the debugger built into Xcode which can help you tackle these problems.

Exception Handling

Let's start off with exception handling. An *exception* is a special object that can be created in one part of a program in order to tell another part that something has gone wrong; this is called "raising" an exception, and in code it might look something like this:

```
// imagine we're in a method that has a parameter "index", whose
// value must not be negative.
if (index < 0) {
  [NSException raise:NSRangeException format:
    @"I can't take all this negativity! (index == %d)", index];
}
```

In this case, we're creating and raising an exception in a single step, using a class method of the NSException class. The first parameter to this method is a string for the exception's name (in this case NSRangeException, which is a predefined exception name defined in Cocoa), which allows for general categorization of exceptions. Unlike many other exception-handling environments, NSException is seldom subclassed, and so its name is used to differentiate between different types of exceptions. The second

239

parameter we pass is a format for the exception's "reason," a human-readable descriptive string. This format is the same sort of list of items you can pass to NSLog, where the first is an NSString and the others are interpolated as specified by the string.

Catching Exceptions

When that code is executed, if index < 0, the program's normal flow is interrupted. Instead of continuing with the rest of the method, the program will start working its way down the call stack, looking for a special code construct called an "exception handler." An exception handler will execute all code contained within a pair of curly-braces prefaced by the @try keyword and, if an exception is raised during that execution, execution will jump to an adjacent block marked with the @catch keyword and execute the code contained there. This is called "handling the exception." Finally, you may optionally include a third block of code labeled with @finally keyword, which will be executed no matter what happens in the @try and @catch section, in order to perform any necessary cleanup.

The following example shows creating the same exception as before, but now within a @try block. We catch it in the @catch block and output an error message, then move on to the @finally section, which is executed no matter what happens. In this simple case, we don't need the @finally section and could just omit it, but it can be useful in situations where some resource is initialized in the @try block and needs to be freed up.

```
@try {
   if (index < 0) {
      [NSException raise:NSRangeException format:
         @"I can't take all this negativity! (index == %d)", index];
   }
}
@catch (NSException * e) {
   NSLog(@"Encountered exception %@ with reason %@",
      [e name],
      [e reason]);
}
@finally {
   // we don't have anything to do here, really.
}
```

This example handles the exception in the same method where it was raised, but that's actually pretty uncommon. More likely, no local exception handler is found, so the system traverses the call stack looking for an exception handler, first in the current method's caller, then *that* method's caller, and so on. This search continues down the call stack until an exception handler is found. If none is found, a special-case scenario can be configured to handle the uncaught exception. By default, a Cocoa app that encounters an uncaught exception will print some info about the exception to the console log, and then try to continue running as usual.

The Limited Role of Exceptions in Cocoa

In Cocoa, exceptions are used to make a method break out of its normal operating flow in case of a serious problem that should not occur while the program is running. In general, if your code causes an exception to be raised, you've got a bug. With few exceptions, a properly written Cocoa program should be able to run forever without a single exception ever being raised.

If you have a background in Java, Ruby, Python, or C++, this may seem a little restrictive. In many other environments, exceptions are used a little more freely, such as a file-reading method raising an exception to tell the caller that it's read to the end of the file (which, if you think about it, is not an exceptional state at all, because every file has an end). In Python, one common idiom for iterating through an array is to increment an index, try to read the indexed value from the array, and catch the resulting exception when you read past the end. In Cocoa, however, this sort of thing is frowned upon, and exceptions are normally used only for reporting unexpected results that are probably caused by a bug in the program.

Because of the rather limited role of exceptions in Cocoa, you don't often see a lot of exception-handling code inside Cocoa apps. Unlike Java, Objective-C doesn't require (or even allow) its methods to specify what kinds of exceptions they may raise, and in theory you don't really *have* to handle them at all. By default, each Cocoa app you create will have a sort of top-level exception handler that simply outputs some information about the exception to the system log, and then lets the app continue on its way as best it can. Unfortunately, this isn't much of a strategy, because whatever your app was doing at the time of the exception was most likely happening in response to the last user action (clicking a button, pressing a key, and the like), and whatever else that action was supposed to be doing after that is just skipped right over, potentially leaving your application in an undefined or inconsistent state!

Some applications install a special top-level exception handler of their own to deal with these situations. Xcode, for instance, occasionally hits an exception (yes, even Xcode has bugs!), at which point it typically gives you to the opportunity to quit the app, recognizing the possibility that something is mucked up.

Create a Test-bed

Let's build a small application that demonstrates some of the kinds of exceptions that Cocoa programmers are likely to encounter. In Xcode, create a new Cocoa application (no Core Data or documents involved this time) and name it "ExceptionCity." If you're running Snow Leopard, the application you create will automatically have a class named `ExceptionCityAppDelegate`, but if you're running Leopard, you'll need to make this class yourself, then use Interface Builder to create an instance of it in *MainMenu.xib* and connect the `NSApplication`'s `delegate` outlet to it, just like you've done before.

Our app delegate is going to be a very simple class, containing the `applicationDidFinishLaunching:` delegate method, which calls three different "utility" methods, each of which demonstrates a common Cocoa pitfall that can result in

exceptions being raised at runtime. If all three methods manage to do their work and
return, you'll be rewarded by the appearance of a congratulatory alert panel (just what
you always wanted). However, each method has a problem that will raise an exception.
Your mission, should you choose to accept it, will be to find and fix each problem.
Here's the complete content of the *ExceptionCityAppDelegate.m* file:

```objc
#import "ExceptionCityAppDelegate.h"
@implementation ExceptionCityAppDelegate
- (void)invalidArgumentException_unrecognizedSelector {
  // The downside of dynamism is the occasional type mismatch.
  // For instance, it's sometimes hard to be sure what's coming
  // out of an array.  Imagine this array is created somewhere...
  NSArray *nameComponents = [NSArray arrayWithObjects:
                               @"Thurston",
                               @"Howell",
                               [NSNumber numberWithInt:3],
                               nil];
  // ... and accessed later on, by code that just assumes all the
  // array's items are strings:
  NSInteger nameComponentLength = 0;
  for (NSString *component in nameComponents) {
    nameComponentLength += [component length];
  }
  NSLog(@"Total length of all name components: %d",
    nameComponentLength);
}
- (void)invalidArgumentException_insertNil {
  // assuming we have an array to put things into...
  NSMutableArray *array = [NSMutableArray array];
  // ... we can add an object to it.
  id object1 = @"hello";
  [array addObject:object1];
  // but suppose we take a method parameter or instance variable
  // whose value we haven't checked to make sure it wasn't nil...
  id object2 = nil;
  // ... and try to add it to the array?
  [array addObject:object2];
  NSLog(@"inserted all the objects I could!");
}
- (void)rangeException {
  // assuming we have an array of things...
  NSArray *array = [NSArray arrayWithObjects:@"one", @"two", @"three",
    nil];
  // ... we can ask for the index of an item...
  NSUInteger indexOfTwo = [array indexOfObject:@"two"];
  // ... and we can later retrieve that value using the same index.
  NSLog(@"found indexed item %@", [array objectAtIndex:indexOfTwo]);

  // But, what if we try to find the index for something that's not
  // there?
  NSUInteger indexOfFive = [array indexOfObject:@"five"];
  // And we forget to check the return value to make sure it's not
  // NSNotFound?
  NSLog(@"found indexed item %@", [array objectAtIndex:indexOfFive]);
}
- (void)applicationDidFinishLaunching:(NSNotification *)aNotification
{
```

```
    [self invalidArgumentException_unrecognizedSelector];
    [self invalidArgumentException_insertNil];
    [self rangeException];
    NSRunAlertPanel(@"Success", @"Hooray, you fixed everything!",
      nil, nil, nil);
}
@end
```

If you run this code, you'll see that the promised alert panel won't appear (but the empty window included in the default nib file will). What will happen, though, is that something like the following will appear in Xcode's debug output:

```
2009-09-14 16:35:35.783 ExceptionCity[4698:10b] *** -[NSCFNumber length]: unrecognized
selector sent to instance 0x109310
```

If you look back at the invalidArgumentException_unrecognizedSelector method and its comments, you can probably see where this is coming from: our array contains an NSNumber, which doesn't have a length method, and as a result an exception is raised. We're not doing anything to explicitly deal with the exception, and it ends up going all the way down the call stack without being handled, which leads to the default behavior mentioned earlier: some info about the exception (specifically, its reason) is logged, and the application skips the rest of the current event. In this case, the event being processed is the application launch, which is already done at this point.

If we hadn't just pointed out that method for you, things wouldn't be so clear. The logged exception info doesn't tell you anything about where it came from, the name of the exception, or anything else that might help you find what part of your code triggered the exception. This is where your new friend, the Xcode debugger, comes in. Every exception that is raised in Cocoa is passed through a C function called objc_exception_throw, so we can set a breakpoint there, and our program will halt in the debugger every time an exception is raised in our application.

THE DEBUGGER

Most developers are probably familiar with the concept of a debugger, which lets you inspect the state of your application while it's running in order to diagnose problems. If you haven't encountered a debugger before, here's a quick rundown of some of the key concepts:

- A *breakpoint* lets you specify, either with a line number in your source code or the name of a method or function, a spot where the program should halt. When your program has halted, you can examine all CPU registers at that spot in the program's execution. If you have the source code for the program, you can also access any variables (local, instance, or otherwise) that are relevant at that spot. All CPU registers and available variables are shown in a table view in Xcode's debug layout.

- The *call stack* is the list of all the nested methods and functions that are in operation at any point in time. This appears in a table view in Xcode's debug layout. When your program is halted, the current method or function appears at the top of the call stack, the method or function that called it appears below it, and so on. You can choose a particular item or "frame" in the call stack in order to switch focus, at which point you'll see the CPU registers and variables as they were when that method or function called the method or function above it in the call stack.

- The debugger contains buttons that let you perform some actions relative to the currently highlighted code line. You can step over the current line (which executes the rest of what's on the line and then halts at the next line), step into the next method or function (which will halt at the beginning of the next method or function that's called), step out of the current method or function, halting in the caller just after returning, or continue or stop the program.

- The debugger contains a command-line interface (a version of the gdb command that is standard on UNIX-based operating systems) which lets you all the functionality mentioned before, as well as execute arbitrary code and examine the results. You can call C functions and Objective-C methods by typing their names just as you would in your source code, and use values from the running program's variables as message recipients and parameters.

For more detailed information on using the Xcode debugger, see the Xcode Debugging Guide included with the Xcode documentation.

In Xcode, open the Breakpoints view by selecting **Run▶Show▶Breakpoints** or by pressing ⌥⌘B. This opens the Breakpoints window (see Figure 12–1).

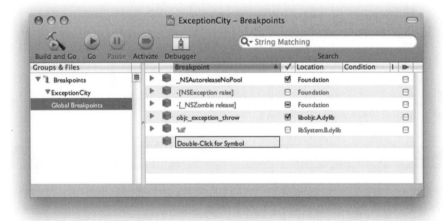

Figure 12–1. *Xcode's Breakpoints window, showing some of the authors' favorite global breakpoints*

On the left side of the window, you'll see a hierarchy of all the breakpoints you've defined, including selections from each open project as well as a list of global breakpoints that will be used for every project you run. On the right you see the breakpoints that fit the left-hand-side selection. We're going to add a symbolic breakpoint, which means we're using the name of a method or function instead of specifying a source code line, to the *Global Breakpoints* group, so it will be present in every project you run. Remember, every raised exception is the result of a bug, probably yours, and you'll want to take every chance you get to stop and see where it's coming from.

Double-click in the space where it says "Double-Click for Symbol," type in objc_exception_throw, and press Enter. This configures a new breakpoint that will stop whenever the program enters the objc_exception_throw function. The *Breakpoint* column shows the name of the symbol you entered (or, if you set a breakpoint directly in a source code file, the name of the method or function containing the line, along with the breakpoint number), and the *Location* column shows the name of the library where the symbol is located, or the name of the source code file, if it's available. There are a number of options available for each breakpoint you configure, but the only one we'll point out right now is the column whose header contains just a checkmark. Clicking a breakpoint's checkbox in this column lets you disable and re-enable the breakpoint.

Now restart the ExceptionCity application by choosing **Run**▶**Debug** from the menu, first quitting it if it's still running. This time, when the application hits the problematic code, it will halt execution where the exception is raised. Figure 12–2 shows roughly what Xcode looks like at this point.

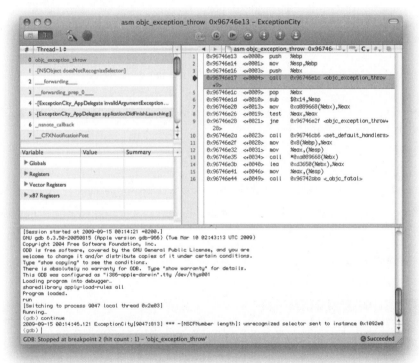

Figure 12–2. *Xcode stops at a breakpoint.*

The upper left shows the call stack, with the location of our breakpoint (objc_exception_throw) at the top and all callers below. Note that the frames for which we have source code available are rendered with black text, while the frames that are stuck in closed-source libraries are shown with gray text. The grayed-out frames are still accessible, but only in the form of assembly language.

The middle left shows all available variables and register values, where you can see some simple values immediately. The upper right shows the source code or compiled assembly code for the chosen stack frame. The bottom view shows you the gdb console interface, where you can both view your program's output (generated by NSLog etc), and enter commands at the gdb prompt. If you're not seeing that bottom view, you can make it appear by selected Run▶Console from the menu.

At this point, having halted right at the start of the function that's used to raise an exception, it would be interesting to see what the exception is. But how? All we see is a pile of assembly code, no variable names or anything else to guide our way. Fortunately, there is a calling convention that we can make use of. In code compiled for Mac OS X (on Intel hardware), the first parameter to any function is, at least at the beginning of the function, contained in a register called eax, which in gdb can be accessed with a special variable called $eax. The first parameter to the objc_exception_throw function is the exception instance itself, so there we go! The version of gdb included with Xcode includes the po command for printing an object's value in a readable format (what it actually does is call the object's description method, which returns an NSString, and print that string value). Try this at the gdb prompt:

```
(gdb) po $eax
*** -[NSCFNumber length]: unrecognized selector sent to instance 0x1092e0
```

Look familiar? That is, of course, the same text we saw in the output earlier on. Knowing that we have access to the NSException here, we can make use of gdb's live Objective-C method execution to ask it some more things:

```
(gdb) po [$eax name]
NSInvalidArgumentException
(gdb) po [$eax reason]
*** -[NSCFNumber length]: unrecognized selector sent to instance 0x1092e0
```

Here we see that the reason method's return value is the same as the description return value, but the name method returns the name, which you may recall is typically used as a sort of type or category for the exception. In this case, we're looking at one of the most frequently encountered exception types in Cocoa: NSInvalidArgumentException.

NSInvalidArgumentException

This exception can in theory be raised by any method which determines that its parameters are invalid in some way. In practice, there are two typical situations where most Cocoa developers will encounter this at some point, and we've just hit the first. Remember that our code loops through all the elements in an array, and tries to call the length method on each:

```
for (NSString *component in nameComponents) {
    nameComponentLength += [component length];
}
```

The problem arises when trying to call length on an object that doesn't have such a method. Our code tries calling the length method on NSCFNumber (the concrete subclass of NSNumber that happens to be used when we create an NSNumber in the usual way), and that class doesn't implement that method, all of which we can reasonably deduce from the exception's reason. We could split hairs now, and complain that Apple really should use a different exception name here that would clearly tell us that the exception is related to a method name, but this seems to be what we're stuck with.

In any case, we can explore further by using the graphical debugger in Xcode. In the table showing the call stack, click on the line labeled "-[ExceptionCityAppDelegate invalidArgumentException_unrecognizedSelector]" to see the last piece of our code that was being executed before the exception was raised. The text editor switches to a view of the relevant source code file, and the variable view now shows the variables available to us at that point in the program (see Figure 12–3).

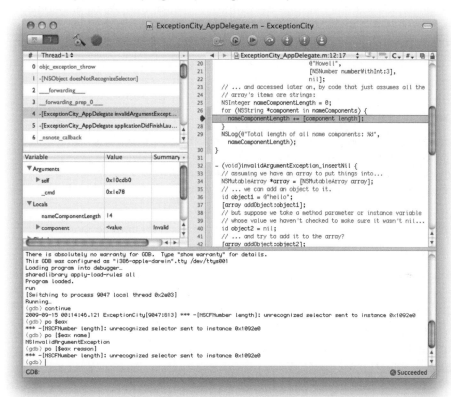

Figure 12–3. *Choosing a different entry in the call stack gives us access to a different part of our running program. Note that the command-line interface at the bottom shows commands that were executed at the top level of the call stack, inside objc_exception_throw. If you entered the same commands with the current stack frame in focus, $eax would have a different value.*

Based on the information we've gotten about the exception and what part of our code triggered it, it's up to us to figure out what the problem is. We can even take additional steps here to examine the current state of our program, such as printing out summary information for the object that the for loop is currently looking at, by typing po component. You can also hover the mouse over a variable in your source code, and a sort of tooltip will appear, where you can see the object's value and examine its structure further. In this case it's pretty simple: our array contains an NSNumber, which doesn't have a length method.

At this point, we have to decide how to fix the problem. We still want to implement the same basic algorithm which adds the lengths of the character strings for each component, we just want to make it so that the value of the NSNumber (in this case, 3) is converted to a string (@"3"). Here we can make use of the description method, defined on NSObject and therefore available in all Cocoa objects. Incidentally, the description method is what's used by gdb whenever you issue a po command to see an object's value. For most classes, calling description will get you the result defined by NSObject's implementation (typically something like <NameOfObjectClass: 0x10cdb0>), but some classes, such as NSString and NSNumber, override this method to return something else. NSString's implementation just returns the NSString itself, while NSNumber's implementation converts the numeric value into an NSString and returns it.

So, to make this work, edit the invalidArgumentException_unrecognizedSelector method, changing the line inside the for loop to the following:

```
nameComponentLength += [[component description] length];
```

Because we know that NSObject, and therefore every object, implements the description method and returns a string, we know that this call will now always work. Even if someone slips another kind of object in there that doesn't give us a nice, compact result like NSString and NSNumber do, at least we know the method is there and will be called!

So do the fix, **Build & Run**, and see what shows up in the Xcode output console:

```
2009-09-16 23:26:11.665 ExceptionCity[8655:10b] Total length of all name components: 15
2009-09-16 23:26:11.667 ExceptionCity[8655:10b] *** -[NSCFArray insertObject:atIndex:]:
attempt to insert nil
```

Dang, another one! Quit the app, and run it again, once again time using the **Run▶Debug** menu item, which enables the breakpoint to halt the program when an exception is raised. When the program halts, you can once again enter some commands at the gdb prompt to get some info:

```
(gdb) po $eax
*** -[NSCFArray insertObject:atIndex:]: attempt to insert nil
(gdb) po [$eax name]
NSInvalidArgumentException
```

And if you scan down the call stack looking for the first location that shows black instead of grey, you'll find -[ExceptionCityAppDelegate invalidArgumentException_insertNil], the location of the piece of our code that triggered the exception. Click that line, and you'll see the code editor window highlight this line in invalidArgumentException_insertNil:

```
[array addObject:object2];
```

Take a look at the code just above that, and you'll see the problem: object2 is a pointer to nil, and NSMutableArray won't allow you to insert a nil into it. In a complex application, you may want to track down the root cause (where did the nil pointer come from, and is nil a valid value for that variable?), but in this case we'll work around the problem by putting a safety check before adding the object, like this:

```
if (object2 != nil) {
  [array addObject:object2];
}
```

That takes care of that. NSInvalidArgumentException is one of the most frequently encountered exceptions in Cocoa, and you've just seen the two most frequent situations that trigger it: calling a method on a class which doesn't implement that method, and trying to insert nil into an array.

Build & Run the app again, and get ready for the next problem.

NSRangeException

The previous exceptions have been cleared up, but look what happens now:

```
2009-09-16 23:44:33.038 ExceptionCity[8881:10b] Total length of all name components: 15
2009-09-16 23:44:33.065 ExceptionCity[8881:10b] inserted all the objects I could!
2009-09-16 23:44:33.066 ExceptionCity[8881:10b] found indexed item two
2009-09-16 23:44:33.066 ExceptionCity[8881:10b] *** -[NSCFArray objectAtIndex:]: index
(2147483647( or possibly larger)) beyond bounds (3)
```

Crikey! That's one big index value. Stop the app, rerun in the debugger with **Run➤Debug**, wait for the halt, and see what we've got:

```
(gdb) po $eax
*** -[NSCFArray objectAtIndex:]: index (2147483647( or possibly larger)) beyond
bounds (3)
(gdb) po [$eax name]
NSRangeException
```

Now look at the call stack, and click on the uppermost item that's within our code: -[ExceptionCityAppDelegate rangeException]. This will highlight the following line in the text editor:

```
NSLog(@"found indexed item %@", [array objectAtIndex:indexOfFive]);
```

This line actually makes two calls: first to the objectAtIndex: method, then to the NSLog function. A glance at the call stack shows that it's the objectAtIndex: method that is complaining. Apparently it doesn't like the value contained in indexOfFive. If you look in the variable view, or type p indexOfFive (note the use of p for standard C types, as opposed to po for Objective-C objects), you'll see 2147483647. That does seem a bit high! If you look at the code where it's set, just two lines earlier, you'll see this:

```
NSUInteger indexOfFive = [array indexOfObject:@"five"];
```

That line is asking array for the index of an object that it doesn't actually contain. In this case, NSArray returns a special integer value called NSNotFound, which is defined to be the maximum possible integer value. On Mac OS X running in 32-bit mode, that turns out to be 2147483647. This value is used to tell the caller that, "Hey, that object you want the index of? I don't have it." Which can be pretty useful to know! A consequence of this is that whenever you get a value from indexOfObject:, you really have to check to make sure that it's not NSNotFound. In our case we know exactly where the problem is, so we could just check that second time, but it's good to make a habit of always checking that return value, so we'll update the entire method like this:

```
- (void)rangeException {
  // assuming we have an array of things...
  NSArray *array = [NSArray arrayWithObjects:@"one", @"two", @"three",
    nil];
  // ... we can ask for the index of an item...
  NSUInteger indexOfTwo = [array indexOfObject:@"two"];
  if (indexOfTwo != NSNotFound) {
    // ... and we can later retrieve that value using the same index.
    NSLog(@"found indexed item %@", [array objectAtIndex:indexOfTwo]);
  }

  // But, what if we try to find the index for something that's not
  // there?
  NSUInteger indexOfFive = [array indexOfObject:@"five"];
  if (indexOfFive != NSNotFound) {
    // Good thing we check the return value to make sure it's not
    // NSNotFound!
    NSLog(@"found indexed item %@", [array
      objectAtIndex:indexOfFive]);
  }
}
```

Make those changes, **Build & Run**, and you'll be rewarded with the congratulatory alert panel. Oh, sweet success!

Having tackled those, you've now experienced and fixed the main types of runtime exceptions that every Cocoa programmer gets at some point. That's it! This may come as a surprise to people come from other, more exception-heavy environments, but like we said, in Cocoa exceptions are used sparingly, and almost always to signal that the programmer has made an error. NSRangeException, and NSInvalidArgumentException (for both of the causes shown above) really make up the bulk of all exceptions you're likely to deal with.

And the Rest

Okay, there are more exceptions that can be raised in a Cocoa app. There are more predefined exception names in *NSException.h*, for example, but chances are you won't encounter any of them. NSGenericException seems to arise sometimes when working with SQLite or Apple Events, and on rare occasions NSInternalInconsistencyException can rear its ugly head if you override a method that you shouldn't (such as when the documentation warns you not to), but real-world examples of those are pretty hard to come by.

The one instance where you're likely to see any exceptions occur is if you're using Apple's Distributed Objects (DO) technology, which uses exceptions in a much more liberal fashion than the rest of Cocoa. For example, DO will raise exceptions to warn you if it loses a connection to the process you're connected to. Most of the predefined exception names defined by Cocoa, in fact, are specifically for DO's use. We're not describing the use of DO in this book, so we won't say anything more about these exceptions, but it's good to be aware of in case you go down that path at some point.

Worse than Exceptions: Death by Signal

Now that you've seen how some bugs can be handled by code-level operations like catching an exception, it's time to look at another kind of problem that arises when object pointers are misused. In Cocoa, every Objective-C object is referenced through a pointer to a specific sort of C struct that defines the basic structure of an Objective-C object. If the pointer isn't pointing either at a chunk of memory containing a valid object, or at nil, then some form of memory access error is almost certain to occur, leading to the creation of a "signal" that ultimately kills your app.

There are two ways that Cocoa programmers inadvertently cause a signal to kill their app. The first way is to try to send a message to an uninitialized object pointer. By default, when you declare a new pointer as a local variable in an Objective-C method, you can't count on it to automatically point at nil or some other harmless thing. In fact, you can usually rely on it pointing at something completely inappropriate, like a memory address that is not even mapped into the system (the situation is different for instance variables, static local variables, and global variables, which are in fact initialized with nil values). We can examine this by adding the following method to your app delegate:

```
- (void)uninitializedObject {
  NSMutableString *string;
  [string appendFormat:@"foo"];
}
```

This method declares a pointer to an NSMutableString, but doesn't actually create the string. So when it tries to call the appendFormat: method, the receiver isn't a valid object. To see the effect of this, add a [self uninitializedObject]; line to your applicationDidFinishLaunching: method, build & debug, and watch. Your program will halt, and you'll see something like this in the Xcode debug console:

```
Running…
Program received signal:  "EXC_BAD_ACCESS".
```

Depending on exactly what this uninitialized pointer is pointing at, you may see a different signal name, such as SIGSEGV or SIGILL. As a bonus bit of wrongness, it's even possible that it could be pointing at some other, valid object in your program, perhaps even an NSMutableString, making it extra-insidious to track down. The specifics don't really matter; the point is that you've got an uninitialized pointer, a problem which would be solved by applying a general rule: Whenever you declare an Objective-C object pointer inside a method, immediately assign it a value, even if it's just nil.

So, fix this by changing the string declaration line to this:

```
  NSMutableString *string = nil;
```

Build & Run, and off you go. It's perfectly okay to send a message to a nil pointer in Objective-C (it's basically a non-operation, and the return value from a nil message is typically nil, 0, or NO), so, although the fixed version of the method won't actually *do* anything, it won't cause a crash, either.

Now, there's one more source of memory problems that we should mention here: Sending a message to an object that's already been freed. Throughout this book, we've been asking you to use garbage collection for every app we've created, which virtually eliminates this kind of bug entirely, but in case you're working at some point on a project without garbage collection, such as a Mac application that uses a library that won't work with GC, or any iPhone project, it can be a good idea to know where it's coming from.

Without GC, memory management for Objective-C objects is handled with manual reference-counting. To make a long story short: any time you create an object with an `alloc` or `copy` method, or mark an object as being "in use" by sending it a `retain`, its retain count is increased. You must at some point (when you're done with the object) send the object a `release` or `autorelease` message, either of which will decrease its retain count. When the retain count hits zero, the object is freed.

The problem that can arise is that if you don't do this quite right, you may end up in a situation where a variable contains a pointer to a space in memory that was formerly occupied by a "live" object, but now may contains a freed object, or may have been reused for some other purpose.

So let's see this in action. When creating the ExceptionCity project, we intentionally refrained from asking you to turn on garbage collection, because it makes no difference for the rest of the code, and will actually prevent us from demonstrating this bug! So if you already went and turned on GC for this project out of force of habit (good for you!), go turn it back off. Now, add the following method to your app delegate class:

```
- (void)freedObject {
    id obj = [[NSObject alloc] init];
    NSLog(@"the object is %@", obj);
    [obj release];
    NSLog(@"the object is %@", obj);
}
```

Then add a `[self freedObject];` line to your `applicationDidFinishLaunching:` method, build & debug, and see what happens. The program will halt, and show something like the following:

```
2009-09-17 23:35:37.677 ExceptionCity[18016:813] the object is <NSObject: 0x1756c0>
objc[18016]: FREED(id): message respondsToSelector: sent to freed object=0x1756c0
Program received signal:  "EXC_BAD_INSTRUCTION".
```

As with the previous signal-generating bug, the program may receive a different signal than the one shown previously, but it'll certainly receive something, and if you look in the call stack for the uppermost stack frame containing your code, you'll see that it's pointing squarely at the final `NSLog()` call in the `freedObject` method.

The way to fix this is, as with the previous case, a matter of self-discipline: any time you send an object a `release` or `autorelease` message, if you still have a pointer to that object in a variable, immediately point that variable at `nil`! Sending `release` or `autorelease` may not always immediately cause the object to be freed (since some other code may have increased its retain count as well), but locally within each method, you should consider anything you've released to be off-limits, and get rid of any dangling pointers to it as soon as you can.

In this case, the solution is to follow up the [obj release]; line with this:

```
obj = nil;
```

Add that line, **Build & Run** again, and you're back to smooth sailing! Again, this type of bug can really only occur if you're not using GC. And, apart from this relatively simple rule of thumb about setting pointers to nil after releasing objects, there are other ways that a non-GC app can wind up in similar situations, such as forgetting to retain an object that you want to use for a while. These bugs can be some of the trickiest to track down, which is one of the strongest reasons for using GC wherever possible.

NSError

Now you know that exceptions in Cocoa aren't typically used for flow control, instead being used primarily to point out bugs. Some other languages and frameworks in use today use exceptions for all sorts of things that aren't bugs but can be side-effects of conditions outside the developer's direct control, such as file-related errors when trying to access a file, or network errors when trying to read data from a socket. In Cocoa, these types of situations are handled more and more often using a class called NSError. In this section, you'll learn about the content of an NSError object, what kinds of situations lead to their creation, and how to deal with them in your code, including giving your application the ability to retry certain kinds of error-triggering operations.

Domains and Codes

Traditionally, every operating system has its own ways of reporting system errors, typically giving you an integer value that you can compare with a predefined list in a header file to determine what to do.

In UNIX-based systems, for example, you can (in fact, *should*) examine the value of errno (which is either a global variable, or a symbol that calls a function, depending on a number of factors we won't get into here) after every system call, including functions to open a file, read from a file, write to a file, and the like. The idea is that if any system function encounters a problem, it will put an integer into errno to let you know the nature of the error.

In "classic Mac OS" programming (everything predating Mac OS X), things were a bit different. Instead of populating a global variable, many system functions have a return type of OSStatus, which again boils down to an integer that you should check after calling each function, to make sure nothing unexpected happened.

Mac OS X is sort of a hybrid OS. Its underpinnings are firmly rooted in UNIX, but it also includes Carbon, a large set of APIs and technologies adapted from older versions of Mac OS. Both of these "worlds" contain functions that need to report back error codes in one way or another, and since these worlds developed in a separate fashion, of course there is some overlap between the sets of error codes. At some point, Apple realized that there could be some benefit to dealing with error messages from these different worlds in a common way, letting each of them continue to use the same error codes they always have (ensuring binary compatibility with existing software) without any risk of confusion by tagging each error with a string specifying its domain.

And that's what we have in the NSError class, which basically wraps a system-level error code in an Objective-C object. Each NSError instance has an NSString to specify the name of its "domain" (generically, which library or framework it came from), an integer to specify the relevant error code, and an optional NSDictionary that can contain additional information about the error. Because these are normal Objective-C objects, they can be dealt with like any other object: passed around, put into an NSArray, and so on.

Cocoa includes some predefined string constants to categorize the main sources of NSError objects in the Cocoa frameworks themselves. The domains you're most likely to encounter as a Cocoa programmer are these:

- NSPOSIXErrorDomain: UNIX errors (those which are part of the POSIX standard).

- NSOSStatusErrorDomain: errors from Carbon functions (which typically return an OSStatus).

- NSCocoaErrorDomain: errors arising directly within Cocoa's own classes.

Whenever a Cocoa method gives you an NSError, its domain will likely be one of these. If you start creating your own NSError instances in your code, you'll probably want to define your own domains and error codes, in order to make it easier for you to handle them in your application.

Each of the predefined error domains also has an associated list of error codes, defined in one or more header files. The error codes applicable to NSPOSIXErrorDomain are found in *errno.h*. Those for NSOSStatusErrorDomain are in *MacErrors.h*; and the error codes in use for the NSCocoaErrorDomain are contained in *FoundationErrors.h*, *AppKitErrors.h*, and *CoreDataErrors.h*. Each of these headers can be found easily in Xcode by bringing up the *Open Quickly* window (⌘⇧D) and typing the name of the file.

Realizing You Have an Error

So now you know a little bit about the NSError class. But, where do they come from? Unlike exceptions, NSError objects don't do anything to change the flow of your code. Typically, an NSError instance is returned to you from a method call, not as the return value but by referencing a pointer you pass in. This form of parameter twiddling is not too uncommon in C, but still fairly uncommon in Objective-C. The idea is that an error-prone method should receive as a parameter a pointer to an NSError pointer. Which means you don't pass in a pointer itself, but the address of a pointer variable so that the receiving method can create an object and assign your pointer to it!

This may sound confusing, but once you see the pattern, things should clear up. As an example, consider the NSFileManager class. The file manager lets you do perform certain disk operations such as creating directories, accessing file attributes, and so on. It has a method whose signature looks like this:

```
- (NSDictionary *)attributesOfItemAtPath:(NSString *)path
    error:(NSError **)error
```

We can use this method to access a dictionary containing a whole lot of relevant file system information about the file or directory specified in the path parameter. Note that the second parameter, error, is of type NSError**, which means that we pass in a pointer to a variable that can point at an NSError. If the method actually encounters an error situation, it will create an NSError, and stick its address in the location specified by error. If you want to ignore any error that a method like this produces, you can pass in the special NULL pointer as the last parameter.

The following method shows what this looks like from the caller's perspective. We create a variable which can point at an NSError, and initialize it to point at nil. Then we pass the address of that variable to a potentially error-generating method, and afterwards check the variable to see whether or not it's still pointing at nil. If not, we know that the method encountered an error, and we ask the application to present the error to the user.

```
- (void)fileError {
  NSFileManager *fileManager = [NSFileManager defaultManager];
  // Declare a variable and point it at nil
  NSError *fileError = nil;
  // Pass the address of the fileError variable to the method
  NSDictionary *attributes = [fileManager
    attributesOfItemAtPath:@"/tmp" error:&fileError];
  // Check to see if the previous method call gave us an NSError
  if (fileError == nil) {
    // Show the attributes
    NSRunAlertPanel(@"Found file attributes",
      [attributes description], nil, nil, nil);
  } else {
    // Report the error
    [NSApp presentError:fileError];
  }
}
```

For simplicity's sake, while exploring NSError we'll continue building onto the project we're already playing with. Add the fileError method shown previously to your app delegate class, and add a [self fileError]; line to the applicationDidFinishLaunching: method. **Build & Run**, and you'll see something like the alert panel shown in Figure 12–4.

Figure 12–4. *No error here!*

Now go back and edit the `fileManager` call, changing the string parameter from `@"/tmp"` to `@"/tmpfoo"` or some other non-existent path. This will cause `fileManager` to encounter an error and give it back to us, in the `fileError` variable whose address we passed in. We notice this error and pass it off to `NSApp`, resulting in the alert panel shown in Figure 12–5.

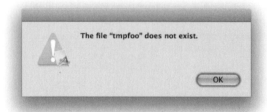

Figure 12–5. *There's the error.*

That's all fine and good, but look at the text in that alert panel: *The file "tmpfoo" does not exist.* Doesn't that seem a little... non-technical? Aren't we used to a bit more jargony language in our computer systems? After all, the error was triggered by a low-level system routine which reported just an error number and nothing else. Where did that text come from?

It turns out that `NSError` has a method called `localizedDescription`, which gives you a nice, human-readable explanation of the error. This description is what's eventually displayed by the `reportError:` method.

Let's explore this a bit by using the debugger. In Xcode, set a breakpoint on the line containing `[NSApp presentError:fileError]` by clicking in the "gutter" to the left of the line in the text editor. The gutter is the space where the line numbers are shown. This is the most straightforward way to set a breakpoint in your own code. Then restart your app, this time in the debugger. The app will halt at the chosen line, leaving you with the gdb prompt in the output console. Let's dig in a bit, asking the error about its domain and error code by executing commands at the gdb prompt:

```
(gdb) po [fileError domain]
NSCocoaErrorDomain
(gdb) p (int)[fileError code]
$1 = 260
(gdb) po [fileError localizedDescription]
The file tmpfoo does not exist.
```

Note that we can print the value of an NSString using the po command, and print the value of any basic C type using the p command. Often when using the p command, gdb will complain that it doesn't know the type of the value you're trying to display, so we put a little (int) just before the method call, which tells gdb what to expect.

Now we know the error code and domain. A quick look in FoundationErrors.h turns up this info:

```
NSFileReadNoSuchFileError = 260,    // Read error (no such file)
```

That still might leave you wondering how this hangs together. As you recall, when you create an NSError, you specify a domain, a code, and optionally a dictionary containing additional info. This dictionary is a key piece of the puzzle. If the dictionary you pass into this method has a value for a key called @"NSLocalizedDescriptionKey", then that value will be returned whenever localizedDescription is called.

So, let's see what the userInfo dictionary contains:

```
(gdb) po [fileError userInfo]
{
    NSFilePath = "/tmpfoo";
    NSUnderlyingError = Error Domain=NSPOSIXErrorDomain Code=2 "Operation could
not be completed. No such file or directory";
}
```

Um. Apparently that's not the answer, either. The userInfo dictionary doesn't specify a localized description, but it does include a couple of other things: the path to the file we were trying to access, and what looks like another NSError. An error wrapped inside an error! Let's see what that inner error's domain, code, userInfo, and localizedError look like. We start off with another gdb command, the x command, which simply executes the statements on the rest of the line, without printing a result like the po or p commands do. In this case, we're assigning the address of the inner error object to a new variable we're calling $inner. This is a nice feature of gdb that lets us hang on to the results of queries we execute, letting values stick around, and saving us some typing later on:

```
(gdb) x $inner = (int)[[fileError userInfo] objectForKey:@"NSUnderlyingError"]
0x175830:   0xa05388c0
```

After assigning the object's address to the new variable, gdb outputs both the address of our new variable, and its content (the address of the object it's pointing at), but you can ignore that. From here on out, we can refer to that inner error as just $inner, like this:

```
(gdb) po [$inner domain]
NSPOSIXErrorDomain
(gdb) p (int)[$inner code]
$3 = 2
(gdb) po [$inner userInfo]
Cannot access memory at address 0x0
(gdb) po [$inner localizedDescription]
Operation could not be completed. No such file or directory
```

This presents us with yet another riddle. When we look at the underlying error, which has no userInfo dictionary at all, it still presents a human-readable localizedDescription that doesn't seem immediately apparent just by looking at the domain and code. In fact, you can make your own inner and outer errors like this:

```
NSError *innerError = [NSError errorWithDomain:NSPOSIXErrorDomain
  code:2 userInfo:nil];
NSDictionary *outerInfo = [NSDictionary dictionaryWithObjectsAndKeys:
  innerError, NSUnderlyingErrorKey,
  @"/tmpfoo", NSFilePathErrorKey,
  nil];
NSError *outerError = [NSError errorWithDomain:NSCocoaErrorDomain
  code:260 userInfo:outerInfo];
```

Those errors will behave *exactly* like the ones generated by NSFileManager, including displaying human-readable text that we're not specifying anywhere! As it turns out, the source of this magic seems to be the NSError class itself. It apparently has enough built-in specific knowledge about Cocoa's error domains and error codes to generate meaningful sentences about many of the errors that a program is likely to encounter. This means that in general, the errors provided to you by Cocoa method calls won't need to be prettied up in order to be shown to users.

Presenting an Error

And how about showing errors to users, while we're at it? Here we've been calling [NSApp presentError:e] to make the application display a modal window, but there are some other choices. In truth, the presentError: method is implemented in NSResponder, NSDocument, and NSDocumentController, which means that whenever an error occurs, you can pass it along to the nearest or most relevant object around, at which point it is passed along a chain of responsibility, similar to the responder chain, until some object actually displays the error. This opens up possibilities for displaying error messages in a different fashion, such as with a document-modal sheet alert.

In Conclusion

You've now seen the primary ways that a Cocoa app can deal with various kinds of unpleasantness, how to avoid some common mistakes, and how to use gdb to help track down problems. You've also seen how methods can use NSError instances to deal with problems in a controlled manner. All of this will come in handy as you delve further into Cocoa programming.

Drawing in Cocoa

By now you've learned lots of powerful Cocoa techniques for dealing with data, optimally arranging your application's classes, and using the wide range of on-screen controls and other views that are included with Cocoa. Now it's time for you to start learning how to use Cocoa to make your own view classes, gaining complete control over the display of text and graphics. Mac applications are commonly known for including "eye candy"—not just for drawing needless graphical flourishes, but also for creating a more immersive interactive experience for the user. The graphics technologies available to you as a Cocoa programmer can help you achieve some of the same kinds of effects with a surprisingly small amount of effort on your part.

Core Graphics gives you rich functionality for rendering paths, manipulating coordinate systems, and more. One major part of Core Graphics is a set of APIs known as Quartz. Quartz, in fact, makes up such a huge part of Core Graphics that the two terms are sometimes used interchangeably. Core Animation takes things even further, letting you animate your views in a remarkably simple way.

In this chapter, we'll cover some of the basics of coordinate systems and drawing into an NSView instance, and show you how to display a view larger than the space available to it in the window by putting it in a scrolling view. We'll also touch on how you can easily add basic printing support to your applications.

Fundamentals

In this section, we'll go through some of the basic concepts used in Cocoa's drawing APIs. If you've done any sort of graphics programming, some of what's available for drawing in Cocoa will be pretty familiar. After all, most of the basic concepts of computer graphics were hammered out decades ago. Where Cocoa stands out is both in the quality of its rendering, including anti-aliasing for both text and graphics primitives, as well as the availability of high-level abstractions for more complex concepts.

The View Coordinate System

Cocoa's drawing systems work with an x-y coordinate system where, by default, the origin point (0,0) is at the lower left, the x-axis points to the right (increasing values take you further to the right) and the y-axis points up (increasing values take you further up on the screen). This is similar to the way graphs are traditionally done in mathematics, but flipped from many other computer graphics systems, where the y-axis points down (increasing values take you further down on the screen). Although it's possible and sometimes desirable to flip the y-axis in Cocoa, we won't be doing so in our examples. Also, by default, one unit along either axis corresponds to one screen pixel.

Drawing is normally done by instances of NSView subclasses. Views exist in a hierarchy. If the top-most view in the hierarchy is set to be the contentView of an NSWindow, then all the views in that hierarchy are displayed within that window. The top-level view in a window, the contentView, can draw across the entire area of the window. For every other view in the hierarchy, the drawing area is limited to its frame, a space within the coordinates of its parent view (see Figure 13–1).

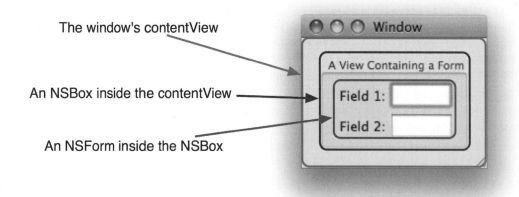

Figure 13–1. *A simple hierarchy of views. The window's contentView contains an NSBox, which in turn contains an NSForm.*

Frame Rectangle vs. Bounds Rectangle

For each view in a window, there are a couple of important rectangles (or "rects" as they are commonly called) that define a lot about its drawing characteristics: its frame rect and its bounds rect. The frame rect simply specifies the view's location and size within its parent view's coordinate space. For example, imagine the top-level view in a window. Let's call it A. If A has a subview called B which extends from point (10,20) to point (40,60), then B's frame rect has (10,20) as its origin and (30,40) as its size.

Apart from its frame, which determines where and to what extent it appears in its superview, each view has a bounds rect, which defines its own inner coordinate space.

For example, view B described previously will by default have a bounds rect whose origin is (0,0) and whose size is (30,40). You can easily change this if you want. For example, say you've got a bunch of points to plot, whose x and y values are all between 0.0 and 10.0. By changing the bounds rect of B, setting its size to (10,10), the points will exactly fill the space occupied by B, no matter how much space B actually takes on-screen (see Figure 13-2).

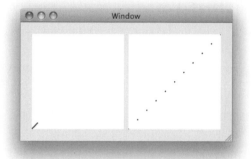

Figure 13–2. *On the left, plotting points from a narrow range in a view with default bounds. On the right, the same points plotted in a view with smaller bounds.*

Rects, Points, and Sizes

In Cocoa, rectangles are represented by a C struct called NSRect, which is composed of an NSPoint containing the origin, and an NSSize containing the size. Both the origin and size each contain two values of type CGFloat, a basic C type used throughout Cocoa's drawing APIs; origin has x and y, size has width and height.

To confuse matters somewhat, many functions in Core Graphics make use of equivalent structures CGRect, CGPoint, and CGSize, which have the same structural layout and are all composed of CGFloat elements. The historical reasons for this divide aren't terribly interesting. Starting with Leopard, these C structs have identical layouts, and can be converted back and forth with inline functions (for example, NSRectToCGRect, NSSizeFromCGSize, and so on) that are really little more than typecasts. In fact, there are a couple of ways you can make their definitions identical, requiring no conversion at all, by either configuring your applications for 64-bit mode, or adding NS_BUILD_32_LIKE_64 to the Preprocessor Macros section of your Xcode target's Build settings, which we'll describe in a page or two.

Path Basics

Cocoa's drawing mechanism includes the concept of paths, which can contain any number of straight or curved line segments. Each path doesn't need to be contiguous. You can "pick up the pen" at one point, and start drawing again at another. Before a path is actually drawn, you can specify values such as line thickness, color, and the like.

Those settings will be applied to every part of the path. Any shapes outlined by parts of the path can also be filled with a separate color or pattern.

Creating an NSView Subclass

Let's start exploring a bit by creating an application that's able to draw a very happy smiley face (see Figure 13–3). In Xcode, create a new Cocoa project named MrSmiley, and do the normal steps to enable garbage collection.

Figure 13–3. *Mr Smiley is very, very happy.*

Now create a new Objective-C class, a subclass of NSView, and name it SmileyView. Xcode will create the class's files for you, including *SmileyView.m*, where all this section's work will take place.

Before getting started on the code, open the project's *MainMenu.xib* file in Interface Builder. Grab a custom view from the Library window, and drag it into the blank window that is created for you by default. Use the Identity Inspector to change the view's class to SmileyView, then use the Size Inspector to change its size to 100×100. Finally, with the SmileyView selected in the window, press ⌘= to make the window resize itself to perfectly fit the view. Then save your changes.

Some C Structures

Go back to Xcode so we can start working on the code itself. A couple of pages ago, we mentioned the distinction between the two sets of geometry structures available in Cocoa: NSRect/NSPoint/NSSize vs CGRect/CGPoint/CGSize. Beginning with Mac OS X 10.5, it's possible to use these interchangeably. In the 64-bit version of the Cocoa framework, these are defined to be identical, but we can achieve the same effect via a simple configuration that tells the compiler to compile code for 32-bit use as if it were compiling for 64-bit use.

Click on the root object in Xcode's navigation pane, the one labeled MrSmiley. Then press ⌘I to open the Inspector panel, and switch to the Build tab at the top of the panel. A popup button lets you choose which configuration (Debug, Release, and so on) you want to modify. Choose All Configurations from the list, because this configuration needs to apply no matter what. In the search field, type "preprocessor," and look for the Preprocessor Macros line in the filtered results. That's where we're going to add a bit of configuration. Double-click the empty table cell to the right of Preprocessor Macros, and add NS_BUILD_32_LIKE_64 to the previously empty list of macros. That's it! Now, any function or method call that specifies NSRect can take a CGRect, and vice-versa. The same applies for the size and point types, as well.

The Basic Drawing Method, drawRect:

Now let's get into the code. The *SmileyView.m* file created by Xcode contains an empty drawRect: method, which is where we'll start writing our code. The drawRect: method is something you usually won't call directly, except for cases where you're implementing a subclass of an existing view, and calling [super drawRect:rect] to let the superclass do its part of the drawing. Instead, the drawRect: method is called automatically whenever the application's main run loop determines that the view needs to be redrawn (typically after a view has been created or resized, or your own code has called setNeedsDisplay: on your view, passing YES as the argument). The drawRect: method takes one argument, a rectangle that indicates which portion of the view is considered "dirty" and needs to be redrawn. This can be used to optimize drawing of complex views, but in our examples we'll just ignore that, and instead make use of the view's bounds rectangle for drawing.

Graphics States

All drawing in Cocoa occurs within a particular context, which is represented by the NSGraphicsContext class. Depending on the context, we may be drawing directly into a window buffer, or drawing into a chunk of off-screen memory for later use. But apart from that, the context has some state information of its own that can change over time, such as the current color to be used for any drawing commands. When it's time for your view to draw itself, it should do so in such a way that the graphics state is put back into the state it was in when drawing started.

Fortunately, NSGraphicsContext provides us with an easy way to do just that. Its saveGraphicsState method will push all relevant state info onto a stack, and the restoreGraphicsState method will pop the state back off the stack. You can use these two method calls to "bracket" your actual drawing code like the following excerpt shows, so you know you aren't leaving the graphics context in an unexpected state.

```
- (void)drawRect:(NSRect)rect {
  [NSGraphicsContext saveGraphicsState];
  // Drawing code here.
  [NSGraphicsContext restoreGraphicsState];
}
```

Path Helpers

To draw the view shown at the beginning of this section, we'll first draw the background, then the face itself. For each of those two elements, we'll first fill in the background, then draw the edge. All of this is done using the NSBezierPath class. A Bezier path allows you to define paths of arbitrary complexity, including straight lines, points, curves, and so on. One of the niceties of the NSBezierPath class is that it gives you nice shortcuts for creating a Bezier path representing common shapes such as rectangles, ovals, and the like.

Let's start by creating a path that defines the visible edge of the view, using a class method on NSBezierPath that gives us a rounded rect. The lines shown in bold below create a path, fill it with white, and then "stroke" the path (draw its edge) in black:

```
- (void)drawRect:(NSRect)rect {
  [NSGraphicsContext saveGraphicsState];

  NSRect bRect = CGRectInset([self bounds], 5, 5);
  NSBezierPath *border = [NSBezierPath bezierPathWithRoundedRect:bRect
    xRadius:5 yRadius:5];
  [[NSColor whiteColor] set];
  [border fill];

  [border setLineWidth:3];
  [[NSColor blackColor] set];
  [border stroke];

  [NSGraphicsContext restoreGraphicsState];
}
```

The first step uses the CGRectInset function to shrink our bounds rect a bit, giving us a little wiggle room so that we can draw a rounded rect with thick lines without having them clipped by our edges. Then we create a path representing a rounded rect, specifying the basic geometry of the rect as well as two numbers defining the size of the elliptical curves used for the rounded corners. After that, we issue simple commands to set colors, a line width, and do some drawing.

Colors and the Graphics Context

Note that specifying which color to use for a drawing operation is a separate step from the drawing operation itself, as is setting the line width. Also, although setting the line width is done through a method on the path itself, setting the color looks like a sort of free-floating operation. You just send any color the set message, and suddenly it's the current color! What's happening is that NSColor's set method interacts with the underlying graphics context, setting the color that will be used for subsequent drawing operations. One consequence of this is that NSColor's set method will only do something useful while there is a current graphics context, such as within a drawRect: method. Another consequence is that the current color is a property (in a general sense, if not an Objective-C language sense) of the graphics context, so whatever color was set before our method is saved at the beginning of our method when [NSGraphicsContext saveGraphicsState] is called, and restored at the end when [NSGraphicsContext restoreGraphicsState] is called, putting everything back in order again.

At this point, if you **Build & Run** the application, you'll see that it draws a white rect with a black outline (Figure 13–4).

Figure 13–4. *The shape of things to come*

Beyond Color

Now let's continue, and start drawing the head. Add these lines to the drawRect: method, toward the end but still before the [NSGraphicsContext restoreGraphicsState] call:

```
NSRect hRect = CGRectInset([self bounds],20,20);
NSBezierPath *head = [NSBezierPath bezierPathWithOvalInRect:hRect];
NSGradient *faceGradient = [[NSGradient alloc]
  initWithStartingColor:[NSColor whiteColor]
  endingColor:[NSColor lightGrayColor]];
[faceGradient drawInBezierPath:head angle:45];
[head setLineWidth:3];
[head stroke];
```

Here we are once again using CGRectInset to make a new rect that is smaller than our bounds, this time to create an oval shape for Mr Smiley's head. After creating a Bezier path, we create something new, an instance of NSGradient, which knows how to take two or more colors and draw a smooth gradient between them. In this example, you see that it can draw itself across the inner surface of a Bezier path. **Build & Run** this code, and you'll see that our view now contains a round "head" with a shaded gradient (Figure 13–5).

Figure 13–5. *The basic head shot*

Manual Path Construction

Now all that's left is to draw the facial features (a simple mouth and eyes). Add these lines to the end of drawRect: (but before the final [NSGraphicsContext restoreGraphicsState] call):

```
NSBezierPath *features = [NSBezierPath bezierPath];
[features moveToPoint:NSMakePoint(35, 30)];
[features lineToPoint:NSMakePoint(65, 30)];
[features moveToPoint:NSMakePoint(40, 40)];
[features lineToPoint:NSMakePoint(40, 40)];
[features moveToPoint:NSMakePoint(60, 40)];
[features lineToPoint:NSMakePoint(60, 40)];
[features setLineCapStyle:NSRoundLineCapStyle];
[features setLineWidth:3];
[features stroke];
```

Here, instead of using one of the convenient class methods on NSBezierPath to get a complete shape right away, we are using some more basic methods to construct a path out of nothing. The moveToPoint: method positions a virtual "pen" at the specified point, without drawing a line to it. And lineToPoint: draws a line from the path's current point to the new point. In reality, these methods don't do any drawing; they simply build up the Bezier path structure that is later drawn by the stroke method.

One additional finesse here is that we set the line cap style. This setting defines what happens at the ends of lines. This is especially important for the eyes, which are drawn as a single point. Using the default setting, which lops off everything precisely where the line segment ends, the eyes were completely invisible, but using NSRoundLineCapStyle gives us a perfect tiny circle for each eye. **Build & Run** to see the final result (Figure 13–6).

Figure 13–6. *Mr Smiley. He really is happy, I'm sure of it!*

Pushing Boundaries

Now that SmileyView is drawing a perfect happy face, naturally we'll want to be able to resize this to fit it into different spots. Switch back to *MainMenu.xib* in Interface Builder, and configure the SmileyView's autosize properties so that it autosizes fully with the window. Do this by selecting the SmileyView, opening the Size Inspector, and clicking the parts of the autosize control so that all the red arrows and lines are "lit". Save your work, go back to Xcode and **Build & Run**, and resize your view (Figure 13–7).

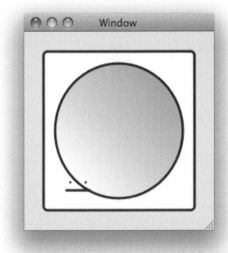

Figure 13–7. *Oops upside your head!*

Now that doesn't seem right, does it? The problem is that our in our drawRect: method, we have a bit of a mix'n'match approach when specifying path geometry. For the outline and the head shape, we base everything on the bounds rect, but for the facial features we're hard-coding numeric pixel widths. When the view resizes, our bounds rect automatically resizes along with it. This makes the outline and head stretch out to accommodate the new bounds, while the facial features are still stuck in their rigid little world.

Also, you'll notice that the lines are the exact same thickness after resizing, which means that their relative thickness, compared to the overall size of the view, has changed. If you made this view really huge, the lines would seem extraordinarily thin.

Fortunately, there's an easy way to remedy all of this. Remember earlier in this chapter, when we mentioned the distinction between a view's frame and bounds rects? The frame, you may recall, defines the view's position and size within its superview. The bounds, however, determines the extent and position of the coordinate system within the view. If we can configure things so that the view's bounds rect never changes, then it will always draw the exact same content, but perfectly stretched to match the actual frame it's drawing in!

To do this, we need to implement two simple steps: grab a copy of the original bounds rect when the view is created, and then manually set the bounds to that original rect every time the view is resized. So, let's add an instance variable (for holding the original rect value) to *SmileyView.h*, complete the initWithFrame: method and implement the setFrameSize: method as shown here:

```
// A portion of SmileyView.h:
@interface SmileyView : NSView {
  NSRect originalBounds;
}
@end
// A portion of SmileyView.m:
- (id)initWithFrame:(NSRect)frame {
  self = [super initWithFrame:frame];
  if (self) {
    // Initialization code here.
    originalBounds = [self bounds];
  }
  return self;
}

- (void)setFrameSize:(NSSize)newSize
{
  [super setFrameSize:newSize];
  [self setBounds:originalBounds];
}
```

The setFrameSize: method is one that gets called during live dragging, while the user is resizing a window. What we're doing here is resetting the view's bounds rect every step of the way, so that when it comes time to draw, all the drawing will occur based on the original bounds. Now **Build & Run**, resize the window, and witness the magic (Figure 13–8).

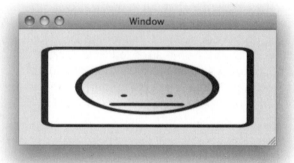

Figure 13–8. *A real stretch*

As you can see, everything stretches perfectly faithfully, including the widths of the lines. Also, everything is rendered to match the actual display resolution. You can stretch that out as big as you want, and you'll always see perfectly anti-aliased curves. Whatever geometry we specify for our bounds, will be adjusted to match the frame we're sitting in. What you're seeing here is, in fact, a two-dimensional transformation.

Apart from being a nice way to deal with resizing, this built-in transformation possibility means that you can do your drawing at whatever scale you're comfortable with, just by setting the bounds rect. If you want to do your graphics at pixel resolution you can do so, but if you're plotting details of a mathematical curve ranging from 0.0 to 0.1, you can set your bounds accordingly, and don't have to multiply all your display values to make them match the screen coordinates.

LOLmaker

Now that you've got a basic understanding of drawing in an NSView and manipulating its geometry, let's move on to a new project: LOLmaker. LOLmaker is a simple application that lets you create your own LOLcat-style imagery by just dragging in an image and typing the text you want it to contain. It's not rocket science, but it will introduce you to a few more issues around drawing in an NSView.

A FEW WORDS ABOUT LOLCATS

In case you've missed out on the whole LOLcat meme, or are reading this book in a future world where LOLcats have been forgotten, a LOLcat is basically a picture of a cat (or other animal) with a humorous caption, typically written in a style mocking the "Internet slang" of the early 21st century.

We like LOLcats simply because they are pictures of cats that make us laugh out loud. Please don't think that we'd stoop to the level of including LOLcats content in our book just to sell more copies! It's a well-known fact that most LOLcats fans are also pirates, and will only read this book in the form of a stolen PDF.

First Steps to LOL

Start by creating a new basic Cocoa project in Xcode, no Document or Core Data support this time. Although both of those could be put to good use in this project, for now we're going to focus on just the drawing aspects. This project won't actually save anything. Name the project LOLmaker, and after creating it use the Inspector panel to turn on GC as usual.

If you're running Snow Leopard, the project will include a LOLmaker_AppDelegate class. If you're still running Leopard, make an NSObject subclass named LOLmaker_AppDelegate, open up *MainMenu.xib* in Interface Builder, pull out a custom object from the Library, change its class to LOLmaker_AppDelegate using the Identity Inspector, and connect the NSApplication's delegate outlet to the object you just created.

Now, edit the *LOLmaker_AppDelegate.h* file to add the bold lines shown below.

```
#import <Cocoa/Cocoa.h>
@class LOLView.h;

@interface LOLmaker_AppDelegate : NSObject
{
  IBOutlet LOLView *lolView;
  NSImage *image;
  NSString *text;
}
```

```
@property (retain) NSImage *image;
@property (copy) NSString *text;
```

```
@end
```

Then, edit *LOLmaker_AppDelegate.m*, adding the following line near the top so that we can use the `LOLView` class:

```
#import "LOLView.h"
```

Add the following lines to the `@implementation` section to complete the properties:

```
@synthesize image;
@synthesize text;
```

These properties will be used with Cocoa Bindings to let the user drag in an image and type in some text which will be automatically attached to our controller object, which in turn updates the view. You'll notice that we're importing a *LOLView.h* header file and declaring an instance variable of type `LOLView*`, even though the `LOLView` class hasn't been completed yet. Solve that problem right away by creating another new set of class files, this time for `LOLView`, an `NSView` subclass.

We'll implement `LOLView` in just a few minutes, but for now let's go configure the GUI. Double-click *MainMenu.xib* to bring it up in Interface Builder, and use the Library to drag a custom view, an image well, and a text field into the empty window. Use the Identity Inspector to set the class of the custom view to LOLView, and the Attributes Inspector to turn on the Editable checkbox for the image well. Finally, connect the app delegate's `lolView` outlet to the `LOLView` in the window. When everything is laid out, your window should resemble Figure 13–9.

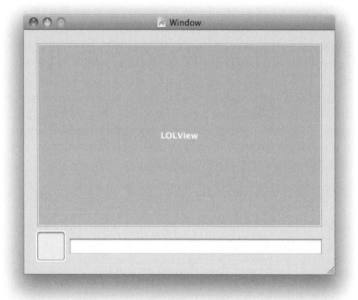

Figure 13–9. *The layout of our LOLmaker window*

This window will let the user drag in an image (to the drag well) and type in a message that will be displayed over the image. The `LOLView` will notice the dragged-in image and edited text, and trigger a redisplay of itself, through the use of Cocoa Bindings. The first half of the bindings will be configured in Interface Builder, the second half in code.

First, select the image well and switch to the Bindings Inspector. Create a binding for the Value attribute, selecting the app delegate in the popup list and typing image into the Model Key Path field. Then select the text field, and create a binding for its Value attribute, again selecting the app delegate in the popup list and this time typing text into the Model Key Path field.

That takes care of the bindings for the controls, but because Interface Builder doesn't know about `LOLView` and what its bind-able values are, we have to set up its bindings in code. Go back to Xcode, and edit *LOLmaker_AppDelegate.m*, adding the following method to the @implementation section:

```
- (void)applicationDidFinishLaunching:(NSNotification *)aNotification
{
  [lolView bind:@"image" toObject:self withKeyPath:@"image"
    options:nil];
  [lolView bind:@"text" toObject:self withKeyPath:@"text"
    options:nil];
}
```

That takes care of the basic communications between all the objects in this application. User edits to the controls in the window are passed along to the app delegate, and from there they'll be passed along to the `LOLView`, all through Cocoa Bindings. The "plumbing" of our app is now complete!

LOLView

So, how about the `LOLView` itself? For starters, it's going to have a couple of properties, just like the properties that the app delegate has, to contain the values that are coming from the user. In this case, however, we want to trigger a redisplay every time one of the values changes, so that the `LOLView` will be redrawn. Therefore, we implement the setter methods ourselves, instead of just using the default setters generated by @synthesize. Note that we're still using @synthesize, but our explicitly implemented setters trump the automatic ones, leaving just the automatically generated getters in place. Add the following to *LOLView.h* and *LOLView.m*, as indicated:

```
// LOLView.h:
#import <Cocoa/Cocoa.h>
@interface LOLView : NSView {
  NSImage *image;
  NSString *text;
}
@property (retain) NSImage *image;
@property (copy) NSString *text;
@end

// LOLView.m:
@implementation LOLView
```

```
@synthesize image;
@synthesize text;
- (void)setImage:(NSImage *)i {
  if (![i isEqual:image]) {
    [image release];
    image = [i retain];
    [self setNeedsDisplay:YES];
  }
}
- (void)setText:(NSString *)t {
  if (![t isEqual:text]) {
    [text release];
    text = [t copy];
    [self setNeedsDisplay:YES];
  }
}
```

In those setter methods, you may notice that we're once again going through the trouble of releasing the old value and retaining the new one, a series of steps that won't really do anything in our garbage-collected world. Really, setText: is doing a copy rather than a retain, which does make a difference (and in general is a good idea when receiving an object such as NSString, because the caller may actually be passing you a mutable string that can be changed by some other piece of code), but even there, the release on the line above it doesn't do anything, so why bother?

We've touched on this before, but it's worth repeating: even though we're encouraging you to use GC in all your applications, there may be times when you can't. You may find that you need to start linking with a framework or library that doesn't work well with GC, or that you want to port your application to iPhone, which (at the time of this writing anyway) doesn't include GC at all. Taking the simple step of writing your accessors from the beginning in a way that will work in a non-GC situation will make such transitions that much easier. With that said, writing your own accessors that properly deal with memory management issues in a non-GC environment can be trickier that you might imagine. If you're not 100 percent sure of how to proceed, you can find a detailed discussion of these issues in *Learn Objective-C on the Mac*, by Mark Dalrymple and Scott Knaster (Apress, 2009).

Drawing a Bitmap

Now let's move on to the "meat" of the LOLView class: drawing the image and superimposing some text. Let's start with the image, which we can copy into place quite quickly by adding a few lines to the drawRect: method that was put in place when you created the class:

```
- (void)drawRect:(NSRect)rect {
  NSRect srcImageRect = NSMakeRect(0, 0, [self.image size].width,
    [self.image size].height);
  [self.image drawAtPoint:[self bounds].origin fromRect:srcImageRect
    operation:NSCompositeCopy fraction:1.0];
}
```

The first thing we're doing here is creating a rect called srcImageRect with origin (0,0) and size equal to the image's size. Then we send a message to the image itself, telling it to draw the portion of the image specified by srcImageRect (in this case, the entire image) into the current graphics context, located at the origin of our view's bounds rect. In short, the entire image is copied, and its lower left-hand corner will be located precisely at the view's lower left-hand corner. The drawing method we're using here also lets us specify an operation, which determines how transparencies in the source and destination images are merged, as well as an integer between 0.0 and 1.0, which acts as an overall alpha level for the entire image. Any value below 1.0 makes the image somewhat transparent; all the way down to 0.0 makes the image completely invisible.

Now, **Build & Run** your app, and let's take a look at what we've got so far. Your app opens, showing you a mostly blank window with the image well and text field at the bottom. Find a nice LOLcat-friendly image somewhere, and drag it into the image well, which will show you something like you see in Figure 13–10.

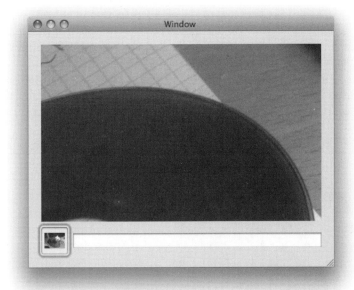

Figure 13–10. *Not much LOL here.*

Hey, that's not very satisfying! All we're seeing is the lower left-hand corner of the picture we dragged in! If only there were some way we could see the whole image...

Let It Scroll

Well, of course there is. Cocoa includes a class called NSScrollView that will help us out here. By putting a view inside of an NSScrollView, you get access to horizontal and vertical scrollbars that the user can use to slide the view around. The scroll view takes care of all the hard work. The drawing code for any views you put in there doesn't need to change at all! Putting the LOLView into an NSScrollView is surprisingly simple. We just need to add a bit of code and make a couple of adjustments in Interface Builder.

The code we need to add is actually one more piece of the setImage: method. What we're going to do is resize the LOLView each time a new image is set, so that the view's size matches the image's size. Later, when the LOLView is enclosed in an NSScrollView, the scrollview will notice the new view size, and automatically re-render everything including the scrollbars. The new code looks like this:

```
- (void)setImage:(NSImage *)i {
  if (![i isEqual:image]) {
    [image release];
    image = [i retain];
    if (image) {
      NSRect newImageFrame = NSMakeRect(0, 0, [image size].width,
        [image size].height);
      [self setFrame:newImageFrame];
    }
    [self setNeedsDisplay:YES];
  }
}
```

Now, go back to Interface Builder to prepare the scrollview itself. Select the LOLView, then select **Layout▶Embed Objects In▶Scroll View** from the menu. Your LOLView is now wrapped in a scroll view, but the positioning and sizing are a little off. Move the scroll view so that it butts up against the top left-hand corner of the window, then resize a little with the lower-right resizing control, making it fill the width of the window and extend just far enough down to leave a decent margin above the other controls (see Figure 13–11).

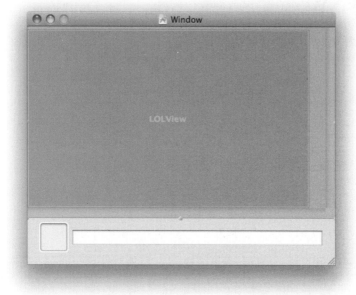

Figure 13–11. *The LOLmaker window, adjusted for scrolling*

Now let's configure the autosizing settings. Doing this will let us not only scroll the LOLView, but resize it along with the window as well. First click the NSScrollView (*not* the LOLView itself), open the Size Inspector, and configure it to be expandable in both directions, and "tied" to all four window edges. In other words, all the red control lines should be lit solid, none of them grayed out. Then, configure the image well to be stuck to the lower left-hand corner, and the text view to be stuck to the bottom, left, and right edges, and horizontally expandable.

Save all your work, **Build & Run**, and you are done with the scrollview! Drag in a large image, and you'll see that it starts off in the lower left, but scrollbars are present, and you can drag around to wherever you want! See this in action in Figure 13–12.

Figure 13–12. *Scrollbars: So simple, even a papier-mâché bird can do it.*

Drawing Text

Okay, so let's get to the final step, drawing the text. It is traditional in the LOLcats community to use a text caption in the Impact font, using white text with a black shadow. This should be a piece of cake. The only mildly tricky part is choosing a font size. Because images can be all sorts of sizes, we need to dynamically choose the font size so that the caption fills up a decent portion of the view without extending off the side. We'll do this by testing several font sizes, starting with 1, and working our way upwards by doubling the size each time, until we hit a point where the size of the text would be wider than the view itself. That we ratchet the font size back down a bit, and draw the text. This is all done by adding the bold lines shown below:

```
- (void)drawRect:(NSRect)rect {
  // Drawing code here.
  NSRect srcImageRect = NSMakeRect(0, 0, [self.image size].width,
    [self.image size].height);
  [self.image drawAtPoint:[self bounds].origin fromRect:srcImageRect
    operation:NSCompositeCopy fraction:1.0];

  if (text != nil && [text length] > 0) {
    NSPoint textLocation = NSMakePoint(0,0);
    NSShadow *textShadow = [[NSShadow alloc] init];
    [textShadow setShadowOffset:NSMakeSize(0,0)];
    [textShadow setShadowColor:[NSColor blackColor]];
    [textShadow setShadowBlurRadius:10];
    NSMutableDictionary *textAttributes =
      [NSMutableDictionary dictionaryWithObjectsAndKeys:
        [NSFont fontWithName:@"Impact" size:40], NSFontAttributeName,
        [NSColor whiteColor], NSForegroundColorAttributeName,
        textShadow, NSShadowAttributeName,
        nil];

    // find the optimal size
    CGFloat fontSize;
    NSSize testSize = NSMakeSize(0, 0);
    for(fontSize=1; testSize.width < [image size].width; fontSize*=2)
    {
      [textAttributes setObject:[NSFont fontWithName:@"Impact"
        size:fontSize]
        forKey:NSFontAttributeName];
      testSize = [self.text sizeWithAttributes:textAttributes];
    }
    [textAttributes setObject:[NSFont fontWithName:@"Impact"
      size:fontSize/4]
      forKey:NSFontAttributeName];
    [self.text drawAtPoint:textLocation
      withAttributes:textAttributes];
  }
}
```

Now, **Build & Run**, drag in an image, and write some text. Voila! You should see something like Figure 13–13.

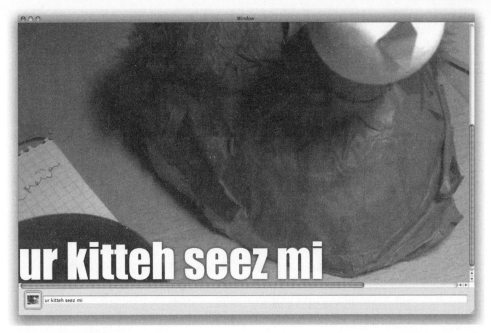

Figure 13–13. *This is not a cat.*

Printing Basics

Most applications that let you do anything interesting on the screen will also let you print your work. On Mac OS X, this is incredibly easy for a developer to implement, thanks in large part to the way that the OS's display system is designed. The Core Graphics methods and functions that we use to draw into a view can actually be used to draw into a variety of contexts, which means that the system can use our existing drawRect: methods to make us draw our content into a context that's ready for printing.

The most basic way to print your content is through the use of the print: method, which is implemented both by NSWindow and NSView. You could, for instance, connect a menu item to the print: method on the First Responder object in Interface Builder. That way, whatever object the user selects will be printed if the menu item is selected. That actually points out the downside of that approach, though: because the method is called on the first responder, invoking the print command would cause the text field to be printed if the user is currently editing in a text field!

Normally, you're probably better off routing your printing through a controller object instead. Presumably, either the window controller, or the document in a document-based application, knows what's the most appropriate thing to print at any point, typically either the entire window, or a single view that is the focus of the window. Using our latest example, the LOLview is what should really be printed, and we'll add a method to MyDocument to make this work. Start off by adding the following to the MyDocument class:

```
// in MyDocument.h:
- (IBAction)printContent:(id)sender;

// in MyDocument.m:
- (IBAction)printContent:(id)sender {
  [lolView print:sender];
}
```

Now, open up *MainMenu.xib* in Interface Builder. We want to connect a menu item to our new `printContent:` method using the First Responder proxy object, but first we have to configure it so that Interface Builder knows that such a method exists! Start by selecting the First Responder proxy. You'll find the list of the First Responder's configured methods in the Identity Inspector. There, a little plus-button lets you add a new item, and give it the name of the method to be called (`printContent:`). Now open the menu from inside the main nib window, and navigate to the existing Print item. Ctrl-drag from it to the First Responder proxy object, and select the `printContent:` method from the popup.

Now save your work, and **Build & Run** your app. In addition to what you implemented earlier, you can now print from the menu, just like nearly every other Mac OS X application. Invoking the print command brings up the standard Mac OS X print panel, letting you choose which printer, open in Preview, and so on. You get all of this for free, just for programming in Cocoa!

Wrapping Up

In this chapter, you've gained a lot of understanding of the workings of NSView and some other classes that deal with drawing. However, there's still lots more you can do with Cocoa's drawing facilities, including drawing more interesting curves, modifying your drawing in response to mouse events, and animating your views, all of which we'll cover in the next chapter.

Chapter 14

Advanced Drawing Topics

In Chapter 13, you gained some basic knowledge of Cocoa's key drawing concepts, such as using paths to describe shapes, copying images to the screen, and rendering text. In this chapter, we're going to expand upon this, getting you comfortable with a few techniques that will bring your graphics to life. In the first section, we'll show you how to make a view respond to mouse events, letting users interact with your customized views. In the second section, we'll give you a brief introduction to Core Animation, an exciting technology that lets you create smooth animations with just a few lines of code.

Editing a Curve

In chapter 13, we introduced you to the `NSBezierPath` class for drawing rounded rectangles, ovals, straight lines, and points. If you've used a Bezier drawing tool in Photoshop or other applications, you may have wondered what those shapes have to do with Bezier curves at all! A Bezier curve is essentially a series of points describing a path, and control points describing the curves between the points. As such, basically any shape that can be drawn with a pen (in the real world, or virtually in a computer graphics system) can be described as a Bezier curve, including straight lines and jagged angles. However, as a layman's term, Bezier curve usually means something more along the lines of what you see here in Figure 14–1.

Here, the black curve is a Bezier curve, defined by two endpoints (the lower-left and upper-right corners) and two control points, depicted here by rather gigantic circles at the end of sticks. By dragging the control points around, the user can change the shape of the curve. A view like this can be useful as a pacing control, determining the rate of change of some value over time, such as the movement of object from one point to another. Make the curve into a straight line to specify a perfectly linear transition, or make a sort of S-shape to make a value start changing slowly, quickly ramp up halfway through, and then slow down as it approaches the target value (sometimes known as an "ease-in/ease-out" transition). This control is what we're going to be implementing in this section.

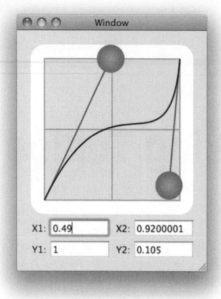

Figure 14–1. *A Bezier curve*

Preparations

Create a new Cocoa project in Xcode and name it CurveEdit. Do the usual steps for turning on garbage collection. If you're running on Snow Leopard or later, the new project will contain a class called CurveEdit_AppDelegate. If you're running on Leopard, you'll need to create the class, and add it to the MainMenu.xib file as usual.

The interesting part of this application will all be in the view object, but first let's take care of the infrastructure surrounding the view. We're going to stick with the MVC architecture for this project, which will help make sure that the view we create will be usable as a standalone component. The text fields for displaying each control point's x and y values will be connected to our controller object with Cocoa Bindings, as will the CurveView itself. The model in this app will just be a set of instance variables in our controller class, but all the views could just as easily be bound to a real model object if we chose to use or create one.

Make a new NSView subclass called CurveView, and leave its implementation as-is for now. We'll get back to it soon enough. Switch over to the app delegate class, and put the following in its .h and .m files:

```
// CurveEdit_AppDelegate.h:
#import <Cocoa/Cocoa.h>
@interface CurveEdit_AppDelegate : NSObject {
  CGFloat cp1X;
  CGFloat cp1Y;
  CGFloat cp2X;
  CGFloat cp2Y;
```

```
    IBOutlet CurveView *curveView;
}
@property (assign) CGFloat cp1X;
@property (assign) CGFloat cp1Y;
@property (assign) CGFloat cp2X;
@property (assign) CGFloat cp2Y;
@end

// CurveEdit_AppDelegate.m:
#import "CurveView.h"
#import "CurveEdit_AppDelegate.h"

@implementation CurveEdit_AppDelegate
@synthesize cp1X, cp1Y, cp2X, cp2Y;
- (void)applicationDidFinishLaunching:(NSNotification *)aNotification {
    // make the CurveView notice my changes
    [curveView bind:@"cp1X" toObject:self withKeyPath:@"cp1X"
      options:nil];
    [curveView bind:@"cp1Y" toObject:self withKeyPath:@"cp1Y"
      options:nil];
    [curveView bind:@"cp2X" toObject:self withKeyPath:@"cp2X"
      options:nil];
    [curveView bind:@"cp2Y" toObject:self withKeyPath:@"cp2Y"
      options:nil];
    // make me notice the CurveView's changes
    [self bind:@"cp1X" toObject:curveView withKeyPath:@"cp1X"
      options:nil];
    [self bind:@"cp1Y" toObject:curveView withKeyPath:@"cp1Y"
      options:nil];
    [self bind:@"cp2X" toObject:curveView withKeyPath:@"cp2X"
      options:nil];
    [self bind:@"cp2Y" toObject:curveView withKeyPath:@"cp2Y"
      options:nil];
    // set initial values
    self.cp1X = 0.5;
    self.cp1Y = 0.0;
    self.cp2X = 0.5;
    self.cp2Y = 1.0;
}
@end
```

As you can see, our controller class is very simple. All it does is declare properties for accessing the control points' x and y values, establish some bindings on behalf of our curveView (because we can't do those in Interface Builder), and set some default starting values for the control points.

Now open MainMenu.xib in Interface Builder. From the Library, drag out a Custom View, and use the Identity Inspector to set its class to CurveView. Resize it to about 240x240. Connect the app delegate's curveView outlet to the new view. Because we've already set up this object's bindings in code, the CurveView instance is now all set (as far as our nib is concerned).

Go back to the library and pull out an NSForm, dropping it below the CurveView. This is a handy control that combines multiple text entry fields, each with its own label, into a single view. This form will show us the x and y values for the first control point in a

Bezier curve. Change its two labels to "X1:" and "Y1:", and create bindings for each of the cells in the form. For each, you want to bind its Value attribute to the CurveEdit_AppDelegate object, using the model key paths cp1X and cp1Y, respectively.

Duplicate the NSForm and place it to the right of the first one. This form will show us the values for the second control point, so rename its labels "X2:" and "Y2:", and set up its bindings similar to the previous form's, but using cp2X and cp2Y as the key paths instead.

Refer to Figure 14–1 to see what you're shooting for, lay things out nicely, and resize the window to match the content you've added. Save your work, go back to Xcode, and **Build & Run** your project, just to make sure you haven't made any errors at this point. The resulting app won't do anything but let you edit four text fields, but we're about to change that!

Bezier Plumbing

Let's get started with the CurveView class by establishing some infrastructure. CurveView needs to keep track of two control points, which we'll set up as four floats, each accessible through a property, just like we did for the controller class. We also want to use a technique similar to the one we used for MrSmiley in Chapter 13, so that the GUI scales to match whatever size it's rendered at. This time, we're going to set up fixed bounds so that we can always draw our curve in a square between (0,0) and (1,1) on the plane, leaving a little extra surrounding space, so we'll add some code that sets the bounds to a square between (-0.1,-0.1) and (1.1,1.1), and maintain those bounds no matter how our view is resized. Take care of all that by adding the bold lines shown here:

```
// CurveView.h:
#import <Cocoa/Cocoa.h>
@interface CurveView : NSView {
  NSRect myBounds;
  CGFloat cp1X;
  CGFloat cp1Y;
  CGFloat cp2X;
  CGFloat cp2Y;
}
@property (assign) CGFloat cp1X;
@property (assign) CGFloat cp1Y;
@property (assign) CGFloat cp2X;
@property (assign) CGFloat cp2Y;
@end

// CurveView.m:
#import "CurveView.h"
@implementation CurveView
@synthesize cp1X, cp1Y, cp2X, cp2Y;
- (void)setCp1X:(CGFloat)f {
  cp1X = MAX(MIN(f, 1.0), 0.0);
  [self setNeedsDisplay:YES];
}
```

```
- (void)setCp1Y:(CGFloat)f {
  cp1Y = MAX(MIN(f, 1.0), 0.0);
  [self setNeedsDisplay:YES];
}
- (void)setCp2X:(CGFloat)f {
  cp2X = MAX(MIN(f, 1.0), 0.0);
  [self setNeedsDisplay:YES];
}
- (void)setCp2Y:(CGFloat)f {
  cp2Y = MAX(MIN(f, 1.0), 0.0);
  [self setNeedsDisplay:YES];
}
- (id)initWithFrame:(NSRect)frame {
  self = [super initWithFrame:frame];
  if (self) {
    // Initialization code here.
    myBounds = NSMakeRect(-0.1, -0.1, 1.2, 1.2);
    [self setBounds:myBounds];
  }
  return self;
}
- (void)setFrameSize:(NSSize)newSize {
  [super setFrameSize:newSize];
  [self setBounds:myBounds];
}
- (void)drawRect:(NSRect)rect {
  // Drawing code here.
}
@end
```

Note that we don't stop at just synthesizing the accessors for our properties. We actually implement setters for each of our properties, and in each we enforce a limited range on the input value, making it fit in the range from 0.0 to 1.0. We also mark the window as "dirty," forcing the system to redraw it whenever a property changes.

Drawing a Curve

Now let's move on to the fun part: drawing the curve itself. We'll use preprocessor #defines to establish values for colors and line widths, making it easier to spot them and change them in order to tweak the appearance. Add these lines somewhere near the top of CurveView.m:

```
#define CP_RADIUS 0.1
#define CP_DIAMETER (CP_RADIUS*2)
#define BACKGROUND_COLOR [NSColor whiteColor]
#define GRID_STROKE_COLOR [NSColor lightGrayColor]
#define GRID_FILL_COLOR [NSColor colorWithCalibratedWhite:0.9 alpha:1.0]
#define CURVE_COLOR [NSColor blackColor]
#define LINE_TO_CP_COLOR [NSColor darkGrayColor]
#define CP_GRADIENT_COLOR1 [NSColor lightGrayColor]
#define CP_GRADIENT_COLOR2 [NSColor darkGrayColor]
```

Now implement the drawControlPointAtX:y: and drawRect: methods as shown in the following example. The code for drawing the control points demonstrates the use of the NSGradient class, which can be used to fill the inside of a Bezier path instead of just a solid color fill.

```
- (void)drawControlPointAtX:(CGFloat)x y:(CGFloat)y {
  NSBezierPath *cp = [NSBezierPath bezierPathWithOvalInRect:
    NSMakeRect(x - CP_RADIUS, y - CP_RADIUS,
               CP_DIAMETER, CP_DIAMETER)];
  NSGradient *g;
  g = [[NSGradient alloc] initWithStartingColor:CP_GRADIENT_COLOR1
                          endingColor:CP_GRADIENT_COLOR2];
  [g drawInBezierPath:cp
     relativeCenterPosition:NSMakePoint(0.0, 0.0)];
}

- (void)drawRect:(NSRect)rect {
  [NSGraphicsContext saveGraphicsState];

  // draw the background
  NSBezierPath *bg = [NSBezierPath bezierPathWithRoundedRect:myBounds
                                   xRadius:0.1 yRadius:0.1];
  [BACKGROUND_COLOR set];
  [bg fill];

  // draw the grid
  NSBezierPath *grid1 = [NSBezierPath bezierPath];
  [grid1 moveToPoint:NSMakePoint(0.0, 0.0)];
  [grid1 lineToPoint:NSMakePoint(1.0, 0.0)];
  [grid1 lineToPoint:NSMakePoint(1.0, 1.0)];
  [grid1 lineToPoint:NSMakePoint(0.0, 1.0)];
  [grid1 lineToPoint:NSMakePoint(0.0, 0.0)];

  [grid1 moveToPoint:NSMakePoint(0.5, 0.0)];
  [grid1 lineToPoint:NSMakePoint(0.5, 1.0)];
  [grid1 moveToPoint:NSMakePoint(0.0, 0.5)];
  [grid1 lineToPoint:NSMakePoint(1.0, 0.5)];
  [GRID_FILL_COLOR set];
  [grid1 fill];
  [GRID_STROKE_COLOR set];
  [grid1 setLineWidth:0.01];
  [grid1 stroke];

  // draw the lines leading to the control points
  NSBezierPath *cpLines = [NSBezierPath bezierPath];
  [cpLines moveToPoint:NSMakePoint(0.0, 0.0)];
  [cpLines lineToPoint:NSMakePoint(cp1X, cp1Y)];
  [cpLines moveToPoint:NSMakePoint(1.0, 1.0)];
  [cpLines lineToPoint:NSMakePoint(cp2X, cp2Y)];
  [LINE_TO_CP_COLOR set];
  [cpLines setLineWidth:0.01];
  [cpLines stroke];

  // draw the curve itself
```

```
NSBezierPath *bp = [NSBezierPath bezierPath];
[bp moveToPoint:NSMakePoint(0.0, 0.0)];
[bp curveToPoint:NSMakePoint(1.0, 1.0)
  controlPoint1:NSMakePoint(cp1X, cp1Y)
  controlPoint2:NSMakePoint(cp2X, cp2Y)];
[CURVE_COLOR set];
[bp setLineWidth:0.01];
[bp stroke];

// draw the control points
[self drawControlPointAtX:cp1X y:cp1Y];
[self drawControlPointAtX:cp2X y:cp2Y];

[NSGraphicsContext restoreGraphicsState];
}
```

This sort of drawing code can make for some pretty long methods, but it's often pretty straightforward, as in drawRect: shown previously. Not a single loop or if construct in the whole method! Note that unlike the Mr Smiley code in chapter 13, this drawing code doesn't refer to our view's bounds rect at all. Because we know that the bounds are always adjusted to contain a square from (0,0) to (1,1), we make use of simple hardcoded values to draw our graphics in and around this unit square.

Compile and run the app, and you should now see something like Figure 14–1. You should be able to edit the values in the text fields (any values between 0.0 and 1.0 work well), and see the control points and curve change accordingly.

Watching the Mouse

But entering numeric values into text fields isn't the point of this exercise, we want to drag those control points around. As it turns out, this is pretty simple to do. NSView contains methods that are automatically called whenever a user interacts with the view by clicking, dragging, and so on. All we have to do is override a few methods, and we can respond to every click, drag, and release of the mouse.

Let's start by adding a pair of BOOL instance variables to our view, to keep track of whether one of the control points is currently being dragged. Add the bold lines below to the interface declaration in CurveView.h:

```
@interface CurveView : NSView {
  NSRect myBounds;
  CGFloat cp1X;
  CGFloat cp1Y;
  CGFloat cp2X;
  CGFloat cp2Y;
  BOOL draggingCp1;
  BOOL draggingCp2;
}
```

Now let's add some methods to the @implementation section of CurveView.m, in order to start intercepting the mouse activity we want to watch. The first method, mouseDown:, will be called whenever a user clicks in our view:

```
- (void)mouseDown:(NSEvent *)theEvent
{
  // get current mouse location, convert to our coordinate space
  // (the one expresed by our bounds)
  NSPoint mouseLocation = [theEvent locationInWindow];
  NSPoint convertedLocation = [self convertPoint:mouseLocation
    fromView:nil];
  // see if the click was on one of our control knobs
  NSPoint cp1 = NSMakePoint(cp1X, cp1Y);
  NSPoint cp2 = NSMakePoint(cp2X, cp2Y);
  if (pointsWithinDistance(cp1, convertedLocation, CP_RADIUS)) {
    draggingCp1 = YES;
  } else if (pointsWithinDistance(cp2, convertedLocation, CP_RADIUS)){
    draggingCp2 = YES;
  }
  [self setNeedsDisplay:YES];
}
```

In the mouseDown: method, we first ask the window for the current mouse location, then use a built-in NSView method to convert the coordinates from the window's coordinate system to our own. This means that a click in the upper right-hand corner of our unit square, for instance, which starts off being the number of horizontal and vertical pixels from the window's lower left-hand corner, will end up being converted to (1,1) or somewhere nearby. Then we do a pair of tests, to see if one of our control points is being clicked on. This test is done using the following function, which you should add to the top of CurveEdit.m, somewhere above the @implementation section:

```
static BOOL pointsWithinDistance(NSPoint p1, NSPoint p2, CGFloat d) {
  return pow((p1.x-p2.x), 2) + pow((p1.y - p2.y), 2) <= pow(d, 2);
}
```

The pointsWithinDistance function makes use of the Pythagorean formula to determine whether the distance between the two points (in our case, the center of a control point, and the location of the mouse) is less than the distance we pass in (the control point radius). Using this, we are able to check to see whether the user clicked on a control point, and if so we set the corresponding flag (draggingCp1 or draggingCp2) to YES.

The next method to implement is mouseDragged:, which is called every time the mouse is moved while the button is held down. Note that this method is called in every view the mouse is dragged over. It's always called in the view where the original mouse click occurred; in a sense, whichever view receives the click "owns" all subsequent dragging. In this method, we once again grab the mouse location from the event, transform it into our view's own coordinate system, and then update the coordinates for the control point that's currently being dragged. If none of them are currently being dragged, then nothing happens.

```
- (void)mouseDragged:(NSEvent *)theEvent
{
  NSPoint mouseLocation = [theEvent locationInWindow];
  NSPoint convertedLocation = [self convertPoint:mouseLocation
    fromView:nil];
  if (draggingCp1) {
```

```
    self.cp1X = convertedLocation.x;
    self.cp1Y = convertedLocation.y;
  } else if (draggingCp2) {
    self.cp2X = convertedLocation.x;
    self.cp2Y = convertedLocation.y;
  }
  [self setNeedsDisplay:YES];
}
```

The final method we need for dealing with the mouse is mouseUp:, which lets us handle the release of the button. Like mouseDragged:, mouseUp: is always called on the view which originated the drag, which means that after the user clicks in our view, no matter where the user lets go of the mouse button, we will receive this message. All we do here is simply set the flags to indicate that nothing is being dragged.

```
- (void)mouseUp:(NSEvent *)theEvent
{
  draggingCp1 = NO;
  draggingCp2 = NO;
}
```

With all that in place, **Build & Run** your app. You should now find that you can drag the controls around, with the curve following every move, and the numbers in the text fields changing as you drag.

A Little Polish

That's pretty cool, but as we've often noticed when toying around with a new GUI design, some enhancements become self-evident with a little use. For one thing, we're always drawing the control points in the same order, so control point 2 is always on top, even if we're dragging control point 1 right over it. This feels pretty unnatural. Fortunately, the fix for this is extremely simple, and this is the real, practical reason we split out the control point drawing into two separate methods. At the end of the drawRect: method, add the bold lines shown here:

```
// draw the control points
if (draggingCp1) {
  [self drawControlPointAtX:cp2X y:cp2Y];
  [self drawControlPointAtX:cp1X y:cp1Y];
} else {
  [self drawControlPointAtX:cp1X y:cp1Y];
  [self drawControlPointAtX:cp2X y:cp2Y];
}
```

That's it! **Build & Run**, and you'll see that whenever you're dragging the first control point, it appears in front of the second.

It would also be nice to highlight the control point that's currently being dragged, maybe by drawing it with a different color. This is also a pretty easy change that gives the user some useful feedback. Start by defining some highlight colors for a new gradient, adding these lines among the other #defines at the top of the file:

```
#define CP_GRADIENT_HIGHLIGHT_COLOR1 [NSColor whiteColor]
#define CP_GRADIENT_HIGHLIGHT_COLOR2 [NSColor redColor]
```

Now, modify the drawControlPointAtX:y: methods, adding an additional parameter to specify whether or not do draw the highlighted variant, and the bold lines shown here:

```
- (void)drawControlPointAtX:(CGFloat)x y:(CGFloat)y dragging:(BOOL)dragging {
  NSBezierPath *cp = [NSBezierPath bezierPathWithOvalInRect:
    NSMakeRect(x - CP_RADIUS, y - CP_RADIUS, CP_DIAMETER, CP_DIAMETER)];
  NSGradient *g;
  if (dragging) {
    g = [[NSGradient alloc] initWithStartingColor:CP_GRADIENT_HIGHLIGHT_COLOR1
                            endingColor:CP_GRADIENT_HIGHLIGHT_COLOR2];
  } else {
    g = [[NSGradient alloc] initWithStartingColor:CP_GRADIENT_COLOR1
                            endingColor:CP_GRADIENT_COLOR2];
  }
  [g drawInBezierPath:cp
    relativeCenterPosition:NSMakePoint(0.0, 0.0)];
}
```

Because we added a parameter to the control-point drawing method, we need to also change the way it's called at the end of drawRect, like this:

```
// draw the control points
if (draggingCp1) {
  [self drawControlPointAtX:cp2X y:cp2Y dragging:draggingCp2];
  [self drawControlPointAtX:cp1X y:cp1Y dragging:draggingCp1];
} else {
  [self drawControlPointAtX:cp1X y:cp1Y dragging:draggingCp1];
  [self drawControlPointAtX:cp2X y:cp2Y dragging:draggingCp2];
}
```

Now **Build & Run**, and you'll see that the otherwise gray control points now light up red while dragging, giving the user a nice visual cue.

Core Animation: A Primer

One of the most exciting technologies Apple includes with Mac OS X is a graphics system called Core Animation, which lets you easily create animated effects in your applications. You can make your views slide, fade, rotate, and scale smoothly and easily, often with just a few lines of code. In essence, Core Animation lets you specify a change in an object—such as changing its location to a different spot in the window—in such a way that, instead of the change happening instantaneously, it's automatically split up into several small movements that are rendered over time by Core Animation. You can specify a transition's length in seconds, as well as the timing or pacing of the change. You can also group animations together, so that they all execute in perfect synchrony.

Core Animation Basics

From a technical standpoint, the basic unit at the heart of all this is a class called CALayer (a pre-release version of Core Animation was even called Layer Kit). Each NSView can optionally have a CALayer attached to it, either by flicking a switch in Interface Builder or setting it up in code. The process of assigning a layer to a view actually begins a recursive process through all the view's subviews, so that when a view has a layer, all its subviews (and all their subviews, and so on) also acquire layers. Once a layer is in place, you can start animating the view.

Under the hood, each CALayer is associated with some OpenGL structures for rendering its graphics. OpenGL does a really great job of quickly drawing rectangles to the screen, even rectangles that are resized, rotated, and the like, so using CALayer lets you have views that do all sorts of on-screen tricks without slowing your application down. The Core Animation APIs shield you completely from OpenGL itself, so it will work away quietly without you having to think about it too much. The only thing to bear in mind is that each layer uses some amount of the memory available to the computer's graphics hardware, so you're better off using layers only for those parts of your application where you actually want to do some animation, instead of applying them to every view in every window.

Implicit Animations

Any layer-backed view can be animated by using its *animator proxy*. This is a special object that acts as a substitute for the view itself, setting up an animation corresponding to the method it's sent instead of making an immediate change. For instance, if you want to animate the movement of a view, then instead of setting its frame like this:

```
[myView setFrame:newFrame];
```

you can set it like this:

```
[[myView animator] setFrame:newFrame];
```

To see this in action, create a new Cocoa project, and name it MovingButton. If you're on Snow Leopard, an app delegate class is created for you; but if not, do the usual steps involved in creating a new NSObject class called MovingButton_AppDelegate and adding it to your nib file. Now, populate the class's .h and .m files as shown here:

```
// MovingButton_AppDelegate.h
#import <Cocoa/Cocoa.h>
@interface MovingButton_AppDelegate : NSObject {}
- (IBAction)move:(id)sender;
@end

// MovingButton_AppDelegate.m
#import "MovingButton_AppDelegate.h"
@implementation MovingButton_AppDelegate
- (IBAction)move:(id)sender {
  NSRect senderFrame = [sender frame];
  NSRect superBounds = [[sender superview] bounds];
```

```
        senderFrame.origin.x = (superBounds.size.width -
            senderFrame.size.width) * drand48();
        senderFrame.origin.y = (superBounds.size.height -
            senderFrame.size.height) * drand48();
        [sender setFrame:senderFrame];
    }
@end
```

This simple action method just calculates a new random location for sender within its superview and moves it there. Open `MainMenu.xib` in Interface Builder, put a button called *Move* in the empty window, and connect it to the app delegate's `move:` action. Save your changes, **Build & Run** your project, and see that each time you click the *Move* button it hops to another location in the window.

Now, let's animate the movement. We just need to edit a single line, changing this:

```
    [sender setFrame:senderFrame];
```

to this:

```
    [[sender animator] setFrame:senderFrame];
```

Build & Run, click the *Move* button, and see what happens. Now, each time you click the button, it slides smoothly into the new location instead of just switching instantaneously. The object returned by the `animator` method is a proxy that responds to each of `NSView`'s setter methods, and schedules animations to apply the change gradually. Behind the scenes, Core Animation does all the work of modifying the relevant value bit by bit until it reaches the target value specified in the call to the setter.

Each thread maintains an animation context, in the form of an instance of `NSAnimationContext`, which among other things lets you set the length of time (in seconds) that an implicit animation will take by first setting a value like this:

```
    [[NSAnimationContext currentContext] setDuration:1.0];
```

If that's all the control you need over your animations, then you can get pretty far using implicit animations. If you need more fine-tuning, such as being able to ensure that several animations occur in a synchronized manner, or trigger some activity when an animation completes, then you'll need something more, such as...

Explicit Animations

Core Animation provides a technique for setting up animations explicitly in your code, instead of using the "magic" of `NSView`'s `animator` method. Each animation you create explicitly is framed by methods that start and stop a section of animation code, making everything a little clearer. Combined with the added capabilities that explicit animations have, it's clear that this is the right approach for all but the simplest of animations.

In order to use Core Animation, you first have to add the QuartzCore framework to your Xcode project. In Xcode, navigate to the Frameworks group, right-click on it, and choose **Add**➤**Existing Frameworks...** from the contextual menu that appears. Then, at the top of `MovingButton_AppDelegate.m`, add the following line:

```
#import <QuartzCore/QuartzCore.h>
```

Now you're ready to refer to Core Animation classes in your own code. Let's start by modifying the previous example to use explicit animation instead of implicit. To do this, we have to create an instance of a Core Animation class called CABasicAnimation, which is capable of animating between values for any CALayer property which can be animated. In our case, rather than animating the frame, we'll animate the layer's position property. We explicitly set start and end locations for the position using the animation's toValue and fromValue properties. Note that these properties expect a proper object, not just a struct like NSPoint, so we have to wrap each NSPoint value inside an NSValue instance. After creating the animation we add it to the view's layer, along with a key. This key doesn't have anything to do with the property we're animating, it's only there to help us in case we later want to identify this animation. Finally, we change the frame on the view object itself, since the animation only affects the drawing of the view's layer. We want the view to actually move as well, so we have to set its target frame manually. Here's the code to do all of this:

```
- (IBAction)move:(id)sender
{
  NSRect senderFrame = [sender frame];
  NSRect superBounds = [[sender superview] bounds];
  CABasicAnimation *a = [CABasicAnimation
                          animationWithKeyPath:@"position"];
  a.fromValue = [NSValue valueWithPoint:senderFrame.origin];
  senderFrame.origin.x = (superBounds.size.width -
    senderFrame.size.width)*drand48();
  senderFrame.origin.y = (superBounds.size.height -
    senderFrame.size.height)*drand48();
  a.toValue = [NSValue valueWithPoint:senderFrame.origin];
  [[sender layer] addAnimation:a forKey:@"position"];
  [[sender animator] setFrame:senderFrame];
  [sender setFrame:senderFrame];
}
```

Note that we also removed the [[sender animator] setFrame:senderFrame]; line from this method, because we don't want to trigger an implicit animation this time. Before this will work, we need to do one more step that the implicit animations took care of for us: establishing layers for the views that need to be animated. Using the animator proxy made this happen automatically, but now we have to turn it on ourselves, for any views that are going to be animated, including the superview of any view that's going to be moving. In our case, this means that the button's superview (the window's content view) needs to be given a layer, and it in turn will establish layers for its subview hierarchy, which is just the button itself. The easiest way to do this is to go back to Interface Builder, select the button in your GUI, and open the Effects Inspector (⌘2). At the top of this inspector, you'll see a section titled Wants Core Animation Layer, which shows a list of view objects (see Figure 14–2).

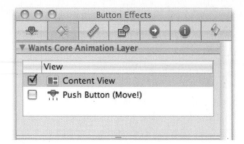

Figure 14–2. *Establishing animation layers*

The selected object (the button) is at the bottom, and all its superviews (in this case just one view, the window's content view) are stacked up above it. Click the checkbox to turn on a layer for the content view. You can leave the checkbox for the button unchecked, since the superview will establish a layer for it.

Now save everything, **Build & Run** your app, and you'll see the exact same behavior as we had before. So, this new version achieves the same result, at the expense of a few additional lines of code. So far it doesn't seem like much of a win here. But wait, there's more! Explicit animation via the animation classes, such as `CABasicAnimation`, lets us do several more key things that we couldn't do with implicit animation.

For starters, we can set the animation's duration. Add the following line just before adding the animation to the layer (with `[[sender layer] addAnimation:a forKey:@"position"]`) to make this animation run a little more slowly:

```
a.duration = 1.0;
```

Build & Run with that in place, and you'll see that the button transitions more slowly. We can also change the pacing of the animation, so that it doesn't go from one point to the next in a strictly linear fashion. Let's set it to an "ease-in, ease-out" motion like this:

```
a.timingFunction = [CAMediaTimingFunction functionWithName:
            kCAMediaTimingFunctionEaseInEaseOut];
```

Build & Run now, and you'll see that when you click the button, it starts moving slowly, then gradually builds up steam and moves more quickly, only to taper off its speed as it reaches its target. Under the hood, these timing functions work by providing a simple mapping for a value shifting from 0.0 to 1.0, using a pair of control points to describe a curve between the two. Does that ring a bell? This seems like the perfect use for the curve editing control we implemented in the first half of this chapter! We can use the curve editor to define the timing that will be applied to the button's movement each time we click it.

Start by adding the `CurveView` class files from the previous project. In the MovingButton project, right-click on the Classes group, then select **Add▶Existing Files...** from the context menu. Navigate to the location of `CurveView.h` and `CurveView.m`, select them both, and click the Add button. In the sheet that appears, click to turn on the Copy items into destination group's folder checkbox, and make sure the MovingButton target is checked in the lower part of the sheet (see figure 14–3).

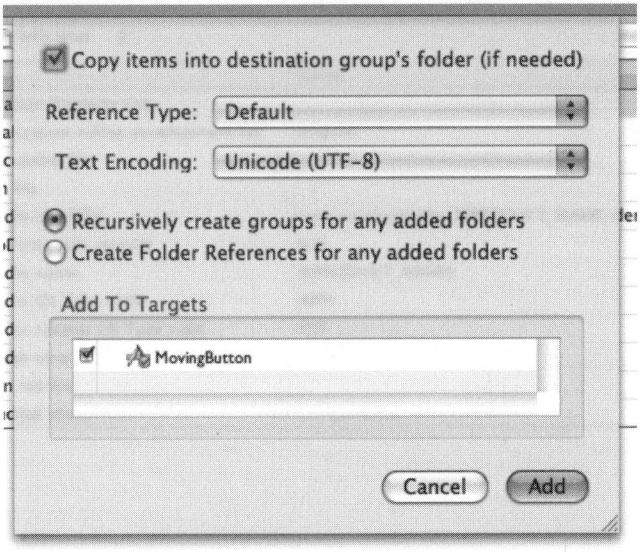

Figure 14–3. *Adding existing files to a project*

This time, rather than setting up bindings to this control, let's just add an outlet in our controller definition so that we can access the CurveView we're going to set up. Modify MovingButton_AppDelegate.h, adding the bold lines here:

```
#import <Cocoa/Cocoa.h>
@class CurveView
@interface MovingButton_AppDelegate : NSObject {
  IBOutlet CurveView *curveView;
}
- (IBAction)move:(id)sender;
@end
```

Now switch back to Interface Builder. We're going to add a small NSPanel which will work as a sort of inspector for our button animation. From the Library, drag out an NSPanel, then drag a Custom View into the new panel. Resize the Custom View to 100×100, and change its class to CurveView. Your GUI in Interface Builder should now look something like Figure 14–4.

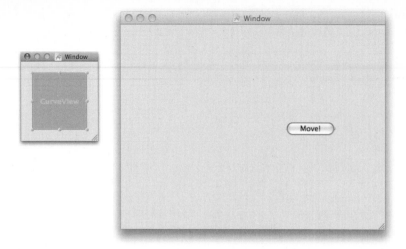

Figure 14–4. *Adding a CurveView for configuring our animation*

Now connect the app delegate's `curveView` outlet to the `CurveView` instance you just created, save your work, and switch back to Xcode. Import the CurveView header somewhere at the top of the app delegate's implementation file:

```
#import "CurveView.h"
```

Update the `move:` method as follows:

```
- (IBAction)move:(id)sender
{
    NSRect senderFrame = [sender frame];
    NSRect superBounds = [[sender superview] bounds];
    CABasicAnimation *a = [CABasicAnimation
                             animationWithKeyPath:@"position"];
    a.fromValue = [NSValue valueWithPoint:senderFrame.origin];
    senderFrame.origin.x = (superBounds.size.width -
        senderFrame.size.width)*drand48();
    senderFrame.origin.y = (superBounds.size.height -
        senderFrame.size.height)*drand48();
    a.toValue = [NSValue valueWithPoint:senderFrame.origin];

    a.duration = 1.0;
    a.timingFunction = [CAMediaTimingFunction
                          functionWithControlPoints:curveView.cp1X
                          :curveView.cp1Y
                          :curveView.cp2X
                          :curveView.cp2Y];

    // Add animation to layer; this also starts the animation
    [[sender layer] addAnimation:a forKey:@"position"];
    [sender setFrame:senderFrame];
}
```

Now, every time the user clicks the Move button, the resulting animation's timing function will be determined by the values in the `CurveView` control. Save your work, **Build**

& Run your app, and you should see this happening. Drag the handles around to create different curve shapes, click the Move button, and see how it moves.

Grouping Animations

You've now gotten a taste of how Core Animation works, but in the somewhat silly context of randomly moving a button around the screen. Not really a GUI design that we'd recommend! In the real world, Core Animation is most often used to animate transitions between different views. Chances are, you've seen this used again and again on the iPhone (the platform that Core Animation was really built for, before being "backported" to Mac OS X). All the smooth slides, scales, and fades that occur throughout the iPhone interface are implemented with Core Animation. In Mac OS X, Core Animation isn't quite so omnipresent, but it's put to good use in places like the "coverflow" view mode, which first appeared in iTunes and is now a part of Finder as well. In this section, you'll see how to implement some nice transitions yourself, by grouping animations together so that they run simultaneously.

In Xcode, by create a new Cocoa project called FlipIt. As usual, turn on garbage collection, and make sure you have a `FlipIt_AppDelegate` class both in the Xcode project, and properly connected in `MainMenu.xib`. What we're going to do is present a GUI where the user can flip between several "pages," and Core Animation will animate nicely between them. We'll use a box in the nib's empty window to show the content pages, which themselves will be held in an `NSTabView`. We won't display the tab view itself, we're just using it as a handy container for our content pages.

Start by defining the interface for our controller class. It contains outlets for the two views we need to manage: `tabView`, the object containing the views we're going to display, and `box`, the on-screen view where we'll be displaying them. It also has instance variables for pointing at the views that are actively transitioning in and out of focus, as well as an array for holding all the available views, and an integer index to identify the current focused view. Finally, our interface declares a pair of action methods that will be used by a matching pair of buttons in the GUI to tell our controller to flip between views.

```
@interface FlipIt_AppDelegate : NSObject {
    IBOutlet NSBox *box;
    IBOutlet NSTabView *tabView;
    NSView *leftView;
    NSView *rightView;
    NSView *middleView;
    NSArray *items;
    NSInteger currentTabIndex;
}
- (IBAction)next:(id)sender;
- (IBAction)previous:(id)sender;
@end
```

Now open `MainMenu.xib` in Interface Builder, where we'll define our views. Start off by dragging a button from the *Library* to the bottom of your GUI's empty window. Then duplicate the button, and title the two buttons Previous and Next. Connect the buttons to the matching action methods in the app delegate, and place the two buttons side by side at the lower center of the window (see Figure 14–5).

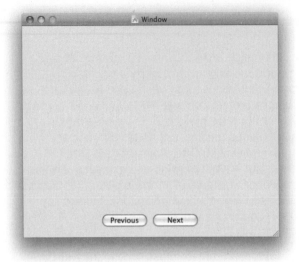

Figure 14–5. *Preparing the window*

Now find an NSBox in the *Library* and drag it to the empty window, placing it above the buttons and resizing it to fill most of the screen. Use the Attributes Inspector to remove the box's title by setting the Title Pos popup to *None* (see Figure 14–6). Then connect the app delegate's box outlet to the NSBox, so that we can reach it from code.

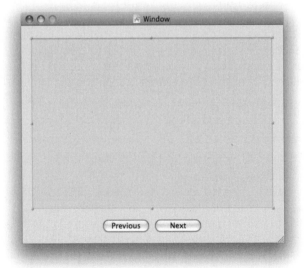

Figure 14–6. *The display window is now ready.*

Our next course of action is to set up a set of views for switching in and out of the main view. We'll use an `NSTabView` for this, simply because it's a convenient way for us to build a series of views in Interface Builder that can later be maintained as a list of off-screen views when our application runs. Find an `NSTabView` in the Library, but drag it to the main nib window instead of the GUI window you've been building. You'll see that the tab view appears as a top-level icon in the nib window, alongside the app delegate, the window, and other items (see Figure 14–7).

Figure 14–7. *It's an unusual place to find a tab view, but there it is.*

A tab view (or any other `NSView` subclass) placed at the top level of a nib file won't be displayed when the nib is loaded, but as long as we have an outlet pointing at it, we'll be able to access it and make use of it in any way we like, including putting it into a window's view hierarchy. In our case, we'll never put the tab view itself on display, just the content views it contains. Connect the app delegate's `tabView` outlet to the tab view so that we can access it later.

Double-click the tab view icon, and you'll see a window appear containing just the tab view. This window is just something Interface Builder uses to give you a structure to edit the tab view in, and does not represent an actual `NSWindow` in your nib file. You can verify this by clicking in the window's title bar and observing the title bar of the *Inspector* window, which always tells you what it's inspecting. In this case, selecting the tab view's window title bar will still show "Tab View" in the *Inspector* title bar, unlike normal windows you edit which will change it to "Window." One side effect of this is that the tab view displayed in this way doesn't have the resize controls on all four sides and all four corners like it would in a normal window. Instead, you can use the resizing gadget at the window's lower-right corner to resize your view. Do that now, making it about the same size as the `NSBox` you put into the window a little while ago.

Now let's put some content into this tab view, the "pages" that we'll be able to flip between. By default the tab view contains just a few content views, but feel free to increase that number (using the *Attributes Inspector*) so that you have even more views to switch between. The actual content isn't that important, as long as something is unique on each page so that you can easily see the content change from one page to the next. A good start is just to grab a label from the *Library*, give it a nice big font, and change its text to the word "One." Then copy this label and paste it into each of the other views (which you can switch between using the tabs at the top, just like otherwise), changing the label accordingly each time. Just for fun, add some unique items to each page as well (a table view here, a set of buttons there) so that when the app is done, you'll see a little more things in motion while flipping between pages. Save your work, and go back to Xcode.

It's time to start implementing our app delegate class in `FlipIt_AppDelegate.m`. This class will have a number of methods for preparing a transition by setting up the next view to be displayed, out to the side of the box; transitioning the new view into position; and transitioning the current view out to the other side. Because we want to be able to do transitions in two directions, depending on whether we're flipping to the right or the left, each of those methods exists in two forms, setting things up and executing a rightward flip or leftward flip. In addition, we'll implement our two action methods that start up the transitions, and a startup method (`applicationDidFinishLaunching:`) that sets up the initial view.

Let's start by creating a preprocessor definition, `ANIM_DURATION`, to define the duration (in seconds) of the animations we're going to create. By putting this in one place, at the top of the file, we can easily experiment, tweaking this setting until we find a speed we like. Define it like this:

```
#define ANIM_DURATION 1.0
```

Now let's move on to the `applicationDidFinishLaunching:` method. Here we grab the list of views from the `tabView`, and set up `currentTabIndex` to point at the end of the array so that the first item will be lined up (more on this later). Then we call the first of our internal methods, `prepareRightSide`, which will set up the next view for display on the right side of the box. Then we make use of the `ANIM_DURATION` value, using it to specify the duration of any animations we create within the current animation context. Then we call another internal method, `transitionInFromRight`, which will start up the animations to move the next view into the right position. Finally we set `currentTabIndex` to point at item zero (the first object in the `items` array).

```
- (void)applicationDidFinishLaunching:(NSNotification *)n {
    items = [tabView tabViewItems];
    currentTabIndex = [items count]-1;
    [self prepareRightSide];
    [[NSAnimationContext currentContext] setDuration:ANIM_DURATION];
    [self transitionInFromRight];
    currentTabIndex = 0;
    middleView = rightView;
}
```

Now let's write the code for the two internal methods referenced here, prepareRightSide and transitionInFromRight. We won't bother putting these methods into a separate protocol or anything. In Objective-C, code can freely call any other methods declared higher up in the same @implementation block, even if those methods aren't declared in any @interface, so all we have to do is put these internal methods somewhere above applicationDidFinishLaunching:, so that the code in there can call these methods. The first of these, prepareRightSide, starts off by determining the index of the next view to display, by adding one to currentTabIndex and then doing a simple bounds check on the new index, resetting it to zero if it's gotten too high. Then we use that index to grab the next view, and set its frame to be the same size as box, shifted off to the right by exactly the width of box so that it's just out of sight. We set its alpha value to 0.0, making it effectively invisible, and finally we add the view as a subview of box, so that it will actually be displayed.

```
- (void)prepareRightSide {
  NSInteger nextTabIndex = currentTabIndex + 1;
  if (nextTabIndex >= [items count])
    nextTabIndex = 0;

  rightView = [[items objectAtIndex:nextTabIndex] view];

  NSRect viewFrame = [box bounds];
  viewFrame.origin.x += viewFrame.size.width;

  [rightView setFrame:viewFrame];
  [rightView setAlphaValue:0.0];
  [box addSubview:rightView];
}
```

The next method, transitionInFromRight, takes rightView and slides it into place so that it fits perfectly into the space provided by box. It also sets the alpha value to 1.0, making it fully opaque. Note that unlike the previous method, this uses rightView's animator method to access the view's animation proxy, so that setting these values actually creates implicit animations for us.

```
- (void)transitionInFromRight {
  [[rightView animator] setFrame:[box bounds]];
  [[rightView animator] setAlphaValue:1.0];
}
```

Before we go any further, let's check our work by building and running our app. This won't quite work as-is, because we declared action methods in our header file but haven't defined them yet. Add the following methods to the .m file:

```
- (IBAction)next:(id)sender {
}
- (IBAction)previous:(id)sender {
}
```

Now, you should be able to **Build & Run** your app, and see the first item from your tab view slide into place and fade in from invisibility to full opacity at the same time, as shown in Figure 14–8.

Figure 14–8. *The first "page" is sliding into view. Note the slightly grayed-out appearance of the objects in the box, which are all at about 50 percent opacity at this point.*

That's a start! Now let's see how we move on to the next item in the list, by providing an implementation for the next: method. Some of this code is similar to what we had in the applicationDidFinishLaunching: method. We prepare the right side, start some transitions (including a call to another new internal method, transitionOutToLeft, which we'll get to soon), and update an index (including another bounds check) and some pointers at the end. The biggest difference here is that the methods that are going to do animation are all sandwiched between calls to [NSAnimationContext beginGrouping] and [NSAnimationContext endGrouping], which work together to form a sort of transaction. Between those two calls, any animations that are added to the default animation context, including all implicit animations, will be set up to run simultaneously. This means that as we create implicit animations in our internal methods, they will all be set up to fire off simultaneously. Without this step, the animations we create would all start running in sequence, one after another as they're created. Normally this won't make much of a difference, but it's entirely possible that some unexpected event could occur just as those animations are being created, such as another process suddenly hogging the CPU, which could lead to these animations running in a slightly staggered manner, starting and ending at different times. By wrapping them in a grouping as shown here, that potential problem is eliminated.

```
- (IBAction)next:(id)sender {
  [self prepareRightSide];

  [NSAnimationContext beginGrouping];
  [[NSAnimationContext currentContext] setDuration:ANIM_DURATION];
  [self transitionInFromRight];
  [self transitionOutToLeft];
  [NSAnimationContext endGrouping];

  currentTabIndex++;
```

```
  if (currentTabIndex >= [items count])
    currentTabIndex = 0;
  leftView = middleView;
  middleView = rightView;
}
```

The `next:` method also calls another internal method, `transitionOutToLeft`, which will take the current view and shuffle it off to the left. Its implementation looks like this:

```
- (void)transitionOutToLeft {
  NSRect newFrame = [middleView frame];
  newFrame.origin.x -= newFrame.size.width;
  [[middleView animator] setFrame:newFrame];
  [[middleView animator] setAlphaValue:0.0];
}
```

With that in place, you're now ready to **Build & Run** once again. This time you'll see that not only does the initial view setup work, but now you can also hit the *Next* button to transition to the next view! Smooth. See Figure 14–9.

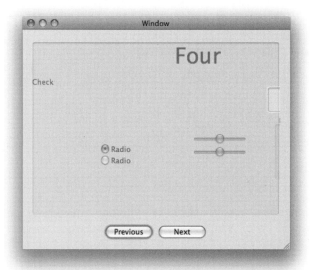

Figure 14–9. *View Three is on its way out, View Four is almost halfway in.*

Now all that's left is to implement matching methods for rightward transitions. These methods are all pretty similar to the others, and are presented here without further comment, except one: you may be tempted to copy and paste the existing methods and make whatever you changes you can spot, but be careful! Some of the differences are subtle but important.

```
- (void)prepareLeftSide {
  NSInteger previousTabIndex = currentTabIndex-1;
  if (previousTabIndex < 0)
    previousTabIndex = [items count]-1;

  leftView = [[items objectAtIndex:previousTabIndex] view];
```

```
    NSRect viewFrame = [box bounds];
    viewFrame.origin.x -= viewFrame.size.width;

    [leftView setFrame:viewFrame];
    [leftView setAlphaValue:0.0];
    [box addSubview:leftView];
}
- (void)transitionInFromLeft {
    [[leftView animator] setFrame:[box bounds]];
    [[leftView animator] setAlphaValue:1.0];
}
- (void)transitionOutToRight {
    NSRect newFrame = [middleView frame];
    newFrame.origin.x += [box bounds].size.width;
    [[middleView animator] setFrame:newFrame];
    [[middleView animator] setAlphaValue:0.0];
}
- (IBAction)previous:(id)sender {
    [self prepareLeftSide];

    [NSAnimationContext beginGrouping];
    [[NSAnimationContext currentContext] setDuration:ANIM_DURATION];
    [self transitionInFromLeft];
    [self transitionOutToRight];
    [NSAnimationContext endGrouping];

    currentTabIndex--;
    if (currentTabIndex < 0)
      currentTabIndex = [items count]-1;
    rightView = middleView;
    middleView = leftView;
}
```

Now **Build & Run**, and you should see that you can flip in both directions.

What Have We Done?

Hopefully, the previous chapter and this one have given you a solid footing in a variety of Cocoa drawing techniques, including a variety of uses of Bezier curves, making your views interactive by using the mouse, and fairly painless animation with Core Animation. The scope of this book doesn't really allow us to delve any further into these topics, especially considering that where graphics and animation are concerned, the only limits are your own imagination! We've given you the basic tools. If you want to do more with graphics, now it's your turn to dig deeper into the areas that interest you most, and see what you can do with the APIs that Cocoa gives you. That's where the fun really begins!

Chapter 15

Working with Files

Most applications will need to deal with files stored on disk in one way or another. So far in this book, we really haven't dealt much with this topic (except for a bit of discussion about Core Data and its data stores), so let's remedy that right now. Cocoa actually includes several useful classes for dealing with files in a number of ways. There are classes that provide APIs mimicking operations the user can normally do in the Finder, and others that represent a file in an abstract way. Still other classes have built-in functionality for reading and writing files.

Implicit File Access

Several classes in Cocoa, such as `NSString`, `NSData`, `NSArray`, and `NSDictionary`, provide methods for reading data directly from a file, or writing their contents directly to a file, using just a string containing the full path to the relevant file. For instance, if you want to read the entire contents of a file into a string, you can do something as simple as this:

```
NSString *myString = [NSString stringWithContentsOfFile:@"/path/to/something"
  usedEncoding:NULL error:NULL];
```

That code will take care of all the busy work of opening the file and reading its contents. It will even tell us what text encoding it used to interpret the contents of the file as a character string, and tell us any errors that occur. But only if we pass in non-NULL values for the second and third parameters. Apart from file-related errors, such as insufficient permissions to access the file, this method can also report back errors related to dealing with data as a character string, such as text encoding errors if the file contains binary data. Later in this chapter you'll see this in action.

`NSArray` and `NSDictionary` have similar methods, which for some reason don't include the sort of error-reporting that `NSString` does, so if they fail, they simply return a `nil` pointer and leave you wondering. Those methods are also much more special-purpose, since they are designed to read values from files stored in Apple's special property-list format. One common use of `NSDictionary`'s `dictionaryWithContentsOfFile:` class method is to read data from a configuration file created in a text editor or in Xcode's plist editor. Cocoa also includes a special-purpose class called `NSPropertyListSerialization` for dealing with the property-list format. If you really need to parse a property-list in a general way, with complete error reporting and more control, you can use its class method `propertyListFromData:mutabilityOption:format:errorDescription:` (try saying that five times in a row).

Of the classes mentioned at the start of this section, NSData provides the most general file access. It can read any sort of data from disk, and represent it as an array of bytes for you to use as you will. This is the ideal way for dealing with binary data. NSData even provides an option for hinting that the file should be mapped into virtual memory (in case you know it's such a large file, you don't want it all in memory at once), like this:

```
NSData *myData = [NSData dataWithContentsOfFile:@"/path/to/something"
  options:NSMappedRead error: &myError];
```

Each of the classes mentioned here also contains a method called `writeToFile:atomically:` whose second parameter is a BOOL specifying whether the data should first be written to an auxiliary file, which then replaces the original after all data is written. The NSString version of this method is actually deprecated, and you're encouraged to use `writeToFile:atomically:encoding:error:` instead, which forces you to specify which text encoding to use, and gives you the chance to inspect any errors that may occur. NSData provides the similar `writeToFile:options:error:`, which also gives you a chance to see any errors that occur when writing to a file.

High-level File Operations

Besides the basics of reading and writing files, Cocoa provides a number of classes that let you deal with files in ways similar to how the Finder deals with files. You can get access to file-system attributes, get the file's icon, see which application will open this file by default, and more. The rest of this chapter will explore some of these capabilities in the context of a new application called "What About That File?" (see Figure 15–1).

This application lets the user choose a file, at which point some information about the file is shown, as well as the file's contents in the form of a string. If the file contains data that can't be represented as a character string, it will tell the user so. Otherwise, the user can use an included popup list to change the text encoding that is used when reading the file from disk, and show the resulting string.

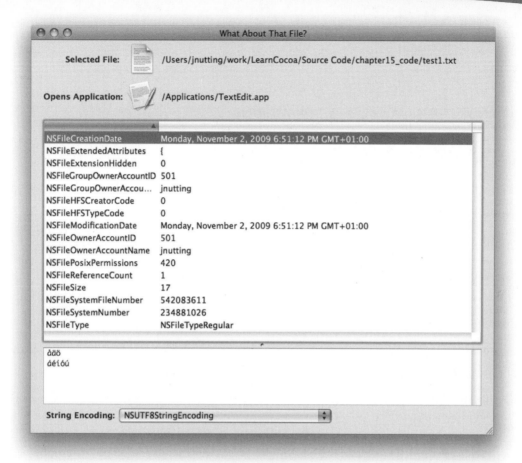

Figure 15–1. *The completed "What About That File?" application*

What About That File: The Code

Start in Xcode. Make a new Cocoa application (no Document support or Core Data this time) named *WhatAboutThatFile*, and do the usual steps of enabling garbage collection and creating a `WhatAboutThatFileAppDelegate` class if Xcode didn't create one for you. In previous chapters, we've assembled applications one step at a time, but now that we're this far along, we think you're ready to take on bigger chunks of application code. So this time, what we're going to do to is present the complete code of the application, with some commentary interspersed, and then describe how to wire up everything in Interface Builder using Cocoa Bindings. For starters, here's the header file of our app delegate, which declares a few instance variables and a larger number of properties, used for accessing values through Cocoa Bindings:

```
// WhatAboutThatFileAppDelegate.h

#import <Cocoa/Cocoa.h>
```

```
@interface WhatAboutThatFileAppDelegate : NSObject {
  NSFileWrapper *fileWrapper;
  NSString *filePath;
  NSStringEncoding chosenEncoding;
}
@property (retain) NSFileWrapper *fileWrapper;
@property (retain) NSString *filePath;
@property (readonly) NSDictionary *fileAttributes;
@property (readonly) NSString *filename;
@property (readonly) NSImage *fileIcon;
@property (readonly) NSImage *opensAppIcon;
@property (readonly) NSString *opensAppName;
@property (assign) NSString *stringEncodingName;
@property (readonly) NSString *fileStringValue;
@property (readonly) NSDictionary *encodingNames;
@property (assign) NSStringEncoding chosenEncoding;

- (IBAction)chooseFile:(id)sender;
@end
```

Now let's move on to the .m file:

```
//   WhatAboutThatFileAppDelegate.m

#import "WhatAboutThatFileAppDelegate.h"
@implementation WhatAboutThatFileAppDelegate
@synthesize fileWrapper, filePath, chosenEncoding;

- (void)applicationDidFinishLaunching:(NSNotification *)n {
  fileWrapper = nil;
  filePath = nil;
}
```

The chooseFile: method uses the NSOpenPanel class to ask the user to choose a file to inspect. If the user actually picks a file, we set all of our instance variables based on the selection. chosenEncoding, a variable of type NSStringEncoding (which is at heart simply an unsigned integer) is set to 0, which is not a valid string encoding type, so that at a later stage we can let the system try to deduce the string encoding type for us. After that, we set filePath based on the selection in the open panel, and finally set fileWrapper, which is an instance of the NSFileWrapper class, which simply wraps a file and lets us get some metadata about it, based on the value of filePath.

```
- (IBAction)chooseFile:(id)sender {
  NSOpenPanel *openPanel = [NSOpenPanel openPanel];
  [openPanel setCanChooseFiles:YES];
  [openPanel setCanChooseDirectories:NO];
  [openPanel setResolvesAliases:NO];
  [openPanel setAllowsMultipleSelection:NO];
  if ([openPanel runModal] == NSFileHandlingPanelOKButton) {
    self.chosenEncoding = 0;
    self.filePath = [[openPanel filenames] lastObject];
    self.fileWrapper = [[[NSFileWrapper alloc] initWithPath:filePath] autorelease];
  }
}
```

Next, we have the filename and fileIcon methods, which will be read by the uppermost GUI objects in our window. Note that this reading occurs via Cocoa Bindings, so we use

the convention of providing class methods named
keyPathsForValuesAffectingFilename and keyPathsForValuesAffectingFileIcon, in
order to ensure that changes made to one bindings-friendly value cause another value
to be re-fetched. We last used this in the context of a Core Data model class, but it
works equally well here, ensuring that any time the filePath or fileWrapper values are
changed, any views binding their content to filename or fileIcon will automatically
reload their content. Both the filename and fileIcon methods use the previously-
created fileWrapper to access the values for display.

```
+ (NSSet *)keyPathsForValuesAffectingFilename {
  return [NSSet setWithObjects:@"filePath", @"fileWrapper", nil];
}
- (NSString *)filename {
  return [fileWrapper filename];
}

+ (NSSet *)keyPathsForValuesAffectingFileIcon {
  return [NSSet setWithObjects:@"filePath", @"fileWrapper", nil];
}
- (NSImage *)fileIcon {
  return [fileWrapper icon];
}
```

We provide similar functionality in order to display info about the application that will be
launched if the user double-clicks the chosen file in the Finder. This time, we're using
the NSWorkspace class, which represents something akin to the Finder itself. NSWorkspace
can do a number of things, such as launching applications and manipulating files. In
opensAppIcon, we first use the workspace to get the name of the application that is the
default "opener" for the chosen file, then ask the workspace for the application's icon. In
opensAppName, we just get the name of the application. Once again, we use the
keyPathsForValuesAffectingXxx convention to make sure these values are properly
refreshed when a new file is selected.

```
+ (NSSet *)keyPathsForValuesAffectingOpensAppIcon {
  return [NSSet setWithObjects:@"filePath", @"fileWrapper", nil];
}
- (NSImage *)opensAppIcon {
  NSWorkspace *workspace = [NSWorkspace sharedWorkspace];
  NSString *appName = nil;
  [workspace getInfoForFile:self.filePath application:&appName type:NULL];
  return appName ? [workspace iconForFile:appName] : nil;
}

+ (NSSet *)keyPathsForValuesAffectingOpensAppName {
  return [NSSet setWithObjects:@"filePath", @"fileWrapper", nil];
}
- (NSString *)opensAppName {
  NSWorkspace *workspace = [NSWorkspace sharedWorkspace];
  NSString *appName = nil;
  [workspace getInfoForFile:self.filePath application:&appName type:NULL];
  return appName;
}
```

Here, the `fileAttributes` accessor returns a dictionary, which it gets from `fileWrapper`. This dictionary contains a dozen or more filesystem attributes, and will be displayed in a table view in the GUI by using an `NSDictionaryController`.

```
+ (NSSet *)keyPathsForValuesAffectingFileAttributes {
  return [NSSet setWithObjects:@"filePath", @"fileWrapper", nil];
}
- (NSDictionary *)fileAttributes {
  return [fileWrapper fileAttributes];
}
```

Now we get into the somewhat hairier issue of string encodings. As we've mentioned earlier, `NSString` provides functionality for reading a string from a file and making a guess at which string encoding it should use. This may be right most of the time, but sometimes it can be useful to see the contents of a string through a different set of goggles, so to speak. It may be enlightening, for instance, to see how a modern UTF8 document may appear if viewed in an archaic application on some other platform that doesn't have any concept of string encodings, and always uses the one and only string encoding available to it.

We start off by defining the `encodingNames` method. This method will provide a list of encoding names to the popup button in our GUI, and will also serve as an internal lookup mechanism for mapping between encoding names and their code-level representation, the `NSStringEncoding` type. For keys, this dictionary uses the numeric value of each encoding wrapped in an `NSString`. You might think that it would make more sense, given the numeric nature of these values, to wrap them in `NSNumber` objects instead, and you'd be right except for one small catch: if you're using an `NSDictionary` in a key-value observer context, such as Cocoa Bindings, you *have* to use strings as keys! Because we're using this dictionary to populate an object via Cocoa Bindings, that's what we're doing.

```
- (NSDictionary *)encodingNames {
  static NSDictionary *encodingNames = nil;
  if (!encodingNames) {
    encodingNames = [NSDictionary dictionaryWithObjectsAndKeys:
      @"NSASCIIStringEncoding", @"1",
      @"NSNEXTSTEPStringEncoding", @"2",
      @"NSJapaneseEUCStringEncoding", @"3",
      @"NSUTF8StringEncoding", @"4",
      @"NSISOLatin1StringEncoding", @"5",
      @"NSSymbolStringEncoding", @"6",
      @"NSNonLossyASCIIStringEncoding", @"7",
      @"NSShiftJISStringEncoding", @"8",
      @"NSISOLatin2StringEncoding", @"9",
      @"NSUnicodeStringEncoding", @"10",
      @"NSWindowsCP1251StringEncoding", @"11",
      @"NSWindowsCP1252StringEncoding", @"12",
      @"NSWindowsCP1253StringEncoding", @"13",
      @"NSWindowsCP1254StringEncoding", @"14",
      @"NSWindowsCP1250StringEncoding", @"15",
      @"NSISO2022JPStringEncoding", @"21",
      @"NSMacOSRomanStringEncoding", @"30",
      @"NSUTF16BigEndianStringEncoding", @"2415919360",
      @"NSUTF16LittleEndianStringEncoding", @"2483028224",
```

```
        @"NSUTF32StringEncoding", @"2348810496",
        @"NSUTF32BigEndianStringEncoding", @"2550137088",
        @"NSUTF32LittleEndianStringEncoding", @"2617245952",
        nil];
  }
  return encodingNames;
}
```

Continuing our efforts with string encodings, we'll now define accessors for stringEncodingName, this time adding a setter into the mix (because this value will be settable from the popup button). As before, we implement keyPathsForValuesAffectingStringEncodingName, this time adding chosenEncoding as one of the keys to watch for.

The stringEncodingName method has two main execution paths. If chosenEncoding has been set (say, the user has picked an encoding from the popup list), we simply look up the name of the chosen encoding in the dictionary we defined earlier. Otherwise, we actually read the file's contents with stringWithContentsOfFile:usedEncoding:error: and use the resulting encoding to look up the name of the discovered encoding (or return a brief problem description if no encoding could be discovered).

The setStringEncodingName: method is quite simple. We do a reverse lookup in the dictionary to find the key (a string containing the integer value of the encoding) corresponding to the chosen encoding. This method is called when the user selects an encoding name in the popup.

```
+ (NSSet *)keyPathsForValuesAffectingStringEncodingName {
    return [NSSet setWithObjects:@"filePath", @"fileWrapper",
      @"chosenEncoding", nil];
}
- (NSString *)stringEncodingName {
    if (!filePath) return nil;
    if (self.chosenEncoding != 0) {
      return [[self encodingNames] objectForKey:
              [NSString stringWithFormat:@"%u", self.chosenEncoding]];
    } else {
      NSStringEncoding encoding = 0;
      NSError *err = nil;
      [NSString stringWithContentsOfFile:filePath
        usedEncoding:&encoding error:&err];
      if (encoding==0) {
        return @"No encoding detected.  Perhaps a binary file?";
      }
      return [[self encodingNames] objectForKey:
              [NSString stringWithFormat:@"%u", encoding]];
    }
}
- (void)setStringEncodingName:(NSString *)name {
  NSString *key = [[[self encodingNames] allKeysForObject:name]
    lastObject];
  self.chosenEncoding = [key longLongValue];
}
```

Finally, fileStringValue and its matching keyPathsForValuesAffectingFileStringValue method. Here we also have a couple of primary code paths. In the first case, where chosenEncoding has been set, we attempt to read a string value from the chosen file, using the chosen encoding. In the other case, where the no encoding has been chosen, we attempt to read a string value but let the system try to figure out which encoding to use. In either case, we do a bit of error checking, and show an alert panel if a particular string encoding error is encountered.

```
+ (NSSet *)keyPathsForValuesAffectingFileStringValue {
  return [NSSet setWithObjects:@"filePath", @"fileWrapper",
    @"chosenEncoding", nil];
}
- (NSString *)fileStringValue {
  if (!filePath) return nil;
  NSError *err = nil;
  NSString *value = nil;
  if (self.chosenEncoding != 0) {
    value = [NSString stringWithContentsOfFile:filePath
      encoding:self.chosenEncoding error:&err];
  } else {
    NSStringEncoding encoding = 0;
    value = [NSString stringWithContentsOfFile:filePath
      usedEncoding:&encoding error:&err];
  }
  if (err)  {
   if ([err code]==NSFileReadInapplicableStringEncodingError &&
       [[err domain] isEqual:NSCocoaErrorDomain]) {
     NSRunAlertPanel(@"Invalid string encoding",
       [err localizedDescription], nil, nil, nil);
   }
   NSLog(@"encountered error: %@", err);
  }
  return value;
}
@end
```

What About That File: The GUI

That's all, as far as the code is concerned. Now let's set up the GUI. Open up *MainMenu.xib* in Interface Builder, and start off by making a connection so that a menu item can call our app delegate's chooseFile: method. Open the menu inside the main nib window, go into the *File* menu, and Ctrl-drag a connection from the *Open* item to the icon representing the app delegate in the main nib window. Then select *chooseFile:* from the small menu that appears.

Now it's time to get started on the window itself. This GUI is completely powered by Cocoa Bindings. Our controller doesn't have any outlets pointing at anything in this window, and nothing in this window calls any action methods in our controller. We'll go through all the bindings piece by piece, but first, Figure 15–2 shows a view of the complete window, as seen in Interface Builder, with all objects selected.

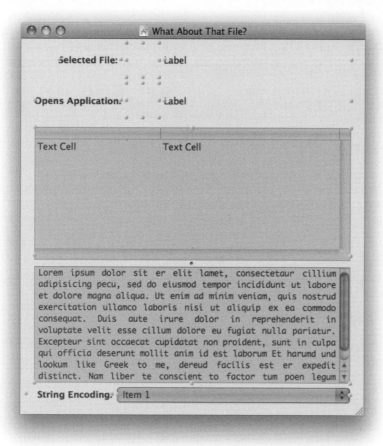

Figure 15–2. *All our window components, highlighted for visibility*

Note that between the table view and the large text view there's a small "dimple." This is actually the draggable control of an NSSplitView, which lets you stack two views vertically or horizontally, and resize both of them at once with a single drag. You've surely seen this used in Xcode and elsewhere, and later you'll see how to set it up here.

For now, let's start off creating this window one section at a time, hooking up all the bindings as we go. At the top, put a couple of labels, and place an NSImageView between them. You'll find this class by searching the *Library* for "NSImageView" or "image well," but not "image view," which actually gives you another class entirely, IKImageView. Make the label on the left appear in bold text by selecting it and pressing ⌘B, and stretch out the label on the right so that it extends almost to the right edge of the window. We want the file icon displayed by the image view to appear to float right over the window background, so use the *Attributes Inspector* to remove its border by selecting *None* from the *Border* popup. While you're in there, change the *Scaling* popup to *Proportionally Up or Down* as well, so that whether the system gives us a tiny icon or a huge one, it will be scaled to fit the available space. Your GUI should look like Figure 15–3 at this point.

Figure 15–3. *GUI for displaying the selected file's icon and path*

Now it's time to set up the bindings for the image view and the right-hand label. Select the image view, open the *Bindings Inspector*, and bind its *Value* to the app delegate using the `fileIcon` key path. Then select the label on the right, and bind its *Value* to the app delegate using the `filePath` key path.

The next portion of the window looks just like what we created above. In fact, the quickest way to add these objects is to select the three shown above by dragging a box over them, pressing ⌘D to duplicate the selected object, and then dragging the new ones down, lining them up above the others. Change the title of the new left-side label and adjust its position if you need to. Figure 15–4 shows what this looks like.

Figure 15–4. *This GUI will let us see with which app the file will launch.*

Reconfigure the new image view's binding, connecting its *Value* to the app delegate with the `opensAppIcon` key path, and then the right-side label's Value to the app delegate using the `opensAppName` key path.

Next, let's move on to the table view. Drag one out from the Library, and resize it to match Figure 15–5.

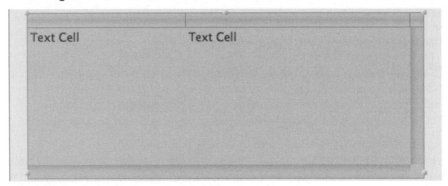

Figure 15–5. *Here we'll display all the file's attributes.*

This table view is going to contain all the file attributes that the system gives us. Those attributes come to us in the form of a dictionary, which is a perfect use of Apple's `NSDictionaryController` class. Using `NSDictionaryController`, we'll be able to display all of the selected file's attributes as key-value pairs in the table view, just by hooking them up with Cocoa Bindings.

Search for NSDictionaryController in the *Library*, and drag one to the main nib window. Rename it *attrDict* so that we can easily identify it when binding to it later on. Like the other included controller classes, the dictionary controller class is able to get its content via a binding. Use the *Bindings Inspector* to bind its *Content Dictionary* (in the *Controller Content* group) to the app delegate's fileAttributes key path.

Now we just have to bind the table view's columns to the new controller. Select the left column, and use the *Bindings Inspector* to bind its *Value* column to *attrDict*, using *arrangedObjects* as the controller key and *key* as the key path. That will make the left column show the keys for each key-value pair in the dictionary. Now select the right column, and bind its *Value* column to *attrDict*, using *arrangedObjects* as the controller key and *value* as the key path.

Next, grab an NSTextView from the *Library*. Use the *Attributes Inspector* to turn off the *Editable* checkbox (we just want to display a file here, not edit it) as well as the *Rich Text* checkbox. Now is as good a time as any to bring the NSSplitView into play, as we hinted at earlier. Make the table view and the text view (actually, the scroll view that contains it) are about the same size, and line them up one above the other. Then select both of them, and choose **Layout▸Embed Objects In▸Splitview** from the menu. Doing so will line them up tightly, and draw the little dimple between them. If you test your interface now by pressing ⌘R, you'll see that you can drag the dimple up and down to resize both views; then press ⌘Q to get back to editing your interface (Figure 15–6).

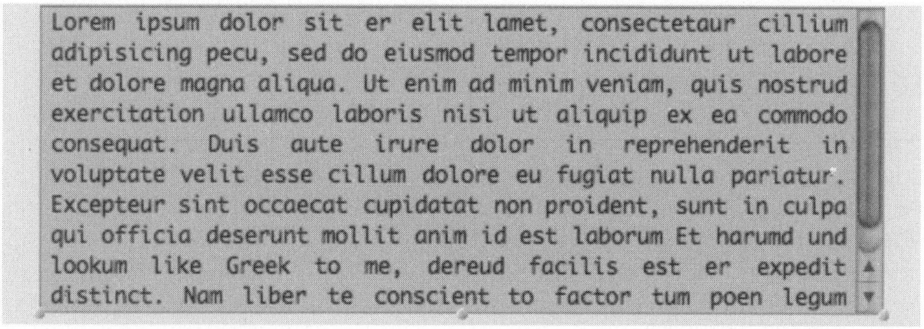

Figure 15–6. *After disabling Rich Text, this is what your text view will probably look like. No need to delete the exhilarating prose that appears here by default; it won't appear in the running application.*

Now select just the text view again. Remember, you can avoid the ambiguity and extra steps involved to select the correct object in the view hierarchy by Shift-Ctrl-clicking the text view and selecting the text view from the stack of objects that's displayed. Switch to the *Bindings Inspector*, and bind the text view's *Value* to the app delegate's fileStringValue key path.

Finally, let's provide a GUI for the list of string encodings that will be used to let us reinterpret the contents of the selected file. For this, you'll need a label and a popup button from the Library. Lay them out as shown, including the extra-wide popup button, since some of the entries in the list will be quite long.

Figure 15–7. *Really, who wouldn't want their popup button wide enough to fully display "NSUTF32LittleEndianStringEncoding"?*

The values for the popup list will be retrieved from the app delegate's encodingNames method, so you don't need to enter them in Interface Builder. Here we'll use NSDictionaryController again, this time to display just the values from the encodingNames dictionary. In order to do that, you need to first of all drag another NSDictionaryController from the *Library* to the nib window, renaming it *strEncs* while you're at it, and bind its *Content Dictionary* to the app delegate's encodingNames key path. Then, bind the popup button's *Content* to *strEncs*, using *arrangedObjects* as the *Controller Key*, and *value* as the *Model Key Path*.

Finally, we need to establish a binding so that the value the user sets in the popup is noticed by the app delegate, making the app delegate redisplay the text using the selected encoding. Do this by binding the popup button's Selected Object to the app delegate, using stringEncodingName as the key path.

Now save all your changes, and **Build & Run** the app. You should see the GUI you've built, including a **File▶Open** menu item that lets you choose a file, and will show you the file's attributes as well as its content. Choosing another encoding from the popup list will make the app redisplay the data in the text view using the chosen encoding.

Filing It All Away

In this chapter, you've seen how to use Cocoa to access files and their metadata. You've also learned a bit about string encodings, and how Cocoa deals with them. What's more, you've seen another example of a GUI powered by Cocoa Bindings. Except for the menu item that opens a file, everything that happens here, happens through bindings, including setting a value in a popup list, which ends up causing the text field to reload. That's a fairly complicated interaction, and until you're used to it, it's not really obvious how it works, because parts of it occur "behind the scenes," thanks to Cocoa Bindings. If you don't quite see how it's working, it may be worthwhile for you to read through this chapter again and see if it brings you any closer to the "a-ha!" moment where it suddenly all makes sense. Otherwise, head on over to the next chapter, where you'll learn how to use concurrency to make your application more responsive.

Chapter 16

Concurrency

One of the biggest challenges in software development is writing software that will do more than one thing at a time. For decades, computers have been able to give an illusion of concurrency by quickly switching between tasks at a high rate, making it seem that they're doing several things at once (when in reality, they're continuously flipping from one task to the next, only "paying attention" to one at a time). Today's computers frequently contain two or more computation cores, so that they really can do multiple things at once, simultaneously executing instructions on all cores at the same time.

However, even if your computer's hardware and OS are capable of working with a multitude of cores, writing application software that can effectively make use of multiple cores is still technically challenging. In most development environments, the default assumption is that the code you're writing is performed sequentially, one operation after the other, and splitting things up so that work can be performed concurrently can be a pretty big task.

In this chapter, we'll present an example of a common situation in which Cocoa applications can benefit from concurrency, and show you how it's done. You're surely familiar with Mac OS X's spinning disk cursor (sometimes called the "spinning beachball of death") which appears whenever an application isn't responding to user actions. This typically appears after you click a button or menu item that triggers any sort of processing that takes more than a few seconds. Mac OS X notices that your process isn't handling input events, and shows the spinning disk cursor to alert the user. This also happens whenever an application has really stopped responding entirely, and is on its way to crashing (or being killed by the user). So when your app stops responding, and starts showing the spinning disk cursor, the immediate reaction for many users is a moment of panic when they suspect that your app is about to crash!

Therefore, it's in your best interests to make sure that any sort of long-running operation in your application is handled in such a way that the user can still interact with your application and not get the spinning disk, by making the operation occur in the background, letting your application still handle user input events as it normally does. This chapter will demonstrate two ways to add this sort of concurrency to a Cocoa application with a minimum of fuss. We'll use the concepts embodied by the NSOperation and NSOperationQueue classes available in Leopard (as well as on the iPhone), and also show you how it can be done using the new Grand Central Dispatch, available only in Snow Leopard.

SlowWorker

As a platform for demonstrating these concurrency options, we'll create a simple application called SlowWorker, which simulates doing some long-running operations such as fetching data from a server, and performing some calculations. This app presents the user with a button to initiate some work, and shows the results in a text view when it's done (see Figure 16–1).

Figure 16–1. *The SlowWorker in action (inaction?).*

Start by making a new Cocoa application (no Core Data or Document support is necessary) in Xcode, and doing the usual steps of enabling garbage collection, and creating a SlowWorkerAppDelegate class and adding it to the *MainMenu.xib* if necessary (say, if you're running Leopard, and Xcode didn't create it for you). Put the following code into *SlowWorkerAppDelegate.h*:

```
#import <Cocoa/Cocoa.h>
@interface SlowWorkerAppDelegate : NSObject {
```

```
    IBOutlet NSButton *startButton;
    IBOutlet NSTextView *resultsTextView;
}
- (IBAction)doWork:(id)sender;
@end
```

This simply defines a couple of outlets to the two objects visible in our GUI, and an action method to be triggered by the button. Now enter the following code for *SlowWorkerAppDelegate.m*:

```
#import "SlowWorkerAppDelegate.h"
@implementation SlowWorkerAppDelegate
- (NSString *)fetchSomethingFromServer {
    sleep(1);
    return @"Hi there";
}
- (NSString *)processData:(NSString *)data {
    sleep(2);
    return [data uppercaseString];
}
- (NSString *)calculateFirstResult:(NSString *)data {
    sleep(3);
    return [NSString stringWithFormat:@"Number of chars: %d",
      [data length]];
}
- (NSString *)calculateSecondResult:(NSString *)data {
    sleep(4);
    return [data stringByReplacingOccurrencesOfString:@"E"
                                           withString:@"e"];
}
- (IBAction)doWork:(id)sender {
    NSDate *startTime = [NSDate date];
    NSString *fetchedData = [self fetchSomethingFromServer];
    NSString *processed = [self processData:fetchedData];
    NSString *firstResult = [self calculateFirstResult:processed];
    NSString *secondResult = [self calculateSecondResult:processed];
    NSString *resultsSummary = [NSString stringWithFormat:
      @"First: [%@]\nSecond: [%@]", firstResult, secondResult];
    [resultsTextView setString:resultsSummary];
    NSDate *endTime = [NSDate date];
    NSLog(@"Completed in %f seconds",
          [endTime timeIntervalSinceDate:startTime]);
}
@end
```

As you can see, the "work" of this class (such as it is) is split up into a number of small chunks. This code is just meant to simulate some slow activities, and none of those methods really does anything time consuming at all, so, to make it interesting, each method contains a call to the sleep() function, which simply makes the program (specifically, the thread from which the function is called) effectively "pause" and do nothing at all for the given number of seconds. The doWork: method also contains code at the beginning and end to calculate the amount of time it took for all the work to be done.

Now, open up *MainMenu.xib*, and put an NSButton and an NSTextView into the empty window, laying things out as shown in Figure 16–1. Connect the app delegate's two outlets to the relevant controls, and connect the button's action back to the app delegate's doWork: method. While you're in there, configure the NSTextView a bit, deleting the example text from the view, and turning off the *Editable* checkbox in the *Attributes Inspector*.

Now save your work, and hit **Build & Run** in Xcode. Your app should start, and clicking the button will make it work for about ten seconds (the sum of all those sleep amounts) before showing you the results. About five or six seconds in, you'll see that the mouse cursor changes to the spinning-disk cursor, and it stays that way until the work is complete. Also, during the entire time, the application's menu is unresponsive, along with the window controls. In fact, the only way you can interact with your application at all, besides killing it with Mac OS X's *Force Quit* window, is to move its window around, because the OS itself handles that. This is exactly the state of affairs we want to avoid! In this particular case it's not too bad, because the application appears to be hung for just a few seconds, but if your app regularly "beachballs" this way for much longer than that, you'll end up with some unhappy users—and maybe even some ex-users!

Threading Basics

Before we start implementing solutions, let's go over some of the basics involved in concurrency. This is far from a complete description of threading in Mac OS X or threading in general. For that, you'll need to look elsewhere. We just want to explain enough for you to understand what we're doing in this chapter.

In most modern OSes (including of course Mac OS X), apart from the notion of a process, which contains a running instance of a program stored on disk, there's also the notion of threads of execution. Each process can consist of multiple threads, which all run concurrently. If there's just one processor core, the OS will switch between executing multiple threads, much like it switches between executing multiple processes. If there's more than one core available, the threads will be distributed among them just like processes are.

All threads in a process share the same executable program code, and the same global data. Each thread can also have some data that is exclusive to the thread. Threads can make use of a special structure called a **mutex** (short for mutual exclusion) or a lock, which can ensure that a particular chunk of code can't be run by multiple threads at once. This is useful for ensuring correct outcomes when multiple threads access the same data simultaneously, by locking out other threads when one thread is updating a value (in what's called a "critical section" of your code). For example, let's say your application implements a banking system, where an account balance can be modified as part of a transaction. In a multi-threaded system, you need to protect the section of code that adds or subtracts from the account balance, to eliminate the possibility that two threads are both messing with it at the exact same time. Otherwise, you might have both threads reading the old balance more or less simultaneously, and both threads later writing back their own ideas of the new balance, oblivious to the changes that the other was trying to make, leading to an incorrect final state; whichever sets the value last is the "winner," and the other thread's change to the balance is simply lost.

A common concern when dealing with threads is the idea of code being "thread-safe." Some software libraries are written with concurrency in mind, and have all their critical sections properly protected with mutexes. Some code libraries simply don't. For instance, in Cocoa, the AppKit framework (containing the classes specific to building GUI applications, such as `NSApplication`, `NSView` and all its subclasses, and the like) is for the most part *not* thread-safe. This means that in a running Cocoa application, all method calls that deal with any AppKit objects should be executed from within the same thread, which is commonly known as the "main thread." If you access AppKit objects from another thread, all bets are off. You are likely to encounter seemingly inexplicable bugs. By default, the main thread is where all the action of your Cocoa app (such as dealing with actions triggered by user events) occurs, so for simple applications it's nothing you need to worry about. Action methods triggered by a user are already running in the main thread. Up to this point in the book, our code has been running exclusively on the main thread, but that's about to change.

Units of Work

The problem with the threading model just described is that for the average programmer, writing error-free, multi-threaded code is nearly impossible. This is not meant as a critique of our industry or of the average programmer's abilities; it's simply an observation. The complex interactions you have to account for in your code when synchronizing data and actions across multiple threads are really just too much for most people to tackle. Imagine that 5 percent of all people have the capacity to write software at all. Only a small fraction of those 5 percent are really up to the task of writing heavy-duty multi-threaded applications. Even people who have done it successfully will often advise others to not follow their example!

Fortunately, all hope is not yet lost. It is possible to implement some concurrency without too much low-level thread-twisting. Just like we have the ability to display data on the screen without directly poking bits into video RAM, and to read data from disk without interfacing directly with disk controllers, software abstractions exist that let us run our code on multiple threads without requiring us to do much directly with the threads at all. The solutions that Apple encourages us to use are centered around the ideas of splitting up long-running tasks into units of work, and putting those units into queues for execution. The system manages the queues for us, executing units of work on multiple threads for us. We don't need to start and manage the background threads directly, and are freed from much of the "bookkeeping" that's usually involved in implementing concurrent applications. The system takes care of that for us.

Operation Queues

Since the release of Leopard, Apple has provided us with a pair of classes called NSOperation and NSOperationQueue that work together to provide operation queues. The idea is that you split your computational tasks into chunks or units of work, wrap each of them up in an NSOperation, and put each operation into an NSOperationQueue. You can also establish interoperation dependencies, specifying that an operation won't begin executing until another one is complete. The NSOperationQueue then takes care of these units the best it can, using the order that operations were added to the queue, along with the dependencies you specified, to determine its course of action. If the dependencies you specify allow some operations to execute at the same time, and there are enough cores available to run them, the operation queue will use multiple threads to execute multiple operations simultaneously.

Vitalizing SlowWorker

To see how operation queues work, let's put them to the test in SlowWorker. Before we start, make a copy of the entire folder containing your SlowWorker project. Later on in this chapter, we're going to use the original version of SlowWorker as a starting point for another way to implement concurrency, so keep a copy of it lying around.

As you will recall, the problem with this app is that the single action method calls several other methods in sequence, the total length of which is enough to make the app feel unresponsive. What we're going to do is put each of those other methods into an operation, put all the operations into a queue, and let the queue do its thing.

In order for this to work, one of the things we have to do is find a way for each operation to get its input from somewhere, and store its return value somewhere. The solution we're going to use here is to make what were previously return values into instance variables in our controller class. Each method will read any input it needs from an instance variable, and put its results into another. Start by adding instance variables and properties for each of the work-methods' return values, along with a new isWorking attribute of type BOOL, which we'll use to keep track of whether the background operations are underway. Because the work-processing is being handled in a different way, we also need to make startTime into an instance variable. Add the lines shown in bold below to *SlowWorkerAppDelegate.h*:

```
#import <Cocoa/Cocoa.h>
@interface SlowWorkerAppDelegate : NSObject {
    IBOutlet NSButton *startButton;
    IBOutlet NSTextView *resultsTextView;
    NSString *fetchedData;
    NSString *processed;
    NSString *firstResult;
    NSString *secondResult;
    BOOL isWorking;
    NSDate *startTime;
}
```

```
@property (retain) NSString *fetchedData;
@property (retain) NSString *processed;
@property (retain) NSString *firstResult;
@property (retain) NSString *secondResult;
@property (assign) BOOL isWorking;
- (IBAction)doWork:(id)sender;
@end
```

Now, in *SlowWorkerAppDelegate.m*, inside the @implementation section, add
@synthesize declarations for the new properties, and replace the old work-methods with
the new ones shown below. We're also going to add a new work-method called
finishWorking, which takes care of updating the GUI when the work is done.

```
@synthesize fetchedData;
@synthesize processed;
@synthesize firstResult;
@synthesize secondResult;
@synthesize isWorking;
- (void)fetchSomethingFromServer {
  sleep(1);
  self.fetchedData = @"Hi there";
}
- (void)processData {
  sleep(2);
  self.processed = [self.fetchedData uppercaseString];
}
- (void)calculateFirstResult {
  sleep(3);
  self.firstResult = [NSString stringWithFormat:@"Number of chars: %d",
    [self.processed length]];
}
- (void)calculateSecondResult {
  sleep(4);
  self.secondResult = [self.processed stringByReplacingOccurrencesOfString:@"E"
    withString:@"e"];
}
- (void)finishWorking {
  NSString *resultsSummary = [NSString stringWithFormat:
    @"First: [%@]\nSecond: [%@]",
    self.firstResult, self.secondResult];
  [resultsTextView setString:resultsSummary];
  NSDate *endTime = [NSDate date];
  NSLog(@"Completed in %f seconds",
        [endTime timeIntervalSinceDate:startTime]);
  self.isWorking = NO;
}
```

Now it's time to update the doWork: method itself. Instead of simply executing each
method directly, it creates an NSOperation for each. Then it defines a set of
dependencies between these operations, so that processData is only called after
fetchSomethingFromServer is done, and the two calculate methods are only called after
processData is done. Here's what it looks like:

```
- (IBAction)doWork:(id)sender {
```

```
    startTime = [NSDate date];
    self.isWorking = YES;

    NSOperationQueue *queue = [[NSOperationQueue alloc] init];
    NSOperation *fetch =
      [[NSInvocationOperation alloc] initWithTarget:self
      selector:@selector(fetchSomethingFromServer) object:nil];
    NSOperation *process =
      [[NSInvocationOperation alloc] initWithTarget:self
      selector:@selector(processData) object:nil];
    NSOperation *calculateFirst =
      [[NSInvocationOperation alloc] initWithTarget:self
      selector:@selector(calculateFirstResult) object:nil];
    NSOperation *calculateSecond =
      [[NSInvocationOperation alloc] initWithTarget:self
      selector:@selector(calculateSecondResult) object:nil];
    NSOperation *show =
      [[NSInvocationOperation alloc] initWithTarget:self
      selector:@selector(finishWorking) object:nil];

    [process addDependency:fetch];
    [calculateFirst addDependency:process];
    [calculateSecond addDependency:process];
    [show addDependency:calculateFirst];
    [show addDependency:calculateSecond];

    [queue addOperation:fetch];
    [queue addOperation:process];
    [queue addOperation:calculateFirst];
    [queue addOperation:calculateSecond];
    [queue addOperation:show];
}
```

Before going on, we'd like to explain the creation of those operations, and offer a way to improve on it. Each operation we create is actually an instance of NSInvocationOperation, which is a subclass of NSOperation. For each of those, we're calling the lengthy initWithTarget:selector:object: method. This method takes as parameters an object to which a message should be sent, a selector specifying the method to call, and an object to pass along to the called method.

> **NOTE:** In Objective-C, a selector is a built-in type (actually called SEL) that lets you deal with Objective-C methods and their names right in your code. In this example, we're using it to specify in code a method name which, at run time, will be used to find the method's actual implementation. The use of selectors, and the run-time method lookup paradigm of which they are a part, enables a lot of interesting architectural patterns in Objective-C that most other compiled languages have a hard time matching. For now, you can just think of a selector as a way to pass a method name as an argument, or assign a method name to a variable.

The problem with this setup is that each operation we create requires quite a big chunk of code, which in our case is also extremely repetitive. We've got the same target for all of them (self) and the same nil parameter, not to mention the huge NSInvocationOperation class name itself!

Extending NSObject

Fortunately, we can wrap this operation-creation functionality inside a method of our own, leaving a much more concise calling syntax. The new method call will be sent to the target object itself, and won't mention NSInvocationOperation or the nil object parameter at all. What's more, we can use an Objective-C category to add this method to NSObject, so that we can, if we want, using this new method to create operations for any object, not just our controller! This powerful technique lets you extend Apple's own classes in ways that Apple never anticipated. You have to exercise caution when doing this, because there is always a risk that method names may clash if both your code and some third-party code include identically-named methods in a category, or if Apple adds a method with the same name in a future version of Cocoa. But that risk is well worth the rewards to be gained by improving your code's readability.

To do this, start by creating a new pair of source files in Xcode, called *FoundationAdditions.h* and *FoundationAdditions.m*. The simplest way to do this is to create a new class called FoundationAdditions, then remove the @interface and @implementation sections from the *.h* and *.m* files. Then add the following code to the two files:

```
// FoundationAdditions.h:
#import <Cocoa/Cocoa.h>
@interface NSObject (SlowWorkerExtras)
- (NSInvocationOperation*)operationForSelector:(SEL)selector;
@end

// FoundationAdditions.m:
#import "FoundationAdditions.h"
@implementation NSObject (SlowWorkerExtras)
- (NSInvocationOperation*)operationForSelector:(SEL)selector {
  return [[[NSInvocationOperation alloc] initWithTarget:self
    selector:selector object:nil] autorelease];
}
@end
```

That code adds a method to NSObject called operationForSelector: which returns an appropriately configured NSInvocationOperation instance. To use this in your controller code, add the following line to *SlowWorkerAppDelegate.m*:

```
#import "FoundationAdditions.h"
```

Then, replace the NSOperation creation code in doWork: with the following:

```
NSOperation *fetch =
  [self operationForSelector:@selector(fetchSomethingFromServer)];
NSOperation *process =
```

```
  [self operationForSelector:@selector(processData)];
NSOperation *calculateFirst =
  [self operationForSelector:@selector(calculateFirstResult)];
NSOperation *calculateSecond =
  [self operationForSelector:@selector(calculateSecondResult)];
NSOperation *show =
  [self operationForSelector:@selector(finishWorking)];
```

Ah, isn't that better? To format things for this book, each operation creation takes two lines, but if you're editing in a window that's just a little bit wider, each of those will fit nicely on a single line.

Demanding the Main Thread

Now, we're still not quite ready to roll. Remember that earlier in this chapter, we mentioned that the AppKit classes (such as all the window and view classes) are generally not thread-safe. All access to them should be performed exclusively on the main thread. However, we have this finishWorking method that runs in an operation, and will in all likelihood be run on some other thread when its time comes!

To get around this problem, we'll drop down to the NSThread class, which provides facilities for checking which thread we're running on, and for calling methods on background threads or the main thread itself. Using NSThread, we can check at the start of finishWorking to see if we're currently running on the main thread, and if not, do so! Here's an initial implementation:

```
- (void)finishWorking {
  if (![NSThread isMainThread]) {
    [self performSelectorOnMainThread:@selector(finishWorking)
      withObject:nil waitUntilDone:NO];
    return;
  }
  NSString *resultsSummary = [NSString stringWithFormat:
    @"First: [%@]\nSecond: [%@]",
    self.firstResult, self.secondResult];
  [resultsTextView setString:resultsSummary];
  NSDate *endTime = [NSDate date];
  NSLog(@"Completed in %f seconds",
        [endTime timeIntervalSinceDate:startTime]);
  self.isWorking = NO;
}
```

Our method now first checks to see if it's running on the main thread already. If not, it relaunches itself on the main thread, and returns so that the rest of the method doesn't go on executing on the non-main thread. Then, when the method is relaunched on the main thread, it continues on through and does its work.

Once you get started working with operation queues, you may find yourself need this kind of functionality in a lot of your worker methods, forcing them to run on the main thread in order to update the GUI. What we've just shown can be improved a bit by putting it into a C preprocessor macro. Because this is essentially adding functionality related to another Foundation class (NSThread), let's go ahead and put this into the *FoundationAdditions.h* file we created earlier:

```
#define DISPATCH_ON_MAIN_THREAD if(![NSThread isMainThread]) { \
[self performSelectorOnMainThread:_cmd withObject:nil \
waitUntilDone:NO]; \
return; }
```

There are two "tricks" to point out in that snippet. The first is that each line (except for the last) ends with a backslash. The appearance of a single backslash in a C preprocessor macro (in case you're unfamiliar with it) causes the preprocessor to ignore the next character it finds. In this case, putting it at the end of the line makes it ignore the following carriage return, so that it goes on to interpret the next line as part of the macro (make sure you don't have any empty space at the end of the line, otherwise this won't work). The second trick is that instead of naming a selector as we did initially, we're using a special variable, available to the preprocessor at compile-time, called _cmd. The _cmd variable always contains the selector of the current method.

With that in place, we can force main thread execution of any of our worker methods by simply starting them off like this:

```
- (void)finishWorking {
  DISPATCH_ON_MAIN_THREAD
  NSString *resultsSummary = [NSString stringWithFormat:
    @"First: [%@]\nSecond: [%@]",
    self.firstResult, self.secondResult];
  [resultsTextView setString:resultsSummary];
  NSDate *endTime = [NSDate date];
  NSLog(@"Completed in %f seconds",
        [endTime timeIntervalSinceDate:startTime]);
  self.isWorking = NO;
}
```

Now you should be able to **Build & Run** your app, and you'll notice something perhaps a little different after pressing the *Start* button: the button immediately reverts back to its non-clicked state, and the menus still work. After about seven seconds (down from the ten seconds the first version used, since some of our work-methods are running at the same time now), the output appears in the text view. That's all well and good, but we can easily make things even more responsive by using Cocoa Bindings and the isWorking property! Open up *MainMenu.xib* in Interface Builder again, and use the *Library* window to find a circular progress indicator. Then add it to your window as shown in Figure 16–2.

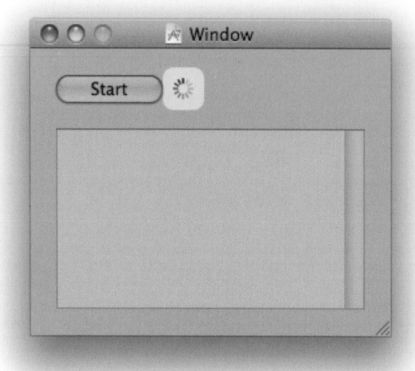

Figure 16–2. *Adding a progress indicator*

With the progress indicator selected, use the *Attributes Inspector* to make sure that its *Display When Stopped* checkbox is turned off. Then switch to the *Bindings Inspector*, and configure a binding for its *Animate* attribute, binding to the app delegate with its isWorking key. Then select the *Start* button in your window, where we'll make a similar configuration. Bind the button's *Enabled* attribute to the app delegate's isWorking key, and this time add an NSNegateBoolean for the *Value Transformer*.

Now, we're even more done with this. Save your changes, **Build & Run**, and you'll now see that when you click the *Start* button, it becomes disabled, and the circular progress indicator appears and starts spinning. When the work is done, the progress indicator disappears, and the button goes back to normal.

Now let's take this just one step farther, and add a horizontal progress indicator, where a horizontal movement tells you that things are happening, such as you may see in a software installer. Our progress view will go from 0 to 4, each work-method upping the number a bit. Like the circular progress indicator, this will be configured entirely with Cocoa Bindings.

Start off by adding a new instance variable and property called completed to our app delegate's *.h* and *.m* files:

```
// SlowWorkerAppDelegate.h
// inside the @interface curly-braces:
NSInteger completed;
// after the @interface curly-braces:
@property (assign) NSInteger completed;
```

```
// SlowWorkerAppDelegate.m
// inside the @implementation block
@synthesize completed;
```

Next, add the following near the top of the doWork: method, to reset it as soon as the user hits the Start button:

```
self.completed = 0;
```

Each work-method now needs to increment this variable when they're done. Our first thought might be to add the following line to each work-method:

```
self.completed = self.completed + 1;
```

However, this is where one of those sticky multi-threaded problems turns up. If you think about that line of code, you'll see that what really happens that it first grabs the current value of the completed property by calling [self completed], then adds one to it, and then stores the result back into the completed property by calling [self setCompleted:]. In a multi-threaded environment, this can lead to incorrect behavior. What if, for instance, two threads execute a line like this at about the same time? Suppose the starting value of completed is 2. If both threads read the current value before either of the writes out their own result, each will add 1 to their own copy of the value, then each of them will write their local sum (3) back into the completed property, which ends up containing the value 3 instead of the correct value, 4.

A way around this is to use Objective-C's @synchronized keyword, which lets us specify that a piece of code can only be run by one thread at a time. Enter the following method at the top of your app delegate's @implementation section:

```
- (void)incrementCompleted {
  @synchronized(self) {
    self.completed = self.completed + 1;
  }
}
```

What we're doing there is taking the same code we thought about earlier and wrapping it in a sort of a safe zone. The @synchronized keyword takes as its one argument an object which will be used to determine the scope of the synchronization limiting. Basically, any calls using the same value will each try to grab the same lock. If some other thread has already claimed it, the current thread has to wait until the other thread is done. In this case, because we're using self, any calls made to this method on the same instance will all try to acquire the same lock. We only have one instance of our app delegate, so this is in practice a global lock, but for our purposes that's okay.

The coding we need to do in order for this to work is to just add this line to the end of each of the work-methods:

```
[self incrementCompleted];
```

And finally, we need to configure the GUI. Go back to the *MainMenu.xib* file in Interface Builder, and search the *Library* for a progress indicator. In addition to the circular one we've already used, you'll also see a horizontal one labeled *Indeterminate Progress Indicator*. Drag that to your window, and lay it out as shown in Figure 16–3.

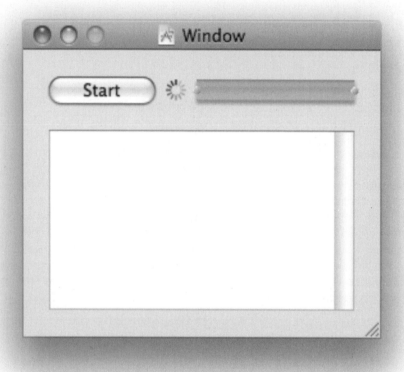

Figure 16–3. *The final GUI touch-up*

Now bring up the *Attributes Inspector*. Click to turn off both the *Display When Stopped* and *Indeterminate* checkboxes, then set its *Minimum* and *Current* values to 0, and its *Maximum* value to 4. Now switch to the *Bindings Inspector*, where you'll configure two bindings. First, bind its *Animate* attribute to the app delegate's isWorking key, just like you did for the circular progress indicator. Then, bind its *Value* attribute to the app delegate's completed key.

Now save your work, **Build & Run**, and click the *Start* button. You should now see that beside the circular progress indicator, a horizontal progress indicator also appears, with a bar moving across as each of the work-methods completes.

And there you have it: relatively painless concurrency. Granted, this contrived example isn't much compared to a large application, but these concepts can scale up to handle more complex situations as well. What we've shown you works well in today's Leopard and iPhone applications, but Apple didn't stop there. Starting with Snow Leopard, most of the design of NSOperation and NSOperationQueue has been reimplemented at a lower level in the OS, resulting in a nice piece of technology called Grand Central Dispatch.

GCD: Low-Level Queuing

This idea of putting units of work into queues that can be executed in the background, with the system managing the threads for you, is really powerful, and greatly simplifies many development situations where concurrency is needed. It seems that once this technology was up and running in the form of NSOperationQueue in Leopard, Apple decided to make a more general solution, that could work not only from Objective-C, but also C and C++. Starting with Snow Leopard, this solution, called Grand Central Dispatch (which we'll call GCD from now on) is ready for use. GCD puts most of the core concepts of NSOperationQueue—units of work, painless background processing, automatic thread management—into a C interface that can be used from all of the C-based languages. This means that it's not just for Cocoa programmers. Now even low-level command-line utilities written in C can take advantage of these features. NSOperationQueue itself was rewritten for Snow Leopard using GCD, and to top things off, Apple has made its implementation of GCD open-source, so that it could be ported to other Unix-like OSes as well.

The main difference between the design of NSOperationQueue and the queues in GCD is that while NSOperationQueue can deal with arbitrarily complex dependency relationships between its NSOperations to determine in what order they should be executed, the GCD queues are strictly FIFO (first-in, first-out). Units of work added to a GCD queue will always be started in the order they were placed in the queue. That being said, they may not always finish in the same order, because a GCD queue will automatically distribute its work among multiple threads.

Another important difference exists between the implementation of NSOperationQueue on Leopard and iPhone, and the implementation of GCD on Snow Leopard (which also defines the implementation of NSOperationQueue on Snow Leopard). In the older implementations, NSOperationQueue starts up a new thread for each operation when it's about to run, and terminates the thread when it's done. In the newer implementations, each queue has access to a pool of threads which are reused throughout the lifetime of the application. GCD will always try to maintain a pool of threads that's appropriate for the machine's architecture, automatically taking advantage of a more powerful machine by utilizing more processor cores when it has work to do.

Becoming a Blockhead

Along with GCD, Apple has released a bit of new syntax to the C language itself (and, by extension, Objective-C and C++), to implement a language feature called *blocks* (also known as closures in some other languages), which are really important for getting the most out of GCD. The idea behind a block is to let a particular chunk of code be treated like any other C-language type. A block can be assigned to a variable, passed as an argument to a function or method, and (unlike other most other types) executed. In this way, blocks can be used as an alternative to the delegate pattern in Objective-C, or to callback functions in C. Much like a method or function, a block can take one or more parameters, and specify a return value. In order to declare a block variable, you make use of the caret (^) symbol along with some additional parenthesized bits to declare parameters and return types. To define the block itself, you do roughly the same, but follow it up with the actual code defining the block wrapped in curly-braces.

```
// Declare a block variable "loggerBlock" with no parameters and no return value.
void (^loggerBlock)(void);
// Assign a block to the variable declared above.  A block without parameters
// and with no return value, like this one, needs no "decorations" like the use
// of void in the preceeding variable declaration.
loggerBlock = ^{ NSLog(@"I'm just glad they didn't call it a closure"); };
// Execute the block, just like calling a function.
loggerBlock();  // this produces some output in the console
```

If you've done much C programming, you may recognize that this is similar to the concept of a function pointer in C. However, there are a few critical differences. Perhaps the biggest difference, the one that's the most striking when you first see it, is that blocks can be defined inline in your code. You can define a block right at the point where it's going to be passed to another method or function. Another big difference is that a block can access variables available in the scope where it's created. By default, the block makes a copy of any variables you access this way, leaving the originals intact, but you can make an outside variable "read/write" by prepending __block before its declaration.

```
// define a variable which can be changed by a block
__block int a = 0;
// define a block that tries to modify a variable in its scope
void (^sillyBlock)(void) = ^{ a = 47; };
// check the value of our variable before calling the block
NSLog(@"a == %d", a); // outputs "a == 0"
// execute the block
sillyBlock();
// check the values of our variable again, after calling the block
NSLog(@"a == %d", a); // outputs "a == 47"
```

As we mentioned a little while ago, blocks really shine when used with GCD. GCD includes a set of functions that accomplish the same sorts of things that NSOperation and NSOperationQueue do, but with a different spin. The main difference is that, instead of explicitly creating a bunch of operations, optionally declaring inter-operation dependencies, and then assigning adding the operations to queues, with GCD you call a function that takes a block and adds it to a queue in a single step; interoperation dependencies don't need to be declared, because the code in the block executes sequentially.

Improving SlowWorker a Second Time

To see how this works, let's take a look at the original form of SlowWorker's doWork: method. To get to it, open up the copy of the original SlowWorker project directory you made earlier, and use that for the rest of the changes we're going to show.

```
- (IBAction)doWork:(id)sender {
  NSDate *startTime = [NSDate date];
  NSString *fetchedData = [self fetchSomethingFromServer];
  NSString *processed = [self processData:fetchedData];
  NSString *firstResult = [self calculateFirstResult:processed];
  NSString *secondResult = [self calculateSecondResult:processed];
  NSString *resultsSummary = [NSString stringWithFormat:
    @"First: [%@]\nSecond: [%@]", firstResult, secondResult];
  [resultsTextView setString:resultsSummary];
  NSDate *endTime = [NSDate date];
  NSLog(@"Completed in %f seconds",
        [endTime timeIntervalSinceDate:startTime]);
}
```

We can make that method run entirely in the background by wrapping all the code in a block, and passing it to a GCD function called dispatch_async. This function takes two parameters: a GCD dispatch queue (conceptually similar to an NSOperationQueue) and a block to assign to the queue. Take a look:

```
- (IBAction)doWork:(id)sender {
  NSDate *startTime = [NSDate date];
  dispatch_async(dispatch_get_global_queue(0, 0), ^{
    NSString *fetchedData = [self fetchSomethingFromServer];
    NSString *processed = [self processData:fetchedData];
    NSString *firstResult = [self calculateFirstResult:processed];
    NSString *secondResult = [self calculateSecondResult:processed];
    NSString *resultsSummary = [NSString stringWithFormat:
      @"First: [%@]\nSecond: [%@]", firstResult, secondResult];
    [resultsTextView setString:resultsSummary];
    NSDate *endTime = [NSDate date];
    NSLog(@"Completed in %f seconds",
          [endTime timeIntervalSinceDate:startTime]);
  });
}
```

The first line grabs a pre-existing global queue that's always available, using the dispatch_get_global_queue() function (Unlike NSOperationQueue, with GCD there's always a global queue available, ready to dispatch work to the background threads). That function takes two arguments: the first lets you specify a priority, and the second is currently unused and should always be 0. If you specify a different priority in the first argument, such as DISPATCH_QUEUE_PRIORITY_HIGH or DISPATCH_QUEUE_PRIORITY_LOW (passing a 0 is the same as passing DISPATCH_QUEUE_PRIORITY_DEFAULT), you will actually get a different global queue, which the system will prioritize differently. For now, we'll stick with the default global queue.

The queue is then passed to the dispatch_async() function, along with the block of code that comes after. GCD then takes that entire block, and passes it off to a background thread, where it will be executed one step at a time, just like it when it was running in the main thread.

Don't Forget That Main Thread

There's one problem here: AppKit thread safety. Remember, messaging any GUI object including our resultsTextView from a background thread is a no-no. Fortunately, GCD provides us with a way to deal with this, too. Inside the block, we can call another dispatching function, passing work back to the main thread! We do this by once again calling dispatch_async(), this time passing in the queue returned by the dispatch_get_main_queue() function, which always gives us the special queue that lives on the main thread, ready to execute blocks that require the use of the main thread.

```
- (IBAction)doWork:(id)sender {
  NSDate *startTime = [NSDate date];
  dispatch_async(dispatch_get_global_queue(0, 0), ^{
    NSString *fetchedData = [self fetchSomethingFromServer];
    NSString *processed = [self processData:fetchedData];
    NSString *firstResult = [self calculateFirstResult:processed];
    NSString *secondResult = [self calculateSecondResult:processed];
    NSString *resultsSummary = [NSString stringWithFormat:
      @"First: [%@]\nSecond: [%@]", firstResult, secondResult];
    dispatch_async(dispatch_get_main_queue(), ^{
      [resultsTextView setString:resultsSummary];
    });
    NSDate *endTime = [NSDate date];
    NSLog(@"Completed in %f seconds",
      [endTime timeIntervalSinceDate:startTime]);
  });
}
```

Concurrent Blocks

We still have one more change to make, in order to make this behave the same and run at least as fast as our previous version that used NSOperationQueue. Remember that when we set up operations in the queue, we allowed calculateFirstResult and calculateSecondResult to run at the same time, through the use of dependencies? We declared that each of them was dependent on the preceding call to processData, and that in turn the following call to finishWorking was dependent on both of them. That left it up to the operation queue to run both of those at the same time if possible. In what we currently have in our GCD version, that's not the case. The code runs straight through just as shown, always calling calculateSecondResult: only after calculateFirstResult: has completed.

Fortunately, once again GCD has a way to accomplish the same thing, by using what's called a dispatch group. All blocks that are dispatched asynchronously within the context of a group are set loose to execute as fast as they can, including being distributed to multiple threads for concurrent execution if possible. We can also use dispatch_group_notify() to specify an additional block that will be executed when all the blocks in the group have been run. Here's what it looks like:

```
- (IBAction)doWork:(id)sender {
  NSDate *startTime = [NSDate date];
  dispatch_async(dispatch_get_global_queue(0, 0), ^{
    NSString *fetchedData = [self fetchSomethingFromServer];
    NSString *processed = [self processData:fetchedData];
    __block NSString *firstResult;
    __block NSString *secondResult;
    dispatch_group_t group = dispatch_group_create();
    dispatch_group_async(group, dispatch_get_global_queue(0, 0), ^{
      firstResult = [self calculateFirstResult:processed];
    });
    dispatch_group_async(group, dispatch_get_global_queue(0, 0), ^{
      secondResult = [self calculateSecondResult:processed];
    });
    dispatch_group_notify(group, dispatch_get_global_queue(0, 0), ^{
      NSString *resultsSummary = [NSString stringWithFormat:
        @"First: [%@]\nSecond: [%@]", firstResult, secondResult];
      dispatch_async(dispatch_get_main_queue(), ^{
        [resultsTextView setString:resultsSummary];
      });
      NSDate *endTime = [NSDate date];
      NSLog(@"Completed in %f seconds",
        [endTime timeIntervalSinceDate:startTime]);
    });
  });
}
```

One complication here is that each of the calculate methods returns a value which we want to grab, so we have to first create the variables using the __block prefix, which means that the values set inside the blocks are made available to the code that runs later.

With all that in place, you should be able to Build & Run your app, and see the same behavior and performance that you saw after the first set of improvements (but not the additional changes we made, where we used Cocoa Bindings to improve the GUI's behavior while the work is being performed; applying the changes to the block-enhanced version of SlowWorker is left as an exercise for the reader). The difference lies in the structuring of the code itself. Remember that in Snow Leopard, NSOperationQueue has been reimplemented using GCD, so your app will have similar performance characteristics either way. It's up to you to decide which way you want to go.

Another Option: NSBlockOperation

Apart from what we've already shown, there's another option for implementing concurrency on Snow Leopard, using a hybrid of the two approaches we've seen so far. Snow Leopard includes a new NSOperation subclass called NSBlockOperation that you create an operation using a block instead of an NSInvocation, like this:

```
NSBlockOperation loggingOperation = [NSBlockOperation
  blockOperationWithBlock: ^{
```

```
    NSLog(@"This is where you'd say something.");
}];
```

Such an operation should be added to an NSOperationQueue in the usual way, where it can be freely mixed with NSInvocationOperation instances. NSBlockOperations are not meant to be used with low-level GCD functions like dispatch_group_async(). The idea is that if you choose to stick with NSOperationQueue instead of GCD queues, you still get the other benefits of using blocks by using NSBlockOperation.

A Little Concurrency Goes a Long Way

You've now seen some concrete examples of how to provide basic concurrency in your applications using both NSOperationQueue and GCD. Our simple example project doesn't do anything interesting, but these techniques can be applied to any situation where you have lengthy activities going on, and don't want to expose your users to the spinning busy-cursor. You've also learned a bit about the new block syntax and how it can be used with GCD's dispatching functions to do work on background threads. Snow Leopard provides even more ways to use blocks, adding dozens of new methods to existing Cocoa classes. You'll learn about some of those, and a whole lot more, in our final chapter: Future Paths.

Chapter **17**

Future Paths

You've now reached the final chapter of *Learn Cocoa on the Mac*, and hopefully by this time you've gotten a good feel for how Cocoa works, and how its various parts can be used to write all sorts of interesting desktop applications. However, the Cocoa frameworks are really huge, and we've only scratched the surface on most of the classes and concepts we've covered. This book was never meant to be an encyclopedic Cocoa reference (you've already got that on your computer, installed with Xcode), but rather a sort of guide to help you find your way. Continuing in that spirit, we're going to wrap up the book with an overview of additional techniques that will help you take your Cocoa development efforts above and beyond what we've covered so far.

We'll start off with a bit of expansion on a few design patterns that we've mentioned, but deserve a little more attention. We'll also take a look at how to use languages other than Objective-C to do Cocoa programming, and finally we'll look at some ways take your hard-earned Cocoa skills and apply them to other realms than just the Mac OS X desktop.

More Cocoa-isms

We've spent a lot of time in this book dealing with the MVC pattern, which helps you partition your application into logical layers, as well as the delegate pattern, which lets you define the behavior of some GUI objects inside your controller layer, instead of subclassing the GUI objects themselves. These techniques use language features and conventions to define patterns of usage. Along those lines, Cocoa has more tricks up its sleeve. One of them is the concept of notifications (referred to as the *observer pattern* in some circles), which lets an object notify a collection of other objects when something happens. Another is the use of blocks (new to C and Objective-C in Snow Leopard) to simplify your code in spots where a full-blown delegate, or even a single method, might be overkill.

Notifications

Cocoa's NSNotification and NSNotificationCenter classes provide you with a way to let one object send a message to a bunch of other objects, without any of the objects needing to know anything about the others. All they really need to know is the name of the notification, which can be anything you like. An object that wants to be notified signs up as an observer of a particular notification name in advance, and the object that wants to broadcast a notification uses that name to send its message out to any observers that are listening.

For example, let's say you have several parts of your application that need to be updated whenever a particular event occurs, such as a piece of networking code reading a response from a web server. Using notifications, your networking code doesn't need to know about every other object that wants the information. Instead, you can define a notification name for both the networking code and the observers to use, preferably in a header file that can be included by all classes involved:

```
#define DATA_RECEIVED @"dataReceived"
```

Observers can sign up to receive notifications at any time, but typically this happens during an object's initialization:

```
- (id)init {
  if ((self = [super init])) {
    [[NSNotificationCenter defaultCenter] addObserver:self
      selector:@selector(receiveNetworkData:)
      name:DATA_RECEIVED
      object:nil];
  }
  return self;
}
```

That tells the application's one and only instance of NSNotificationCenter that it should notify the caller by calling its receiveNetworkData: method whenever anyone posts a DATA_RECEIVED notification. Note the final parameter, where we're passing a nil: if we instead specified an object there, that would limit the notification-observing to only apply to that particular object. Any other object posting the same notification wouldn't have any effect on us. To make this work, the observer also needs to implement the method it specified when registering. This method always receives the NSNotification itself as a parameter:

```
- (void)receiveNetworkData:(NSNotification *)notification {
  NSLog(@"received notification: %@", notification);
}
```

Finally, any object that sets itself up as observer should usually remove itself from the observer list later on. If you're using GC as we have in most of this book, it's not such a big deal; but if you're not using GC, you really have to do this in order to avoid run-time errors. A common pattern is to do something like the following in the dealloc method of any class that ever registers as an observer:

```
- (void)dealloc {
  [[NSNotificationCenter defaultCenter] removeObserver:self];
```

```
    [super dealloc];
}
```

Now, what about the notifier itself, in our case the network-reading object that's going to broadcast its status? That's taken care of as simply as this:

```
if (some condition is met) {
  [[NSNotificationCenter defaultCenter]
    postNotificationName:DATA_RECEIVED
    object:self];
}
```

The idea is that the notifier can fling out a notification like that, and the notification center takes care of the actual delivery. The notifier can also pass along additional information, in the form of a dictionary which can be retrieved by an observer, like this:

```
// in the notifier
NSDictionary *info = [NSDictionary dictionaryWithObject:someData
                        forKey:@"data"];
[[NSNotificationCenter defaultCenter]
  postNotificationName:DATA_RECEIVED
  object:self userInfo:info];

// in the observer
NSLog(@"received data %@", [[notification userInfo]
  objectForKey:@"data"]);
```

Blocks

In Chapter 16, we introduced you to blocks, an addition to C that Apple has come up with and included in Snow Leopard. We brought up blocks in the context of the concurrency features provided by Grand Central Dispatch, where blocks fit in really well, but there are many more uses for blocks. In Snow Leopard, Apple extended several Cocoa classes, adding dozens of new methods that take blocks as parameters. Let's take a look at some of them.

Enumeration

Let's start with something simple: enumeration. You're probably familiar with the standard C-based ways of stepping through a list, and perhaps the use of NSEnumerator and even the new fast enumeration ("for – in" loops) that's been available since the release of Leopard. Now, blocks provide us with yet another way to do the same thing:

```
NSArray *array = [NSArray arrayWithObjects:@"one", "two", @"three"];

// C-style enumeration
int i;
for (i = 0; i < [array count]; i++) {
  NSLog(@"C enumeration accessing object: %@",
    [array objectAtIndex:i]);
}

// NSEnumerator, the "classic" Cocoa way to enumerate
```

```
NSEnumerator *aEnum = [array objectEnumerator];
id obj1;
while ((obj1 = [aEnum nextObject])) {
  NSLog(@"NSEnumerator accessing object: %@", obj1);
}

// "Fast enumeration", released as part of Leopard
id obj2;
for (obj2 in array) {
  NSLog(@"Fast enumeration accessing object: %@", obj2);
}

// "Block enumeration", new in Snow Leopard
[array enumerateObjectsUsingBlock:^(id obj3, NSUInteger i, BOOL *stop) {
  NSLog(@"Block enumeration accessing object: %@", obj3);
}];
```

The block we pass in to enumerateObjectsUsingBlock: takes three arguments, and returns nothing. That's the block signature declared by the method, and that's what we have to follow. The three arguments sent into our block are an object from the array, an integer containing that object's index in the array, and a BOOL passed by reference that lets us halt the enumeration by setting its value to YES.

Looking at it that way, it may not be obvious at first why the block version is any better than the others, but the fact is that it really combines the best of all the other ways of enumerating. For one thing, it gives you the index of the current object, which is really handy if you want to do something like print out a numbered list of the items in an array. We can't tell you how many times we've dropped down to C-style iteration just for easy access to each object's index value! Also, there's a variant of this method that lets you specify options defining how the enumeration runs, such as make it run concurrently:

```
[array enumerateObjectsWithOptions:NSEnumerationConcurrent
  usingBlock:^(id obj3, NSUInteger i, BOOL *stop) {
  NSLog(@"Block enumeration accessing object: %@", obj3);
}];
```

That method actually uses GCD to spread the work around to all available processor cores, which will make your app run more quickly and better utilize system resources. And you get it for free!

Similar enumeration methods exist for the NSSet class, but without the index parameter (because the objects in a set are, by definition, unordered). NSDictionary has also gotten some good block action, with new methods such as enumerateKeysAndObjectsUsingBlock: (and its options-taking variant that allows for concurrency), letting you specify a block that gets the key and value together. This is much better than previous ways of enumerating the contents of a dictionary, which typically involved stepping through all the keys, and looking up the value for each key.

Observing Notifications Using Blocks

We realize that we just threw notifications at you a few pages ago, but guess what: Apple's already taken the block concept and applied it to the NSNotification class as well, which boasts a new method in Snow Leopard that lets you specify a block rather than a selector, like this:

```
[[NSNotificationCenter defaultCenter] addObserverForName:DATA_RECEIVED
  object:nil queue:nil usingBlock:^(NSNotification *notification){
  NSLog(@"received notification: %@", notification);
}];
```

This is cool in a couple of ways. For one thing, it frees you from the burden of creating a method for your notification-handling code, letting you instead put it inline with the code that's setting it up, which can make your code easier to read. The other cool thing, which is true of all blocks, is that because the block you create picks up its context from the location it's defined in, it has access to not only instance variables, but also local variables defined earlier in the same method. That means that you can defer access to some values until a later time, without needing to explicitly put them into instance variables or pass them along in some other manual way.

Filtering

Another use of blocks that Apple has added to Cocoa is NSArray's indexesOfObjectsPassingTest: method. This method lets you declare a block that will examine an object, and based on your own criteria determine whether it should be included in the set of indexes that comes out (which can in turn be used to extract the "successes" from the original array. For example, assuming you have an array of people, you can find all the people named "Bob" like this:

```
NSArray *people;  // <- assume this exists
NSIndexSet *bobIndexes = [people indexesOfObjectsPassingTest:
  BOOL ^(id obj, NSUInteger idx, BOOL *stop){
  return [obj.firstName isEqual:@"Bob"];
}];
NSArray *bobs = [people objectsAtIndexes:bobIndexes];
```

Although the use of blocks may seem tricky at first, after a while they become second nature, and once you get started, you'll probably find more and more ways to use them. They are a really important tool for every Cocoa programmer moving forward.

Cocoa in a Foreign Language

As much as some of us love Objective-C, it's not the only game in town, and some people would rather use another language for developing Cocoa apps. Maybe you have a particular code library you want to make use of, or maybe you just prefer some other language. The good news is that there are some languages out there that can interface with Objective-C well enough to allow for some Cocoa development, through the use of what's called a "bridge" between the other language and Objective-C.

The bad news, for some people at least, is that two of the biggest, most popular languages, C++ and Java, aren't among them. You may be wondering why not. Well, without getting too deep: C++ and Java are just too inflexible. They don't have the sort of runtime introspection capability that's required for fully interfacing with complex Objective-C class libraries like Cocoa. Maybe, technically, Java has got what it takes. In fact, Apple included a Java bridge for building Cocoa apps in the first several versions of Mac OS X. But the fact that programmers weren't lining up at the gates to use it, combined with the technical challenge of implementing and maintaining the Java bridge, just made it not worthwhile for them, and Apple abandoned the project several years ago. And because you can actually combine Objective-C and C++ together in the form of Objective-C++, the need for bridging there is somewhat reduced. There are some real limitations there. You can't, for instance, implement an Objective-C delegate in the form of a C++ class, so you'll need to create some "glue classes," typically paired up across the border (one C++, one Objective-C) that are each able to deal with their own world and translate things for one another. It works, but believe me, that sort of code is not much fun to write or maintain.

Back on the good news side of things, some of the languages whose usage is still increasing year-by-year, such as Python and Ruby, have solid, working bridges that let you do real Cocoa work with them.

PyObjC

One of the earliest projects to bridge a non-Objective-C language with the Cocoa frameworks is PyObjC, which lets you do a significant amount of Cocoa development in Python. As you're well aware by this point, Objective-C's syntax, in particular the intermixing of method names and arguments, is somewhat unusual, and most other languages don't have any equivalent. What PyObjC does is provide mappings for all methods in all Objective-C classes included in Cocoa, so that you can call them from Python. The mappings are determined by a pretty simple formula: the entire Objective-C method name is pushed into a single symbol, with each colon in the method name replaced by an underscore character. All the method arguments are sent between parentheses, just like a standard C function. All objects are automatically bridged, so that you can use all the standard Cocoa classes right from Python. For example, let's look at a line of code we showed earlier, when talking about notifications. Here's the Objective-C version:

```
[[NSNotificationCenter defaultCenter]
  postNotificationName:DATA_RECEIVED object:self];
```

The Python version, using PyObjC, looks something like this:

```
center = NSNotificationCenter.defaultCenter()
center.postNotificationName_object_(DATA_RECEIVED, self);
```

As you can see, the lack of intermixed method-name-parts and arguments really impacts the readability. Also, on the whole it's rather "un-Pythonic," so, while it works well for what it does, there are things for all sides to be somewhat unhappy about.

PyObjC is included in both Leopard and Snow Leopard, and Xcode even has templates for making application projects using this right out of the box.

MacRuby

On the Ruby front, there are a couple of ways to bridge to Objective-C. For several years, a project called RubyCocoa has been available that works similarly to PyObjC in many ways. However, RubyCocoa seems to have stagnated, with most forward momentum having shifted to a newer project called MacRuby. This Apple-sponsored project aims to bring Ruby syntax to Cocoa in a whole different way. Instead of bridging between similar classes, MacRuby takes a different approach, basically jettisoning all the existing Ruby standard library classes, and using the Cocoa equivalents instead, often giving them new methods whose names match their equivalents in the Ruby world. This means that experienced Ruby developers who jump on a MacRuby project may find that lots of their favorite classes and methods are missing or subtly different.

One interesting difference between MacRuby and both PyObjC and RubyCocoa is that MacRuby goes the extra mile to make method calls feel similar to the way they do in Objective-C, while still working within Ruby syntax. This works is by a smart use of Ruby's keyed arguments, using the name of the Ruby method being called, and the argument keys, to look for a matching Objective-C method. Returning to our previous example:

```
[[NSNotificationCenter defaultCenter]
  postNotificationName:DATA_RECEIVED object:self];
```

In MacRuby, this would be written like this:

```
center = NSNotificationCenter.defaultCenter
center.postNotificationName(DATA_RECEIVED, object:self)
```

When MacRuby hits that second line, it uses the method name (postNotificationName) and the argument key (object) to look for an Objective-C method called postNotificationName:object: in the receiver (center), finds it, and calls it. If we didn't include a keyed argument for object, or included other keyed arguments that aren't part of the underlying method we're shooting for, this method call wouldn't find a matching Objective-C method, and would fail.

On top of all that, MacRuby offers some other interesting features, such as compilation to native code, both just in time and ahead of time. It has also moved away from the traditional Ruby VM, instead sporting a new runtime built atop of LLVM, which some of you will recognize as the most modern of the compilers that Xcode can use.

All of this is still pretty new. At the time of writing, MacRuby is less than two years old, and hasn't produced a 1.0 version yet, but it's definitely something to keep an eye on. http://www.macruby.org is the place to do so.

Nu

Another interesting language in this context is Nu. Unlike PyObjC and MacRuby, here it's not a matter of interfacing an existing language to Objective-C. Instead, Nu is essentially a whole new language (really a Lisp variant) that is designed specifically for interoperation with Objective-C, so it features the same interwoven method and argument syntax. Let's bring back that example one more time. Objective-C:

```
[[NSNotificationCenter defaultCenter]
  postNotificationName:DATA_RECEIVED object:self];
```

Nu:

```
((NSNotificationCenter defaultCenter)
  postNotificationName:DATA_RECEIVED object:self)
```

How about that! Of course, it's not completely identical. Even ignoring the change from square brackets to parentheses, there are lots of other syntax changes when declaring classes, methods, and so on, often stemming from Nu's origins as a Lisp-based language. However, in general there's a lot here that's immediately recognizable to an Objective-C developer.

Apart from the language itself, Nu also includes a command-line shell (nush), a make-like tool (nuke), and more. These tools add up to a package that lets you fire up a shell, and do some ad-hoc scripting using the Cocoa classes you know and love. You can interact with live objects, and take an exploratory approach to the Cocoa frameworks. Head on over to http://programming.nu to download it and see more about this interesting crossover between Cocoa and Lisp.

JavaScript

The odd-man out here, in some sense, is JavaScript. Everyone knows that JavaScript can be used to script web pages, but did you know that you can script your app with it? The WebKit framework included with Mac OS X won't let you create an entire app in JavaScript, but it does let you build in a scripting layer, with or without a web view, that lets someone familiar with JavaScript define some of what happens in your application.

This is something you're most likely to use in conjunction with a web view. Using the WebView class from WebKit, you can "reach through" to a WebScriptObject, which lets you call JavaScript functions from Objective-C, and also lets you expose an Objective-C object to the JavaScript interpreter, so that the JavaScript code can call Objective-C methods, using a method-to-function mapping similar to what we described for PyObjC. This is primarily useful if you want to use a WebView to lay out your GUI, but still include controls in your GUI that can affect things outside of the javascript environment.

But wait, there's more! Besides the JavaScript support that WebKit gives you, there's a third-party option called JSCocoa, which fully bridges JavaScript with Cocoa, using the same JavaScript engine (JavaScriptCore) that's a part of WebKit. This lets you write complete Cocoa applications in JavaScript, much like you can in Python or Ruby. One nice feature of JSCocoa, which it shares with Cappuccino (described in the final section of this chapter) is that, in addition to the translation between JavaScript-style function names and Objective-C method names, JSCocoa actually lets you write your javascript in a syntax that is hauntingly similar to Objective-C:

```
[[NSNotificationCenter defaultCenter]
  postNotificationName:DATA_RECEIVED object:self];
```

JSCocoa:

```
[[NSNotificationCenter defaultCenter]
  postNotificationName:DATA_RECEIVED object:self]
```

That's right, the only difference is the absent semicolon, because you don't need a semicolon at the end of a line of JavaScript if the end of the line is also a valid statement ending. We're the first to admit that this seems like a JavaScript miracle: we don't have the JavaScript knowledge to have the slightest idea how this trick was pulled off, and probably never will, but that's okay. If you want to learn more about this, http://inexdo.com/JSCocoa is the place to look.

F-Script

No discussion of alternate languages for programming in Cocoa would be complete without mentioning F-Script. Unlike most of the language bridges, which are ultimately meant to let you build Cocoa apps in a different language, F-Script seems to have a couple of complementary purposes. First of all, you can embed F-Script into your applications, providing an easy way to add user scripting to your apps, including GUI components for entering and trying out scripts written in the F-Script language, which is based on Smalltalk and therefore pretty similar to Objective-C.

The other, perhaps even more useful features of F-Script are the tools it provides to you, the developer, in the form of an interactive command shell that lets you explore your running application. This includes a graphical browser that lets you navigate among the objects in your application, inspecting their properties, traversing relationships to other objects, and so on. It's like taking the interactivity you have in gdb, and turning it up to 11.

Not only that, you can also inject F-Script into any running Cocoa application, and use the same tools to explore its objects! Although this functionality is not as useful as having another app's source, being able to browse the structure of other applications can be highly educational, and fun as well. This is really a tool that all Cocoa developers should have some familiarity with. Run, don't walk, to http://www.fscript.org to try this out for yourself.

Ported Cocoa

This book is primarily about making Mac software (it's right there in the title), but we'd be doing you a disservice if we didn't point out the other areas where Cocoa and Cocoa-ish technologies may be applied.

Cocoa Touch

These days, with iPhone development growing by leaps and bounds, presumably everyone reading this book knows a bit about the iPhone development model, and the fact that it's based around Objective-C. In fact, it's a pretty safe bet that you probably did some iPhone development before testing the Mac waters. In spite of that, it's worth mentioning the iPhone's Cocoa Touch frameworks, and how it differs from the Cocoa frameworks we've been covering.

Cocoa's core classes are split between two frameworks: Foundation contains all the fundamental classes that can be useful in every type of development (NSString, NSArray, and so on), and AppKit contains all the classes that are specific to desktop GUI app development (NSApplication, NSView, NSWindow, and so on). In Cocoa Touch on the iPhone, the Foundation framework is about the same, but the AppKit is gone, and UIKit has taken its place.

Many of the fundamentals of UIKit are similar to AppKit, with a few twists to make it work easily on a small, accelerometer-enabled, touch-screen device. Each application has a single UIWindow where all drawing occurs, and that UIWindow contains a hierarchy of UIView subclasses (such as UIButton, UITextField, and the like). Although AppKit's only native user input methods are mouse and keyboard, UIKit also provides similar event-based input for handling multiple onscreen touches as well as movement of the device.

In some other ways, UIKit is sort of "AppKit 2.0." Apple took the opportunity to toss out some baggage in the form of APIs and classes that may have seemed like a good idea a decade or two ago, but now seem unnecessary. For instance, the whole concept of cell classes, distinct from views (as exhibited by the NSCell classes) is now gone. The only UIKit class with *Cell* in its name is UITableViewCell, which is really an NSView subclass used to draw a chunk of a table view (hence the name). Also, UIKit embraces Objective-C 2.0's properties in a way that AppKit never has, providing declared properties for most of the configurable attributes.

Apart from that, there are some important parts of Cocoa that aren't available in Cocoa Touch (at least, not as of this writing). First of all, there's no garbage collection on the iPhone, so any code meant for iPhone needs to use the retain/release/autorelease reference-counting system that we've mostly been avoiding in this book. Second, there are no Cocoa Bindings in Cocoa Touch, though KVC and KVO are there, so, if you're feeling ambitious, the underpinnings for building your own bindings-like technology are there. Finally, there are no blocks on iPhone. It's entirely possible that Apple will port these technologies to iPhone on its own at some point, but don't hold your breath!

GNUstep and Cocotron

Another platform that can run Cocoa-like apps is GNUstep, and its more recent brother-in-arms Cocotron. The GNUstep project has been around for a long time, and its original goals were centered on providing a desktop application programming environment for Linux and other Unix machines. The development libraries were based around the

OpenStep API, a published standard which lists classes and APIs that are a subset of today's Foundation and AppKit frameworks. That, in turn, came from a collaboration between NeXT and Sun in the mid-1990s, when Sun wanted help providing an application development environment for their Solaris OS, all of which preceded Apple's later acquisition of NeXT, whose OS and software later morphed into Mac OS X.

So here we are today, and GNUstep is still out there in the wild. GNUstep continues to grow, acquiring new APIs as volunteers re-implement the latest things that Apple adds to Mac OS X, but its main goal has always been to implement the old OpenStep APIs, with the new additions being just a bonus. So far, there's not much for GNUstep to shout about in terms of big-name projects, but if you are looking for a way to port your Cocoa app to another Unix variant or to Windows, GNUstep is worth looking into.

A few years ago, a new alternative called Cocotron turned up. Cocotron has a slightly different focus (trying to keep on top of all of Apple's latest classes and API changes) and a different deployment target (it's focused primarily on Windows instead of Unix), but it may also be worth thinking about if you're looking for a way to port your app to Windows. It also has a less stringent license than GNUstep, which means you're free to build Cocotron into your own closed-source applications. You'll find more about GNUstep at www.gnustep.org, and for more Cocotron info, www.cocotron.org is the place to go.

Cappuccino/Objective-J

Another interesting development from the past few years is the Cappuccino development environment. Unlike the other environments we've mentioned, Cappuccino is all about making web apps, not desktop apps. Cappuccino contains class libraries that mimic much of Foundation and AppKit in name and functionality, and even manages to pull off the amazing trick of implementing much of Objective-C's syntax in Javascript, as we described when we mentioned JSCocoa. The applications you create using Cappuccino can then be published on any web server and run in any modern browser, just like any other web application. This implementing of Objective-C in Javascript is called Objective-J, and is a crucial part of what makes Cappuccino tick. The company behind this, called 280 North, is also working on a tool called Atlas to help you manage your Objective-J source define the GUI of your Cappuccino app, somewhat like Xcode and Interface Builder. Of course, following the spirit of the project, Atlas is itself a Cappuccino application, which runs in a web browser. As of this writing, all of the Cappuccino technology is still in its infancy (in fact, Atlas is only available as a private beta at this time), but it looks very promising indeed. Go to http://280north.com to follow the action.

Here at the End of All Things

That wraps up our discussion of future paths for you to take as you develop your Cocoa skills, and also concludes this book. We hope this book has taken you to a place you wanted to get to, but let's not assume that stopping place is the final destination! Visit the *Learn Cocoa on the Mac* web site, where you'll find forums for discussing with other Cocoa developers, source code for all the examples in this book, and more. Come and visit us at http://learncocoa.org where we'll do our best to help you learn even more!

Index

You Need the Companion eBook